VOICE

Leonardo

Roger F. Malina, Executive Editor

Sean Cubitt, Editor-in-Chief

Uncanny Networks: Dialogues with the Virtual Intelligentsia, Geert Lovink, 2002

Information Arts: Intersections of Art, Science, and Technology, Stephen Wilson, 2002

Virtual Art: From Illusion to Immersion, Oliver Grau, 2003

Women, Art, and Technology, edited by Judy Malloy, 2003

Protocol: How Control Exists after Decentralization, Alexander R. Galloway, 2004

At a Distance: Precursors to Art and Activism on the Internet, edited by Annmarie Chandler and Norie Neumark, 2005

The Visual Mind II, edited by Michele Emmer, 2005

CODE: Collaborative Ownership and the Digital Economy, edited by Rishab Aiyer Ghosh, 2005

The Global Genome: Biotechnology, Politics, and Culture, Eugene Thacker, 2005

Media Ecologies: Materialist Energies in Art and Technoculture, Matthew Fuller, 2005

New Media Poetics: Contexts, Technotexts, and Theories, edited by Adalaide Morris and Thomas Swiss, 2006

Aesthetic Computing, edited by Paul A. Fishwick, 2006

Digital Performance: A History of New Media in Theater, Dance, Performance Art, and Installation, Steve Dixon, 2006

MediaArtHistories, edited by Oliver Grau, 2006

From Technological to Virtual Art, Frank Popper, 2007

META/DATA: A Digital Poetics, Mark Amerika, 2007

Signs of Life: Bio Art and Beyond, Eduardo Kac, 2007

The Hidden Sense: Synesthesia in Art and Science, Cretien van Campen, 2007

Closer: Performance, Technologies, Phenomenology, Susan Kozel, 2007

Video: The Reflexive Medium, Yvonne Spielmann, 2007

Software Studies: A Lexicon, Matthew Fuller, 2008

Tactical Biopolitics: Theory, Practice, and the Life Sciences, edited by Beatriz da Costa and Kavita Philip, 2008

White Heat and Cold Logic: British Computer Art 1960–1980, edited by Paul Brown, Charlie Gere, Nicholas Lambert, and Catherine Mason, 2008

Curating New Media Art, Beryl Graham and Sarah Cook, 2010

Green Light: Toward an Art of Evolution, George Gessert, 2010

VOICE: Vocal Aesthetics in Digital Arts and Media, edited by Norie Neumark, Ross Gibson, and Theo van Leeuwen, 2010

Enfoldment and Infinity: An Islamic Genealogy of New Media Art, Laura U. Marks, 2010

See <http:mitpress.mit.edu> for a complete list of titles in this series.

VOICE

Vocal Aesthetics in Digital Arts and Media

edited by Norie Neumark, Ross Gibson, and Theo van Leeuwen

The MIT Press
Cambridge, Massachusetts
London, England

For information about special quantity discounts, please e-mail special_sales@mit-press.mit.edu

This book was set in Stone Sans and Stone Serif by the MIT Press. Printed and bound in the United States of America.

Library of Congress Cataloging-in-Publication Data

Voice : vocal aesthetics in digital arts and media / edited by Norie Neumark, Ross Gibson, and Theo van Leeuwen.
    p. cm. — (Leonardo books)
Includes bibliographical references and index.
ISBN 978-0-262-01390-1 (hardcover : alk. paper)
1. Communication—Social aspects. 2. Voice—Social aspects. 3. Technology and the arts. 4. New media art. I. Neumark, Norie. II. Gibson, Ross, 1956– III. Van Leeuwen, Theo, 1947– IV. Title: Vocal aesthetics in digital arts and media.

P95.54.V65 2010
302.23—dc22
                                                                    2009038444

10 9 8 7 6 5 4 3 2 1

Contents

Series Foreword

The arts, science, and technology are experiencing a period of profound change. Explosive challenges to the institutions and practices of engineering, art making, and scientific research raise urgent questions of ethics, craft, and care for the planet and its inhabitants. Unforeseen forms of beauty and understanding are possible, but so too are unexpected risks and threats. A newly global connectivity creates new arenas for interaction between science, art, and technology but also creates the preconditions for global crises. The Leonardo Book series, published by the MIT Press, aims to consider these opportunities, changes, and challenges in books that are both timely and of enduring value.

Leonardo books provide a public forum for research and debate; they contribute to the archive of art-science-technology interactions; they contribute to understandings of emergent historical processes; and they point toward future practices in creativity, research, scholarship, and enterprise.

To find more information about Leonardo/ISAST and to order our publications, go to Leonardo Online at <http://lbs.mit.edu/> or e-mail <leonardobooks@mitpress.mit.edu>.

Sean Cubitt
Editor-in-Chief, Leonardo Book series
Leonardo Book Series Advisory Committee: Sean Cubitt, *Chair*; Michael Punt; Eugene Thacker; Anna Munster; Laura Marks; Sundar Sarrukai; Annick Bureaud
Doug Sery, Acquiring Editor
Joel Slayton, Editorial Consultant

Leonardo/International Society for the Arts, Sciences, and Technology (ISAST)

Leonardo, the International Society for the Arts, Sciences, and Technology, and the affiliated French organization Association Leonardo have two very simple goals:

1. to document and make known the work of artists, researchers, and scholars interested in the ways that the contemporary arts interact with science and technology and
2. to create a forum and meeting places where artists, scientists, and engineers can meet, exchange ideas, and, where appropriate, collaborate.

When the journal *Leonardo* was started some forty years ago, these creative disciplines existed in segregated institutional and social networks, a situation dramatized at that time by the "two cultures" debates initiated by C. P. Snow. Today we live in a different time of cross-disciplinary ferment, collaboration, and intellectual confrontation enabled by new hybrid organizations, new funding sponsors, and the shared tools of computers and the Internet. Above all, new generations of artist-researchers and researcher-artists are now at work individually and in collaborative teams bridging the art, science, and technology disciplines. Perhaps in our lifetime we will see the emergence of "new Leonardos," creative individuals or teams that will not only develop a meaningful art for our times but also drive new agendas in science and stimulate technological innovation that addresses today's human needs.

For more information on the activities of the Leonardo organizations and networks, please visit our Web sites at <http://www.leonardo.info/> and <http://www.olats.org >.

Roger F. Malina
Chair, Leonardo/ISAST
ISAST Governing Board of Directors: Roger Malina, Jeffrey Babcock, Greg Harper, Meredith Tromble, Michael Joaquin Grey, John Hearst, Sonya Rapoport, Beverly Reiser, Christian Simm, Joel Slayton, Tami Spector, Darlene Tong, Stephen Wilson

Preface

There are some questions about the voice and technology that do not go away. What happens, for example, when the distinction between the human voice and the voice of the machine is blurred? Can we still distinguish between genuine and synthetic affect? Should we? Can we still distinguish between the uniqueness of an individual's voice and the social and cultural determinations that shape its performance? Should we even try to do so? This book is an interdisciplinary investigation of questions of this kind as they have been articulated and investigated by historians, philosophers, cultural theorists, film scholars, and artists and designers working in fields such as dance, poetry, music, film, and computer games. The book examines the recording, distribution, and synthesis of the voice, the way voices perform in contexts of technology, and the influence of changing voice technologies on mainstream media such as recorded music, film, and computer games, as well as a range of other themes relating to the ongoing power and centrality of the voice in social and cultural life.

We will focus on digital culture, but our concern is not primarily with the actual way the voice is digitally produced—although that is of interest to a number of the contributing authors. Our primary concern is with the way the voice and its uses are shaped by and help shape digital culture. Our approach therefore avoids technological determinism, attending instead to the complex relations between technology and culture. Many of the chapters in the book demonstrate how the constraints and affordances of digital voice technology were already adopted by artists before digital technology made them seem commonplace or inevitable, thus demonstrating Lewis Mumford's (1939) thesis of the "cultural preparation" that precedes technological innovation, of the way that socially important new technologies are foreshadowed in philosophy, in the arts, and also in seemingly trivial everyday pastimes and playthings. There is no total and abrupt rupture between the idea and its realization, or between different kinds of technology that may realize it.

The chapters in this book approach this theme from a number of angles. Some are written in a theoretical or historical voice; others in a critical voice, elucidating the ideas articulated in the works of artists; and others by the artists or sound designers themselves, explaining their practice and reflecting on it. Ideas about the technological mediation and recreation of the voice are not only formulated in the language of the academic paper or the critical essay, but also in the languages of art, by artists who experiment with voices and their uses in their work. For this reason, we have included first-person narratives by artists and designers and experiential accounts of art and design practices.

We have structured the book in four sections. The first section, "Capturing VOICE," focuses on the recording, synthesis, and distribution of the human voice, touching on technologies such as voice mail, podcasting, and digital musical instruments that seek to approximate the sound of the human voice. The chapters in this section show that contemporary voice technology has a prehistory going back to at least the time of Descartes, with its interest in the body as a mechanism. They also show that as the "disembodied" voice—the voice that is made transportable through time and space, or even artificially produced—voice still has material qualities, although quite different ones from those praised by Roland Barthes in "The Grain of the Voice." (1977)

The second section, "Performing VOICE," focuses on performance and performativity, for the most part in dance, poetry, and media arts. Several themes tie this section together: the performativity of the voice, which many see as having exchanged authenticity for performativity; the separation between the voice as a vehicle for language and the voice as phonetic material for a possible new "syntax of sounds" explored, for instance, in sound poetry; and, again, the role of art as "cultural preparation," borne out by the way many artists already incorporated key aspects of digital media such as modularity and remixability into their work before digital tools for semiotic production became available. The section also shows artists and essayists grappling with contradictory impulses to disconnect and reconnect the voice with the body.

The third section, "Reanimating VOICE," focuses on mainstream media such as recorded music, films, and computer games. In these media, in contrast to the media art discussed in the previous section, the voice reasserts the human. In the world of machinima, computer games, and computer animations, the image has radically moved away from photographic indexicality, but voices remain recorded voices, and designers working in these fields stress that they should be "real," "emotional," and so on. If new technologies such as 3D sound and voice processing are used, it is for purposes of characterization or to signify disorientation or unreality. Although many artists question the authenticity of the voice, in these media the impression of authenticity—the "as if not digital"—appears to be unchallenged, at least for the time being.

The final section, "At the Human Limits of VOICE," addresses a number of other themes that have long haunted discourses of the voice, such as the magic, creationary power of the voice, the voice that can call things into being; the "ghostliness" of disembodied voices; and the threat of machine voices acquiring emotions and a will of their own, which has haunted fiction since *Frankenstein*, and now takes on different forms in the work of contemporary artists.

The pleasure of editing this book has been to immerse ourselves in a rich diversity of voices—philosophical, psychological, musicological, anthropological, practice-based, and much more. We will let them speak for themselves and not attempt to synthesize them into a unified set of conclusions. But we hope that in bringing this collection together we have opened up the field for new mediations and new meditations in the coming decade of digital and networked culture.

References

Barthes, R. 1977. "The Grain of the Voice." In R. Barthes, *Image, Music, Text*. London: Fontana.

Mumford, L. 1939. *Technics and Civilization*. London: Routledge and Kegan Paul.

Acknowledgments

The strong history of audio, art, and sound studies in Australia, and particularly at the University of Technology, Sydney, has provided the intellectual and artistic basis for this book. The audio arts departments of the Australian Broadcasting Corporation (ABC) must especially be acknowledged for supporting the practice of a number of the contributors and for providing a cultural hub for radio and sound art locally and internationally. The extensive and lively sound art community in Sydney has also provided much inspiration for this project, and while we cannot list everyone, we would like to thank Alessio Cavallaro, Shaun Davies, Frances Dyson, Eddy Jokovich, and Annemarie Jonson, editors of the seminal journal *Essays in Sound*, and particularly for their permission to reprint Thomas Y. Levin's essay.

We would like to acknowledge the intellectual engagement and practical support of our colleagues at the University of Technology, Sydney, and Sydney College of the Arts. We would also like to thank the contributors, whose commitment has been unwavering over the several years of gestation of the book. Their generosity in sharing their ideas and self-reflections has been remarkable. For those whose first language is not English, we are grateful for the care and time they took to write their own texts in English.

We are particularly grateful to our editors at the MIT Press. Doug Sery as always has provided astute and knowledgeable advice and encouragement. His openness to a breadth of material and authors has allowed us to bring together a richness of voices in the book. Nancy Kotary and Sandra Minkkinen edited the final manuscript with care and insight. Katie Helke provided invaluable and patient organizational assistance.

Finally, Norie Neumark would like to gratefully acknowledge Maria Miranda for her profound engagement with the project and for her unswerving intellectual and personal support.

Introduction: The Paradox of Voice

Norie Neumark

Voice, with all its paradox, has at last returned to the theoretical agenda. In the first decade of 2000, several key books about voice appeared—resuming discussions that had been somewhat deferred since Derrida's deconstruction of phonological voice thirty years earlier. Voice is also back on the artistic agenda, now that (sound art) noise has somewhat spent its modernist force. Witness, for example, *Lipsynch*, the remarkable production in 2008 by Robert LePage, which took more than nine hours to explore voice's "many manifestations, declensions, and implications through different procedures that convey and reproduce it."[1] But is this the same voice that was earlier hushed, in theory and art, as somehow too present, too interior, too presumptuously authentic? Or have the developments of digital and networked culture shifted the artistic and everyday terrain so that we now listen to voice in a different way? Can we now hear embodied voice as fundamentally paradoxical, rather than evoking some straightforward and originary presence, identity, or interiority?

To introduce this volume, I will approach the paradox of voice from three different directions. I will begin by addressing the issues of embodiment, alterity, and signification, as a way to think about voice. Next, I will focus on techniques of voice and examine how voice is both shaped by techniques and is also itself a technique that constructs bodies and relations. Finally, and more concretely, I will explore vocal modalities that disturb, distort, and thus make evident the *normal* operations of voice.

Thinking Voice: Embodiment, Alterity, Signification

The writing of Jacques Derrida has been particularly influential in thinking about voice across a number of discourses, from philosophy to cultural studies and media and sound studies. Derrida famously critiqued phono-centrism and logocentrism, which he presented as symptomatic of the emphasis in the western philosophical canon on voice and speech—at the expense of writing—from Plato through Rousseau to Heidegger. Derrida deconstructed the "self-presence, immediacy, identity, interiority" of vocal speech—calling on the "difference and mediation and metaphoricity" of writing to do so.[2] Derrida's work has, of course, been important to get past invocations of voice as true, unmediated, and authentic. However, I sense that his critique also somehow inhibited subsequent discussion of voice until recently, when works by scholars such as Adriana Cavarero, Mladen Dolar, and Steven Connor have breathed new life into thinking about voice. These theorists, from quite different perspectives, have foregrounded an ambiguity and paradox of voice, a supplementarity, which—while actually resonating with Derridean concepts—draw out potentials of voice on which he himself did not focus.

It is not my intention to summarize these works or the various other earlier and also important theories of voice; that would require a volume all its own. Rather, I will be guided more by the interdisciplinarity of much thinking about voice and a shared concern with a number of key questions that, in various ways, are also crucial for a number of other authors in this volume. How do voices relate to bodies and subjectivity—how do voices speak to, from, and of embodied subjects? What happens to embodied voice when it is mediated? How do voices speak of alterity—performing intersubjectively, and sounding out the physical, affective, signifying, and psychic spaces between subjects? I will address these questions through three intertwined figures that run across a number of disciplines: embodiment, alterity, and signification.

Embodiment

The relation of voice to embodiment raises the question of aesthetics. For instance, citing Terry Eagleton, Susan Buck-Morss argues that "'Aesthetics is born as a discourse of the body.' It is a form of cognition, achieved through taste, touch, hearing, seeing, smell—the whole corporeal sensorium. The terminae of all of these—nose, eyes, ears, mouth, some of the most sensitive areas of skin—are located at the surface of the body, the mediating boundary between inner and outer."[3] We might then hear the voice as aesthetically bearing the marks of the body, in Buck-Morss's sense, somewhat like the "expressive face" (from which the voice emerges); that is, the voice is always/already written by the body. And, as such, it is also a site of excess"[4]—both of the body and supplemental to the body.

In relation to embodied voice, it was Roland Barthes who most famously drew attention to its aesthetic qualities with his figure "grain of the voice":

> The "grain" of the voice is not—or not only—its timbre; the signifying it affords cannot be better defined than by the frictions between music and something else, which is the language (and not the message at all).[5] . . . The "grain" is the body in the singing voice, in the writing hand, in the performing limb.[6]

Barthes's "grain of the voice" has become very familiar in sound studies, though it is perhaps less well-known outside this area. Although Barthes deployed this figure to explore singing, its attention to the body was and remains vital more broadly in relation to voice. And I would suggest that this figure continues to evoke issues of embodiment and signification in complex ways, providing a useful point of departure for examining the aesthetics of voice in digital arts and media.

For many others, however, the embodiment of voice is not so much or simply an aesthetic matter as a philosophical or psychoanalytical concern, and one that is deeply paradoxical. For Steven Connor and for Mladen Dolar, for instance, ventriloquism is the doubling figure that most keenly expresses the paradox of voice emanating *from* a body yet not quite being "disembodied." The fact that their books *Dumbstruck* and *A Voice and Nothing More* both had the same cover image (Michael Redgrave and his dummy Hugo, from the film *Dead of Night*) speaks volumes. In a way, the figure of ventriloquism strangely extends Marshall McLuhan's approach to voice as a medium, and as such, an extension of man. Whereas Connor's approach to voice is more cultural-historical, Dolar writes within a different, psychoanalytic discourse—though he too invokes the figure of ventriloquism to attend to voice's "spectral autonomy" and its paradoxical and "acousmatic" relationship to the body.[7]

Attention to the ambiguity and paradox of the embodied voice is particularly important, because both provide rich veins for media artists themselves and for scholarly understanding of what artists are doing with voice. Equally important is a recognition of the in-between, uncanny, and hinging qualities of the voice.[8] Indeed, the uncanny is another frequently recurring figure in relation to voice: the uncanny voice is also a haunted voice, ghostly or zombie like. As writer and philosopher Mark Fisher, aka k-punk, argues about haunting,

It is not accidental that the word "haunting" often refers to that which inhabits* us but which we cannot ever grasp; we find "haunting" precisely those Things which lurk at the back of our mind, on the tip of our tongue, just out of reach. . . .

*Haunt is a perfectly uncanny word, since like "unheimlich" it connotes both the familiar-domestic and its unhomely double. Haunt originally meant "to provide with a home," and has also carried the sense of the "habitual."[9]

The embodiment/disembodiment question in relation to voice has long haunted sound and radio theory and practice. In the early 1990s, for instance, Gregory Whitehead famously figured radiophonic space as a sort of zombie space, a dead space, of disembodied voices.[10] Whitehead's metaphor was important for experimental radio art, because he foregrounded the uncanny quality of voices that had been recorded and mediated—the uncanniness resulting from the passing through a technological process, be it analog or digital. However, I would argue that the emphasis on disembodiment risked losing the paradoxical simultaneity of presence and absence that a Derrridean approach foregrounds, which would allow us, in a sense, to defer a choice between radio voice as either embodied or disembodied.

Further, it is important to remember that although electronic mediation and reproduction's reconfiguring of "the body" has had very significant effects, a focus on electronic mediation can risk masking other always/already present mediations, such as the way that the voice is mediated culturally, through techniques, for instance, as discussed shortly. Culture colors the voice, contours its performative capacities, and leaves deep imprints on its character—it *mediates* the voice, in terms of its accent, intonation, timbre, cadence, and rhythm. And these mediations and their performances matter and are just as powerful as and underpin the electronic effect, be it analog or digital. Further, it is noteworthy that although disembodiment has been a key figure for scholars of radio voice, it has been less pivotal in film discourses. This suggests that what is noticeably different with radio voices, as compared to onscreen film voices, is that the listeners cannot *see* the body—so in some ways, the loss of body in radio seems to be particularly the loss of the *sight* of the body.[11] In an ironic twist, the notion of radio's disembodiment thus once again privileges vision, which sound studies has been so rightly concerned with problematizing.

Alterity

The figure of alterity speaks to the question of embodiment: it points to the importance of the embodied subject, but focuses attention on the way that voices connect these subjects. Kaja Silverman, a seminal theorist of filmic voice, noted that "the voice is capable of being internalised at the same time as it is externalised, to spill over from subject to object and object to subject, violating the bodily limits upon which classic subjectivity depends."[12]

Voice, then, not only exceeds subjects, it interconnects them. Walter Ong, one of its early theorists, highlighted the way voice establishes relationships between people—binding interiors to one another within a total sensual/spatial/temporal situation.[13] More recently, in *For More Than One Voice*, Adriana Cavarero foregrounds voice's intersubjectivity and call to alterity, suggesting that these offer a way to get past the *presence*, which so worried Derrida. Associating the sonorous with a particular embodied person, Cavarero focuses on the sonorous voice as relational and proposes alterity as the key for listening to voice:

What it communicates is precisely the true vital and perceptible uniqueness of the one who emits it. At stake here is not a closed-circuit communication between one's own voice and one's own ears, but rather a communication of one's own uniqueness that is, at the same time, a relation with another unique existent. It takes at least a duet, a calling and a responding—or, better, a reciprocal intention to listen, one that is already active in the vocal emission and that reveals and communicates everyone to the other.[14]

In attending to its relationality, to its call to alterity, Cavarero asks philosophy to listen to voice as exceeding *both* sonority and signification.[15] The call and response of Cavarero's duet of alterity, with its ethics of reciprocity, should not, I would note, be confused with the vocal interpolations of political speech, such as the very different call and response of fascism's exhortations.[16]

Alterity also has a spatial dimension. This is particularly important to remember when listening to voice, which, as sound, is defined by and defining of the space in which it resonates. The spaces of alterity include the bodily and social space of affect—affect in the sense of more than just feelings, but rather "the very engagement between body and world from which these feelings arise," as Andrew Murphie and John Potts put it.[17] Similarly, Sara Ahmed, "in examining ... affective economies, ... argue[s] that emotions *do things*, and they align individuals with communities—or bodily space with social space—through the very intensity of their attachments."[18] Thus in signaling alterity as a dimension of voice and an important figure in its discourses, one recognizes the affective qualities of voice, which has implications for aesthetics as well as for intersubjectivity.[19]

Signification

Adriana Cavarero's idea that alterity frames communication as a "duet" has important implications for signification. She argues that the problem with Derrida's figure of speech is that it joins the sonorous and the meaningful into a *unitary* figure—speech as meaningful signification—in a way that makes it difficult to think the difference and specificity of voice.

Voice is paradoxically, ambiguously, and uncannily at the intersection of subjectivity, intersubjectivity, and signification. In one way, we could hear voice as a hinge, holding the sonorous and signifying together and apart—preventing them from collapsing into a unity. As Steven Shaviro notes,

The voice always stands in between: in between body and language, in between biology and culture, in between inside and outside, in between subject and Other, in between mere sound or noise and meaningful articulation. In each of these instances, the voice is both what links these opposed categories together, what is common to both of them, without belonging to either.[20]

Dolar too explores the paradox of voice, arguing that the Derridean "deconstructive turn tends to deprive the voice of its ineradicable ambiguity by reducing it to the ground of (self-) presence."[21] Dolar brings into play a Lacanian psychoanalytic perspective to disturb the critiques of *voice as presence* that rest on an opposition between writing and speech and that too easily deploy the figure of phonocentrism to recuperate writing at the expense of voice.[22] Thus we return to the critique of the Derridean impasse—which Dolar, Cavarero, and Connor renegotiate, without losing the many and important insights of Derrida's deconstructions—to rethink voice.

Techniques of Voice

Technique, which is commonly said to be a response to a preexistent object or technology, actually helps to construct that object and to shape that technology. From anthropology to history to cultural studies, theorists have worked with the concept of technique to understand how culture shapes subjectivities through bodies and their gestures. Technique thus offers a way to think about voice in relation to bodies and spaces and culture; technique is where subjectivity, technology, and culture intersect. Techniques from preanalog moments of culture may still operate in digital times, despite inflecting bodies and technology differently and specifically over time.

The anthropologist Marcel Mauss was a key theorist of technique. He understood the "biological" body as gendered, cultural, historical, and sexual—as a product or expression of what he called "habit" or "habitus"—*techniques* of the body. Every society, he argued, has its own special habits, which are not just external but internal and constructive of body and psyche, though not in some unalterable way. As habits, they tend not to be noticeable to those in that society and culture, because they are "naturalized" by it. That is, in their naturalizing of sex, gender, and class, techniques do not have to be named or directly spoken of. Although they are often experienced as a "natural" product of a biological nature, they are actually constructive of "biology" and "nature" itself.[23] Following Carl Jung, François Dagognet also contributed a significant understanding of technique. In relation to voice, in particular, he foregrounded it more in terms of "the mind-body juncture" of psycho-architecture—breathing, diaphragm, muscles. Dagognet heard voice as one of the body's "mirrors" or, in a way, performances of the mind—a witness, sediment of a history, indicator, collection of marks or traces."[24] Mauss and Dagognet help us attend to the effects on voice of the techniques through which someone learns to walk, breathe, and run—affecting how much oxygen she gets, how she develops her nerves and muscles, how she nourishes and shapes her organs.

In the second half of the twentieth century, cultural historians have also been working with technique in ways that are useful for understanding voice. Michel Foucault has been a major influence here, with his thinking about how bodies, techniques, institutions, discourses, and social space intersect. Writing within a Foucauldian paradigm, historian Adrian Forty, for instance, focused on the differentiation of commodities and the organization of social space. He examined how bodily postures and gestures are constructed with and through items of clothing, furniture, accoutrements, that distinguish by sex, by age, as well as by class.[25] Forty's work directs us to an understanding of how tight clothing, for example, produces a thinness of voice heard as if essentially female and as "appropriately" feminine.

Similarly, historians Peter Stallybrass and Allon White studied habits and techniques of class; they examined how bourgeois morality was (and still is) incorporated and habituated into the body. In relation to voice, their analysis is most useful where they look at the history of the techniques, which introjected morality into the body by differentiating between improper and proper sounds and noises. Proper bourgeois behavior, for instance, was learned through the proper relation of voice, lungs, tongue, mouth, glottis, and saliva.[26] The result was one's own, proper voice.

Steven Connor has recently approached techniques of voice through the figures of exercise and strain, providing a sense of how the strain—indeed "pathos"—is an inevitable part of techniques of voice:

Everything that is said about the exercise of the voice—by coaches, experts, trainers, and voice professionals of all kinds—implies that it should be easy and relaxed, an effortless effect of the breath. The voice must be produced without inordinate stress, which will damage or distort it. Coaches and gurus offer exercises and visualisations designed to free your voice from the cramping, vampiric grip of its bad habits. But there is no voice without strain; without the constraining of sound in general by the particular habits and accidents that, taken collectively, constitute a voice, and the constraining of the body to produce voice. The breath is drawn as a bow is drawn, by applying a force against the resistance of the diaphragm and intercostal muscles. The power of the voice is the release of the kinetic energy stored in these muscles as they return to their resting positions.[27]

There are numerous technologies that could be discussed here to illustrate the complex relationship between vocal techniques and their related technologies. One with a well-documented history, and with significant implications for gender, is the telephone. For instance, in *The Telephone Book*, Avital Ronell recounts the history and ramifications of boy operators being replaced by girl operators—the soft and patient female vocal techniques replacing the boys' shouting:

The voice, entering the intimate borders between inner and outer ear, was soon feminized, if only to disperse the shouting commands of a team sport. Nowadays, it is said, when a military aircraft finds itself in serious trouble, the voice command switches to the feminine.[28]

Among other significant technologies shaping and shaped by vocal techniques that are particularly relevant to media are sound recording and mixing technologies for radio, film, and other broadcast and distribution media. Because microphones are a crucial technology across a number of media, I'll turn to them as my example of the intersection of technique and technology and their effect on producing, reproducing, and listening to (filmic) voices. Film sound studies—particularly the important work of Rick Altman—have elaborated the effects of miking and sound mixing in film and how these produced cinema's voice and the viewer's relationship to it. Sound recording and mixing techniques—through highly directional mics and through postproduction techniques (such as isolating the voice and mixing it higher than other sounds)—foreground certain voices at a higher level than the original performance. They place the voice in tune with the selection and focus characteristics of the camera, instead of the space of performance. Through such techniques, a sense of interiority, involvement, and intimacy with the audience could be created, and voice could work to tie the audience into the narrative. With such film miking, then, we can hear technique and technology working together to produce voices that call out to us, that call us in, in ways we experience as faithful.[29]

It would be remiss to conclude a discussion of technique and technology of voice without at least brief mention of two key, if controversial, theorists of media technology: Marshall McLuhan and Friedrich Kittler. One could read McLuhan, for instance, as understanding voice itself as a medium, determined in part by techniques of language—as mothers' tongues impart mother tongues:

The patterns of the senses that are extended in the various languages of men are as varied as styles of dress and art. Each mother tongue teaches its users a way of seeing and feeling the world and of acting in the world that is unique.[30]

McLuhan's work might thus underline the sensuous complexities of voice, as a medium itself, prior to electronic mediation.[31]

Friedrich Kittler, a follower of McLuhan and an equally rhetorical and controversial scholar, also foregrounds the materiality and mediality of media. His focus is not on the content of the mediated voice, but its emergence within particular discourse networks—at the intersection of "physical, technological, discursive, and social systems."[32] Even though Kittler gleefully announces the ultimate end of sonority, he also remembers that *meanwhile* media, entertainment, and therefore aesthetics are still operative.[33] And, though his is not a call to hear the aesthetics of voice's grain, nevertheless one could argue that Kittler's concern with a noisy, bodily Lacanian "real" and the materiality of media do open up to thinking about sonority.

Modes of Voice

In this section, I will attempt to amplify and distort "normal" voices in order to throw them into relief. I will listen at the edges that bound and help frame normal voices through examples of several vocal modes: voice at its ground zero of breath; cracked, broken, and bent voices; and voice screaming at its limits. These amplified and distorted modalities point to the complex and varied relations of voice to body and of bodily voice to signification and intersubjectivity: they make sensible the ways in which the sonorous and signifying aspects of voice supplement and disturb each other, and they make evident the aesthetic and affective potentials of voice.

Breath as Ground Zero

In relation to embodiment, the ground zero of voice is breath. Voice begins with the breath, and breath serves as a constant and physical reminder of the ephemerality, intimacy, and alterity of the voice. An essential condition and part of voice, breath is compelling and intriguing in that it is both bodily and not. Breath starts in one body and then connects to—communicates with—another.

Adriana Cavarero turns to Emmanuel Levinas to understand breath, as the ground zero of voice, as relational:

Nothing more than the act of breathing is able to testify to the proximity of human beings to one another; nothing else better confirms their communication as reciprocal exposure that precedes any initiative. Breathing. For breathing is not subject to a decision, but is rather involuntary and passive—it is a profound communication of oneself, an exchange in which one inhales the air that the other exhales. The proximity of the other in breath, is "the fission of the subject, beyond the lungs, to the very nucleus of the 'I,' to what is indivisible in the individual."[34]

With its intimate relation to voice and the body, its ephemerality, and its testament to alterity, it's not surprising that breath has long been a popular medium for sound and performance artists. My own fascination with breath started back in the analog days, doing radiophonic work, cutting and putting aside bits of tape with people's breath—in case I needed it later to reinvigorate the rhythm of a voice I had edited. The whole intimate process of editing a voice and holding someone's breath in the tangible yet very alien piece of magnetic tape felt both exhilarating and uncanny.

But breath is also tinged with an edge of undecidability and ambiguity: how can you hear—or see in a digital editing track—the difference between an exhalation (carrying CO_2) from an inhalation (bearing O_2)? What is the direction of this connection through breath? This undecidability between an expiration and an inspiration—two movements, in different directions, of the "same" breath—is reminiscent of Marcel Duchamp's *infrathin*, which he used to describe the separation between two things that are the "same," but not. He presented the infrathin through examples because he saw it— heard it—as indefinable. Marjorie Perloff cites one of his examples, particularly relevant to breath, "When the tobacco smoke smells also of the / mouth which exhales it, the two odors / marry by infra thin (olfactory / in thin). (#11)"[35]

Broken, Cracked, and Bent Voices

Broken voices operate at thresholds and boundaries, often in familiar ways— for instance, the boy's voice breaking into manhood. Broken voices speak of a transitional moment that can be both "normal," as in this case, but also uneasy—reminding us of the uncertainties of transition, throwing into doubt the "normal" (gender, say) that precedes and follows that moment. Wayne Koestenbaum hears the broken voice in opera, for instance, as a reminder of the uncertainties of "normal" manhood. Furthermore, he suggests it actually becomes the aural sign of and for the abnormal man—the opera-loving male homosexual.[36]

In 2008, in the more mundane realm of popular news media, the United States experienced the different effect of the cracked female voice when then-Senator Hillary Clinton's breaking voice brought her temporarily back to an acceptable femininity and into the running in the primary campaign. Her breaking voice was replayed over and over on broadcast and Internet media. In Australia, however, we were already familiar with the affective power of the cracked female voice in politics—the power to break a sense of cold political calculation, which can be worrying in anyone and certainly not befitting a woman. We'd heard it here a decade before, in the 1990s, with a politician of a very different hue, Pauline Hanson. Hanson was a racist, right-wing politician whose popular appeal was too quickly dismissed by left-wing critics unable to understand and counter the populist appeal that she voiced with a notable tremor. Her voice cracked and broke through familiar political speech, plucked the heartstrings of her audience, and pulsed not just in the body of speaker but agitated the responsive bodies of its audience. Its cracked quality made it feel not just heartfelt, but also "real," as I have discussed elsewhere.[37] We might wonder whether the potency and appeal of the crack in a polished veneer also suggests a broader disquiet with the cold smoothness of the digital (voice), to which (do-it-yourself) aesthetics in media art, for example, also appeals, with an opening to intimacy.

A different sort of broken voice is the one that coughs or hiccups, for example, which opens "an intrusion of physiology into structure," as Dolar puts it. Apparently an "involuntary voice rising from the body's entrails," it is, however, not external to structures of meaning: "it means that it means," he says.[38] Signifying with its very physical brokenness, such voices evoke for Dolar the complexities of the relation between physiology, or sonority, and signification in vocal expression. As Dolar says of the cough or the hiccup, the stutter, too, is without the intention or will of the utterer and a disruption of speech and meaning, "but an intriguing reversal takes place here: those voices, somatic and unattractive as they may be, are hardly ever simply external to the structure—quite the opposite, they may well enter into its core or become its double."[39] With the stuttering voice, smooth signification is interrupted, set at unease, even dis-ease. It is the move from stuttered signification to a nonsignifying stutter that Alvin Lucier plays with in his famous recorded/rerecorded vocal work *I am sitting in a room*.[40] In Lucier's work, the ambiguity of the stuttering voice, its move between signification and sonority (from sound speech to noise), moves the work forward. And it is a movement, by the way, that technology both enables and demonstrates—a comment on the tape recorder and a play at the edge of voice, sound, and, ultimately, music. A stuttering voice makes speech elusive, painful, never quite or wholly or transparently present, never easily or fully graspable.

Martin Heidegger developed a now well-rehearsed argument that tools reveal their being, which is normally masked, when they are broken. And, as Steven Connor implies, it's the convulsions of broken voices that remind us how the voice normally coheres, despite its inherent tensions.[41] Laughter, too, as it breaks into the voice is an outburst of physiology and culture—both individually and infectiously from one body to another. Laughter has both an immediate and mediated relation to voice. Because laughter is voice out of control—released at the edge of voice—controlled laughter, from the individual's forced laugh to the TV laugh track, can feel particularly disturbing. There is a memorable scene in *Lipsynch*, LePage's 2008 homage to voice, in which one of the main characters conducts and records a laugh track chorus. The performing of laughter on stage, evoked by the seriously professional gestures of a conductor, provoke not altogether easy laughter in the audience. The scene also reminds us of laughter's performative play within and across bodies. Remix culture, too, has delighted in playing with laugh tracks, and from art galleries to YouTube, numerous videos add laugh tracks to serious genres, disturbing our position as media audience and our relation to the voices they overlay.[42]

When it's the normal cohering of a technologized voice that is broken or bent, we are reminded how strangely familiar, functional, and banal the synthesized voice has become. The Australian experimental electro rock group Toy Death provide a powerful example of this effect as they bend the circuits of cheap commercial dolls, toys, and other objects: they produce cranked-up and distorted voices that unsettle our normal relation to these familiar objects.[43] As Toy Death distort the toys' "normal" performance, they make us aware of what Natalie Jeremijenko analyzes as the usual *static* and commodified dynamics of our quotidian human-machine interactions.[44] Because children's toys, according to Jeremijenko, are one of the most widespread users of voice chips, it is not surprising that artists like to play with their voices. Another celebrated example is that of Artmark's Barbie and GI Joe interventions in 1993. The story is that somehow they swapped the voice mechanism of Barbie and GI Joe in the factory, letting loose these gender-bent icons on unsuspecting consumers. This early hactivist intervention humorously focused attention on the relation between voice, gender, and commodification.[45]

Voices at the Limit

When the normally phatic becomes overly emphatic, we hear the voice as scream. For Dolar, such a voice is the expression of desire—of demand over need—and as such, a call to the other.[46] Like broken voices, these liminal voices can disturb the seemingly natural relations between biology and culture.

The scream is voice at the extreme of signification. It is a vocal gesture that in some ways appears to be outside signifying structures, but may be understood as revealing those structures. To lower the voice is to gain authority, but to allow it to rise in a scream is to open the body to be read as hysterical, infantile, out of control, uncivilized. The scream is the sort of improper vocal gesture that proper bourgeois subjects learn not to emit. Once you've controlled your tongue, lips, mouth, you're ready to control your voice, to sublimate extremes like the scream, which would reveal a body out of control.[47]

Though we have become used to associating hysterical screaming with women (the voice of hormones or genes, depending on the decade), Sander Gilman provides a musical example of how this modality has also been heard to reveal something seemingly essential about ethnicity:

Jews argue; they don't make sense. Their music is basically out of key. . . . Both in the opening scene of the opera and in the quintet, Strauss follows shrill Jewish cacophony with deep-voiced Christian response and diatonicism.[48]

"Christian tonality" and cacophonous Jewish "screaming" and "howling"—the inexorability of ethnic and religious difference screaming out to be heard. Voices at these limits doubled ethnic perversity with sexual perversity in the ears of conservative Christian Germans at the time, according to Gilman, with their myths of sick and abnormal Jewish bodies and their representations of (circumcised) Jewish males as feminized—inherently hysterical, perverted, and homosexual.[49]

Decades later—different times, different ethnicity—Yoko Ono's singing screaming of John Lennon's songs evoked similar extreme responses. For instance, on the *Dick Cavett Show* in the 1970s, a cool Cavett made tongue-in-cheek reference to foreigners and hysteria in response to Ono's performance; today, YouTube comments on the video of that event, and other Ono videos, are far less polite and less subtle in their negativity toward her screaming as singing. Ono, who had performed a lung- and throat-achingly performative 32-minute, 31-second *Cough Piece* in 1961, was well aware of the significance of playing with modalities of voice. For this occasion, she simply noted with calm aplomb that "many people hate my screaming"—including particularly sound engineers, whom it drove from the room.[50] Ono's singing screaming throws into relief the normal mode of singing voice—which does not disturb, but appeals easily, familiarly, directly, sometimes even mystically to its listeners.

A final female scream that cries out for attention is that of horror films—a familiar yet still disturbing scream that has become emblematic of the genre. Like the presence of other bodily emissions, especially mouth sounds that sound designers would normally cut or avoid but which they leave in for this genre[51]—the scream suggests unclean and unclear boundaries—moving us beyond the frightening, into the horrific. Not all cinematic screams are female, of course, or horrific. The infamous Wilhelm scream entered film history in 1951 and since has moved from voice actor to sound effect. With the ease of digital editing, it has appeared in well over 130 films, many of which are not horror, as well as in games. As the numerous YouTube videos devoted to the Wilhelm scream suggest, it has been both a convenient part of a repertoire of special effects (SFX) as well as a (now no longer secret) cult. In a way, the Wilhelm scream has become a zombie sound—as much as the sound of zombies—signifying itself and its "lost" body along with the voice of the sound designer.[52]

Conclusion

What I have tried to open up with this introductory discussion are the paradoxes and potential that sound out and play out with voice. The fundamental paradoxes of voice—embodied and moving between bodies, sonorous and signifying—have become even more complex as voice, always/already culturally (and politically) mediated, is remediated and remixed in networked and digital culture. Listening to voice in digital art and media, we can think the uncanny and complicated relation between embodiment, alterity, and signification. We can hear the intricate ways in which voice is shaped by technique and how it shapes techniques—not just of production and reproduction, but also the habits of everyday life. And, listening to amplified and distorted voices, we can sense the undecidability, tensions, and ambiguity that subtend the normally coherent voice. Complex and paradoxical, voice once more calls out for theoretical and artistic exploration.

Notes

1. *Lipsynch*, Sydney Festival 2009, catalog (no pagination).

2. Steven Shaviro, "A Voice and Nothing More," *The Pinocchio Theory*, http://www.shaviro.com/Blog/?p=489 (posted Friday, April 14, 2006; accessed January 3, 2008).

3. Susan Buck-Morss, "Aesthetics and Anaesthetics: Walter Benjamin's Artwork Essay Reconsidered," *new formations*, 20 (Summer 1993): 125. She cites Terry Eagleton, *The Ideology of the Aesthetic* (Oxford: Blackwell, 1990) 13.

4. Ibid., 129–130.

5. Roland Barthes, *The Responsibility of Forms: Critical Essays on Music, Art, and Representation*, trans. Richard Howard (Berkeley: University of California Press, 1991), 273

6. Ibid., 276.

7. Mladen Dolar, *A Voice and Nothing More* (Cambridge, MA: MIT Press, 2006), 70. Dolar cites Slavoj Žižek, *On Belief* (London: Routledge, 2001), 58.

8. Ibid., passim; see, for example, 7–8, 61, 96, and 102–103.

9. k-punk, "Hauntology Now," http://k-punk.abstractdynamics.org/archives/0072 30.html (posted January 17, 2006; accessed February 5, 2008).

10. See, for instance, Gregory Whitehead's seminal piece "Who's There? Notes on the Materiality of Radio," *Art & Text* 31 (December–February 1989), 11.

11. Of course, even in film, this can occur with what Michel Chion called *acousmatic sound*—where we don't see the originating cause. Michel Chion, *Audio-Vision: Sound on Screen*, ed. and trans. Claudia Gorbman (New York: Columbia University Press, 1994), 71.

12. Cited in Brandon LaBelle, *Background Noise: Perspectives on Sound Art* (New York and London: Continuum, 2006), 63.

13. Walter J. Ong, *Orality and Literacy: The Technologizing of the Word* (New York: Routledge, 2000). Though the religious undertones of Ong's concept of interiority has taken it out of favor, it did play a noteworthy major role in early sound studies (and still does for some).

14. Adriana Cavarero, *For More Than One Voice: Toward a Philosophy of Vocal Expression*, trans. Paul A. Kottman (Stanford, CA: Stanford University Press, 2005), 5.

15. Cavarero, op. cit., passim. See especially "Introduction," 7–16.

16. Technologically, radio and the loudspeaker were important in enabling the vocal call of fascism, and with it the interpolation of the fascist subject. New media technologies like radio and amplification gave fascism a voice—loud and intimate (in penetration), omnipresent, and exhorting—a quality of voice that made it easier to hold together contradictory ideologies (including violent and revolutionary change plus disciplined order and national unity; capitalist development with anti-bourgeois sentiments); to speak to deep libidinal needs; and to mobilize consent and support. Following Julia Kristeva, Alice Kaplan argues that libidinally, fascism made use of a certain quality of voice (rhythm, tone, repetitiousness) that was reminiscent of the maternal voice, in order to generate the virile fascist male subject. See Alice Yaeger Kaplan, *Reproductions of Banality: Fascism, Literature, and French Intellectual Life* (Minneapolis: University of Minnesota Press, 1986), especially chapter 1.

17. Andrew Murphie and John Potts, *Technology and Culture* (New York: Palgrave Macmillan, 2003), 87.

18. Sara Ahmed, "Communities that Feel: Intensity, Difference and Attachment," *Conference Proceedings for Affective Encounters: Rethinking Embodiment in Feminist Media Studies*, ed. Anu Koivunen and Susanna Paasonen (Turku, Finland: Media Studies, University of Turku), http://media.utu.fi/affective/proceedings.pdf (accessed January 15, 2007), 10–11.

19. Affect, in the way Ahmed figures it, as *doing things*, also evokes the performativity of voice, which I deal with at length in chapter 6, "Doing Things with Voices: Performativity and Voice."

20. Shaviro, op. cit.

21. Dolar, op. cit., 42.

22. Ibid., passim; see especially 36–42.

23. Marcel Mauss, "Techniques of the body," [1934] in *Incorporations, Zone 6*, ed. Jonathan Crary and Sanford Kwinter (Cambridge, MA: MIT Press, 1992) See Norie Neumark, "The Well Tempered Liver," in *Writing Aloud: The Sonics of Language*, ed. Brandon LaBelle and Christof Migone, (Los Angeles: Errant Bodies Press, 2001).

24. Francois Dagonet "Towards a Biopsychiatry," in Crary and Kwinter, op. cit., 522, 529, 534, 540.

25. Adrian Forty, *Objects of Desire: Design and Society from Wedgwood to IBM* (New York: Pantheon Books, 1986).

26. Peter Stallybrass and Allon White, *The Politics and Poetics of Transgression* (London: Methuen, 1986); see for example chapter 2, 89–90, 94; chapter 3, 125–133; and chapter 5, 154–155, and 167–168.

27. Steven Connor, "The Strains of the Voice," http://www.bbk.ac.uk/english/skc/strains/ (2004; accessed January 20, 2008), 1.

28. Avital Ronell, *The Telephone Book: Technology-Schizphrenia-Electric Speech* (Lincoln and London: University of Nebraska Press, 1989), 302.

29. See especially Rick Altman, "The Technology of the Voice: Part I," *Iris*, vol. 3, no. 1 (1985) and "The Technology of the Voice: Part II," *Iris*, vol. 4, no. 1 (1986). See also Rick Altman, "The Material Heterogeneity of Recorded Sound," in *Sound Theory, Sound Practice*, ed. Rick Altman (New York: Routledge, 1992), passim; see especially 23–27. Classic and seminal texts include this edited volume of Altman's; Elisabeth Weis and John Belton, eds., *Film Sound: Theory and Practice* (New York: Columbia University Press, 1985); and Michel Chion, op. cit.

30. Marshall McLuhan, *Understanding Media: The Extensions of Man* (Cambridge, MA: MIT Press, 1999), 80.

31. Ibid., 78–79.

32. Friedrich A. Kittler, *Gramophone, Film, Typewriter*, trans. Geoffrey Winthrop-Young and Michael Wutz (Stanford: Stanford University Press, 1999), xxiii; see also xiv–xv, xxxi, xxxix.

33. Ibid., 2–3, 16.

34. Cavarero, op. cit., 31.

35. Marjorie Perloff, "But isn't the same at least the same? Translatability in Wittgenstein, Duchamp, and Jacques Roubaud," *JACKET* 14 (July 2001), http://jacket magazine.com/14/perl-witt.html.

36. Further detail in Neumark, op. cit. and Wayne Koestenbaum, "The Queen's Throat: Or How to Sing," in Wayne Koestenbaum and Tony Kushner, *The Queen's Throat: Opera, Homosexuality, and the Mystery of Desire* (New York: Vintage Books, 1993), passim.

37. See Neumark, op cit., 97–98. For an analysis of the contrasting vocal techniques of Margaret Thatcher and their appeal, see Max Atkinson, *Our Masters' Voices: The Language and Body Language of Politics* (London and New York: Methuen, 1984), 115, 120, 113.

38. Dolar, op. cit., 24–25.

39. Dolar, op. cit., *A Voice and Nothing More* (Cambridge, MA: The MIT Press, 2006), 24.

40. LaBelle, op. cit., 25.

41. Steven Connor, "The Strains of the Voice," 3.

42. More "serious" video art also plays with laugh tracks; for example, Melbourne-based artist Arlo Mountford's 2007 digital animation *Stand Up* punctuated a serious voice reciting homilies about art ("Art will . . . destroy the museum, reinvent the museum," and so on) with laugh tracks of outbursts and whoops of laughter.

43. See http://www.toydeath.com/info.html (accessed June 15, 2008). "Circuit bending is the creative, DIY (Do It Yourself) short-circuiting of electronic devices such as low voltage, battery-powered guitar effects, children's toys, and small digital synthesizers to create new musical instruments and sound generators." Also see the Wikipedia article, http://en.wikipedia.org/wiki/Circuit_bending (accessed April 22, 2008).

44. Natalie Jeremijenko, "If Things Can Talk, What Do They Say? If We Can Talk to Things, What Do We Say?" in *First Person: New Media as Story, Performance, and Game*, Noah Wardrip-Fruin and Pat Harrigan, eds. (Cambridge, MA: MIT Press, 2004). See especially 264, 266–268, 277.

45. When media artists like this excessively and playfully crack the code of synthesized voices, they also, by the way, provide an antidote to the normalizing effect of

much scientific use of synthesized voice, such as affective computing's robot, Kismet, whose so-called "expressive synthesized speech" in fact epitomizes dull functionality, masquerading as cute.

46. Dolar, op. cit., 27–29.

47. Gregory Whitehead, whose extensive radiophonic play with voice has been most important, explored the scream in *Pressures of the Unspeakable*, which had very thought-provoking implications in relation to gendered and national (Australian) articulations of the scream. Commissioned and broadcast by the Listening Room, ABC Radio (1992), http://mediamogul.seas.upenn.edu/pennsound/authors/Whitehead/Gregory_Whitehead-Pressures_of_the_Unspeakable_1992.mp3 (accessed May 28, 2008).

48. Gilman, op. cit., 172.

49. Ibid., 160, 169, 173–174.

50. http://www.youtube.com/watch?v=1TiDNrsTv7c. Accessed May 20, 2008. Ono's *Cough Piece* is downloadable from ubu web, http://www.ubu.com/sound/ono.html.

51. This has been pointed out to me by film sound designer Andrew Plain.

52. See for example, http://www.youtube.com/watch?v=4YDpuA90KEY and http://www.youtube.com/watch?v=_PxALy22utc&feature=related (accessed May 20, 2008).

VOICE

I Capturing VOICE

This section focuses on the recording, synthesis, and distribution of the human voice, including voice mail, podcasting, and digital musical instruments that seek to approximate the sound of the human voice.

Theo van Leeuwen describes how instrument makers for centuries have been trying to build instruments that sound like the human voice, moving from mechanical contraptions to modern digital instruments. In doing so, they did not seek to deceive the ear, but to create a discourse of "humanness," and a sound that would musically express the key themes of this discourse—subjectivity, individuality, and emotionality.

Thomas Levin's chapter is a fascinating history of technologies that allow the voice to travel through time and space. It elegantly demonstrates Lewis Mumford's idea of the "cultural preparation" that precedes the introduction of new technologies. For example, in 1656 Cyrano de Bergerac offered an account of traveling to the moon, in which he told of books that are "'read with one's ears' . . . in order to grasp the contents one simply placed a needle on the desired chapter and, as if spoken by a human voice, one would hear it, loud and clear." Levin then shows how, from the nineteenth century onward, that same idea was pursued in a range of different technologies, each characterized by quite different material qualities.

Virginia Madsen and John Potts focus on podcasts, which "like seed pods are released to drift through cyberspace, awaiting that moment of connection in which they may begin to take root and multiply." They evoke the way podcasts, in a new form and a new age, revive the participatory nature and programming diversity of radio before its descent into music formats, and how they can accommodate the amateur and the enthusiast as well as the public broadcaster and the archivist.

Clearly, voice capturing (and voice synthesis) technologies have a long history (and prehistory) going back to the days of Descartes. And their ability to dissociate the voice from the body does not mean that they are not material. On the contrary, each technology brings its own materiality, albeit in ways that are very different from the materiality of the voice eulogized by Roland Barthes.

Theresa Senft's beautifully written chapter weaves these strands together in a first-person narrative—the disembodied fantasies of telephone scx, the use of audio tapes to prepare for invasive surgery, teaching a computer to recognize one's voice, meditating about a work of sound art in which the voice is rerecorded until all meaning is gone and only rhythm remains.

Voice technologies are described experientially here, as the writer interacts with the multiple disembodied voices surrounding her and reflects on the often ambivalent and complex emotions they call up.

Finally, Martin Thomas's resonant piece describes how sound-capturing technologies have allowed Australian indigenous peoples to keep their knowledge and traditions alive, despite language loss, and to "write" their stories without having to inscribe them into a semiotic modality that divests them of their fundamental oral qualities.

1 Vox Humana: The Instrumental Representation of the Human Voice

Theo van Leeuwen

Introduction

I am a jazz pianist and church organ player as well as an academic. Two years ago I bought a new digital piano, a Roland RD300-SX. Its hundreds of voices imitate the whole range of traditional musical instruments, but also include "human voices": Aah Choirs and Oooh Choirs, Jazz Scat, Space Voices, and more. As a church organ player, I knew this was nothing new. Church organs have included *vox humana* ("human voice") stops for centuries. I became intrigued. Is there a continuity between analog and digital musical representations of the human voice, or has digitality introduced a new dimension? It is this question that I will explore in this chapter.

Writing about instrumental representations of the human voice, it is impossible not to touch on the question of authenticity. To do so, I will use "modality theory," an approach that asks not whether voices actually are "authentic," but *as how* "authentic" they have been represented. As it turns out, musical representations of the human voice have always been relatively abstract, perhaps in the first place seeking to provide a kind of discourse about the human voice, rather than seeking to be heard as realistic representations of human voices.

The Vox Humana

Already in the course of the sixteenth and seventeenth centuries, church organs were beginning to include voices representing other musical instruments, natural sounds, and also the human voice.

"Does it not suffice," wrote Pierre Trichet in his *Treatise on Musical Instruments*, published in 1640, "to have found a way that in the same organ

. . . one can hear the song of the lark, the twittering of the nightingale, the drone of the pedals ("bourdonnement"), the noise of drums, trumpet fanfares, the echoing of clerons, the clanking of cymbals, the tolling of bells, the buzzing ("nazardement") and grating sound of the régales or voix humaines; in short the sound of almost all musical instruments, such as the playing of soft flutes, fifes, flageolets, arigots, oboes, bassoons, cornets, cromornes, musettes, violins? . . . All these all together, if desired, or by combining them and separating them alternately."[1] And Father Mersenne, a friend of Descartes, wrote in his book *Harmonie Universelle* (1636): "If the violin stop is added . . . it seems that there will be nothing more to desire in the organ, unless it be that the pipes should sound the vowels and the syllables. This it seems must not be hoped for because of the great difficulty encountered."[2]

This vision of an instrument on which one player could command a whole orchestra continues to inspire instrument makers to the present day. And at the same time, another vision and another project emerged: the representation of the human voice by musical instruments. Organ builders began to create a new organ stop, the "vox humana" or "voix humaine," developing organ pipes that would imitate the human voice. For this they used reed pipes, which have within the pipe a resonating metal tongue that is wind-driven, and tunable by means of a clip that presses against it. Soon these pipes would be given a separate wind supply, so as to allow a kind of vibrato, by means of "tremulants," or valves covered in leather that were suspended in the wind conduit and started to flap as the wind entered the conduit, causing fluctuations in the wind supply, and hence in the sound of the pipes. The size and weight of the valves determined the rate and depth of the vibration.

Why did they use reed pipes, which sound rather thin and hollow, a little like an oboe, and not at all like a human voice? Perhaps the organ builders knew their classics. Reed instruments had been equated with the emotive aspect of music since antiquity. In the fifth century BC, the poet Pindarus told how Athena invented the *aulos* after hearing the lament of Medusa's sisters at the beheading of the Medusa. The aulos was a kind of oboe and would become the key instrument in Greek drama and tragedy because of its capacity for emotive expression through dynamic shading and tonal coloring. Reed instruments may not have sounded like human voices, but they were nevertheless conventionally associated with human voices because of their emotive expressiveness. In the context of church organs, powered by large bellows and unable to vary the dynamics and timbres of their individual voices, this was a novelty.

But a close imitation of the human voice it was not, and the way the organ was played had to help make the imitation more convincing. Organists warned each other to play "compassionately and very legato"[3] and to make sure they did not use too wide a range. "The voix humaine must not be played lower than the first F ut fa, not higher than the fourth G re sol, because natural voices do not ordinarily pass these limits," wrote Dom Bedos de Celles in the eighteenth century, adding that using the tremulant was particularly important: "Without the tremulant the Voix-Humaine does not truly imitate the human voice. I know of only two Voix-Humaines which have achieved that quality. I believe the perfect success of these two Voix-Humaines must be attributed principally to the quality of the Tremblant-Doux." [4] And according to Mersenne, "such a 'Tremblant'" had to "beat in such a way that it imitates the vibrato of human voices in the stops of the organ," and for this reason it had to be "close to the [wind]chest, where the wind does not vibrate too fast."[5]

Music, Emotion, and the Voice

The Baroque period foregrounded the music of drama and tragedy, and, as Curt Sachs describes it in his insightful history of musical instruments:

The new generation strove for strong emotion: it tried to appeal to the listeners' hearts. "What passion cannot Music raise and quell," sings Dryden. Father Mersenne relates that Italian singers of his time expressed passions so violently that the audience would think they themselves were involved; and when, in an opera by Monteverdi performed in 1608 at the Mantuan court, Arianna, forsaken by Theseus, sang her heart-rending lament, the listeners burst into tears.[6]

As a result, polyphony receded and homophony—a form of music in which a single expressive melody stands out against a background of chordal accompaniment—began its ascendance. Homophony was thought to be more suited to the expression of emotion than polyphony, especially in opera. This happened first of all in singing, but it also caused radical changes in instrumental music. Instruments that, like the human voice, could produce a wide range of pitch, dynamics, timbral variation, vibrato, and so on were kept and further developed, especially strings. Other instruments disappeared in the space of a few decades—for instance, wind instruments in which the reed could not be grasped by the lips and that therefore did not allow "overblowing" in a higher octave, instruments such as the ranket, the cromorne, the schryari, and the rauschpfeife. The organ is also such an instrument, and organ builders sought to remedy its lack of expressiveness by creating voices like the "Viola da Gamba" and of course the "Voix-Humaine," putting them in a separate section of the organ, the *Rückwerk*, which was positioned behind the organist at the front of the organ gallery and looked like a mini organ all by itself. Voix-humaines also acquired their own windchests and their own, separate tremulants, and sometimes they were enclosed in thin-walled boxes to allow them to be played softer and louder, all to enhance the organ's potential for emotive expressiveness, and all for the divine instrument to become human—and for humans to become divine.

Developments of this kind have continued to the present day. The keyboard continues to reign and to be developed as a kind of master instrument—a compendium of all musical and other sounds. In the late nineteenth century, when Dutch clergyman Ten Kate heard in the organ of his church "the shepherd's flute, the wind, thunder, rain, streams, the nightingale, storms,"[7] the first theater organs had already been built, allowing an even wider range of sound effects, including doorbells, steamboat whistles, railroad bells, sirens, bird calls, and car horns, as well as many different musical instruments.[8] Wurlitzer theater organs also introduced the "double touch," whereby another voice could be introduced by pressing the keys harder, and the "pizzicato" touch, for a staccato or plucking effect. In 1927, one company, Marr and Colton, began to build organs with "symphonic registrators," presets with labels such as "Love (mother)," "Love (romantic)," "Love (passion)," "quietude," "jealousy," "hatred," "anger," "excitement," "agitation," "mysterious," "gruesome," "happiness," and "sorrow."[9] The violin and the cello continued to be key solo instruments and key instruments for the expression of emotion. In the twentieth century, the saxophone would play a similar role in jazz. Using elements of brass and woodwind, and combining the key arrangement of the oboe with the mouthpiece of the clarinet, the saxophone has an unrivalled capacity for the expressive variation of timbre, ranging, as Sachs put it, "from the softness of the flute, through the mellow tone of the cello, to the metallic strength of the clarinet."[10]

My own digital piano, the Roland RD300-SX, follows the tradition. Many of its voices imitate musical instruments, and others represent natural sounds, such as Seashore, Rain, Thunder, Wind, and Stream; animal sounds, such as Bird, Dog, and Horse Gallop; and mechanical sound effects, such as Cars, Trains, Planes, Gunshots, Machine Guns, and Explosions. Voice effects such as Laughter, Applause, and Screaming are also included. Like eighteenth-century European church organs, which featured different kinds of human voice stops such as the German *Jungfernregal* (Girls' Voices) and *Singendregal* (Singing Voices), and the Spanish *Viejos* and *Viejas* (Voices of Old Men and Women), *Vox pueri* (Boys' Voices), and *Vox tauri* (Bulls' Voices),[11] the Roland piano includes a range of human voices—Female Choirs, Aah Choirs, and Ooh Choirs, Humming, Jazz Scat, Solo Vox, Synvox, Analog Voice, and Space Voice. It also has a "humanizer" effect that can be added to every single one of the instrument's 270 voices, adding "a vowel colour to the sound" and "making it similar to the human voice."[12] Father Mersenne, living in a mechanical age, had not been able to foresee how the difficulty of producing vowel sounds and syllables might ever be overcome. Two-hundred and fifty years later, in the digital age, his vision was finally achieved. Or was it?

Abstract and Sensory Modality

To discuss how the modern Roland piano imitates the human voice, I will need to briefly recapitulate the theory of "modality" I introduced in an earlier publication.[13]

The idea of modality originated in philosophy as a term for the study of the truth conditions of propositions. When it was taken over in linguistics by linguists such as Lyons and Halliday,[14] an important shift occurred. While philosophers asked, "How likely is it that this proposition is true?" linguists asked "*As* how likely has this proposition been represented?" Linguistic signifiers of probability, such as the modal auxiliaries ("may," "will," "must") can be, and are, equally used for true and untrue propositions. Untrue propositions can be affirmed with great certainty, and, as evidenced by the case of the Holocaust deniers, doubt can be cast on true propositions. Language alone cannot guarantee truth, and linguistic analysis can therefore only bring out *as how* true something has been represented.

The idea of modality as apparent truth or verisimilitude has subsequently been applied to modes of communication other than language, including images[15] and can also be applied to representation by means of sound and music—for instance, the representation of musical sounds, natural sounds, and speech by musical instruments such as the Roland RD300-SX. In the case of sound and music, degrees of verisimilitude are signified by the degree to which certain means of auditory expression are used. Pitch range is one of these. You could, for instance, represent rain by means of a "pitter patter" rhythmic pattern on pizzicato strings with a very narrow and restricted range of just two pitches. This would not be very realistic, but it would nevertheless get the idea across. It would be a relatively abstract representation. You could also use an appropriate electronic sound with a good deal of hiss, increase the pitch range, and include dynamic variation and glissandos to suggest sheets of rain. This would not only be more naturalistic, but would also have a greater emotive effect. It would not only get the idea across, but also "feel" more like rain. And if the range of pitch, and of dynamic and timbral variation, is extended even further, the experience can become "more than real" and emotionally overwhelming. The cline of verisimilitude is not just a cline of verisimilitude, but also a cline of emotional involvement, a cline that runs from relatively "abstract" representation, through "naturalistic" representation, to what Kress and I have called *sensory representation*.[16] In the case of abstract representation, the truth criterion is conceptual: "to which degree does this sound represent the essential, constant qualities of what it represents, e.g., the 'idea of rain'?" In the case of naturalistic representation, the truth criterion is perceptual: "to which degree does this sound represent what we would have heard if we could have heard the real thing, under specific acoustic conditions?" In the case of sensory representation, the truth criterion is emotive: "to which degree does this representation engender the feelings that accompany an intense experience of what is represented?"

The same auditory parameters serve not only to indicate degrees and kinds of truth in representation, but also to indicate what Martinec[17] has called "presentation," for instance, the presentation of the identity of a speaker or a particular kind of action or event. In speech, a limited pitch range, for instance, is often used to present the "*not* human," such as the divine or the mechanical, as in stylized forms of ritual chanting or the monotonized speech of robots.

The key indicators of modality include not only pitch range, but also dynamic range. Instruments that do not allow dynamic variation are again a touch more abstract, a touch less emotive. As we saw, the organ is such an instrument, and eighteenth-century German organ builders therefore looked for ways to make the *vox humana* the only stop capable of dynamic variation.

Degrees of fluctuation form a third parameter, ranging from completely steady sounds to a maximally deep and/or rapid vibrato. Vibrato, as long as its speed and depth resemble the fluctuations the human voice is capable of, is a very effective signifier of emotive expression. Emotions can make our voice waver and tremble, and for this reason tremulants or tremblants played a key role in creating convincing imitations of the human voice in church organs.

Degrees of friction constitute a fourth parameter. "Friction" here refers to anything we hear besides and in addition to the tone itself—friction, hoarseness, harshness, rasp, sibilance, breathiness. This again increases verisimilitude. The guitar sounds of the Roland piano, for instance, lack the sound of the plectrum and of the fingers sliding along the fret board. This makes the sound inevitably less realistic and a little more abstract. Unlike musical instruments, the sound of the human voice is affected by different emotive states, and also by physical states such as fatigue, intoxication, health, and age. Different kinds of vocal friction can evoke different meanings, different emotions, and different associations. A rough, hoarse voice can signify having lived a rough, hard life. A breathy voice can signify exertion or excitement, and, combined with a soft whisper, it is a standard signifier of sensual seduction.

Degrees of absorption should also be mentioned. They range from the completely "dry" to the maximally spacious sound. Beyond a certain point, reverb can create an effect of dread, as in representations of extraterrestrial landscapes.

These parameters are not only capable of fine-grained degrees, but may also be combined in many different ways, providing a rich range of resources for the creation of verisimilitude and the expression of emotion. It is perfectly possible that some parameters of the same sound are "abstract" and others "sensory." The reed pipes of the church organ, for instance, are a fairly abstract and not very realistic representation of the human voice. At best, they put across the idea of a human voice, but they do not really sound like one. The sound of the tremulant, on the other hand, is both more realistic and more able to pull the heartstrings.

Musical representation always combines the abstract and the sensory. In Honegger's *Pacific 231*, for instance, the sound of the locomotive engine is played by brass, strings, and timpani, alternating between two pitch levels, first low and slow, then gradually faster and higher as the machine gathers speed, and the whistle is played by strings abruptly sliding up. There is no friction, no grinding of wheels on rails, no squeaks, no hissing, no shrillness in the whistle. The music gives the idea of the locomotive and the whistle, but it does not aim at realistic representation. At the same time, it is music, and therefore emotively engaging. It does not only represent the machine, it also makes us *feel* its power as the energy level of the music increases. "What I was looking for," said Honegger in 1924, "was not so much to imitate the sounds of the locomotive, but to translate visual impression and physical enjoyment with a musical construction." [18]

The Human Voice According to Roland

The instrumental basis of the "human voices" in the Roland RD300-SX remains that of a musical instrument. In some voices, it in fact reminds of the thin, reedy sound of the old *vox humana*. As in the church organs, it is the added parameters, not the tone itself, which makes the voice "human."

In the Aah Choir, for instance, a vowel sound is added to the instrumental sound, but only as a kind of flavor. Although speech synthesis or sampling techniques would make it perfectly possible to use an actual "aah," this is not what Roland has provided. The voices of the Aah Choir do not aim to "be" human voices, only to represent them in a way that—like Honegger's representation of a locomotive—is both abstract, and, because the Roland remains a musical instrument, sensory. Also added is "friction," in the form of a hiss. Again, it is not clear what this represents. Breath? It is difficult to say. Perhaps it forms a relatively abstract representation of the idea of friction, the idea of the "grain of the voice."[19] Finally, there is a slight and slow vibrato, to suggest the fluctuating timbre of the human voice. As in eighteenth-century church organs, these effects work only in the middle two octaves. They must be complemented by the way the instrument is played.

The Ooh Choir too has a quite thin and reedy instrumental base, sounding, perhaps, somewhat like strings. The "ooh"-like vowel sound is stronger here and has a consonantal attack which, if played forcefully, staccato, and not too slowly, makes for a relatively convincing "doo" (sustaining the tones destroys the illusion in less than a second). Unlike the Aah Choir, hiss is absent here and the vibrato is slight. In other words, the Ooh Choir relies more on its vowel sound and less on friction and fluctuation. Again unlike the Aah Choir, this voice also works at two octaves below the middle C, producing relatively convincing male voices.

The Jazz Scat voice makes use of the piano's "humanizer" effect, which alternates different vowels (this can be done at twenty-one different frequency levels, making it hard to use). Different pressure produces different vowels. A soft touch yields "doo doo doo," more pressure produces "pah pah pah" and sometimes a fast descending glissando. Some of the variation is preset and hard to predict for the player. To create a convincing instrumental imitation of scat singing, players quickly learn to restrict themselves to a fairly circumscribed pitch range, tempo, and attack (again, only staccato). Only a stereotyped version of scat singing can be produced in this way, and, as with so many imitative voices, it is difficult to use the voice for anything other than clichés.

The Space Voice, finally, uses the same "ooh" sound as the Ooh Choir and also has a hiss. But its fluctuation is fast and shallow (therefore "*not-human*") and its reverb strong. This voice reminds of the wordless choirs used to evoke desolate landscapes, such as in Vaughan Williams's *Antarctic Symphony,* or dark and sinister themes, such as in Benjamin Britten's evocation of Auden's "A Summer Night" in his *Spring Symphony,* or, to use a more recent example, John Williams's music for the movie *Harry Potter and the Prisoner of Azkaban.* At once human and *not*-human (because of the rapid vibrato and reverb), choirs of this kind evoke *not*-human landscapes and events while at the same time infusing them with the human emotion of dread.

Clearly, the Roland RD300-SX stands in a long tradition of instruments that on the one hand strive for greater emotive expressiveness and on the other hand use technologies that impel them to reduce human vocal expression to codifiable forms that inevitably strip away its unique "grain" and reduce it to a more abstract idea of "the" human voice. In this, it resembles the paradoxes of contemporary digital images that strive for ever greater realism, yet can achieve this only by codifying the very phenomena which, in older media, escaped codification and provided the realism of unpredictable randomness and grit. This struggle between the urge to retain a romantic emotivism and realism on the one hand, and the technological imperative of total codification on the other, is likely to continue for some time.

What then constitutes the "human" in this instrument's human voices? Clearly, on the one hand, we have the time-honored qualities of subjectivity, individuality, and emotionality. But on the other hand, humanity has become a surface phenomenon here—a dressing up of a mechanical and relatively character-less foundation. What was once the core, the very vibration of the vocal cords, the very articulation of the vowel sound, now becomes a surface phenomenon, a bit of spicing added to an essentially characterless substance.

A heart no longer beats inside.

Notes

1. Quoted in Fenner Douglass, *The Language of the Classical French Organ—A Musical Tradition Before 1800* (New Haven: Yale University Press, 1969), 95.

2. Ibid., 175.

3. Ibid., 186.

4. Ibid., 210.

5. Ibid., 177.

6. Curt Sachs, *The History of Musical Instruments* (New York: W.W. Norton, 1940), 351.

7. A. Bouman, *Nederland . . . Orgelland* (Leiden: Spruyt, Van Mantgem & De Does, 1964), 100.

8. John Landon, *Behold the Mighty Wurlitzer—The History of the Theatre Pipe Organ* (Westport, CT: Greenwood Press, 1983), 4.

9. Ibid., 28.

10. Sachs, *The History of Musical Instruments*, 415.

11. Peter Williams, *The European Organ 1450–1850* (London: B.T. Batsford, 1966), 288.

12. *RD-300SX Owner's Manual* (Roland Corporation, 2004), 55.

13. Theo van Leeuwen, *Speech, Music, Sound* (Basingstoke, Macmillan, 1999).

14. See, for example, John Lyons, *Semantics Vol. 2* (Cambridge: Cambridge University Press, 1977), and Michael Halliday, *Introduction to Functional Grammar* (London: Arnold, 1985).

15. See Kress and van Leeuwen, *Reading Images—The Grammar of Visual Design* (London: Routledge, 1996).

16. Ibid., 170.

17. Radan Martinec, "Types of Process in Action," *Semiotica* 130, no. 3/4 (2000): 243–268.

18. Sleeve notes of CD of Honegger's *Rugby* and *Pacific 231*, Erato 2292-45242-2. 1985.

19. Roland Barthes, *Image-Music-Text* (London: Fontana, 1977).

2 Before the Beep: A Short History of Voice Mail

Thomas Y. Levin

We shall deal here with humble things, things not usually granted earnest consideration, or at least not valued for their historical import. But no more in history than in painting is it the impressiveness of the subject that matters. The sun is mirrored even in a coffee spoon.

In their aggregate, the humble objects of which we shall speak have shaken our mode of living to its very roots. Modest things of daily life, they accumulate into forces acting upon whoever moves within the orbit of our civilisation.

—Siegfried Giedion[1]

Before the Beep

A dramatic advance in voice storage, processing, and retrieval technologies took place during the early 1990s, a transformation that first began to show up in appliances that suddenly started to "talk," announcing with uninvited familiarity that "you have twenty-three messages" or reminding one, as a rented cars suddenly began to do in an annoyingly insistent manner, to fasten one's seatbelt. In America, the futuristic thrill of navigating a complex of touch-tone menus in order to avoid an interminable hold and the resulting Muzak migraine is by now commonplace. Prompted by prerecorded, synthetic voices, we are increasingly encountering and exploiting all sorts of interactive, remote-controlled, intelligent data-processing machines. What I am referring to, of course, is the conjunction of affordable, high-speed computing power and sophisticated, as well as affordable, analog-to-digital (AD) and digital-to-analog (DA) conversion devices, i.e., contraptions that translate sound into digital information and vice versa. Among the more visible of the various products that this alliance has produced, in conjunction with the telephone, for example, is the phenomenon of voice mail, that is, the move from the electromagnetic answering machine to the digitalized storage of analog traces which can be retrieved (re-analogized) upon command.

Even more state-of-the-art in the early 1990s was voice email. Transmitted via the already widespread networks for electronic mail, voice email allows one to: (1) play back email as acoustic information, (2) transmit voice messages via a computer network (send someone a greeting that they will "hear" when they "read" their "mail," (3) verbally annotate a file as it scrolls by on somebody else's screen, and, then still in its very initial stages, (4) speak data into the computer rather than typing it.

Sound is thus slowly breaking into the domain of digital information processing systems, expanding a computer age still largely dominated by text (i.e., data and word processing) and (increasingly) image (AutoCAD and the like). As an unabashedly logocentrist author in *PC Magazine* put it in a 1990 article that rehearses a litany of photocentrist clichés:

Why would you want to hear voices over your network? Because, as humans, we used verbal expressions years before we began writing, and for many people verbalizing is easier and more satisfying than jotting thoughts down on paper. Speaking potentially evokes greater emotion, conveys greater sincerity, and promotes a higher level of trust than writing.

What this means is that, most likely, in the years to come people will be using more and more voice in their "documents," including, of course, dispatches of electronic voice mail. The computer is becoming a site of telephony, a sending of the voice as data. But for your voice to be sent, it must be translated into a form that can be stored, transported and reproduced; it too must, in other words, become writing.[2]

However strange the idea of writing with sound, I think most people do have some memory of a primitive voice mail experience, probably that now charmingly anachronistic use of the post to send friends recorded "letters" (acoustic epistles) on audiocassette tape, or, depending upon your age, on records recorded in booths specially outfitted for that purpose (figure 2.1). I describe these as primitive, of course, only because of the dramatic discrepancy between the speed and quality of the recording and the much slower rate of their subsequent transmission—a frustrating inequality that may well be one of the reasons for their ultimate failure.[3] Nevertheless, it is just this sort of rather literal voice mail or acoustic sendings that concern me here, that is, voice mail understood as the inscription, storage, and retrieval of acoustic traces on material media physically sent to a destination, for this sort of seemingly retrograde voice transmission may well explain a lot about the more sophisticated voice mail systems that so many of us increasingly revel in, resist, and/or resent today. What follows is a provisional archeology of this sort of voice mail, a history that culminates with the beep of that currently most widespread type of voice mail technology: the answering machine.

The answering machine itself, however, is hardly as "completely modern" as most people assume. Indeed, this now so widespread domestic technology was in fact invented in 1898 by the Danish physicist and engineer Valdemar Poulsen (1869–1942), pioneer of wireless or radio telegraphy and the man who broke the Marconi monopoly in the British Empire. Poulsen first presented his device to the public at the Paris Exhibition in 1900, officially divulging the details of his discovery in the September 22, 1900, issue of *Scientific American*[4]—the same year Freud published *The Interpretation of Dreams*. And yet this late-nineteenth-century contraption—known variously as the recording telephone, the telegraphone, the telegraphophone, or the telephonograph—did not differ in any fundamental technical way from our contemporary answering machines. Patented in 1899 as a means of "storing up speech or signals by magnetic influence," the telegraphone employed a steel wire or band (and soon thereafter a steel disc) instead of the now ubiquitous magnetic tape, recording acoustic information in the form of electromagnetic impulses and allowing for the indefinite storage or subsequent obliteration of these inscriptions on a medium whose inscribability was in no way compromised by being erased. In fact, the quality of the recordings was lauded by contemporary science writers as being significantly better than those of the phonograph. Even the employment of this device was from the start hardly different from that of today. But why, if the answering machine was effectively invented in the nineteenth century, did it take so long to get developed? Why, for example, did it take thirty years before an article in the *New York Times* of June 27, 1931, announced the impending marketing of the first telegraphone in the United States, with the headline "Phone Messages to Be Recorded"?

Of crucial concern here is the fact that the invention of the answering machine marks an important shift in the voice mail paradigm, belonging to a technological episteme in which the voice itself travels *per* telephone and activates a remote inscription device. Here, in other words, the sending, the *epistellein* of the epistle, the materiality of the transmission, appears

Figure 2.1
Voice-O-Graph record from the early 1940s for home recording of audio messages on 6" records at 45 or 78 RPM. This particular "voice letter," sponsored by GEM razors and blades during WWII as a "contribution to the morale of America's armed forces and the folks back home," depicts various aspects of the recording process which usually took place at USO shows and other military locations and was usually introduced by an operator who controlled the machine. Collection of Thomas Y. Levin.

to have been dramatically transformed, having become as rapid as the act of recording.

Despite this seemingly instantaneity, however, I would suggest that it is a mistake to succumb to the temptation of considering telephonic or digital voice mail as no longer material, since—as anybody who has had a "bad" telephone connection knows—the media of such inscriptions must still be understood as having a materiality, albeit one whose phenomenality is of a very different order, and no longer tangible. In other words, the missives of telephonic and digital voice mail still get lost, misdirected, damaged, delayed, and so on, just as did their more primitive predecessors. What the newer forms allow one to overlook, however, is the very fact of that materiality and the practice of inscription which is their condition of possibility. The ur-history of that materiality, of the long-standing dream of voice mail, will hopefully make clear that the history of voice mail cannot be understood apart from the history of the attempts to capture the acoustic, to render sound as writing, the history of the *graphe* or *gramme* of *phone*, which is to say, the history of the phonograph and gramophone (figure 2.2).

The vision of voice mail is a motif that dates back not three decades, as one might expect, but almost three centuries.[5] According to some accounts, this rather long history of voice mail begins in China during the reign of K'ang-hsi in the seventeenth century. A device, invented by Chiang Shun-hsin of Hui-chou, which became known as the "thousand-mile speaker" allowed a sender to speak into a wooden cylinder, which was then sealed and sent sometimes thousands of miles. On arrival, the recipient broke open the seal and the voice message resounded. Basically, the idea here is that because sound is a spatial phenomenon (a vibrating mass of air), if you could capture that vibrating air mass in some sort of container, you could liberate it from its tie to the body, to presence. A similar image of sound conserved in tubes recurs on a number of occasions, such as the seemingly well-known speaking-tube described in the Greek scholar Giovanni Battista Porta's *Magia Naturalis* of 1589.[6] The primitive model of physical conservation here is given a subtle (and literal) twist by Johann Joachim Becher's 1682 description of the stentrophonium,[7] which this adviser to Prince Ruprecht of Pfalz is reported to have discovered in the workshop of a Nuremberg optician and mechanical artisan named F. Gründler. This machine, so Becher claims, was capable of "catching many words as an echo by means of a spiral line within a bottle in such a way that one could

Figure 2.2
Demonstration Disc from circa 1948 for the Wilcox-Gay Coin Recordio, a sonic equivalent to the photo-booth for on-the-spot production of 78 RPM recordio-gram voice letters, manufactured starting in the late 1940s by the Wilcox Gay Corporation of Charlotte Michigan. Collection of Thomas Y. Levin

carry it for almost an hour over land" and then, upon opening, the words would sound anew. Even Becher describes the idea as fantastic, but notes that one ought not fail to attempt to make it a reality (note here the invocation of another important proto-gramophonic form: the spiral).

Or take the following example from 1632. In the Bibliotheque Nationale there is a thin little book with the title *Le Courrier Veritable* (the true mail!): no author, no publisher, but just a note indicating the date of publication to be April 23, 1632. In this mysterious document, the anonymous author—someone researching Australia—tells the story of a land of people with bluish-black skin that has no art and no science nor any written exchange. Nature has, however, given them a marvelous alternative means of communication, providing them with sponges that soak up all sounds and human language as well. People simply speak into the sponges and then send them to the person for whom the message is destined; they in turn lightly press on the sponge in order to hear the words they contain.

The sponge-model of voice mail assumes that the materiality of the acoustic is somehow liquid: sound is something that can be soaked up. A similar liquidity of sound informs another proto-voice mail fantasy: storage by means of freezing and reproduction by subsequent thawing. Perhaps the most famous version of this rather widespread sixteenth-century folkloric topos, besides the one by Munchhausen, is the rather amusing episode in Rabelais' *Gargantua and Pantagruel* (chapter LVI, book IV), in which a battle takes place during a winter so cold that the sounds of combat freeze and fall to the ground, only to thaw in the spring:

[Pantagruel] threw on the deck before us whole handfuls of frozen words, which looked like crystallized sweets of different colours. We saw some words gules, or gay quips, some vert, some azure, some sable and some or. When we warmed them a little between our hands, they melted like snow, and we actually heard them, though we did not understand them, for they were in a barbarous language. There was one exception, however, a fairly big one. This, when Friar John picked it up, made a noise like a chestnut that has been thrown on the embers without being pricked. It was an explosion, and made us all start with fear. "That", said Friar John, "was a cannon shot in its day".[8]

Even more amazing is the Moon book described by Cyrano de Bergerac in 1656 in his *Histoire comique des États et Empires de la Lune*. Recounting his arrival on the Moon, Cyrano tells of being given two strange books that one did not read, but instead listened to. Each contained a complex of watch-like gears and the pages had no letters. One read them "with one's ears," he explains.[9] In order to grasp the contents, one simply placed a needle on the desired chapter and—as if spoken by a human voice—one would hear it, loud and clear, albeit in the lunar language, of course.

The crucial step that moved voice mail from the domain of (science) fiction to that of experiment was made, surprisingly enough, in the context of German Romantic physics, still abuzz with the aphorist and researcher Georg Christoph Lichtenberg's 1777 findings that tiny metal particles formed distinct figures on positively or negatively charged fields. Here the mysterious phenomenon of electricity had finally become palpable; that is, electrical force had been translated into a visible—and thus readable—medium![10] An even more dramatic breakthrough of a very similar sort was the discovery in 1787 by Ernst Florens Friedrich Chladni—now considered the father of acoustics—of the visual patterns produced by acoustic waves. Chladni's experiment consisted of spreading quartz dust on glass plates that were then made to vibrate. Depending on the rate of the vibration, the dust distributed itself into lines, curves, and hyperbolas, gathering in those areas that were free of movement. Here, for the first time, one could associate acoustic phenomena with specific graphic figures which, most importantly, were "drawn" by the sounds themselves! These "tone figures," as Chladni explained in *Die Akustik* (1802), were not arbitrary but rather stood in some sort of a "necessary"—indexical—relation to the sounds. In the graphic traces of these "script-like ur-images of sound," one could see what another German physicist, Johann Wilhelm Ritter, called "the notation of that tone which it has written by itself."[11]

Barely a generation later, there began a series of attempts to translate this idea of sound writing itself into a practical technology. Consider, for example, the apparatus that measures the vibrations of sounding bodies described by Thomas Young in his 1807 "Course of lectures on natural philosophy and mechanical arts": here Young takes a tuning fork made to sound by bowing, and affixes to it a pen that draws the wave form corresponding to the pitch on a rotating cylinder. The same basic translation of sound into graphic traces also informs the appropriately named "phonautograph" invented by the typographer Leon Scott de Martinville in 1858. In the mid 1850s, Scott replaced the tuning fork with a sensitive membrane and a horn, rendering his device capable of capturing the acoustic waves in the air produced by various types of sound and translating them into wiggly lines inscribed on a charcoal-blackened paper mounted on a turning cylinder. Crucial here is to note that this apparatus was—true to its name—only an autograph, that is, a self-writing as traces of sound. This is, of course, only the realization of the first part of the tube voice mail fantasy: the capturing of the sounds as potentially transportable and then potentially readable inscription.

With the invention of photography, the realization of the essential second stage of voice mail—the restoration or retranslation of these traces back into sound—begin to proliferate. Typical in this regard was how Nadar himself in 1856 came up with the idea of a *daguerreotype acoustique* which would faithfully record *and reproduce* sounds with a fidelity comparable to that of the photograph. In 1864, he again mused:

One of these days it will come to pass that someone will present us with the daguerreotype of sound—the phonograph—something like a box within which melodies would be fixed and retained, the way the camera surprises and fixes images. To such an effect that a family, I imagine, finding itself prevented from attending the opening of a *Forza del destino* or an *Afrique*, or whatever, would only have to delegate one of its members, armed with the phonograph in question, to go there. And upon his return: "How was the overture?" "Like this!" "Too fast?" "There!" "And the quintet?" "Don't you think the tenor screeches a bit?"[12]

It was not Nadar, however, but another Frenchman, Charles Cros, a brilliant French poet, artist, and scientist (author of the first two-color photographic process), who took Scott's idea and pushed it one step further, proposing in a dossier deposited at the Paris Academy of Sciences on April 30, 1877, that one replace the charcoal paper with a wax cylinder onto which a needle would engrave the traces transmitted to it by the sensitive membrane. This is a major step, for by incising these waves, they could subsequently be retraced by another needle—or another stylus—which could translate them back into an acoustic event. Here was the principle for a machine that accomplished both inscription and subsequent reproduction. The only problem was that the poor poet Cros—a friend of Verlaine's, and favorite son of the Surrealists—was just that: poor. He thus did not have the money to actually build his device, which he christened the Parléophone. Then, to Cros's dismay, the November 17, 1877 issue of *Scientific American* announced that work was being done in Menlo Park on the bold and original idea of recording the human voice upon a strip of paper, from which at any subsequent time, it might automatically be redelivered with all the vocal characteristics of the original speaker accurately reproduced. Fearing—and rightly so—that he would not be credited as having been the first to propose such a device, Cros demanded that his dossier be opened and read at the Academy, which it finally was on December 5, 1877. Two weeks later, Edison, who had been able to actually build a working model of his phonograph, applied for a patent.

What is crucial here is to consider for a moment the consequences already anticipated by Scott's "phonautograph," which was an attempt to produce, as the machine's subtitle explained, an "Apparatus for the Self-Registering of the Vibrations of Sound." The resulting "natural stenography" would, in turn, be sound writing itself.[13] Similarly, during the first half of the nineteenth century, phonography—understood as a "system of phonetic shorthand invented by Isaac Pitman in 1837" (OED)—was heralded as a "natural method of writing" and was arduously defended by workers' groups as a means of making writing more widely accessible.[14] But in what sense could the gramophone function as a "natural stenography," as a type of "phonography" in the Pitmanian sense?

To answer this question, it is crucial to recall that one of the most popular—but forgotten—uses of the early phonographs was to record one's own voice. Through the use of the gramophone, illiteracy would be eliminated by substituting listening and speaking for reading and writing, since the first generation of gramophones could both play and record. They not only played prerecorded music, but could also be "erased" and reinscribed with new music or a spoken message. The most widespread commercialization of this capability, of course, occurred in dictating machines, such as Dr. Seward's phonograph diary in Bram Stoker's *Dracula*, and in gramophones customized for learning languages. The use of gramophones as domestic music machines was developed only much later. During both the initial and later phases, however, there were also attempts to market the new read/write 'talking machines' (as they were called) for other purposes, among them postal correspondence. Although the phonograph would eventually become almost exclusively a playback technology for musical entertainment, Edison himself had conceived the device first and foremost as a tool for business correspondence:

The main utility of the phonograph [is] for the purpose of letter writing and other forms of dictation, the design is made with a view to its utility for that purpose.[15]

Edison envisioned that "phonogram" sheets containing as much as four thousand words each would eventually become the primary epistolary form. What we have here is nothing less than the first, literal, voice mail, the birth of what elsewhere would come to be known as the Phonopostal (figure 2.3).

The "phonopost"—speaking postcards that one could record and send through the mail—made writing superfluous, a fact stressed by advertisements that invited potential users to drop their dictionaries and "Speak! Don't write any more! Listen!" The ambivalent political consequences of what is effectively a vision of instantaneous universal literacy—similar in this regard to the esperantist discourse surrounding the advent of cinema—are quite dramatic. Advertisements frequently staged the figure of the young woman or girl juxtaposed with the dictionary-toting, bespectacled old man, clearly casting her as the figure of the paradigmatically disenfranchised—that class of illiterates or semiliterates excluded from the privilege of correspondence by their inability to read and write. Indeed, women did become the primary users of the new dictation technology, marking, as Friedrich Kittler has pointed out, a dramatic shift in the gender of the previously male scribe class, with the proviso that although women did then largely dominate the material production of writing, it is most often the writing of a male voice.[16] Female secretaries took dictation, translating voice to writing, phone into graphemes. Thus it is hardly surprising that women not only became identified with the phonographic correspondence, but actually became the figure for the phonographic technology itself, as in the logo of *Phonographische Zeitschrift*, where the device that translates the acoustic into writing is nothing other than a woman's body.

Unlike the cylinder phonographs used for dictation machines, the phonopost apparatuses were often disc machines, a flat medium, based on the gramophone model developed by Emile Berliner in Washington in 1887, and preferable less because of its resemblance to traditional writing surfaces than for the ease with which it could be mailed. The apparatuses marketed especially for this purpose included the Phonopostal, a small, rather low-quality machine, and Pathé's Pathépost machine, introduced in 1908 and sold in limited quantities through WWI after which its name was changed to Pathégraph. The phonopost, effectively the first not merely phantasmatic but actually functional voice mail, unfortunately had problems: the inferior quality of the phonographs produced recordings that were difficult to understand (to which it must be added that few people knew the proper way to speak into the horn in order to get the maximum clarity), and the recording medium itself was quite fragile.

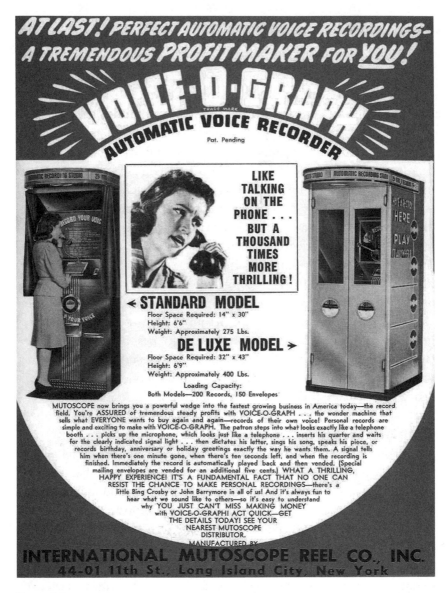

Figure 2.3

"It's a fundamental fact that no one can resist the chance to make personal recordings." 1957 Advertisement for the Voice-O-Graph Coin Operated Recording Booth, manufactured by the International Mutoscope Reel Company in Long Island, NY. Collection of Thomas Y. Levin.

The subsequent history of phonopost is short-lived; voice mail would have to wait for the advent of the next popularly available read/write technology: the tape deck. In the meantime, a commercialized variant of phonopost appeared; the largely gimmick-oriented fad in the late 1940s and 1950s for gramophonic postcards—images that one could play on a phonograph. These curious artifacts—fascinating in that the two systems of their doubly inscribed surfaces (photographic and gramophonic) in no way interfere with each other, despite the exponential increase in the density of information—are not acoustic epistles in the same sense, for here sound (and image) are prefabricated, leaving only the traditional obverse space of the postcard for a penned missive. However, as a transportable materialization of sound, they are nevertheless part of the tradition of postally transmitted acoustic inscriptions.

The late 1950s saw the birth of yet another type of sendable acoustic data: the first acoustic news magazine, *Sonorama*. This complex artifact, composed of image, text, and 33 RPM discs to be "read with the ear," effectively adds (so we read in the premier issue of October 1958) a new sensory dimension to print media, giving radio news a memory trace—a duration that exceeds its transmission. Spiral-bound and punctured in the middle with a hole, one turned the pages of this journal, reading articles, and then placed the entire object on the gramophone in order to listen to the acoustic documents, music, and interviews contained in the other "pages." Made possible by the development of high-quality record pressing on very thin vinyl (flexidisks), the multimedia journal *Sonorama*, which continued well into the 1960s, never provoked the dramatic revolution in the history of the press that its founders anticipated. In its juxtaposition of text, image, and sound, and in its insistence on the status of sound as text, it did, however, make an important point about the condition of possibility of the material storage, transmission, and reproduction of sound—namely, that it too is, in an important sense, writing. The proximity of the photographic, textual, and gramophonic traces in *Sonorama* served only to foreground their semiotic heterogeneity. Unlike the photographs and articles, which usually can be read by means of our "built-in" apparatus (along with the necessary technological supplements such as glasses and the like), the acoustic "texts" usually did require an external interface in order to be read (indeed, one that—through its spinning—momentarily rendered the others unreadable). Even the latter condition seems only contingent, if one is to take seriously the case of Tim Wilson, a 33-year-old Englishman who made the rounds of British and American talk shows in 1985 demonstrating his particular ability to "read" unlabeled records simply by looking at them, ostensibly reading the patterns of the grooves with his eyes! Alas, this rather hilarious confirmation of Moholy-Nagy's vision of a gramophonic "groove-script" remains unavailable to most people, for whom the phonograph "pages" remain undecipherable without the required technical prosthesis. Although recognizable as inscriptions in their concentric spiral form, it is these very traces that are being obliterated and/or reconfigured in both the pop-cultural and the avant-garde variants of the turntablist practice of scratching.

After the Beep

What then can one learn in the school of scratch? Many things, surely, but among them, a lesson about the historicity of the inscriptional status of sound, a point also explored by contemporary work on the gramophone by artists such as Stuart Sherman or Maurizio Kagel. With the elimination of the literal grooviness of sound, acoustic writing has entered a new episteme, a new paradigm called the digital. Today sound, image and text are all "written" in the same digital language, a language whose fidelity and longevity depends—as voice mail always has—on the particular qualities of its mode of inscription.

What we see here in this field of pure difference (zero or one)—which is to say the condition of writing as such—is also, of course, sound as writing, but it is an inscription of a significantly different sort. No longer an indexical trace, this digital code abandoned the order of the analogic that characterized both the photograph and the gramophone, revealing the hidden semiotic solidarity between the two elements of the gramophonic postcards: a now anachronistic indexicality. If both the photo- and the phonographs bore some sort of existential semiotic relation to the information they contained—this being their analogic character—digital code is a writing that forsakes that economy entirely, providing us with reliability of transmission by transforming analogy into information, a sampling of the acoustic curve approximately 44,100 times per second, which is then translated into 14-, 16-, or 18-digit strings of zeroes and ones. It is this that allows us, with contemporary voice mail systems, to not only record, revise, and/or erase a message remotely, but also to literally send it elsewhere and to multiple addresses.

This is not the place to explore in detail the semiotic specificity of digital sound. Rather, the more modest goal of this meditation has been to establish that for sound to travel across distance and time, it must first be translated into something else that is the condition of possibility of that transmission. Indeed, as the voice and sound in general becomes increasingly transmitted, as phonetic inscription seems to displace the practice of writing, the history of phonopost reminds us—as does the auratic indexicality in contemporary hip-hop culture's practice of scratching—that, before the voice can be mailed, it must first be written. Voice mail, in other words, reveals speaking as inscription, as translation, as writing.

Acknowledgments

This article is reprinted from Alessio Cavallaro, Frances Dyson, Shaun Davies, and Annemarie Jonson, eds., *Essays in Sound 2: Technophonia* (Sydney: Contemporary Sound Arts, September 1995), 59–67. A much longer version was published as "Vor dem Piepton: Eine kleine Geschichte des Voice Mail," in: Ulrich Raulff and Gary Smith, eds., *Wissensbilder: Strategien der Überlieferung* (Berlin: Akademie Verlag, 1999), 279–318.

Notes

1. Siegfried Giedion, *Mechanization Takes Command* (New York: W.W. Norton, 1948), 3.

2. Frank J. Derfler, Jr., "Voice E-Mail: Building Workgroup Solutions," *PC Magazine*, July 1990, 13.

3. To get a sense of just what sort of memory demands we are talking about here, it might be helpful to point out that the file size of a spoken text depends both on the sampling rate of the AD (analog to digital) converter and the speech rate of the person speaking, but for email it is between 50 and 100 kb/minute—the higher the sound quality of a recording, the more memory it takes up.

4. "Poulsen's Telegraphone," *Scientific American*, September 22, 1900, 178.

5. On the prehistory of the gramophone, see Eugene H. Weiss, *Phonographes et Musique mécanique* (Paris: Hachette, 1930) and W.Weiss-Strauffacher, *Mechanische Musikinstrumente und Musikautomaten* (Zurich: Orell Füssli Verlag, 1975).

6. Giambattista della Porta, *Magiae naturalis libri XX in quibus scientiarum naturalium divitiae et deliciae demonstrantur* (Naples: Apud Horatium Salvianum, 1589), vol. 16, chap. 12.

7. Two of the earliest references to this account can be found in F. M. Feldhaus, "Der Phonograph im 17.Jahrhundert," *Phonographische Zeitschrift* vol. 6 no. 43 (1905), 949, and in Rudolf Lothar, *Die Sprechmaschine. Ein technisch-Aesthetischer Versuch* (Leipzig: Feuer-Verlag, 1924), 11.

8. François Rabelais, *The Histories of Gargantua and Pantagruel*, trans. by J. M. Cohen (Harmondsworth: Penguin, 1955), 569.

9. Cyrano de Bergerac, *Voyages to the Moon and the Sun*, trans. by R. Aldington (New York: The Orion Press, 1962), 136.

10. On the details of Lichtenburg's discovery, see Walter D. Wetzels and Johann W. Ritter, *Physik im Wirkungsfeld der deutschen Romantik* (Berlin/New York: Walter de Gruyter, 1973), 88ff.

11. Cited in Walter D. Wetzels, *Johann Wilhelm Ritter: Physik im Wirkungsfeld der deutschen Romantik.* (Berlin: Walter de Gruyter, 1973), 91.

12. F. Nadar, *Les Mémoires du géant* (Paris: E. Dentu, 1864), p. 1, cited in Jacques Perriault, *Mémoires de l'ombre et du son: une archéologie de l'audio-visuel* (Paris: Flammarion, 1981), 133–134.

13. Édouard-Léon Scott de Martinville, *Le Problème de la parole s'écrivant elle-même* (Paris: La France, l'Amerique [chez l'aute], 1878). In 1849, Scott had published a study of stenography entitled *Histoire de la Sténographie depuis les temps anciens jusqu' a nos jours.*

14. Isaac Pitman, *Phonography, or Writing by Sound: A Natural Method of Writing, Applicable to All Languages, and a Complete System of Shorthand* (London: S. Bagster and Sons, 1840).

15. Thomas A. Edison, "The Phonograph and Its Future," *North American Review*, June 1878.

16. See the section titled "Typewriter" in Friedrich Kittler, *Gramophone, Film, Typewriter.* Geoffrey Winthrop-Young and Michael Wutz, trans. (Stanford: Stanford University Press, 1999), 183ff.

3   Voice-Cast: The Distribution of the Voice via Podcasting

Virginia Madsen and John Potts

Contemporary audio media have been transformed by the advent of digitization and the ready downloading and distribution of digital audio files on the Internet. Podcasting, which emerged with unexpected rapidity in 2005, has achieved wide popularity due to two of its characteristics: time-shifting, which allows users to listen to audio items when and where they choose; and mobility, due to the portability of the iPod and other MP3 players. Another core feature of podcasting is the central role of the voice: many podcasts comprise voice only, or voice accompanied by minimal music and audio effects.

In this chapter, we consider the significance of this new distribution of the voice through podcasting: a distribution that extends voices—and voice performances in particular—not only through space, but also potentially through time. As we will argue, one of the key attributes that may be genuinely new and even revolutionary to podcasting lies in its creation of a new and extended sphere for the performance of the essentially *acousmatic* voice. By acousmatic, we mean the transmission and reception of voices (people and things) without their origin being visible.[1] And far from being disembodied or disincarnate, the acousmatic voices activated through podcasting carry the traces of their bodies with them, or more correctly, they become their own "voice-bodies"—set adrift in space and now also in time. Like seed pods, perhaps, as light as air and global in their reach, these "voice-bodies" from the past as well as the present are released to drift through cyberspace, awaiting that moment of connection in which they may begin to take root and multiply. Podcasting thus opens up a new sphere of voicings and of words in motion and "in suspension": through the MP3 download of the "voice-cast" an ever growing reservoir of old and new voices await activation as they find listeners. This means that a genuinely new extended auditory space for these acousmatic voices has emerged. It is a voice-talk sphere which draws on traditions of radio talk and radiophony, distinguishing itself from that other audio sphere extended by the MP3 download: music.

Podcasting is a singular audio media form then with potentially revolutionary qualities; at the same time, its closest kin remains an "old media" form, the radio. This is why we choose to assess podcasting in the context of the long history of radio dissemination and radiophony, particularly the tradition incorporating amateur radio, community radio, and other manifestations of the citizen voice. These communications utopias founded on the broadcast voice continue to resonate with their private and more public longings, intersecting in the age of the MP3 download, with contemporary ideas of user-generated content within a digital commons, or expanded public sphere. But, as John Durham Peters also reminds us, "democracy and eros remain the twin frames for the popular reception of each new medium."[2] In this way, podcasting recalls attempts at communication with potential lovers or the dead, just as it is also an extension of broadcast radio, literally, with all its utopian democratic and profane commercial entertainment baggage. It also may return us to an earlier vision of "crystal set" communications and "listeners-in," of a radio or even radiated telephony (and the "party line") where transmission and reception were perhaps as uncertain as they were unregulated.

Our study of podcasting also considers this phenomenon within the history of the technologizing of the voice: its "faithful" and playful recording, reproduction, and distribution. It is in this context that we explore further this explosion of trained and unruly voices' acousmatic effects. What gives these voices their particular power and weight? As a means of gleaning the potential of the digitized podcast voice, we survey recent applications of podcasting in various forms, including its recent massive uptake by the public service radio sector—which appears to be constituting a revitalization of the public radio (and public institutional) voice.

A Short Genealogy of Podcasting

The word "podcasting," a fusion of "broadcasting" and "iPod," began to be used three years after Apple's launch of the iPod in 2001. An early reference to the new form of audio distribution was made by the journalist Ben

Hammersley in 2004. Remarking that Apple's iPod and other MP3 players were already "in many pockets," and that weblogging had become "an established part of the internet," Hammersley observed that these factors, combined with the availability of free or cheap audio production software, created "all the ingredients" for "a new boom in amateur radio." His attempt to name this new form was tentative: "But what to call it? Audioblogging? Podcasting? GuerillaMedia?"[3] Later that year, a weblog item posted by Doc Searls anticipated a new form of radio "where we choose what we want to hear." Searls entitled his blog "DIY radio with PODcasting."[4]

The contrast between these tentative mentions of a possible audio distribution platform in 2004, and the actuality of podcasting only a year later, is remarkable. Dan Gilmour states that whereas a Google search for "podcasts" in September 2004 yielded only 24 hits, the same search in October 2005 elicited over 100 million hits, "growing daily." By the end of 2005, tens of thousands of individuals and organizations had made podcasts available for downloading, and traditional radio stations were already releasing podcasts of programs on their websites.[5] The neologism "podcast," uncertainly floated at the beginning of 2004, was in such widespread use by August 2005[6] that it was included in the *Oxford English American Dictionary*.[6]

The explosion in use and awareness of podcasting can be traced to the middle of 2005.[7] This extremely rapid emergence of a new type of audio production, distribution, and reception was closely connected to technological developments. In June 2005 Apple added a podcasting feature to its popular iTunes software, at the same time making more than 3,000 podcasts available for no cost. Apple declared that more than one million subscriptions to podcasts via iTunes were made in just two days in that month.[8] The appeal of podcasting transcended the consumption of audio files by computer users: iTunes also allowed users to create and publish their own podcasts. Podcasting thereby incorporated, from the moment of its entry into wide cultural awareness, aspects of both production and consumption. Apple capitalized on its marketing momentum (its iPod brand name had, after all, been absorbed into the generic name of this new medium) by trumpeting podcasting as "the next generation of radio."[9] This particular technological and marketing innovation was the culmination of a series of technological developments, including compressed audio files, the Really Simple Syndication (RSS) file format, and podcasting software.[10]

However, it would be a mistake to focus exclusively on technological innovation in attempting to explain the popularity of podcasts and their adoption by a variety of media organizations and individuals. The broader social context of podcasting includes the culture of weblogging into which the new audio platform emerged, and a rhizomatic "links" culture helping to extend the podcast through space and time. The journalist Stephen Baker observed in the middle of 2005 that "the heart of the podcasting movement is in the world of blogs, those millions of personal Web pages that have become a global sensation."[11] The easily constructed and maintained personal websites, and nontraditional circuits of communication available on the internet allowing greater freedom—the subject of recent theoretical work in "distributed aesthetics"[12]—were part of the cultural matrix in which podcasting could flourish. In 2005 a BBC news item stated: "There are now thousands of different podcasts—from gardening programs, film and TV review programs, shows about motherhood, wine, religion and technology—with the overwhelming majority of them made by ordinary people in their own homes."[13]

Listeners in the United States, who were in particular disaffected with commercial radio's conservative programming and "plague" of advertising,[14] could now create their own podcasts ("from back rooms, sheds and even cars")[15] while accessing a far broader range of audio materials (and voices) than found on traditional radio. Podcasts such as the now long-running "The Dawn and Drew Show!" (2004–), to which we return later, feature the shenanigans of "two self-described ex-gutter punks who now podcast from a 19th century dairy farm in southeast Wisconsin and talk raunchy about love, sex and even farm animals."[16] Much of the early excitement surrounding podcasting then concerned the use of these new technologies to challenge or bypass traditional communication and media channels.[17] Podcasting in 2005 was about "reclaiming the radio," "refreshing the radio," ignoring the hierarchical "gate-keeping" role of mass media, and developing instead a "horizontal"—even rhizomatic—media form where consumers were also producers (*prosumers*) engaged in ongoing conversations with other producer/consumers.[18] In this first stage of podcasting, as we might now label it, a "raw naïveté and quirkiness of such programming" could be "appealing and refreshing to jaded listening ears."[19] Adam Curry, a pioneering voice in podcasting in the United States (previously well known as an MTV Veejay) declared that: "Using the theater of the mind, using sound as art—this is something we've forgotten how to do in radio."[20]

Though much-maligned vertical media—including commercial radio networks in the United States and elsewhere—were construed as the "old media" against which the grassroots-led "new media" were pitted, it is noteworthy that radio as a medium was not rejected by the new audio practitioners. Even Apple, while marketing podcasting and iTunes, used terms such as "Radio Reborn" to capture the appeal of the new format.[21] Podcasting here was thus explicitly associated with an earlier, potentially more spontaneous, democratic, anarchic form of radio expression: first the amateur-led two-way radio communications of the 1920s and earlier, talk- and voice-based, and then later pirate radios and community "access" broadcasting from the 1970s onwards.

A new call to creativity in audio programs might also be understood as a harking back to the middle "golden age" period of radio drama and performance, relegated to the realm of nostalgia and amnesia with the arrival of television in the 1950s.[22] The new podcasters in America also cited the loss of their more edgy nonconformist DJing tradition in popular music radio (originating in the pirate radios of the 1960s), the Wolfman Jacks now discarded by increasingly conservative networks who feared listeners becoming too distracted to attend to their advertising content or station jingles. The heavily formatted and syndicated radio dominant in the United States for many years had become so stultifying, critics argued, that any real individual creativity or spontaneity had become virtually impossible. Wolfman Jack (who also would appear in the movie *American Graffiti*) was the "daddy" of all these unorthodox yet highly influential DJs. His gravelly voice persona is perhaps worth recalling from the vaults as one progenitor for some of the wilder amateur podcaster offerings today. Becoming a cult figure on XERF "border" radio, he was first renowned for his provocative anarchic radio presentation and his unmistakable "voice-body" with its grainy breathy, sexy, sometimes screaming antics. Of course he wasn't born with that name. He grew up as "plain old Bob Smith in the tough New York neighborhood of Brooklyn"[23] where "neglected by his parents," he sought communion and perhaps inspiration from those illicit "voices he heard on the radio at night beaming up from the Mexican border."[24]

The Long Tail Prehistory of Podcasting

The trope of "rebirth" links podcasting to a more innocent time of experimentation in radio voice transmission and programming; first, the time of radio "hams" with crystal sets, headphones, and dials in the dark, enthusi-asts throwing out new-sounding lines into the unexplored *ether*—the first "geeks"?—trawling for productive connections or couplings with unknown speakers and listener-operators. In this vision of a new hope opened by pod-casting (beyond standardized models of entertainment based on pure prof-itability), we are returned to this prior or insufficiently explored medium in its experimental phase (broadcast wireless) and its earlier dreams of a specifically democratic two-way communication across distance. Much to the disappointment of early radio critics, like Bertolt Brecht in his oft-cited article "The Radio as an Apparatus of Communication" (1932),[25] the radio industry's reduction to the one-way flow of broadcasting (the one-to-many model) meant the loss of radio's potential as a two-way civic and democra-tizing voice. Brecht castigated and advised:

[R]adio is one-sided when it should be two. It is purely an apparatus for distribution, for mere sharing out. . . . Change this apparatus over from distribution to commu-nication. The radio would be the finest possible communication apparatus in public life. . . . That is to say, it would be if it knew how to receive as well as transmit, how to let the listener speak as well as hear, how to bring him into a relationship instead of isolating him.

Brecht's next words are almost uncanny today: "[R]adio should step out of the supply business and organize its listeners as suppliers."[26] Along with Brecht, who was also responding to the growing demagoguery of the time in Germany and the rising tones of the dictator, the earliest utopian visions of radio embodied in ham radio and "the listener-in" experience advocated active "production"/participation by individuals and an anarchic unregu-lated interactive, dialogic communication. Sabine Breitsameter describes the experience in these terms: "Every night, hundreds of radio amateurs would assemble in the ethers. Call and answer occurred on the same fre-quency—by the dozens, simultaneously. The whole thing was like a mod-ern day Internet chat scenario, but you could hear every bit of it."[27]

We can hear these earlier voices once more resounding in the new DIY podcasting sphere of enthusiastic amateurs and dabblers who today have become for all intents and purposes their own radio stations, and are able to produce their own small (or extremely large and profitable) "radio" net-works and shows through RSS, the iPod, and the Web's implicit "link" cul-ture.[28] The media artist Richard Kriesche appeared prophetic in 1988 when he talked of the new "radio man" in his performance "Radiozeit":

The electric man no longer listens to the radio—he himself is radio . . . he creates around himself the postmodern aura of an omnipresence. His exterior is radiant . . . [and] his interior is embedded in the electronic community of the data background.[29]

The almost-forgotten dreams of an unfettered community of voices, made visible to each other communing through the ether, disembodied but yearning for other bodies, can be heard as a sympathetic vibration with the audio bloggers and audience activism voices now populating cyberspace. Much of the utopian "talk" generated around podcasting, blogging, and online citizen journalism and other emergent *participatory* new media forms is centered around this new release of voices *and presence* into everyday life. The viral or rhizomatic libertarian potential of this activity is a contribution to what Pierre Lévy has called "collective intelligence."[30] The related explosion of democratic dialogs occurs through the Internet's deterritorialization of mainstream media, its activation of a dialogic two-way "citizen voice" and through time-shifting capacities enabled within Internet media communications.[31]

But perhaps there are also losses and missed connections here in the tangled thicket of voices on display, voices we can never really follow or "sound out." Jean-Luc Nancy refers to voices as possessing weight when he asserts that the voice "is not a thing, it is the means by which something-someone-takes distance from the self and lets that distance resonate."[32] In the wake of podcasting, there is an almost delirious abundance of voices in the crowd, a glossolalia with many unable to germinate or extend themselves efficiently enough to be heard beyond their own small niche communities. These are voices without sufficient resonance or weight to find a community or bridge the gap of distance (the potential vacuum) that threatens no matter how persuasive our beliefs in connectivity might otherwise be. They are voices that speak to anyone—or no one—voices in the babble, in Babel, which may leave us with little more than a half-tuned twitter to decipher. They fail to become "favorites" in the exploded media environment that counts "successes" increasingly in "hits" and through the new aggregating possibilities of social networking.

Podcasting undoubtedly offers new hope for some of these voices, through sidestepping the gatekeepers and building on (multiplying) communities of like-minded listeners. Sometimes it can even surprise the podcasters how far their voices can actually be carried, and to how many. Dawn and Drew of "The Dawn and Drew Show"—the previously mentioned couple podcasting from their Wisconsin country barn since 2004 ("a gou-lash of hotness" or "Studio B Studio Barn" as they describe it)—commented on the occasion of their hundredth show: "Yeah, there are not many shows who have reached 100 and we've come onto you 100 times." While listen-ing to some of their own uncensored highlights handpicked from their last hundred programs, Dawn reflects, "Who'd have thought anyone would listen?" "Take this, Big Brother! I don't need you. I don't need your fucking contracts. I've got my own radio show!" Referencing themselves in their program as being in the "Top 10" on Podcast Alley,[33] this pair can be heard to speak with increasing confidence as they witness their niche audience growing beyond locals, friends, and family, as it presumably started. Dawn and Drew had uploaded nearly nine hundred programs as podcasts by the end of 2009, starting from their opening episodes recorded with little more than a cheap laptop, Apple's GarageBand software, and a poor-sounding internal microphone. Drew even sounds like an early amateur radio ham operator (and the quality of the "transmission" is almost as bad) when he "IDs" their very first podcast with the words "So, this is September 23. It's 10:19 p.m., broadcas . . . [slip of the tongue] podcasting from Allington, Wisconsin."[34]

Since program No. 100, the couple has professionalized their outfit, with higher-fidelity recordings and inclusions of radio style stings, signature tunes, and use of sound effects and music (not to mention sponsors). Nev-ertheless, they still offer us a perfect example of the unregulated voice made possible by podcasting and rarely even heard on pirate radio. As they sign off "Goodnight everybody, goodnight Internet,"[35] one can still hear that this voice and production, no matter how illicit—or, for some, risqué—with explicit sex talk, is modeled on their hearing of the traditional radio chat show format. Only here the "radio" of the podcast comes from the private vernacular world of the couple, the bedroom, the home, complete with the occasional family member and even their dogs. Dawn in particular, playing with the sense of a private space revealed (on exhibition) to the listener's imagination through acousmatic sound (private voice to private ear), enjoys the salacious play made possible by this kind of radio persona invisible to the eye. Performing herself (simulating or performing real sex or recounting stories that we cannot be sure are true), Dawn's voice can be recognized as being both a marker of an identity and a mask (masque) for it. Both a sense of authenticity and performed play enter these "real-ity" home-studio podcasts—although one might complain of an excess of self-indulgence or narcissism. One of the explanations for the show's popularity may also lie here, in the show's slippage between reality and artifice, matched with the "characters'" pronounced ordinariness—heard in their apparently "unproduced" voices and in the equally unscripted feel of their presentation.

The Technologized Voice

Why is the voice so prominent in podcasting? One reason no doubt is the ease with which a microphone can now be connected to a computer with Internet access (and most computers now have built-in microphones, although these do not as effectively produce the desired "presence" and rich voice capture as custom-built external high-fidelity microphones). For little extra expense, the computer easily becomes a recording studio and editing suite, as we have seen.[36] Copyright regulations are also a factor, to date preventing the use of copyright-protected music on many amateur podcast productions and on many professionally made programs.[37] Many podcast programs comprise then a simple spoken word delivery imparting information on the interests or enthusiasms of the program-makers. Programs made available for download by radio stations are frequently spoken word: current affairs, analysis, interviews, comedy, and other genres. The range of subjects and themes available on spoken word podcasts is vast, resulting in a new spectrum of voices available to listeners when they want to hear them. This distribution of voices should be considered, however, within the broader context of the history of developments in the technologizing of the voice.

Thomas Edison's recording and playback of the words "Mary had a little lamb" in 1877 preserved the spoken word in the form of a recording; successive technical developments improved the quality of recording and replay, refining the process of the technological displacement of the voice first displayed by Edison. R. Murray Schafer coined the term "schizophonia" to denote the splitting of a sound from its natural source by the means of recording technology.[38] Such a technology is also "schizochronic," in that it splits a sound from its time;[39] in the case of the voice, a recording splits it from the time of its utterance. The recording comprises spoken words preserved as a past sequence of time; these recorded words constitute a past waiting to be returned to the present, in the act of replay. The recorded voice is thus split across time: when it is played back, it is marked by the technological intervention of recording; it is also marked by its displacement in time.

The archival dimension of podcasting enhances the schizochronic aspect of the recorded voice. The array of podcasts assembled by any listener, or arranged on any website, constitutes a library of voices waiting to be returned to the present. The spoken word is stored and "time-shifted," accessed and played back whenever required by the listener. In this way, voices are summoned from their storage and reactivated; later, they are returned to a "suspended" archival state, awaiting further invocation.

Much of the extraordinary popularity of podcasting may be attributed to this time-shifting capacity. Listeners are enabled to download and store audio items to be listened to whenever—and in whichever sequence—they choose. This is potentially an empowering process that allows consumers to program their own listening experience. Here the contrast with traditional radio broadcasting is sharp: the listener to a radio station is dependent on the station producers and programmers for the succession of audio items. Podcasting operates in a manner contrary to the principle of sequence or flow, which Raymond Williams identified as "the defining characteristic of broadcasting."[40] For Williams, the "planned flow" of programming introduced by radio (and then television) broadcasting was a formal departure from all previous communications systems, in which "the essential items were discrete."[41] Podcasting thus returns audio communication to a pre-broadcasting condition, assembling audio items as "discrete" and separated from any sense of sequenced flow. In some cases, these programs have become works-in-progress, with listeners invited to tinker and transform the podcast. A new development in this area is the virtual studio, a tool to be offered to the prosumer of a program or station, opening the podcast to multiple versionings and remixes.[42]

Portable audio playback devices add the element of mobility to the character of recorded sound, further expanding the technological displacement of the sound from its source. The mobile facility of MP3 players takes its place within the history of portable recorded audio, which includes the transistor radio of the 1960s and the Sony Walkman of the 1980s. These portable devices were principally used, however, for the mobile enjoyment of music. The ghetto-blaster prominent in the 1980s and 1990s, for example, was often used to mark out urban territory through the means of the loud and confronting presentation of music.

Podcasts, in the sense of radio programs and speech downloads, may be auditioned in the home or played from a personal computer or an MP3 player; frequently, listeners choose to transfer podcasts to their portable players and carry them outside the home or office environment. As we have stressed, a key dimension of podcasting is the ability of a listener to "subscribe" to a web feed (through syndication software such as iTunes and others) and to have audio files transferred automatically to their portable MP3 player every time they connect player to computer. The listener or consumer becomes here more like an editor of a broadcasting organization as they make choices about what to listen to from a frequently huge array of options. The prevalence of the spoken word in podcasts has also allowed the voice to be transported along with portable MP3 players. Listeners may travel through cityscapes listening to spoken-word podcasts on iPods and other devices, in the manner in which music has been enjoyed from various portable devices since the 1960s.

The audition of spoken-word podcasts on portable MP3 players is consistent with the trend toward personalized mobile media in the early twenty-first century. Communications technology has followed the imperatives of convergence, miniaturization, and portability, as evident in the success of mobile phone and other devices incorporating a range of applications. Wireless portable communications devices have engendered a new type of public space, labeled "hertzian space" by Anthony Dunne, an "electro-climate" (and data-immersed sphere, recalling Richard Kriesche's electric "radioman") that fuses the natural and artificial environments to create "a hybrid landscape of shadows, reflections, and hot points."[43] This notion of public space entails a conception of urban space as criss-crossed by a variety of agents and entities: citizens, cars, and public transport; electromagnetic transmissions, and frequencies. The iPod listener, walking or traveling through a cityscape while engrossed in a spoken-word podcast, is traversing a hybrid social space, made more complex when the issue of public and private space is taken into consideration.

The Inner Voice

The iPod listener traveling through urban space is occupied in a private sound-world, listening to a voice apparent solely to that listener. This cocooning aspect of the mobile iPod experience has generated some critical reflection on the impact of portable audio technologies on the public sphere. Nigel Helyer, for example, has remarked on the "retreat" from the "sonic commons" represented by the "myriad imploded private sound-scapes" evident in contemporary urban settings.[44] Helyer regards this tendency as commensurate with a political and cultural shift "away from the collective and personal and toward a valorisation of the individual and the privatised."[45] In contrast to the assertive claim on public space once made by the carriers of ghetto-blasters, iPod users enact a "serial withdrawal" from public space, into "micro-acoustic-ecologies":[46] an audio world of one's own. There is, nevertheless, a diversity of headphone types and sizes used by the mobile iPod listener, ranging from full-size high-fidelity head-phones to small earbud sets. The nonenveloping quality of the earbuds suggests some potential porosity between public and private—the porosity typical of networked digital culture.

Within this private sound-world, the voice features prominently. Spoken word podcasts fill this psychic (and often erotic) space of the listener, occupying the intimate audio space with the grain and warmth of the human voice. The functioning of the voice in this space draws on long traditions of sonic experience. Religions have reserved a special place for the inner voice as the expression of divine presence, whether as the Voice of God or as the spiritual manifestation available to certain attuned individuals: shamans, prophets, or other inspired holy men and women. Social authority has often been represented as a spoken voice, whether externalized as the voice of the leader, or internalized as the voice of conscience. Indeed, many spoken-word podcasts entail a form of voiced authority, in the form of expert commentary, self-help "guru" advice, or political or religious oratory. The Vatican issues podcasts, many termed "Vatican Radio," which sound like BBC-style radio features. All forms of religious and mystical instruction are available as spoken-word downloads. Yet much spoken podcast material aims not for religious authority but the smaller authority of the "expert" in a particular field: amateur enthusiasts use podcasting as an outlet to vocalize their enthusiasms, pastimes, and hobbies.

In all these manifestations of the spoken word, the close intimacy of the voice through earphones is a constant factor. The emotional contours of the voice may foster a sense of trust in the listener; the distinctive qualities of the voice may induce sensations of pleasure. Radio has always exploited the intrinsic qualities of the human voice, building relationships between host and audience on the desirable aspects of a voice. As Susan Douglas has remarked, sound transmitted over radio "envelops us, pouring into us, whether we want it to or not, including us, involving us."[47] The podcast listening experience accentuates this process: the acousmatic voice is poured into the ears without disruptions from the exterior world, enveloping the listener with the intimate expression of its character—its grain—before the content of its message is even considered.

This audio "pouring" effect, especially pronounced when the listening experience involves the intimate effect wrought by the use of headphones, participates in the erotic nature of the voice—or, rather, the potentially erotic relationship between speaker and listener. Many podcasts draw on this erotic quality, focused as they are on the spoken voice as auditioned through headphones by individuated listeners. Certainly not all podcasts can be said to cultivate an intimate, erotic delivery of the voice: many are poorly constructed, with little attention to the quality or recording of the spoken voice, and many feature crude production values and intrusive sponsors' messages. Yet it is not difficult to find podcasts that present the spoken voice as a central feature—appealing, alluring—conveying the message through an intimate encounter with the listener.

This approach is typical of the self-help, spiritual life-counseling genre of audio instruction. One example is the podcast by the American "alternative career counselor" Rick Jarow, "Honoring Your Calling to Find Your Life's Work."[48] It begins with a piece of music in the style common to meditation and relaxation environments: a vaguely subcontinental flute melody accompanied by a drone and languorous keyboard. This musical introduction fades underneath a female voice whose function is to introduce the main speaker. This female voice is calm, midrange, and pleasant in a reserved manner. The brief introduction directs us to the speaker's authority by emphasizing the importance of voice: "The voice of a gifted spiritual teacher carries authenticity, inspiration, and insight, all of which are transmitted in an instant." These preliminary comments underline the significance of the speaker in communicating the messages of spiritual empowerment and guidance. The "transmitted in an instant" remark refers to the quality of the instructor's voice, as if it embodied the wisdom of its owner. The introduction concludes: "Professor Rick Jarow takes you on a journey to find the work you were born to do."

After a brief reprise of the flute music, Jarow's voice is heard. It is, as we have been led to expect, an assured voice of spiritual authority—a "voice of wisdom." It has a rich timbre and a soothing delivery. Jarow speaks in calm, measured cadences. The tempo is slow; the effect is calming, although the subject matter refers to matters of spiritual power: "There is a vitality, a life force, a quickening, that is translated through you into action, and because there is only one of you in all time, the expression is unique." Jarow speaks throughout the podcast with a controlled vocal manner, occasionally injecting a little emphasis into his monologue through minor increases in volume or pace. At all times, he maintains the audio sensibility of the spiritual guide: assured, authoritative, benevolent.

This effect is achieved not solely by the timbre and rhythm of Jarow's voice. Unlike many podcasts made by amateur operators, Jarow's effort has high production values. The voice is close-miked, without any audio distractions such as mouth noises. The sound quality is good, unmarred by extraneous studio noises or poor audio. The result is that Jarow's voice occupies the center of the podcast: it is the assured presence pouring continuously into the ears of the headphoned listener. The consequence, over an extended period, is a hypnotic effect of the spoken word, aimed in this instance to connect the listener to the "authentic life force" of empowerment. Jarow's podcast, like many others of the spiritual self-help/guidance genre, partakes of both a religious dimension and the erotic quality of the voice. Indeed, the two are connected. Jarow is a modern guru or spiritual master; he is introduced by a female acolyte who endorses his authority as spiritual guide. The sensual nature of his voice, with its calming qualities and gentle assurances, conveys the message of contemporary wisdom to the listener with an intimate ease. The success of Jarow's podcast is measured, presumably, by the increased sales of his various books, meditation CDs, and spiritual courses on CDs, which are available for purchase from his website.

The listening experiences aimed for in certain more intensive radiophonic productions—audio documentary and performance work most notably produced by public broadcasters for radio and podcast, and also podcast by web radios like ARTE radio—also appear to explore the intimate voice, although here the motivation is connection and a kind of revelation opened through listening. Some of these works appear to transfer the body in the voice, transmitting to us a felt sense of presence and co-presence.

They propose a metaphysics of voice, perhaps, which is paradoxically a material as well as psychic property of the transfer of voice sound. At least this is how the radio producers Kaye Mortley and Rene Farabet have described the effect of this kind of "documentaire de creation" and the recording and the listening they hope it engenders. The voices heard in Mortley's works are often a kind of witness to a life lived in a place and in time, with all the marks of place and time (suffering, humor, joy) upon it. They are offered perhaps as a gift to the listener, one that can be shared without theft or exploitation, a kind of exquisite transfer of spirit and breath, sensitive as it is to the body who grants us access to it. They point to a quality of voice, moving from one person to another, from speaker to auditor, that is giftlike.

Public Service Podcasting as Gift Culture

Another point to consider in this long history of negotiating a space for a richer communication between bodies, citizens, and voices (now enabled by the podcast and webradio "streaming" on the Internet) is the history associated with the democratic thrust unleashed through institutional public broadcasting radio forms. Most recently, this has concerned their exponential adoption of podcasting (and "webcasting" or "radio on demand") to create and extend their voice to new audiences. In this light, we need to consider the increasingly powerful potential of podcasting as it is being harnessed to extend these institutions' already rich audio diffusions. Podcasting on the one hand is an atomized affair involving a host of individual podcasters. They rise above the babble, come to prominence or not. But it is also a form, within a surprisingly short time span, that promises to transform more institutionalized versions of radio—in particular, that sector known internationally as public service broadcasting (PSB). Perhaps more than Digital Audio Broadcasting (DAB radio), podcasting appears most likely to offer renewed opportunities for this huge sector of publicly funded and supported radio, either as a way to revitalize existing services directed toward "time-poor" but hungry-for-content listeners, or bringing new listeners to these services, especially those avid for the content-rich forms unavailable on most mainstream commercial radio or through other kinds of podcast services. The major public service broadcasters had no or little podcasting in 2005, but today thousands of hours weekly are podcasts, with increasing numbers of downloads recorded and new subscribers.[49] The BBC and large cultural PSBs like it are more than media outlets through this convergent technology: they are searchable libraries, not only of data, but of voices.

Using the metaphor of the pod (as a collection of seeds encased in some protective yet permeable form to be set free from the parent as a gift—of life), we might say that podcasting continues the "gift culture" tradition already established—but threatened—of public broadcast dissemination. This tradition has been to distribute freely to all, no matter what the waste, for the common good. Program pods containing these voices in suspension disperse like so many seeds (through links, RSS feeds, and downloads) finding a place to settle or open their full contents supported by a new and richer ecology of revitalized broadcast audio and radio talk. These podcasting programs are able to offer access to a wider range of voices from all sectors and fields. They offer public service broadcasting listeners in particular, beyond the boundaries of nation states and niche markets, much greater accessibility to their unique "richmix"[50] programming ecology, designed to be scattered to all without any desire for an immediate return. Podcasting, in terms of these cultural institutions, and if recognized within the gift culture of a cultural commons,[51] has the potential to revitalize public broadcasting (and the "public sphere") in a time of frequently unreliable babble where voices speak more to their own kind than a broad and diverse "public," in what many critics see as nothing more than niche forms of radio. Public broadcasters and other respected cultural and educational institutions are likely to remain key players—and voices—here because of their larger resources, already substantial archives (of voices and visions) to draw upon, and their obvious aggregating power as institutions and their historical claims (still justified) to deliver quality and independence of thought.

There is without doubt a hunger there too for the voices that these services provide, and the diverse and often eloquent voices that public broadcasters are able to bring together across space and time, keeping alive a notion of the public sphere (and the public voice), indeed extending it by opening up actual material conversations to a larger and more inclusive public, or by challenging preconceived opinion. And as many radio and audio producers who work on a daily basis with voices as material objects know, words alone do not do this; the voice—with all its tones, pauses, pitch changes, tremors, and stutters—can be highly revealing. A voice can be caught off guard no matter how well trained; inauthenticity detected; artifice and fabrication unmasked.

There is also the possibility of reconsidering those more intense listening experiences produced by certain forms of PSB radio not pursued elsewhere for financial reasons, even among blogger podcasters. Contrary to previous predictions, podcasting may favor those more intensive forms of listening experience and audio storytelling/sharing built on PSB radio forms. The question of voice and the auditory imagination is raised once more here.[52] In 2005, Dearman and Galloway wrote that "podcasts are not listened to live. But what they lose in immediacy they may well gain in intimacy."[53] We might add the potential already well in evidence for more intensive listening experiences—something that relates especially well to the more expensive and intellectually demanding talk and audio content provided by cultural radio (and television) channels internationally.[54] These stations, scattered across Europe, the Americas, and Australia, continue to foster the creative and skilled program making traditions established in the "golden age" of radio and prior to the introduction of mass television. These too have been developed to new sophistication within these organizations with the advent of enhanced technologies of recording and audio con-struction. With their maintenance of content-driven "block programming" and unique radiophonic forms such as the radio feature and documentary (abandoned or left unexplored by almost all of the commercial organiza-tions), PSB radio can offer a diversity of distinct program packages for pod-cast—driven less by music than the voice—eminently suitable for replay or reauditioning wherever and whenever a listener chooses to listen.[55]

These programs might also be heard with greater levels of attention, rather than the more usual and familiar mode of everyday radio listening—oscillating between high levels of attention and distraction, foregrounding and backgrounding.[56] In the age of podcasting, we can imagine this kind of PSB programming to be ideally suited to this expanded and intimate, yet exploded, dissemination environment.[57] The rich *pod-ecology* that some PSB forms appear to favor may mean also that we are no longer wedded to the present tense and the once-only real-time (essentially evanescent) broadcast. Podcasting promises not only to put diverse individuals and communities in contact, but also to connect the living with the "creative commons" of the dead.

The Voice Archive

With the podcast, time is no longer a restricting condition; as with the seed (frozen in time) distributed, or rather the pod awaiting activation of its distribution, programs and voices long disappeared may now be renewed with possibly limitless chances at redistribution or activation. The BBC was one of the first public and cultural institutions to recognize this potential of the archive (the dormant seed awaiting new conduits and potentialities of distribution) and it now proclaims a new and ambitious project to put all its programming up (first as web pages, later as audio and video files) into the public domain on the Internet.[58] Long inaudible and therefore invisible, audio archives when coupled with podcasting may be given "new voice" in much the same way as an old text when rediscovered. Only here the actual voice imprint (digital or analog at source) carries something more, and that is the traces of its body, its life through the body, in time, in a place, in a context (language and accent are two markers here, but there are many other less quantifiable traits to consider). And other institutions beyond public broadcasters are also becoming "media outlets": echo chambers for voices, offering up the living voice and the dead, as with Pennsylvania State University with its support of the UbuWeb site (http://ubu.com), which was created using Creative Commons licensing (in the English, French, Italian, German, and Portuguese languages).[59] This site offers podcasts (MP3 files) of the work and voices of poets, dramatists, and audio artists[60] electrifying the archive into something more like a radio station. Here you can listen to Apollinaire's turn-of-the-century French voice emerging five years before his death from the white noise of an old acetate disc recording incanting his most famous poem, "Le Pont Mirabeau" from 1913. Or Marshall McLuhan talking almost in monologue in a refined Canadian-English deep "dons" voice about the medium being the message with Truman Capote (in a radio show from the 1960s), whose real voice (distinct southern inflections, feminized, "camp," high-pitched) is remarkably like the voice Philip Seymour Hoffmann resurrected in the film *Capote*.[61]

Stirring new life out of the once-dormant but latent archive is something that all kinds of cultural institutions, including broadcasting institutions, can participate in and activate if the ecology (and ethics) are right. This is why a wide range of cultural and educational institutions internationally are taking up podcasting as ways of expanding their voice. Through

Princeton University, UChannel is a podcasting/vodcasting site that acts as an aggregator and "host" for intellectual debate and "thought," giving us the voices of major "thinkers."[62]

Recent intersections between radio, podcasting, the archive and "the ethical," and the public broadcasting project, come together also in the mammoth StoryCorps project initiated by public radio documentary maker David Isay, working for the Macarthur Foundation and the American Library of Congress. On the website for this not-for-profit project, where the voices of ordinary and not-so-ordinary folk may be downloaded, it is offered: "Listening is an act of love." The heart of StoryCorps is this:

The conversation between two people who are important to each other: a son asking his mother about her childhood, an immigrant telling his friend about coming to America, or a couple reminiscing on their 50th wedding anniversary.[63]

The StoryCorps goal is "to make that experience accessible to all, and find new ways to inspire people to record and preserve the stories of someone important to them."[64] StoryCorps is one of the largest oral history projects of its kind, creating an accumulating portrait of American life by the means of American voices. The first StoryBooth opened in 2003 in New York City's Grand Central Terminal and from there the recording and interviews began, moving around the country to other sites like these, and to the Internet, where the recording can be uploaded for posterity. This is a reversal of what radio (and particularly public broadcasting) has continued to do from its early days in the 1920s: offering "access to a public world."[65] StoryCorps works in reverse on two levels, bringing the private into the public sphere (in the present) and the past into a future archive, and then making the (public) event of the private voicing/witnessing/history-writing the ongoing and future project itself (as a subject for mass and privatized listening in the present and the future). This voice-writing grows rhizomatically (written as Barthes has it, with the grain of the voice), creating a diverse texture: a rhapsodic weaving of voices. Again, the voices are of ordinary people, with all their differences heard in each voice, each unique and picked up through age, gender, culture, language, education, historical, physical, and psychological circumstances that are never simple and on various levels can be heard in the voice. These ordinary Americans speak into a microphone, gifting us their not-so-ordinary stories of lost sons, childhood battles, and recollections of worlds faded. One old lady is so shy that she is happy only to speak with her granddaughter; another whose loss of a son is so raw, even after many years, that her story is meant as an act of witnessing. Her voice tells us (whoever we are) that he was real, he was alive, he too was a voice-body.

Podcasting's "Logosphere": The Reanimation of Listening and the Radio Voice

In 1957, the eminent French poet Jean Tardieu, who was then art director of the French Public/State broadcaster's Club d'Essai and of the Centre d'Études de Radio-Télévision, Radiodiffusion–Télévision Française (RTF), described radio in these terms:

Radio, which sends this rain of exact impressions and words, of authentic voices and works of art, is like a cloudburst that waters the human soil.[66]

Tardieu invoked Gaston Bachelard's conception of radio as setting up "permanent circulation, about the earth, of words in suspension which transport an important part of human knowledge," noting that Bachelard's name for this "sphere endowed with the gift of speech" was the "logosphere." Tardieu believed that the purpose of cultural broadcasting is to "enrich" this logosphere, so that:

Anybody at any time may be able to draw upon this wealth of culture and art, to receive the initiating shock, that fragment of poetry, music or learning which sometimes suffices to arouse the mind to higher forms of curiosity or—who knows?—to the discovery of a vocation.[67]

Podcasting reactivates possibilities of the creative commons as reservoir of cultural wealth for all—as owned by all: not in the limited sense of allowing unfettered dialog and remix or information, but allowing voices, space, and time to resound, in a new environment/ecology—through time/space shifting and dissemination.[68] This process involves voices engaged in time-shifted dialog.

In keeping with the rhizome metaphor, voices transformed by MP3 technologies available for download also potentially extend themselves—and possibly indefinitely—not only into space but forward through time. This is a new and revolutionary quality in the logosphere not possible previously with traditional broadcasting "real-time" audio. There the voice with rare exception must disappear on its enunciation, remaining as a trace in the listener's memory. We are currently witnessing the creation and activation of a vast new reservoir of voices, no longer "dead letters" or confined to the closed circuit of the activist couple, or even of a generation of receivers. These are voices that may well keep speaking into the future, revived from their long slumbers of the past.

Notes

1. Pierre Schaeffer, *Traité des objets musicaux* (Paris: Le Seuil, 1966). The term *acousmatique* was first used by the French musique concrète composer Pierre Schaeffer. Derived from *akousmatikoi*, the outer circle of Pythagoras's disciples who heard their teacher only as he was speaking from behind a veil, it refers to sounds separated from their source as through radio, loudspeaker, or some film sound.

2. John Durham Peters, *Speaking into the Air: A History of the Idea of Communication* (Chicago: University of Chicago Press, 1999), 224.

3. Ben Hammersley, "Audible Revolution," *Media Guardian*, quoted in Richard Berry, "Will the iPod Kill the Radio Star?" *Convergence* 12, no. 2 (2006): 143.

4. Cited in Dan Gilmour, *We The Media: Grassroots Journalism by the People, For the People* (Sebastopol, Calif.: O'Reilly, 2006), xiii.

5. Ibid., xiii–xiv.

6. Berry, 104, citing S. Miles, "Podcast Makes the Dictionary."

7. The BBC began their seven-month podcasting trial in May 2005 with a *Radio 4* History program "In Our Time," presented by Melvyn Bragg. It "averaged 30,000 download requests a week," according to BBC News, becoming the public broadcaster's "most popular podcast." And "overall, the BBC had more than 100,000 download requests each week in July of 2005." BBC NEWS, September 1, 2005, http://news.bbc.co.uk/go/pr/fr/-/1/hi/entertainment/tv_and_radio/4204008.stm.

8. Sheri Crofts, John Dilley, Mark Fox, Andrew Retsema, and Bob Williams., "Podcasting: A new technology in search of viable business models," *First Monday* 10, no. 9 (September 2005): 3, citing Apple Computer releases of June 2005. http://firstmonday.org/htbin/cgiwrap/bin/ojs/index.php/fm/article/view/1273/1193

9. Ibid., 3.

10. Crofts et al. provide an account of these developments (ibid.), 2–3.

11. Stephen Baker, "The Lowdown on Podcasting," *Business Week*, quoted in Crofts et al. (ibid.), 2.

12. Examples of theoretical essays on distributed aesthetics may be found in *Fibreculture Journal* 7 (2005), edited by Lisa Gye, Anna Munster, and Ingrid Richardson, http://journal.fibreculture.org/issue7/index.html.

13. Darren Waters, "Digital Citizens: The podcaster," BBC NEWS, July 19, 2005, http://news.bbc.co.uk/go/pr/fr/-/2/hi/entertainment/4626445.stm.

14. Crofts et al. refer to the appeal, in the United States, of podcasting for listeners keen to escape "the advertising that plagues traditional radio broadcasting" (5).

15. Philip Dearman and Chris Galloway, "Putting Podcasting into Perspective," *Radio in the World: Papers from the 2005 Radio Conference* 2005, (eds) Sianan Healy, Sianan, Bruce Berryman, and David Goodman, (Melbourne: RMIT Publishing), 536. Conference dates were July 11–14, 2005. The authors, citing Timothy McNulty, also refer to "roadcasting" as another form of podcasting, allowing "music sharing in and between cars," 544 n10.

16. http://thedawnanddrewshow.com/ (Original citation from dawnanddrew. mevio.com/ accessed Jan 12, 2008, no longer operational. See also http://articles latimes.com/2006/may/21/entertainment/ca-podfather21?pg=2

17. Dearman and Galloway, "Putting Podcasting into Perspective," 535.

18. Berry, 4–5, citing J. Twist on "reclaiming the radio."

19. Dearman and Galloway, "Putting Podcasting into Perspective," 535.

20. Cited in ibid., 540. Citation from Daniel Terdiman, "Podcasts: New Twist on Net Audio," *Wired News*, October 8, 2004. Curry's current and popular podcast site, "Daily Source Code," gives us a summary of what his podcasts are all about: "The challenge to mainstream media—and the voice of independent media—starts here. Podfather Adam Curry scours the globe for the hottest new mashups, podcast highlights, and podsafe music." Available at http://www.dailysourcecode.com (accessed May 25, 2008).

21. Apple release, August 2005, cited by Crofts et al., 3.

22. At least this is the case in the United States. This picture is not entirely applicable in the United Kingdom and much of northern and western Europe, where public service radio continues to disseminate and produce rich content in the form of comedy, drama, serials, documentaries, and features. And this continues in the contemporary context.

23. In Sarah Cuddon "What made Wolfman Jack great?" http://news.bbc.co.uk/2/hi/uk_news/magazine/7307738.stm accessed October 15, 2008. Interestingly, Wolfman Jack's listeners had no idea of the face behind the microphone. Many believed he was black, especially as he played all the latest black music that was not being heard on commercial radio. Cuddon sites Durell Roth, Border radio historian: "He could talk the soul language of a black man with the dialect. . . . I thought he was black for many years and that's the beautiful thing about radio, [that] it's totally color-blind." This also should alert us to the "play" always involved with acousmatic voices—as personas, or masks.

24. Cuddon (ibid.) also writes, "As the name suggests, the Wolfman was a creature of the night. He loved the midnight hour—"the bewitching time," as he called it—and the time when a hungering young audience could feed on his tidbits. Young people hanging out late at night in their cars would tune into his broadcasts and feed off his reckless, free spirit. And as his young fan base grew, the Wolfman became the leader of a generational movement."

25. In Neil Strauss and Dave Mandl (eds.), *Radiotext(e)* (Brooklyn, NY: Autonomedia, 1993), 15–17. Originally published as *Der Rundfunk als kommunikationsapparat in Blattaer der hessischen landestheaters* (Darmstadt, no. 16, July 1932).

26. Brecht in Strauss and Mandl, *Radiotext(e)*, 15.

27. Sabine Breitsameter, "From Transmission to Procession—Radio in the Age of Digital Networks," in Erik Granly Jensen and Brandon LaBelle (eds.), *Radio Territories* (Los Angeles: Errant Bodies Press, 2007), 61.

28. This occurs via Web 2.0 convergence and links, email, and Internet "favorites" sites like "Delicious," allowing individual favorites to be seen by many and cross-referenced. Hugely successful podcasters like Adam Curry appear to be building small empires of podcasting in this way. His "Daily Source Code" show, one of many hosted by his company Pod Show Inc., (now Mevio) was cited as averaging more than 1 million downloads a month in December 2005. Martin Miller, *LA Times*, http://pressroom.mevio.com/2006/05/23/podfather-plots-a-radio-hit-of-his-own-la-times/ (accessed June 1, 2008). In the column Heard on the Street titled "Podcasting will change radio, not kill it" (*The Economist*: April 22, 2006), it was suggested he had "several million listeners" (12).

29. Cited by Heidi Grundmann, "Beyond Broadcasting: The Wien-Couver series," in Erik Granly Jensen and Brandon LaBelle (eds.), *Radio Territories* (Los Angeles: Errant Bodies Press, 2007), 215.

30. Pierre Lévy, *Collective Intelligence: Mankind's Emerging World in Cyberspace* (New York: Plenum, 1994).

31. See also Howard Rheingold, "Using Participatory Media and Public Voice to Encourage Civic Engagement," in W. Lance Bennett (ed.), *Civic Life Online: Learning How Digital Media Can Engage Youth* (Cambridge, Mass.: MIT Press, 2008).

32. Jean-Luc Nancy, *The Birth to Presence* (Stanford: Stanford University Press, 1993), 20.

33. Dawn and Drew make this claim in their hundredth show. They were not listed in the Top 10 when this essay was being written, but enthusiastic bloggers post comments like: "The most natural down to earth podcasters I have ever heard." and "They complete me. The world's best podcasters. There will never be any better in my lifetime." http://www.podcastalley.com/podcast_details.php?pod_id=195 (accessed July 27, 2008). All shows can be heard from http://thedawnanddrewshow.com/archives/.

34. Accessed at http://thedawnanddrewshow.com/archives/ August 14, 2009.

35. This homely sign-off references the American classic children's bedtime picture book *Goodnight Moon* by Margaret Wise Brown (New York, Harper), 1947.

36. Sound production and editing software are comparatively cheap compared to the old analog "hardware" days, and some systems are completely free on the Internet, such as Audacity (http://audacity.sourceforge.net/).

37. The Australian Broadcasting Corporation, for example, rarely distributes podcasts of its music programming, or even other talks and feature programs that may contain large sections of copyrighted music. In Australia and the United Kingdom, dramas with professional actors have also been mostly off-limits due to the lack of copyright agreements to date. Many podcasts are also limited in terms of download accessibility time periods. The BBC limits many podcasts to European audiences only and subscribers may access them for only one week after broadcast. With the French public broadcaster and the ABC, the podcast is usually available for at least one month after broadcast, with programs increasingly made available in a permanently accessible archive.

38. R. Murray Schafer, *The Tuning of the World* (Philadelphia: University of Pennsylvania Press, 1980), 90.

39. John Potts, "Schizochronia: Time in Digital Sound," in S. Davies, F. Dyson, A. Jonson, A. Cavallaro (eds.), *Essays in Sound 2: Technophonia* (Sydney: Contemporary Sound Arts, 1995), 20.

40. Raymond Williams, *Television: Technology and Cultural Form* (London: Fontana, 1974), 86.

41. Ibid., 86–87.

42. There are numerous examples of this. The Australian Broadcasting Corporation's "Orpheus Remix Project" offered a selection of MP3 micro opera works to be offered as podcasts for download and future remix by prosumers (http://www.abc .net.au/classic/orpheus/). The ABC's latest "Pool" project promises an online virtual studio and is proposed as a "file sharing system which allows users to share or collaborate on sound-visual-text works that can be posted on a public access site and/or broadcast by the ABC." The authors describe this new space as "New ways of making radio for a wireless world." In Sherre DeLys and Marius Foley, "The exchange: a radio-web project for creative practitioners and researchers," *Convergence* 12, no. 2 (2006): 129–135.

43. Anthony Dunne, *Hertzian Tales*, (London: Royal College of Art, 1999), cited by Maria Miranda, "Uncertain Spaces: Artists' Explorations of New Socialities in Mediated Public Space," *Scan Online Journal of Media Arts Culture* 4, no. 3 (December 2007): 6, http://scan.net.au/scan/journal/display.php?journal_id=101. Quotations

regarding hertzian space are from the Future Farmers website, 2007, quoted by Miranda.

44. Nigel Helyer, "The Sonic Commons: Embrace or Retreat?" *Scan Online Journal of Media Arts Culture* 4, no. 3 (December 2007): 1, http://scan.net.au/scan/journal/display.php?journal_id=105.

45. Ibid.

46. Ibid., 2.

47. Susan Douglas, *Listening in: Radio and the American Imagination: from Amos 'n' Andy and Edward R. Murrow to Wolfman Jack and Howard Stern* (New York, N.Y.: Times Books), 30.

48. Accessed from iTunes, July 24, 2008.

49. American National Public Radio (NPR) launched its first podcasts on August 31, 2005, after having "received e-mail requests from listeners for months," according to blogger Mark Glaser. "The term 'podcast' was one of the most searched terms on NPR.org," Glaser noted, during this early period, and it took only six days after launch for NPR's "Story of the Day" podcast to reach the no. 1 spot on iTunes for most-downloaded podcast. On November 21, NPR's podcasts held eleven spots on the iTunes Top 100—more than any other media outlet. In "Will NPR's podcasts birth a new business model for public radio?" November 29, 2005, http://www.ojr .org/ojr/stories/051129glaser/ (accessed June 1, 2008). The BBC's first trials in 2005 revealed a similar success story, which has only helped to grow its audiences nationally and internationally and consolidate recognition of its "brand." The same requests by listeners for downloadable programming were noted by most public broadcasting organizations, with now vast quantities of programming available for limited periods as MP3 files and RSS feeds.

50. David Hendy, *Radio in the Global Age* (Cambridge: Polity Press, 2000).

51. In *The Gift*, Lewis Hyde advocates a freeing up of the cultural wealth found and never depleted in the commons. Lewis Hyde, *The Gift: Imagination and the Erotic Life of Property*, 1983 (New York, N.Y.: Random House).

52. Virginia Madsen, "Cultural Radio at the Crossroads: 'When I Hear the Word Culture I Switch on My Radio': Reflections on an Underestimated Form, 'Cultural Radio,'" *Southern Review* 39, no. 3 (2007): 16–37.

53. Dearman and Galloway, "Putting Podcasting into Perspective," 536.

54. New forms of cultural radio are emerging also beyond the major public service broadcasting institutions. An example is ARTE radio, a podcaster and web radio site, part of the larger ARTE organization, known for its huge contribution to independent film and television production of high quality.

55. Many programs are presented as "the original"; others are compiled into special podcast programs offering highlights or new mixes of content from the existing material. The ABC's *Radio National* channel has a "shuffle mode" program that gives the user a random selection of programs of the day or the week or even the month.

56. Andrew Crisell, *Understanding Radio* (London: Routledge, 1994), and Martin Shingler and Cindy Wieringa, *On Air: Methods and Meanings of Radio* London: Hodder Arnold, 1998).

57. "Radio will give a rhythm and a human touch to the digital traffic of the 21st century," Raina Konstantinova, European Broadcasting Union (EBU) Radio Director, in her opening speech to the 2005 "Radio Day of European Culture: the unification of Europe—on air," Potsdam, October 15, 2005, http://www.prix-europa.de/publish/n_subnews.html (accessed May 10, 2006). Link no longer active. (Information recorded in Prix Europa Publicity, 2005).

58. Radio 4 of the BBC already offers a majority of its programs, cultural and informational, for podcast (see http://www.bbc.co.uk/podcasts/radio4/) or they can be heard on the BBC's "i-player". The BBC World Service, for example, now has a documentary archive available for download anywhere in the world (http://www.bbc.co.uk/radio/podcasts/docarchive/).

59. Creative Commons (CC) is a nonprofit organization devoted to expanding the range of creative works available for others to build upon legally and to share. The organization has released several copyright licenses known as Creative Commons licenses. These licenses allow creators to communicate which rights they reserve and which rights they waive for the benefit of recipients or other creators.

60. The not-for-profit UbuWeb site, a site where the mostly "boundary rider" but "electric" voices of a range of twentieth- and twenty-first-century artists and poets are being made audible through podcasting, vodcasting, and Creative Commons copyright licensing (see http://creativecommons.org/). Through their voices, returned to us via old analog and new digital recording, playback, and storage technologies, we can experience the grain in the voices of Apollinaire, Samuel Beckett, Ezra Pound, Gertrude Stein, Antonin Artaud, and Gregory Whitehead.

61. http://www.ubu.com/sound/.

62. http://uc.princeton.edu/main/index.php/home-mainmenu-1. Vodcasting, is the distribution of video for download via the web in a similar way to podcasting.

63. David Isay, 2009 StoryCorps website, "Listening is an act of love," http://www.storycorps.org/about.

64. Digital Storytelling was pioneered by the BBC, notably with their digital story bus in Wales. Here they deliberately sought the unmediated stories of ordinary people, offering an opportunity to all to tell their own stories in their own voices. Digital storytelling projects have been initiated all over the world, often in relation-

ships with public libraries. In this, they are iterations of previous oral history collections like those initiated by the Smithsonian, the Library of Congress, and so on. However, the recent digital audio projects invite speakers in, rather than ethnographically collect their material.

65. Kate Lacey, "Toward a periodization of listening: Radio and Modern life," *International Journal of Cultural Studies* 3, no. 2 (2000): 285.

66. Tardieu, "The 'Club d'Essai'", 25. Referenced in Madsen 2004, *Cultural Radio at the Crossroads*, 21.

67. JeanTardieu, "The 'Club d'Essai' and Its Contribution to the Cultural Effort of RTF," in UNESCO Dept. of Mass Communications, (ed.), *Cultural Radio Broadcasts; Some Experiences* (Paris, Unesco Clearing House, Dept. of Mass Communications, 1956), 25.

68. As expanded by Lewis Hyde in *The Gift* and as championed by Creative Commons (CC) and this organization's founder Lawrence Lessig.

4 Four Rooms

Theresa M. Senft

We would not give a page of Artaud for all of Carroll. Artaud is alone in having been an absolute depth in literature. . . . But Carroll remains the master and the surveyor of surfaces—surfaces which were taken to be so well-known that nobody was exploring them anymore. On these surfaces, nonetheless, the entire logic of sense is located.

—Gilles Deleuze, "The Schizophrenic and the Little Girl"[1]

(1)

I am sitting in a room different from the one you are in right now. I dial the telephone. The phone rings, and then connects. The background music dumps into my ear. My shoulders drop. A year ago, it was great music, some sort of calypso tune that seemed to shout, "Glad you've made it. Have a frosty drink and relax!" Now the music is faster, whiter, something that might be Michael Bolton's next easy listening smash. I don't like it, but I do like this phone service, mostly because "every night is Ladies' Night." Women call free.

"Welcome to the Night Exchange," the digitized female voice coos, in a manner I now emulate whenever I want faster, nicer, or smarter service during my day. The automated voice asks me for my first name, which the system records, and plays back for me. To "accept my name" and continue, I press "1." The electronic lady asks me to record a brief description of myself. "Remember, this is your first impression," she reminds me. "So be honest, and have fun!" I consider telling the nice lady that I am exhausted from a night of teaching a computer to speak. I wonder if she will care that it has now been one year and two weeks since my mother has died, that I am feeling bloated and premenstrual, that my throat hurts and I just want to come, already, but decide that this type of information does not fit the injunction to have fun.

"Hi," I breathe into the phone, trying to sound at least as desirable as the background music that continues to play, providing my phone sex mise en scène. "I am looking for a dominant man." It's pretty common knowledge among users of automated phone sex services that the hardest-working people on the chat lines are the dominants. In real-life domination, the top barks out orders once in awhile, and the sub runs around doing things. On the phone, however, the dom does all the work, all the imagining, while the sub moans, "Oh, yes. . . ." Tonight, I just want to oh-yes my way to an orgasm, and then get some sleep.

After I record my message, there is the pause. The pause means that somewhere, a computer is listening, assessing, and processing the sound of my voice. I have a theory that everywhere, all pauses are related: the pause between punching my PIN into the bank machine and hearing the cash rustle. The electronic silence between songs on the radio. The emotional space that hangs in the air after the words "I love you" come out. I hear the faintest bleeds from the old calypso music in my mind, scoring this telephone pause, and I remember why my mother hated to hear music play during her last weeks in the hospital. It's wrong to pollute the pause with sound.

Finally the lady returns. "If you are looking to meet in person, press 1, " she murmurs. "If you are looking for conversation, press 2. If you are look-ing for intimate conversation, press 3." I press 3. The Michael Bolton music plays for less than 15 seconds. "You have a message," I am told. The nice lady moderates all incoming phone messages. There is no way to get rid of her voice.

"Hoyah," some person with a Long Island diphthong problem breathes, "You want a dominant guy, you got him, baby. I am not into head games, so press '1' and let's tawk, LIVE."

Wondering just what would constitute "no head games" during phone sex, I decide to skip this caller. I don't really like going live, for the same rea-son I don't like real-time computer bulletin boards, or leaving my answer-ing machine off. I like to stay on the surface and surf the phone systems, hearing a little bit of this, a little bit of that, pressing and rubbing and press-ing and rubbing. The men, who pay for this service, hate the women who surf. Time is money for the men, but time for ladies is not even cheap—it's free. As if we shouldn't all live, breathe, come, pay, and die the same way. I will never press "1" for this guy, and later, I know, I will skip his messages entirely. He is not my type. But for now, I want to keep him calling back, so I press the button to respond, only to be interrupted by the nice lady's voice: "You have made an improper selection. Please try again."

I press "2" and breathe back into the phone, "How would you handle me?" and then send the message. On the phone, I like to think of myself as something to be handled, tied up, tortured. Why not? I make pictures in my mind of women I would like to be, and then play them on the telephone. The nice lady tells me that I now have ten phone messages, from ten different men. I listen and press, listen and respond and press, listen and press.

And always, the lady moderates. She listens to vocal tone. Sometimes women use the men's line (for which they are billed) to search for other women. I always respond to female phone ads. I respect the ability to pay for what one desires. But not everyone gets to use the lines creatively. The transgendered women I talk to tell me that when trannies call on the Ladies' Line, the electronic lady throws them off, telling them they are being removed from the system for being "unclear." The lady does the same thing if I say anything obscene, telling me my voice cannot be heard. One user of the system told me the Night Exchange hates prostitutes (for the obvious competition). Obscene women are probably prostitutes—or at least that's the feeling of the folks at the Night Exchange. I suspect that the nice lady does not cut off the paying customers as quickly as she does the trannies and the whores on the Ladies' Line.

Because I know my continued calling privileges are being monitored, I try to straddle a space between naughtiness and vulgarity on the phone, feeling the answers of my male callers back for obscene intent, which is really what I want, after all. I listen, reply, punch a number, hear a new message, and reply. It feels more like shopping than anything else. This man sounds okay, he wants to hang me from a hook and whip me in front of the neighbors, but there may be a better one, a faster one, a slower one. When I am exhausted enough, I agree to go live, or as alive as one is during phone sex. The lady helps me through it, by letting me know that from here on in, I will only hear a bell, a bing-bong bell that lets me know when other men are trying to reach me with messages.

I am excited every time I leave the eavesdropping lady. I can finally be as filthy as I want to be. But strangely, at that moment when I leave her, I want to hear her again, pacing my phone messages, narrating my sexuality for me to the bad rock 'n' roll background. "Hi," says some mystery guy. "Hi," I say back, and we begin. It's fun, but I know the rest will be predictable in a way the automated Law of the Lady never really is.

(2)

I am sitting in a room, different from the one you are in right now, holding my mother as she weeps. She can no longer write her own name. Visual symbols don't make sense to her. After my mother's second brain surgery, the doctors stop talking about whether she will ever read again. Living through the pain, learning to walk, avoiding blood clots—these were the more pressing concerns of the Roswell Cancer Institute staff, which of course made sense. Because she can no longer read, people bring my mother audio tapes to play on her Walkman. One day, someone gives her a Bernie Siegel Cancer Care tape. After one hearing, she asks me to buy her the entire collection.

Bernie Siegel is an oncology surgeon who now specializes in self-help literature. His tapes have titles like, "Strengthening Your Immune System," "Preparing for Surgery," and "Time for Meditation." I don't understand these tapes very much. For one thing, Bernie Siegel sounds uncannily like George Bush, and my mother has always hated Republicans. My mother believes in what the Republicans call Big Government. Now that she is being taken care of in a Big Government cancer ward, she believes in it even more. My own politics are likewise to the left of Cuba, but I still want my mother to be a little more suspicious of the Roswell Cancer Institute. I don't exactly know what it is I expect her to do about her situation, as she is more or less at the mercy of a series of doctors who have cut and stitched her brain on five different occasions. Still, I hate the tedium of her complacency, and I hate her stupid Bernie Siegel tapes.

Sometimes I demand her medical charts, but can make no sense of the information written down there. I try to talk about this with my mother. No, just give me the Walkman, she says. When the nurses change her IVs, boring me with their attempts at small talk, when the smug doctors usher themselves in to draw spinal fluid, when the helpful orderlies turn on the never-ending television news, my mother smiles at them wanly and says, "I can't hear you. I am listening to my tapes." Even her children know it after a while. The headset on means, "Don't disturb."

After my mother's death, I use Dr. Siegel's tapes to keep me company. Lots of the advice on the tapes is practical. "Ask for a room with a window, where you can see the sky," Dr. Siegel counsels. "And if they say none is available, calmly tell them you will wait to check in until one is available." Actually, this is good advice. Many times, patients check in to cancer wards and never leave. Having a window is the last chance for them to see the sky. It happened to my mother that way. The tapes, as Dr. Siegel intones over and over, are not meant to be substitutes for adequate medical care, but rather they should be used to strengthen and aid the patient. In one of the tapes, "Preparing for Surgery," Dr. Siegel tells patients (with a synthesized Pachelbel's Canon background) that in order to help to prevent dangerous post-surgical blood clots they must "Feel the blood getting thinner, and concentrate on that feeling throughout and after the surgery." After my mother's second surgery, she began to hemorrhage, and my Aunt Penny blamed it on "that damn blood thinning tape."

I am sitting in my room, different from the one you are in right now, and I am listening to my mother's cancer care tapes. I do not even pretend to understand what these tapes meant to her. When she was alive, I fantasized that while the doctors irradiated and cut up my mother's body, she resisted through a place that medicine couldn't reach. I would look at her, drifting in and out of sleep, and pray that something good and powerful was going on inside her body. I would fantasize that if I stayed in her room long enough, I could absorb all the sounds of pain in this place, and that my Momma's tapes will take care of her insides. I listened to the tinny sounds of a hundred televisions blaring down the halls. I listened to the IV machine beeping, busy emptying bag after bag of antibiotic into dying bodies. I listened to the retching noises of chemo patients. Between the interior and the surface, between my mother and I, surely we can take on her illness, her madness, and her death, I thought. I was wrong.

(3)

I'm sitting in a room, different from the one you are in right now. The year is 1994 and the location is my friend Dana's apartment in the East Village.

Dana, a male-to-female transsexual (we didn't really use the word "transgender" then) and a Certified Voice Recognition operator, has offered to show me how I can get computers to respond to my voice. The wall to my right is thumping. Salsa music, I realize. The computer suddenly boots up, out of nowhere. I look at Dana, perplexed. "Oh, it's the damn vibration from the music," she tells me, and walks over to the terminal, picks up a microphone and says, "Go to sleep!" The machine shuts off, and we eat our dinner.

"Computer, wake up!" Dana tells the computer, and it begins to boot up. "Console on!" Dana yells, and the screen flashes on to an empty page. "Start Word! Good. Start letter! Insert date! Address book! Find Senft! That's it! Insert that! Dear Terri. Colon. New paragraph. Insert thank you paragraph. Insert no money paragraph. Insert get in touch paragraph. Love, comma, Dana. Save! Print!"

Dana is demonstrating a program called Law Talk, a voice recognition system that she sells to law firms. To run Law Talk in 1994, you needed a 486 MHz computer with a sound card installed in the back. On the sound card were 1200 prerecorded and coded phonemes.

"Do you want to try?" she asks me, and hands me the microphone device. "Uh, computer, wake up!" I say, trying to mimic Dana's intonation. Nothing. "Computer, wake up!" Nothing again.

"Hah. It is resisting you. It doesn't know your voice. You have to train it to understand you. You sound like a weather lady. You need to practice your trannie voice!" Dana starts up the tutorial program for me. I speak into a microphone, and teach the computer to recognize my voice as it combines phonemes into words. The Law Talk initialization software consists of two hundred thousand words. My job is to speak into a microphone, pronouncing each word that appears on the screen, until the computer recognizes my voice, and spells out the words I speak without error. To do this, the Law Talk tutorial makes me recite passages from *Alice in Wonderland* for about three and a half hours. I also recite extraneous words like "plus" and the Arabic numerals three times each. There are four hundred extraneous words that must be recited into the computer before I can even begin to address this system. It is like teaching a child to speak, I imagine. Only I can't imagine having a child.

I begin to dictate to the machine, and the sounds I make then appear on screen as a word. I visually register each word printed, and then correct the computer when it is wrong, by saying the word "oops." At the oops prompt, a bar comes up on the computer screen describe the bar of choices—visual arrangements of my spoken words all in a row, complete with "default choices," and I say, "Move left, choose three, okay." And then the computer replaces the word it thought I said with the one I tell it that I really did say. I spend the rest of the evening this way, marking the computer up with the sound of my voice, demanding that it yield text for me—and not just any text, but the right text. I am reading *Alice in Wonderland* out loud to this machine, and watching it get my words right, gloating like some stupid parent or doctor or phone dom when I realize that the machine has got it! It's with me! It is telling me exactly what I always already commanded it to hear.

(4)

"I am sitting in a room, different from the one you are in now. I am recording the sound of my speaking voice and I am going to play it back into the room again and again until the resonant frequencies of the room reinforce themselves so that any semblance of my speech, with perhaps the exception of rhythm, is destroyed. What you will hear, then, are the natural resonant frequencies of the room articulated by speech. I regard this activity not so much as a demonstration of a physical fact, but more as a way to smooth out any irregularities my speech might have."

This is the complete text of Alvin Lucier's "I Am Sitting in a Room."[2] The piece, which is a dreadful technical exercise in 1980s sound art, consists of forty minutes of the paragraph above, spoken at least three hundred times. That's it. As promised, the sound of Lucier's voice grows more and more distorted, until a huge acoustical flood of noise fills the room, blurring anything that might have given this piece meaning. I am sitting in a room, a classroom, being instructed that Lucier is a genius, and frankly, I just don't get it. I hear nothing in this piece that could ever move or interest me. The last twenty minutes of the piece consists of nothing but audio feedback. The stereo blares into my face. I look at my classmates. One student is doodling. Another is sleeping. I am getting angry, really angry; I don't know why.

"I used to go to every new show Alvin Lucier did," my friend Phil James chats to me from his computer terminal. "He was like a cross between Mr.

Wizard and the Wizard of Oz, demonstrating with each new work some magical principle of the physics of sound. But it eventually left me cold. As you can see from the score, the meaning of the spoken words is close to irrelevant; it's very frustrating if something human is hinted at and then you're only left with an exercise in science-art. For me, anyway, being pretty much a wordaholic."

A fat housefly lumbers across the chalkboard. There is no air circulating in this classroom. I feel sweat pooling in my bra. I am sitting in a room. Bah bah BAH bah ba ba bahm. Lucier is right; nothing in this piece matters, save the rhythms of his voice. As the repetition builds into extended feedback and then a white roar, discerning rhythm becomes an act of blind faith on my part. I don't know how you ever endured it all without a pause. Perhaps it all seemed like one long pause, washed with sound?

I am sitting in this room, different from the one you are in right now, and while you sleep, I take your hand in mine. Your arms are blue as fresh plums. Your chest rises. The bags beep when they are done. Every night is Ladies' Night. You are too proud to ring, and I don't blame you. If the nurse won't come, then I will change your needles. Everyone has their own way of fighting. Remember, this is your first impression, so relax and have fun. I will not leave. Faith is not a substitute for medicine, but an addition to it.

My classmate looks up from her doodle to watch me sobbing over the sound art. As I type my response to my friend Phil, I hear an angry voice silently raise itself in my head. When did we decide that "psychological" art is the kind that "means" something, versus "science-art," which is supposedly about nothing but technique and surface? Why would the art critics not trade a page of Artaud for all of Carroll? I am sitting in a room, different from the performance spaces in which people ordinarily exclaim "so brave" at the finish of my psychological, text-driven monologues. I am at my computer, arguing in silence with my friend, remembering Lucier, and I am shocked to realize that I have lost all interest in performance work based on words. Except, perhaps, science-art based on words. I wonder if the Law Talk program could be trained to recognize my voice in anger. I don't want to do another monologue without a computer. I don't want to do art that "means" something. I can tell you precisely what about Karen Finley's work "means," what moves me, what does not, where her mythologies overlap mine, where they don't. I still cannot explain what happened to me the day I listened to Lucier.

I was sitting in a room, different from the one I am in now, when the line noise on my computer cued me into the fact that someone was tying to reach me over the phone. The call was from my brother. My mother had finally died, after hanging on in the hospice with a pulse rate that baffled the doctors. The end of the Lucier piece sounds like bells, just highly pitched bells, over and over. And then it ends. There is nothing rich and wordy about certain types of art, sex, or death. Which is not to say there is no sound. My brother told me that he believed my mother was truly gone only when he stopped hearing the chugging of the machines keeping her alive.

Notes

1. Gilles Deleuze, "The Schizophrenic and the Little Girl," in *The Logic of Sense* (New York: Columbia University Press, 1990), 93.

2. Alvin Lucier. *I Am Sitting in a Room*, Lovely Music, Ltd. 1981/1990.

5 The Crackle of the Wire: Media, Digitization, and the Voicing of Aboriginal Languages

Martin Thomas

In 1763, when the long friendship between Samuel Johnson and James Boswell was still in its infancy, their conversation turned to the poems of a clergyman named Ogilvie who was visiting London. Unlike his future biographer, Dr. Johnson had a low opinion of Ogilvie's writings, which he criticized for want of originality. "[W]hat might be called imagination in them was, to be sure, imagination once; but it is no more imagination in him than the echo is sound." Like so many of Johnson's epigrammatic utterances, the fact that we can access this curious distinction between a sound and an echo is the direct consequence of Boswell's habit of creating echoes of his own by transcribing Johnson's words (or at least his recollection of them) into his diary. So this remnant of Johnson speaking becomes uncannily self-reflexive—as Boswell might have realized when he recorded it. Enthralled as he was by the wit of Johnson, he was unpersuaded by his argument. Boswell's diary says of Ogilvie: "I cannot help, however, thinking that he has more merit than this great censor will allow."[1]

A Johnsonian pronouncement might seem a peculiar launching pad for a discussion about the relationship between sound recording, language, and digital technologies in Arnhem Land, a tract of Aboriginal-owned country, 97,000 square kilometers in size, situated to the east of Kakadu National Park in the far north of Australia. Readers of *The Life of Samuel Johnson* will recall that for all his humanist tendencies, the literary leviathan of Enlightenment England had a low opinion of traditional societies. "[O]ne set of Savages is like another," he said to Boswell as he waved dismissively at Parkinson's account of journeying with Cook. "These Voyages . . . will be eaten by rats and mice before they are read through. There can be little entertainment in such books."[2] Yet this lack of sympathy for "savages" (and even the writers who described them), which is at least somewhat inconsistent coming from a man who made an ex-slave from Jamaica the chief beneficiary of his will, is among the reasons why it is so intriguing to ponder Johnson's notion of an echo being devoid of the originality or authenticity that he ascribed to sound. The publication that defined his transformation from Grub Street hack to literary eminence was *A Dictionary of the English Language* (1755), a work of record, trace, and echo that won him the moniker "Dictionary Johnson" and made him one of the most famous figures of his era.

Johnson's was not the first dictionary, even of English, but the thoroughness with which it furrowed English as a linguistic territory made it the lexicon par excellence, at least until the publication of the *Oxford English Dictionary* in the early twentieth century. The Johnson *Dictionary*, with its 42,000 definitions, involved the wholesale transformation of units of sound into visual signs. Now of course that transformation is not in itself special to Johnson; it is the alchemy at the heart of all writing. But the *Dictionary*, an icon of the encyclopedic eighteenth century, packaged and regularized the manifold vagaries of English in a way that could scarcely have been imagined by earlier generations. To invoke the resonant term used by Walter J. Ong, dictionaries enabled a new "technologizing" of the word that in an era of imperial expansion had cascading effects. It influenced the pronunciation of English, just as it facilitated the exponential growth of both its vocabulary and sphere of influence. English, as Ong argued, became a "grapholect"—"a transdialectical language formed by deep commitment to writing."[3] As much as the culture of printing affected the *sound* of language (encouraging the standardization of grammar and diction), it also provided new avenues for the containment of social difference—a phenomenon (to use an appropriately visual metaphor) that can be counted among the many long shadows cast by the Enlightenment. The critic Bruce Johnson has argued that Samuel Johnson's exclusion of the lexicon of the underclasses was "part of their progressive criminalisation." The *Dictionary* was both the symbol and the instrument of a social order that "stiffened the disenfranchisement of non-literate cultures (within and beyond 'the nation')."[4]

Ong argued that oral traditions are imperiled when they clash with typographic cultures. The experience of Aboriginal Australia, like that of so many indigenous societies around the world, confirms the general substance of this claim. In the early 1990s, the Australian Institute of

Aboriginal and Torres Strait Islander Studies, reviewing the status quo of Australian languages, reported that of the estimated 250 tongues spoken at the time of British settlement in 1788, only about ninety are still in use and of those a mere twenty are in a relatively healthy condition. Ninety per cent of Aboriginal people no longer speak an indigenous tongue.[5] More recent reportage, based on 1996 data, is also pessimistic. It claims that of the 20 languages found to be healthy in 1990, a further three had become "endangered," and it predicted that unless intervention is taken, all the Aboriginal languages of Australia will be extinct by 2050.[6] To attribute this grim history of linguistic genocide entirely to the impact of print would be simplistic. The loss of some languages was due to the outright annihilation of their speakers. But it can be said of the contact experience that the status of English as a language of the literate affected its efficacy as an instrument of coercion. That English carried textual authority affirmed the sense of entitlement and superiority of those who spoke it. (Many colonials were themselves barely literate, but this did not dent, and arguably heightened, their linguistic chauvinism.) As the historian Diane Collins has remarked, Aboriginal speech was regularly typecast as "noisy jabbering" and "dreadful shrieks" in colonial accounts. Aboriginal Australians, she writes, were "portrayed as aural primitives."[7] So it is not surprising that the supplanting of Aboriginal languages with English became a central objective in the "civilizing" of colonial subjects. Unlike most of the arriving Britons, Aboriginal people were typically multilingual. This was essential for conducting the trade and ceremonial relationships with neighboring communities that were standard throughout the continent. Doubtless, their grounding as polyglots affected their proficiency in acquiring English. (English speakers, in contrast, have shown little flare for learning Aboriginal tongues.) But inevitably, Aboriginal people spoke English in a manner inflected by their own linguistic heritage. From the language of their colonizers, they created a dialect, a "lingo," that in the culture of white Australia became the butt of endless jokes and caricature. When, as I have often heard, Aboriginal people utter the refrain, "Lost my land, lost my language," they cogently express this doubled sense of displacement. To convey the loss of identity and self-esteem caused by this invidious process is ultimately impossible, but its effects are evident in the frequently catastrophic condition of Aboriginal society today.

Often unwittingly, Anglophone Australians use Aboriginal terms, or derivatives of them, in day-to-day speech. Loans from Aboriginal languages, about four hundred of which are common in modern Australian English, give the vernacular much of its presumed national flavor, as an Aboriginal man once pointed out to me as we sat by a billabong under a coolabah tree. But as a team of linguists discovered when they did interview-based research into how people perceive and define such words, public awareness that they are rooted in indigenous language is at best minimal.[8] To adapt Samuel Johnson's phraseology, Aboriginal loan words have become echoes; they are frequently heard, but their origins remain unsounded.

In the mass media, and in public discourse more generally, it is remarkably rare that we hear an Aboriginal language being spoken or sung fluently on its own terms—the important moves in this direction of Aboriginal rock groups such as Yothu Yindi and the Warrumpi Band notwithstanding. The extent of this was brought home to me during a recent experience while driving through Kakadu National Park on the threshold of Arnhem Land. At a service station, a car pulled up and four young Aboriginal men got out. They bought fuel, cigarettes, soft drinks, and ice creams, loudly speaking all the while in Kunwinjku, the most common language of the west Arnhem Land region. Only when speaking to the cashier, who was non-Aboriginal, did they use English. If it were Italian, Turkish, Vietnamese, or Lebanese that I had heard in a similar scenario, it would not provoke comment. For several decades after World War II, Australia opened its doors to mass immigration and to an extent the populace—although *not* the public culture—became linguistically diverse. Of course it is the fact that it was an *Australian* language that I overheard that gave cause for reflection. In the north or "Top End" of the country, and in the arid center, what I experienced is utterly normal. But most Australians, who live in the southeast of the continent, could go to their graves without having even this degree of exposure to a living Aboriginal tongue.

The history that I have summarized perhaps too briefly—in which the technologization of language has helped shape an aural landscape in which the Aboriginal presence is contained and for the most part muted—has a specific bearing on the issue that concerns us here: the relationship between digitization and the mediated voice. An indication that digitization is having a material effect upon the standing of Aboriginal language can be discerned in Rolf de Heer's *Ten Canoes* (2006), a feature film that has been rightly celebrated for breaking significant ground in Australian cinema. Its spirit of collaboration and profit-sharing arrangements with Aboriginal performers and knowledge-holders is unprecedented in the history of mainstream filmmaking. Another distinctive aspect is that *Ten Canoes* is the only feature to be set in Australia at a time predating the arrival of Europeans. Related to this, and particularly pertinent to this discussion, is the fact that the film is enacted in various languages indigenous to Arnhem Land, most of which fall under the umbrella term *Yolŋu Matha* (a descriptor for the family of clan-based dialects spoken in the northeast of Arnhem Land).[9] Although the film has been subtitled in English and other languages for cinema and DVD release, the drama and off-screen narration (spoken by the veteran Aboriginal actor David Gulpilil) are performed entirely in Aboriginal tongues. Most are part of the Yolŋu Matha group, although Crusoe Kurddal, a lead player, speaks Kunwinjku in the film. So to say, as most commentaries have done, that the film is performed in "an" Aboriginal language is to miss a fundamental point about the polyglot quality of Arnhem Land life. *Ten Canoes* marks a particular milestone, as it is the first feature film to be made entirely in indigenous Australian languages.

To get a grasp of the particular achievement of de Heer and his Yolŋu collaborators, and to understand the very specific role played by digitization, some historical and technological context is required. We need to consider how Arnhem Landers have been represented in time-based media, an issue that cannot be divorced from the question of how time-based media have been presented to Arnhem Landers, frequently as emblems of Westernization. An outsider could readily assume that de Heer's decision to work collaboratively on a film project with the residents of Ramingining, the settlement where *Ten Canoes* was shot, marks an introduction of cinema to this isolated community. Yet nothing could be further from the truth. *Ten Canoes* should be recognized as a recent chapter in a long and complex process of engagement, going back for at least a century, in which cameras and sound recorders have played a distinctive role in mediating the interactions between Balanda (as white people are known in this part of the country) and the communities of Arnhem Land. W. Baldwin Spencer, the first visitor to the area who had anything in the way of anthropological training, set the scene when he made films and phonographic recordings during his 1912 research trip to Oenpelli in the western part of Arnhem Land.[10] Later,

a movie was produced during Herbert Basedow's Second Mackay Exploration Expedition in 1928 (although its whereabouts are unknown).[11] Donald
Thomson's outstanding photography from the 1930s—the acknowledged
catalyst for *Ten Canoes*—I will discuss shortly. These are but a few examples.

Since the 1960s, when sound-to-film cameras became readily portable
and affordable, ethnographic filmmaking has blossomed in Arnhem Land,
as it has in other parts of Australia where sizable Aboriginal populations
reside. Filmmakers including Ian Dunlop and Kim McKenzie worked within
communities to document ceremonial traditions as well as more prosaic
aspects of social life. During this period, the electronic tape recorder was
also introduced, and it rapidly became a tool of trade for linguists, anthropologists, ethnomusicologists, and other fieldworkers. The tape recorder
had unique attributes that suggested new possibilities for media participation, most notably its playback mechanism.[12] This allowed performers to
conduct on-the-spot monitoring of how they sounded—a feature that did
not apply to the movie camera (although this changed with the advent of
video).[13] The reception of these technologies was influenced by the rate of
literacy, which in Arnhem Land has never been high. This rate is due to
a variety of factors: the lack of educational resources and opportunities;
resistance to the authoritarianism of missionary educators (some of whom
compelled children to wash their mouths out with soap if they spoke Yolŋu
Matha on school grounds); and the ill-suitedness of the Latin alphabet to
the notation of Aboriginal phonetics.[14] So it is not surprising that Aboriginal people seized upon the tape recorder as an instrument for furthering
their own agendas. Examples of this can be found in the audio archives
of A. P. Elkin, Australia's best known anthropologist of the mid-twentieth
century, which contain several recorded missives in which senior Arnhem
Landers express to Elkin their concern about the way secret-sacred information, confided to visiting researchers, had fallen into unauthorized hands.[15]

These attempts to regulate cultural property are indicative of a wider
trend. Aboriginal people became increasingly aware that Western media
could assist in the preservation of knowledge during an era of rapid change
(within their own society and beyond). Yet these sorts of initiatives are
seldom recognized in histories of anthropology or postcolonial critique,
partly because sound archives have never attracted the same level of interest as ethnographic film and photography. As a consequence, *observational
practices* have been privileged over the *dialogic interactions* that are basic to

the ethnographic project. The dominance of sight over the other senses (trumpeted by R. Murray Schafer and later sound scholars) offers a possible explanation for this. But there is cause for a certain skepticism about the presumed evanescence of the auditory in comparison to other types of experience. As Jonathan Sterne argues, "[t]o say that ephemerality is a special quality of sound, rather than a quality endemic to any form of perceptible motion or event in time, is to engage in a very selective form of nominalism."[16]

Recorded dialog between ethnographers and their subjects has in fact been extensively archived and thereby rendered "permanent." These archives are no more evanescent, or difficult to access, than films and photographs. The fact that such sources have been so comprehensively overlooked suggests to me that critics have found a comfort zone in this space of silencing. By perennially emphasizing how ethnographic subjects are constituted as objects of visual scrutiny, they turn a deaf ear to the voices of the people whom they purport to defend. The one-eyed fixation on the gaze of the camera, resting at the surface of whatever it surveys, forms a dramatic contrast to an encounter with the recorded voice, emanating, it seems, from the very inside of the speaker. The intimacy of so many recordings, augmented by the frequent transparency of the speakers' conversational strategies, brings to the forefront the question of agency. I can think of numerous examples of Aboriginal recordists who purposefully used the medium of audio to create resources for future generations. Recently I auditioned some remarkable 1970s recordings made the by Yolŋu artist and political activist Wandjuk Marika.[17] During a series of visits to Sydney, he spent many hours at the Australian Museum. Sitting in a quiet back room, speaking in a measured and considered English, he recorded detailed interpretations of scores of bark paintings, collected from his own country in northeast Arnhem Land. Some he had painted himself and some were done by his late father, Mawalan Marika, one of the greatest painters of the region. Wandjuk was the principal player in Ian Dunlop's film, *In Memory of Mawalan* (1971), a documentation of the elaborate memorial ceremony that Wandjuk coordinated as a tribute to his father. The film, still watched on video in the Marikas' home community of Yirrkala, is an example of how that dialogic exchange could be played out in the audiovisual medium of cinema. As he oversaw the preparations and the ceremonies themselves, Wandjuk was ever mindful of the filmmaker whose craft was allowing him to memorialize his memorial, so to speak.[18] At an almost subtextual level, this contributes to the elegiac quality of the film. Ethnographic documentaries helped pave the way for film and video produced fully by Aboriginal people, some of it intended solely for Aboriginal audiences. As Eric Michaels and others have discussed, Aboriginal TV production began in the 1980s as equipment became cheaper and more user-friendly and as funding from government and other sources became available.[19]

The fact that Aboriginal people have assumed a degree of control over their own media image does at least complicate the history, as old as the camera, in which technologies of reproduction have been used to stigmatize and objectify those whom Westerners have classified as primitive. Indeed, as Bruno Latour has argued, that juxtaposition of "modern" and "primitive" has been pivotal to modernity's self-definition.[20] Very frequently that contrast between "the West and the Rest" is articulated by setting up a theater of technological difference. One of the subtleties that gets overlooked in this scenario is the extent to which media images provide resources for Aboriginal people to apprehend and interpret their own historical reality. *Ten Canoes* is a vivid example of this process, since it was inspired by the photography of Donald Thomson (1901–1970), the renowned anthropologist, photographer, and ethnological collector, who became friendly with the Yolŋu during an extended residence in their country during the mid-1930s. Thomson, a fervent advocate of Aboriginal rights, was well memorialized in oral traditions. But his memory assumed new life when researchers such as the anthropologist Nicolas Peterson began to publish Thomson's photography and circulate it among the Yolŋu, some of whom were inspired to visit the Museum of Victoria in Melbourne where they could view the vast array of material culture that Thomson had collected from their forebears. It was a Thomson photograph, showing men in ten canoes, that David Gulpilil singled out to de Heer as especially significant to Yolŋu, and that steered the production of the film. De Heer later claimed that knowledge of traditional canoe-making had entirely disappeared in Ramingining and that the Yolŋu were able to manufacture the bark vessels used in the film only by studying examples collected by Thomson.[21] The latter's impact on Yolŋu historical consciousness is reflected in certain structural devices that were adopted as a result of the extended liaison between the filmmaker and the community, most notably the decision to create a narrative within a narrative. In the first instance, *Ten Canoes* is a period drama, set at a time prior to European settlement during the annual hunt for eggs of the migratory magpie goose (*Anseranas semipalmata*). A young man named Dayindi (Jamie Gulpilil) is being told a story about another young man rather like himself—a story that is apparently set in the ancestral period of creation, the time of "the Dreaming" as it is known in English—the epoch when the land and its founding narratives were created by the ancestral beings. As much as the Dreaming is conceived as something that went before, it is nonetheless thought to exist in the here and now. The practice of ceremony, song, and storytelling brings it constantly into the present. This complex temporality is expressed in the film by the contemporary "look" of the mythical sequences, which are shot in color, many of them using aerial photography. In contrast, the "historical" component where Dayindi and his companions are hunting for eggs is shot (à la Thomson) with a fixed camera in black and white. As film critic Therese Davis explains, this was in accord with the expectations of the Yolŋu whose "history as it now exists in and through the Thompson [sic] photographs needed to be depicted accurately, that is, in 'black and white.'"[22]

All of this is evidence of the way Western media have inflected the Yolŋu sense of time and history. But what of the human voice and the exclusive use of Aboriginal language in a feature film? Why suggest that David Gulpilil's mellifluous storytelling in his own tongue is somehow a product of the digital age? After all, Gulpilil has been a presence in Australian cinema for more than a generation. He made his screen debut in *Walkabout* (1971) after being "discovered" at the age of thirteen by the British director Nicolas Roeg. His many credits include *Storm Boy* (1976), *Crocodile Dundee* (1986), *Rabbit-Proof Fence* (2002), and an earlier de Heer film, *The Tracker* (2002). Gulpilil is easily the best-known Aboriginal actor in the history of film. The clarity with which we hear the dialog, the narration, and the highly evocative soundtrack of *Ten Canoes* is of course due to digital recording and studio production. But there is no technical reason why a feature film in an Aboriginal language could not have been made at the beginning of Gulpulil's career or earlier. As we have seen, ethnographic filmmakers have been doing just that for decades.

So the higher fidelity of digital audio is almost a distraction at this point. It is for quite different reasons that the computer is central to the assertion of the Yolŋu that their language should be heard publicly on its own terms. To understand these reasons, it is necessary to think within the full time frame of modernity's trajectory, beginning back in those black-and-white days when the oral and typographic traditions encountered each other— a meeting so destructive to oral societies. It continued with the arrival of cameras and recorders, and as Aboriginal people learned about these technologies and eventually began to acquire or control them, a shift occurred. In ways that were inscriptive, although they sat outside the troubled sphere of writing, these media brought techniques of encoding language and other aspects of the culture. The computer marks the current chapter in this narrative, and its distinction, as Friedrich Kittler discerned in *Gramophone, Film, Typewriter* (1986), is not that it added a further element to the three great strata that constitute the media of modernity (sound reproduction, moving pictures, and print).[23] Rather, its triumph is one of packaging and integration. Access to what had formerly been discrete media is now integrated in a single machine; the machines themselves are integrated through adaptation of the old infrastructure of telephony.

The significance of this phenomenon lies in its twofold act of compression: the compact size (and hence the portability) of the machine and the reduction of the effective distance between machines (through instantaneity of communication). These two types of compression have transformed our experience of the computer's antecedent media. (We no longer depend on the cinema for film, the postman for mail.) For the people of Arnhem Land, whose survival as a people owes much to their geographic distance from Australia's major centers of population and political power, this change is as unmistakable as the turning of the tide. As we have seen, their contribution to media history has been extensive, but almost invariably it has resulted in the export of their cultural property to distant institutions and repositories where in many cases it has lain dormant, unseen or unheard. To appreciate how digitization is playing a role here, we must think about the logistics of how Donald Thomson's archives, and those of many other outsiders, are finding a route to their place of origin. We need to get outside the stereotype of an Aboriginal people forever bypassed by the highway of modernity, and acknowledge, as the anthropologist Melissa Hinkson argues, that these "remote" communities have been thoroughly "caught up in the telecommunications revolution which has swept the world in the past two decades."[24] If the twenty-first century is broadening the bandwidth of the voices we hear in public culture, the reason is very much to do with the connectivity facilitated by digital systems.

The dialog that is axiomatic to genuine inquiry between cultures has been extended in new directions by digitization. When the contents of media archives are dislodged and returned to their place of origin, discussions from the past can speak to the present—a process that forces the very conception of an ethnographic archive to be "reimagined," according to the musicologist Linda Barwick. Formerly, as she points out,

the sound archives' primary relationship was with the individual collector, who typically travelled to remote places to collect the recordings for deposit in the archive. Relationships between the archives and the individuals whose speech or performances were recorded were typically limited by geography, technological differentials, and sometimes language barriers.[25]

With the advent of facilities such online access to institutions and an increasing move toward the establishment of digital knowledge centers within Aboriginal communities, the orientation of the archive can be turned from servicing the researcher to serving the people (or their descendants) who provided the content of collections. This alters the role of the researcher as much as it affects the focus and responsibilities of the archivist.

Here I can write personally—as a historian interested in cross-cultural transactions and as a media practitioner. In an earlier age, I might have been content to write a history of Arnhem Land, or make a documentary about it, by excavating and interpreting archives in much the same manner as historians have been doing for centuries. But in an era when the prospect of transit from a colonial to a postcolonial paradigm looms as a tantalizing possibility (though not, alas, as a concrete reality), it seems not only unethical but woefully uninteresting to ignore the views of the people whose cultural heritage is encoded in those spools of tape and film. My work on northern Australia began in the archives of the Australian Broadcasting Corporation (ABC) in Sydney, where I auditioned some recordings that postdate Donald Thomson's time with the Yolŋu by a little more than a decade. They were produced at the then mission settlement of Oenpelli, now a predominantly Aboriginal town called Gunbalanya in the western reaches of Arnhem Land. The people there are known as the Bininj and the most common of their many languages is Kunwinjku. The recordings I have been studying date from 1948, a time when the magnetic wire recorder, a short-lived predecessor of the tape recorder, was the machine of choice for location recording. Colin Simpson, an ABC producer (and later a well-known travel writer), and Raymond Giles, a staff technician, liaised with local Bininj who performed song and ceremony for the recorder. These presentations of culture were prompted by the visit of a roving party of naturalists, anthropologists, biochemists, and photographers known as the American-Australian Scientific Expedition to Arnhem Land.[26]

The wire recordings were transferred to acetate discs soon after Simpson returned to Sydney. Some of the material he used in a radio documentary about the expedition, broadcast in late 1948.[27] The rest of it was archived, and seems to have been left largely untouched until the discs were duplicated onto magnetic access tapes in the 1980s. These were the tapes that I auditioned—and as I did so, I copied them onto a computer where I saved them as audio files. The recordings were the thread that led me to contemporaneous film and still photography, taken by members of the Arnhem Land Expedition and held in a variety of institutions.[28] By the time I traveled to west Arnhem Land in 2006, a virtual truckload of film and tape was compactly stored on my laptop.

Figure 5.1
Colin Simpson (far right) and Eric Giles with unidentified men around a Pyrox wire recorder at Oenpelli, 1948. Photograph: Howell Walker. NLA MS5253/133. By permission of the National Library of Australia.

It was the late Lofty Bardayal Nadjamerrek, a senior law man and renowned west Arnhem artist, who had opened the door to much of the material I gathered. Because some of it portrays restricted ceremonies, or is in other ways culturally sensitive, the archival institutions rightly insist that research can occur only with the support of traditional owners. Bardayal (circa 1926–2009), whose life began as a hunter-gatherer on the Arnhem Land Plateau, and who did not read or write, dictated authorization that I could access the films and recordings. This was relayed to the Australian Institute of Aboriginal and Torres Strait Islander Studies by the linguist Murray Garde, who works part of the year with Bardayal at Kabulwarnamyo, a tiny settlement within his ancestral country. I met up with Bardayal at the airport in Darwin, capital of the Northern Territory, where he had flown for a day to formalize what is known as the West Arnhem Fire Management Agreement, a partnership involving a liquid gas company, the Northern Territory government, and traditional owners of west Arnhem Land. The agreement provides Aboriginal owners with income of about $1 million a year to implement their traditional knowledge of the country by managing bushfires and burn-offs, and thereby minimizing the release of greenhouse-producing gases.[29] That the economics of power supply—a carbon emissions offset program—are providing the means for Aboriginal people to maintain connection with their ancestral country is further evidence of the complex web of relationships between antiquity and modernity being renegotiated at the present time.

Through a light haze of bushfire smoke, we flew over Kakadu and the heavily weathered sandstone of the Arnhem Land Plateau in a six-seater aircraft, bouncing down to land on a rutted slash in the forest that passes as a landing strip. Kabulwarnamyo, whose population numbers about 30, owes its position to an increase ceremony, performed for time immemorial, that involves a particular tree beside the spring that waters the settlement. In Kunwinjku the species is known as *djarduk* (native apple or *Syzygium suborbilulare*). As the term suggests, an increase ceremony encourages the abundance of living things, typically foodstuffs. In this case, the ritual involves singing a song and striking the tree with an axe. Although the *djaruk* at Kabulwarnamyo is recovering from fire damage, a cluster of tight little scars, formed by both stone and steel hatchets, is discernible upon the bole. The ritual is designed to increase the numbers of *norne*, a wasp-imitating fly. Bardayal is custodian of the Honey Dreaming, which explains his personal identification with this *norne* site. The *norne* is valued not as a comestible, but for its power of signification. Because the insect seeks native honey hives in which to lay its eggs, it can be followed in the hope that it will lead to a supply of *sugarbag*, as the exquisite native honey is plainly known in Aboriginal English.

Lest this conjure an Arcadian impression of life on the plateau, I should mention that a *norne* shares the air with signals and signifiers more typically associated with the twenty-first century. With solar panels mounted on the A-frame-and-tarpaulin structures that serve as dwellings, and a satellite dish that allows telephone service and internet connection for the communal computer, the settlement is wired up—or should I say *beamed in*—to the digital world. Life in the camp allows for a range of media experiences that could include, within the time frame of an hour or two, perusal of the rock art that crowds cave and boulder, a session auditioning historic recordings of Kunwinjku song (installed on the camp computer by visiting

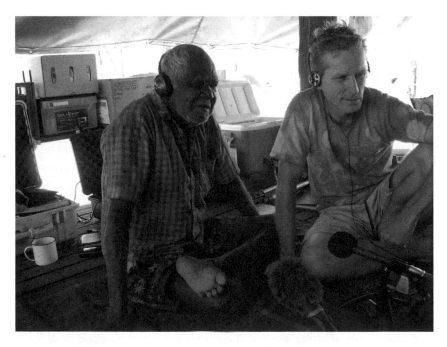

Figure 5.2
Lofty Bardayal Nadjamerrek and Murray Garde auditioning the archival recordings in 2006. Photograph: Martin Thomas. Permission of the author.

researchers), followed by an evening's diversion with Bruce Lee (the favored DVD at the time of my visit). This was the locale for studying the historic media images produced during the visit of the Arnhem Land Expedition in 1948. On successive days, Murray Garde and I convened discussion sessions, which we recorded. Some involved men only; others included men, women, and children. It all depended on the content of the material. While the audience gathered cross-legged on the ground, we cued iTunes or the file on the laptop and let it play.

Of the many remarkable things that occurred during that process, the most fascinating was Bardayal's response to documentation of an initiation ceremony known as *Wubarr*. In this culture of gender specificity, the documentation, like the ceremony itself, is out of bounds to women and children. Wubarr is the ceremony into which Bardayal and other older men in the west of Arnhem Land were first initiated as youths. The ritual has long been known to anthropologists through the work of Ronald Berndt, who observed it at Oenpelli in 1949.[30] For contemporary Arnhem Landers, the significance of the documentation is heightened by the fact that Wubarr has not been performed since the 1970s. Post–World War II, it was gradually displaced by *Kunapipi*, an entirely different initiation ceremony, associated with the Rainbow Serpent cult. Berndt witnessed Kunapipi in northeast Arnhem Land in 1946 and made it the subject of a famous monograph.[31] Although the locality of Kunapipi's origin is a matter of conjecture, all evidence attests to the rapidity with which it spread across the Top End during the middle of the twentieth century. In the Oenpelli case, the presence of the ethnographer seems to have influenced its introduction. Bardayal explained that although some residents of the mission had attended Kunapipi further east, it was performed at Oenpelli only on Berndt's request. Bardayal recalled that the appropriateness of performing a ceremony then foreign to the region was fiercely debated by senior men. But Berndt was pressing in his demand, made at a time when the authority of Balanda was not readily challenged. Bardayal stated that the request was lubricated by a substantial payment of food and tobacco to the performers—a detail that Berndt neglected to mention in his published account.

The circumstances that led to the recording of the Wubarr ceremony are another story.[32] Of interest here is the way the documentation was received on the Arnhem Land Plateau—a reception that I have occasionally revisited while writing. Through headphones attached to my computer, I can hear the register of birdsong, the buzz and splutter of a chainsaw, and here and there the abrupt and truly awful distortion of a southerly breeze that swelled up randomly to set the microphone vibrating and coating the keyboard with dust. There is the sound of the 1948 recordings playing: the song, didgeridoo, and clap sticks, so much tinnier now than it seemed then when we were all ears, crowded around the computer. And amidst it all are the ecstatic cries of appreciation that Bardayal and others uttered in unison as a song or dance came to its conclusion. I later established that these exclamations are the typical mode of applause used at ceremonies. It was only natural that the formal gestures of appreciation should greet the documentary records.

Difficult to pick up in the field recordings, but bleedingly obvious when I return to the sound files dubbed from the ABC archives, is the crackle and interference that I like to think originate from the magnetic wire recorder, the instrument that allowed the preservation of these performances sixty years ago. Yet perhaps I am being nostalgic in connecting the crackle with the wire alone. For surely it is a composite distortion: each decaying generation in the analog chain (the steel wire, the acetate disc, the plastic tape) must have left a muddied accretion. Like static to the ear, I can hear it now, undiscriminatingly reproduced in the sequence of ones and zeroes that constitute the digital copy. Presumably, the digital reproduction has its own sound also, but this is harder to discern. The ear, and indeed the entire body, rapidly adjusts to the current notion of "high fidelity," as Barthes reminds us in "The Grain of the Voice"—his argument neatly periodized by his contemplation of how musical performance has been altered by the clarity and extended duration of a medium that now seems short and scratchy, the LP record.

Technically, it would be possible to "clean up" the 1948 recordings using digital processes and thereby eliminate much of the "crackle in the wire" (or whatever it is). In the record industry, digital recording and production are comparatively recent arrivals. The computerized processing of the sound image was first introduced for the purpose of "remastering" earlier recordings (this being a euphemism for expunging the residue of analog processes that were becoming aurally unacceptable). In a world without budgetary restraints, the Arnhem Land recordings might be similarly cleansed. Yet whether this is desirable is far from certain. The Bininj seemed perfectly happy to filter the distortion with their ears, as they did the wind and other distractions. And it occurred to me then that the whoosh and hiss have their own poetry; they are worth preserving, because they delineate the confluence of such dissimilar technologies and traditions. Conscious of this paradoxical melding, I hear, in the production suite that is my mind's ear, the appreciative gasps of those older men, applauding the virtuosity of long-dead dancers and singers. Somewhere along the way, their utterances find harmony with the crackle in the wire, as distinctive as the patina that coats any artifact—and equally redolent in meaning.

Many contradictions emerge when you begin to sound these echoes from the past. The belief that racial termination loomed provided the impetus for Westerners to document Aboriginal traditions. As R. H. Mathews, the early Australian anthropologist, candidly explained: the "native tribes are disappearing rapidly before the advancing tide of European population, and unless some person qualified for the task shall take up this highly important subject, the languages and the customs of an interesting primitive people will be lost to science."[33] The phraseology differed over time, but the apprehension of impending disappearance was the motivation for much ethnographic recording in the twentieth century. It gave rise to the unwieldy mass that fills the media archives. Yet even as we recognize that predictions of extinction were ill founded, a further threat presents itself: the impermanence of the wax, acetate, celluloid, magnetic tape, and other media on which all this material was recorded.

Strategies for dealing with the frailty of media heritage are the subject of intense debate among the archivists who specialize in this field. An increasingly common practice is to digitize collections, even those that run to hundreds of thousands of hours of recorded data. There is no fast-tracking this process. To be faithfully reproduced, the recordings must be played in what is referred to as "real time." They must speak to the computer at the tempo at which they were made. Whether our huge ethnographic archives and collections of oral history can be preserved before they rot is a moot point. Yet there is something majestic about those spools set in ceaseless revolution, steadily disgorging memories that will otherwise be eaten by rats and mice before they are heard through. As the case study of Arnhem Land reveals, a plethora of signals converge when they meet with the computer. A temporal panorama, rooted in antiquity, though engaged with modernity in its many manifestations, is opened up by the course of this technological migration.

Acknowledgment

We thank the family of the late Mr. Lofty Bardayal Nadjamerrek for allowing us to name him and publish his photograph so soon after his passing.

I am indebted to Murray Garde for his valuable criticism and for helping me understand the linguistic diversity of *Ten Canoes*.

Notes

1. James Boswell, *Boswell's London Journal 1762–1763* (London: William Heinemann, 1951), 289.

2. James Boswell, *The Life of Johnson* (Ware, Hertfordshire: Wordsworth Editions, 1999), 917.

3. Walter J. Ong, *Orality and Literacy: The Technologizing of the Word* London: Routledge, 2000), 8.

4. Bruce Johnson, "Voice, Power and Modernity," in Joy Damousi and Desley Deacon (eds.), *Talking and Listening in the Age of Modernity: Essays on the history of sound* (Canberra, Aus.: ANU E Press, 2007), 115.

5. Annette Schmidt, *The Loss of Australia's Aboriginal Language Heritage* (Canberra, Aus.: Aboriginal Studies Press, 1993).

6. Patrick McConvell and Nicholas Thieberger, *State of Indigenous languages in Australia—2001*, Second Technical Paper Series No. 2 (Natural and Cultural Heritage) (Canberra, Aus.: Department of the Environment, 2001), 2–4.

7. Diane Collins, "Acoustic Journeys: Exploration and the Search for an Aural History of Australia," *Australian Historical Studies* 37, no. 128 (2006), 11.

8. Gerhard Leitner and Inke Sieloff, "Aboriginal words and concepts in Australian English," *World Englishes* 17, no. 2 (1998), 153–169.

9. *Yolŋu Matha* is a term meaning "people's language." It includes a number of discrete languages (some unintelligible to other Yolŋu Matha speakers) and their dialects.

10. D. J. Mulvaney and J. H. Calaby, *"So Much That Is New": Baldwin Spencer, 1860–1929: A Biography* (Carlton, Aus.: Melbourne University Press, 1985), 294.

11. The existence of the footage is known from press coverage: "[a]n excellent instructional film, 'Through Unknown Arnhem Land,' has been presented to the Imperial Institute by the British Film Institute. The film was taken by the Mackey Exploring Expedition." See F. L. Minnigerode, "London Screen Notes," *New York Times*, March 31, 1929, 107.

12. As I have discussed elsewhere, earlier audio technologies such as phonography and magnetic wire recording *did* allow playback in the field. But their size and expense were among the factors that generally prevented Aboriginal people from acquiring and controlling them. See my article "The Rush to Record: Transmitting the Sound of Aboriginal Culture," *Journal of Australian Studies* 90 (2007), 105–121.

13. Until the advent of the digital camera, the results of ethnographic still photography were usually unavailable to the people depicted. But there were exceptions to this. When photographer Axel Poignant worked in Arnhem Land in the early 1950s, he dispatched his film by plane for immediate processing and had reference prints flown back so the subjects of the photographs could see how they were being depicted. See Roslyn with Axel Poignant, *Encounter at Nagalarramba* (Canberra, Aus.: National Library of Australia, 1996).

14. For discussion of linguistic research and notation, see my article "Word Territory: Recording Aboriginal Language with R. H. Mathews," *History Australia* 5, no. 1 (2008) and William B. McGregor (ed.), *Excavating Australia's Linguistic Past: Studies in the history of Aboriginal linguistics* (Canberra, Aus.: Pacific Linguistics, 2008).

15. The elders are Douglas Daniels and Lazarus Lami Lami. Recordings among A. P. Elkin Papers, University of Sydney Archives, P130/Series 19/Box 136.

16. Jonathan Sterne, *The Audible Past: Cultural Origins of Sound Reproduction* (Durham, N.C.: Duke University Press, 2003), 18.

17. The fullest account of his life is his autobiography, itself an example of his strategic use of recording technology, as it is based on memoirs that he autonomously recorded. See Wandjuk Marika, *Wandjuk Marika: Life story as told to Jennifer Isaacs* (St. Lucia, Qld.: University of Queensland Press, 1995). The recordings I auditioned are in the Archives of the Australian Museum, Sydney.

18. Ian Dunlop (dir.), *In Memory of Mawalan* (Film Australia, 1971).

19. For an account of Aboriginal television in the Warlpiri community of Central Australia, see Eric Michaels, *Bad Aboriginal Art: Tradition Media, and Technological Horizons* (St. Leonards, NSW: Allen & Unwin, 1994). Contemporary video in Arnhem Land is addressed in Jennifer Deger, *Shimmering Screens: Making Media in an Aboriginal Community* (Minneapolis: University of Minnesota Press, 2006).

20. Bruno Latour, *We Have Never Been Modern* (Cambridge, Mass.: Harvard University Press, 1993).

21. Linguist Murray Garde thinks this claim is exaggerated. He points out that relatives of actors in *Ten Canoes* were filmed making bark canoes in the 1990s. These vessels and associated documentation are in the collection of the Djómi Museum, Maningrida. Garde, pers. comm., June 24, 2008.

22. Therese Davis, "Remembering our ancestors: cross-cultural collaboration and the mediation of Aboriginal culture and history in *Ten Canoes* (Rolf de Heer, 2006)," *Studies in Australasian Cinema* 1, no. 1 (2007), 9.

23. Friedrich A. Kittler, *Gramophone, Film, Typewriter* (Stanford: Stanford University Press, 1999).

24. Melissa Hinkson, "New Media Projects at Yuendumu: inter-cultural engagement and self-determination in an era of accelerated globalization," *Continuum: Journal of Media & Cultural Studies* 16, no. 2 (2002), 207.

25. Linda Barwick, "Turning It All Upside Down . . . : Imagining a distributed digital audiovisual archive," *Literary and Linguistic Computing* 19, no. 3 (2004), 253–254.

26. See Colin Simpson, *Adam in Ochre: Inside Aboriginal Australia* (Sydney: Angus & Robertson, 1951).

27. Colin Simpson (writer/producer), *Arnhem Land Expedition*, November 1948, ABC Radio Archives 83/CD/1239.

28. The major repositories are described in Martin Thomas, "Taking Them Back: Archival media in Arnhem Land today," *Cultural Studies Review* 13, no. 2 (2007), 20–37.

29. Details at http://www.atns.net.au/agreement.asp?EntityID=3638 (accessed February 20, 2008).

30. Ronald M. Berndt and Catherine H. Berndt, *Man, Land & Myth in North Australia: The Gunwinggu People* (Sydney: Ure Smith, 1970).

31. Ronald M. Berndt, *Kunapipi: A Study of an Australian Aboriginal Religious Cult* (New York: International Universities Press, 1951).

32. See Thomas, "Taking Them Back."

33. R. H. Mathews, "Languages of the New England Aborigines, New South Wales," *Proceedings of the American Philosophical Society* 42 (1903), 249–250.

II   Performing VOICE

This section focuses for the most part on the voice in contemporary arts—in dance, poetry, and media—and on how art, in its own languages, articulates and theorizes the place of the voice in today's digital culture.

Several themes recur throughout the section—the performativity of the voice, which can no longer be seen as natural or authentic; the dissociation of voice-as-speech and voice-as-sound, of voice as subjugated to the syntax of language and voice as material for a "new syntax of sound"; and, again, the arts as "cultural preparation," as the prefiguration of constraints and affordances in technologies yet to come.

Norie Neumark focuses on an uncanny "embodiment that the voice brings forth in the making"—listening to the voice in digital media and media art through a wide range of examples, including amateur YouTube videos and machinima as well as Igor Stromajer's Internet operas, Mark Hansen and Ben Rubin's *Listening Post*, and Janet Cardiff's audio walks. All of these, she argues, are characterized by performativity rather than authenticity, and by intimacy and intensity, rather than by the immersiveness of the spectacle. Drawing on the performative to evoke a way of "doing things with voices," Neumark points to "an *authenticity effect* through voice and in voice."

Meredith Morse takes us back to the predigital era, with remarkable new insights into the dance performances of Simone Forti and Yvonne Rainer, who, in the 1960s, introduced the voice into an art form hitherto silent. Even though it was not yet fully understood at the time, their work, Morse argues, prefigured the digital in a number of ways—through Forti and Rainer's interest in the material qualities of nonlinguistic sounds, through their exploration of vocal sound as bodily movement, through their focus on process rather than product and on modularity rather than cohesion.

Brandon LaBelle elucidates similar themes in relation to sound poetry, another speculative form that prefigured the digital. He discerns the reduction of sound to phonetic material replete with modularity and "cut-up-ability," ready to be shaped into a "new syntax" different from that of language. Discussing a range of writers and artists, including 1920s sound poets such as Hugo Ball, Kurt Schwitters, and others, as well as William Burroughs, Brion Gysin, François Dufrêne, and Henri Chopin, he reveals the double movement of the voice in contemporary sound poetry and art that on the one hand seeks to make the body enter language again, and on the other hand plays with the way technology allows the voice to be radically separated from the body.

Amanda Stewart also explores these themes, but as a poet rather than as a critic. Like that of Theresa Senft in the previous section, her account is experiential, describing her engrossing trajectory from analog to digital as a process of discovery that both confounded and exhilarated her, and a development that would lead to the elimination of meaning and the search for the same kind of "syntax of sound" that LaBelle also signals in his chapter. Writing as a vocal performer, Stewart explores the multifarious feedback loops that activate between the voice and language.

Mark Amerika's chapter, finally, is also "autobiographical," though through the voice of "Professor VJ," an "appropriation artist" who declares himself not to have a "self," and approvingly quotes Kathy Acker, who, in a radio interview, answered the question "Where do you find your voice?" with "What voice? I just steal shit." Voice for Professor VJ is something mashed together of singing and talking, of speaking and breathing, of reading and writing. Although Amerika describes his work as a "performance poet" and "spoken word artist," "voice" is here also synonymous with identity, conceived of as "character." In Amerika's account, the survivor cannot afford a voice, a fixed identity, just as the martial artist Bruce Lee, by his own admission, cannot afford "character": "Once you have a character your behavior becomes petrified, predictable and you lose your ability to cope freely with the world with all your resources ... the most productive, creative person is a person who has no character."[1] Amerika's chapter is itself a vigorous aesthetic performance of this paradoxical voice function—it is an *act* of digital/remix of his voice, demonstrating that what we think of as our *authentic* voice is always/already inherited, a sampling of others, a remixing of our own.

Note

1. Bruce Lee, *Artist of Life* (North Clarendon, VT: Tuttle Publishing, 2001), 42.

6 Doing Things with Voices: Performativity and Voice

Norie Neumark

A specter is haunting digital media—the specter of authenticity. You hear the voice of authenticity everywhere—from the direct address videos on YouTube to the home-style performances of DIY media and art. Or do you? In this chapter, I will analyze specific examples of media and media artwork to argue that what we are hearing is not the authentic voice staging a comeback (if it ever disappeared), but rather that something else—performative—is going on.

Although debates about authenticity per se are too complex and varied to summarize here, I would just note that the authenticity of media voices has long been troubled by analog technology—in ways that provoked extensive theoretical and artistic examination during (and even before) the twentieth century. And although the digital has further and specifically disturbed the authenticity of its voices, the digital relationship to authenticity is itself particularly complex and paradoxical. On the one hand, the digital enables better quality, which might suggest better fidelity, greater authenticity. On the other hand the digital is also more manipulable and flexible—as well as more abstract—thus undermining a sense of vocal fidelity and authenticity. From another angle, however, we might focus not so much on the digital voice as somehow post-authentic, but rather ask how in digital media and art there is an *authenticity effect* through voice and in voice. Indeed, I will suggest in this chapter that "authenticity" itself may be heard as performative.

I will work with the concept of performativity to go beyond well rehearsed debates about authenticity and essentialism—to think about an aesthetics of intimacy and intensity. For, as Adriana Cavarero's *For More than One Voice* would suggest, when voice works performatively, it is not necessarily a call to (or from) essentialism or authenticity; a performative voice can instead call the other into an intimate relationship—it can performatively effect intimacy. This happens not by speaking about intimacy, but through vocal qualities and vocal performance—through the performativity of voice. In media art, this may be the voice of Janet Cardiff as she whispers in your ear or the stuttering, singing voice of Igor Stromajer, as he channels the Internet, as I shall discuss shortly.

In this chapter, I will begin by discussing performativity and voice, focusing on the *uncanny* quality of performative voices, as they are haunted by the media from which they emerge—and as they haunt that media. I will then turn to specific examples of performative voices across a range of media and media art works, including machinima, Internet works, and installation art, to hear how these voices perform intimacy and intensity.

Performative Voices: Uncanny Disturbances of Sense and Identity

Performativity suggests something that doesn't just describe or represent but performs or activates—acting as "a material force to change something."[1] Theoretical approaches to performativity have focused not on voice but more on the spoken word and its effects: they have thought about *how to do things with words*.[2] In recent decades, influenced by Foucault and following the work of Judith Butler, scholars have concentrated particularly on the effects of performative acts on the construction of gender. Performativity now also has significant traction beyond gender studies in performance studies.[3] From the point of view of digital media art, performativity might also perhaps be understood as typical of what Jacques Rancière analyses as the aesthetic regime of art: that is, performative works enact and make evident, rather than represent or express.[4]

I realize there has been much debate, and even some ennui, around the concept of performativity, but I consider it still useful to approach voice as gesture and event—and to point to what voices *do*, how they *create and disturb* meaning and "identity" rather than just conveying or expressing it. On the one hand, voice needs to be recognized as carrying (out) the performative effects of words, in Austin's sense. And on the other hand, there is an important performative quality of voice itself. Indeed, verbs such as *provoke*, *invoke*, *evoke*, and *convoke* resonate etymologically with the performative action of voice. We can, thus, listen to voice as fundamentally performative when, as Brandon Labelle writes, it works "to embody through action rather than point to through representation."[5]

Performativity is a useful concept for thinking about the embodiment and intimacy of voice without falling into essentialism or phonocentrism. Emerging from the body, voice is marked by that enculturated body. That is, *embodied* voices are always already mediated by culture: they are inherently modified by sex, gender, ethnicity, race, history, and so on. Through its performative quality, voice does not directly express or represent those cultural characteristics, it *enacts* them—it embodies them through its vocal actions. And, when media come into play, those performative voices are not only marked once more, by mediation, but they enact and mark mediation itself.[6]

The performative voice also works to interpolate the other. In relation to the space of media art, for instance, performativity implicates the viewer/auditor in particular ways. As John E. McGrath explains:

Whereas non-performative representations allow the viewer an external relationship to the represented via representation, performative space brings the viewer into the space constructed. As in performative language, in which one of the key factors in "happiness" of the performative utterance is the status of the auditor . . . so in performative space, the space does not exist without the viewer/auditor's implication.[7]

Following McGrath, the performative voice also offers a way to think about intersubjectivity in media and media art that goes beyond the notion of interactivity. That is, rather than call to or call forth an audience as interactors, voice can instead performatively interpolate them as players and/or performers who bring the works into existence.

Finally, the performative voice is quintessentially paradoxical in Mladen Dolar's sense and uncanny in Freud's sense of *unheimlich* or unhomely.[8] It carries a trace of its "home," the body of the speaker, but leaves that home to *perform* speaking.[9] And, if we consider voice in digital media, it is even more uncanny, in that it has a second home—the digital realm of ones and zeroes—yet must leave that home, and indeed the digital realm, to perform differently, to sound analogically. In a way, we are haunted by the uncanny sense that we know where the digital voice lives, even if it must leave there to perform. On the one hand, we can listen to the way in which the media can shape the very performativity of the voices we hear there, rather than transparently communicating voices and meanings. On the other hand, though, as I have suggested, we might hear these voices as already performative and thus shaping the media in turn, so that what haunts digital media is the very performativity of voice.

Performing Slash

Picture this: two tough, armored Quake 3 Arena characters campily voicing this dialog:

Anarki: Keel, why do I always clean up; why do you always tell me what to do?

Keel: Oh, come on, Anarki, we both know how much you love it when I take command, like last night.

Anarki: What about last night?

Keel: You know, down in the dungeon, when I gave you a good fragging with my gauntlet.

Anarki: Eww, yes.

Keel: The way I wielded my hard weapon against your live torso, the way I made you groan.

Anarki: Mmmm, okay, I'll clean up.

This is the opening of Rebecca Cannon's machinima[10] *The Buff and the Brutal* (2002–2004). Because performativity has done much important conceptual work in cultural studies around the idea of gender, I'll start with this machinima example of gender bending that is performatively effected largely through voice.

The Buff and the Brutal, produced out of SelectParks Australia, was described by its maker as

a Machinima soap-opera parody. In it the very tough, mutant characters of Quake 3 Arena become emotionally vulnerable, jealous, gay lovers caught in an intricate web of treachery and deceit. Fragging is synonymous with sex, linking in-game pleasure/pain responses to S&M sexuality.[11]

The story is convoluted, baroque, and highly camp, as the revoiced Quake characters circle round each other—trading insults and stirring up jealousies. Anarki is Keel's lover and they get into some pretty heavy fragging in the dungeon. Meanwhile Anarki's ex, Ranger, is plotting to get him back. Razor, who fancies Keel, also wants to break up the pair. The spanner in the works is Major, a female character about whom Anarki complains, "You can't trust a woman who thinks she's got balls." Which she does.

The Buff and the Brutal has a split-level home in games, machinima, and soap opera, as Cannon describes. I would argue, however, that there is something *unheimlich* or uncanny here, to do with the "slash" aesthetic of its voices as they performatively enact the gay characters out of familiar tough bodies. (Briefly, slash fan fiction creates sexual relationships between two or more male characters, who are depicted as not gay in their home media.) According to slash reader and writer Sheenagh Pugh, slash fiction is a "genre of subtexts and possibilities . . . a genre of filling in the gaps" and working with potentials in the canon texts.[12] She cites slash writer Ika's take on the male-to-male relationships of normally normal men in slash:

> I think the pleasure of it for me is that interaction between them marks out a space, which for me is a very erotic space, but then doesn't fill it, so that you're free to imagine any sort of relationship, without having to subject it to your men-act-this-way, women-act-that-way heterosexual grid. (Ika, on "Arts Today," Radio National, Australia)[13]

In a way, there seems to be a certain conscious performativity to the gender of slash characters in general, because by performing gayness or homoerotica, romantic and sexual, they bend their gender.

Is it convincing to listen to *The Buff and the Brutal* as a performative slash work, rather than a simple parody—to hear the voices as both performatively regendering the iconically masculine-gendered game characters, and in so doing, reminding us more generally of the performativity of their "original" gender? Certainly the male-to-male sexual relations of characters coming from a canon that is highly heterosexual fits the slash model—the canons here being both Quake 3 and soap operas. At first glance, the lack of buddy relations among the screen avatars in Quake 3 take it outside of slash/able territory, but at another level, I would suggest that any environment that is predominantly male and action-packed does seem ripe for slashing. Ultimately, however, this question probably hinges on whether Cannon's machinima enables the Quake 3 characters to "explore their own subtexts and possibilities."[14]

I would argue that it does, and that it is voice that plays the crucial role in performatively fleshing out the slash potentials of Anarki, Keel, Ranger, and Razor. Though voice clearly plays a major part in *The Buff and the Brutal*, in the Quake 3 Arena game itself, the use of voice is limited:

> The different character voices (each model has its own set of sounds) are pretty good, though you may become annoyed with Orbb the eyeball's screeching noises—all the more reason to kill him quickly. But the real problem with the audio is the announcer, who says things like "five minutes remaining" or "impressive" when applicable. Id obviously tried to duplicate the sound and style of the announcer's menacing voice from the Mortal Kombat games. But instead of hiring an appropriate voice

actor, id simply took a typical voice (specifically, that of level designer Christian Antkow) and pitched it down a few octaves to make it sound sinister. Instead, it just comes off as amateurish. Given the frequency with which the announcer speaks during the game, you'd think that the voice would have received a bit more attention.[15]

In Cannon's work, the pitch-shifting techniques go in the other direction, up to stereotypically gay pitches, twangs, and intonations that remind us of the power of that vocal edge to perform and signal gay (and of the pitch down to perform straight).[16] These qualities of voice evoke the gender bending of slash, though unlike written slash fiction, it's the performative voices, as much as the written script, that are crucial in bending this work.

The immediate impact of *The Buff and the Brutal* is the uncanny disjunction of voice and body of both Anarki and Keel. Keel is a Schwarzenegger type whose gayness is signified by the slight pitch up of his hunk voice. The "enhanced and augmented" Quake 3 character Anarki speaks in a mismatched singsong voice with a stereotypical Latin accent, gay laugh, and exaggerated and elongated pronunciation. One of the interesting things about this voice-body disjunction is the relation of voice to the movements and gestures of the armored avatars. The looping animations render all the movements of the characters strange: counterpointed to the lilting camp script and the gay voices, the avatars jump in an abrupt and repetitive fashion—which in this vocal context performs something else, readable as sexual overexcitement. The looping, repetitive movements seem to open the gestural, sexual gap that the voices speak from and to.

In *The Buff and the Brutal*, the characters are familiar, either directly to gamers or more generically to nongamers. Their Arena game space is familiar. Their movements are familiar, though strangely almost in slow motion. And out of these familiar straight characters in familiar digital places come familiar, but different voices—voices uncannily mismatched to the bodies and space. Thus, while Cannon presents her work as parody, it seems to me that there is something more here, something uncanny, especially in relation to voice; that is, we sense that it is the voices that performatively bend the characters' gender in an uncanny way. In so doing, they also remind us of the performativity of straight gender in media and media art—and the role of voice in evoking it.

A precursor to Cannon's work might be heard in the uncanny gender bending of Laurie Anderson, which is also performative but within a more traditional media and performance context. With her uncanny, doubling techniques, Anderson has destabilized identity since the 1980s; through voice-altering technology, Anderson often performs a vocal persona with a deep and commanding voice, a persona that is neither male nor female—nor androgynous. We hear the voice, but it does not feel as if it could be coming from the small figure of Anderson, despite what we see: there is a slippage between her, her identity, and our senses. Yet there is a difference between Cannon's piece and Anderson's work not just in regard to genres but also in part to digital culture. Though Anderson in a sense disturbs her "own" and therefore our identity, *The Buff and the Brutal* disturbs our identity through disrupting the identity of its avatars and their performers. Unlike Anderson's persona, the avatars are already at a further remove from the body as part of a media work, located in the coolly abstract digital domain. At the same time, the performers of these archetypal digital avatars sound out intimately with hot analog voices. Playing with our doubled embodiment through digital-looking avatars and analog-sounding voices, *The Buff and the Brutal* doubles the uncanny effect.

Performing YouTube

What's wrong with simply putting an unknown up on YouTube, letting her do all the "personal and authentic" things that appeal in this vlog age, things like singing unaccompanied in your living room and making video blogs that speak directly to your fans?[17]

This rhetoric from vlog.blog.com expresses in typical blog fashion what seems to be a commonplace desire for the "personal and authentic," but those scare quotes perhaps betray a sense that the "personal and authentic" are not quite what they seem in networked culture.

The Web 2.0 era has witnessed a multitude of YouTube performances and vlogs (video blogs) which appear to reinstate (at least the desire for) a straightforward, very much at-home presence, identity, and authenticity. Through their reliance on direct address and performances in one's living room, kitchen, or bedroom, this at-home location seems at first very far from the uncanny. The direct vocal and visual address, which is almost a signature of a whole genre of YouTube videos, also initially feels far from the uncanny, as if they are giving us access to identity through authentic performance.

But how "authentic" are these vlogs' performances? Or are they performatively evoking authenticity—producing an authenticity effect—as they play out Web 2.0's intimate and intense aesthetics? In one way, the vlogs and YouTube videos are in tune with what's happening in other media, particularly Reality TV's apparent sense of authenticity, through an endless "witnessing" and "revelation" of private information in a public setting. It has become commonplace to criticize these Reality TV and Internet performances as inauthentic—playing out narcissistic and voyeuristic desires or, alternatively, "exhibitionist" practices.[18] I would suggest, however, that these concepts (and the call to authenticity that frames them as inauthentic) fail to come fully to terms with complexities of what Theresa Senft argues is the particular digital "culture of performance" and "the postmodern brand's crisis of authenticity in the West."[19] That is, these criticisms do not recognize the performativity of "authenticity." Nor do they address the way Internet culture produces and responds to a desire for intersubjective intimacy on one hand and self-conscious playfulness with mediation on the other.

YouTube abounds with amateur and everyday play with famous singers and songs—cover versions—but also with other covers of others' covers—covers of covers of covers. If you search YouTube for "cover version" as I did in January 2009, you can choose from about 98,200 results. "Bedroom wannabes" is how musicradar.com describes the thousands of amateur covers.[20] Perhaps, but I would instead listen to these covers not as inauthentic or unprofessional, or even as authentically amateur—rather, I would stress that they are remediations and reworkings of this well-known musical mode, the "cover" version. What seems significant to me as I hear the singing voices reverberate through YouTube in playlist-able variations is the number of performances at home, with people performing themselves, performing a "self." The subjects in these videos, who might seem to perform an authentic self, also uncannily and paradoxically disturb the line—and, perhaps more importantly, even the sense that such a line matters—between authentic identity/performed self, public/private, mediated/immediate.[21] This recalls what Senft names as a "theatrical authenticity,"[22] where "rather than a voyeuristic gaze, the Web operates through an aesthetic of the "grab," allowing viewers to take what they see in bits and pieces, out of sequence, and to re-make it according to their own desires."[23]

To turn to the voice, intersubjectivity, and intimacy on the Net, I'd like to ask, what is it about the Internet that makes you want to sing?

What Is It About the Internet that Makes You Want to Sing?

Surfing through YouTube playlists, listening to cover versions, I came across Oprah, at "home" in her studio, being filmed for her first YouTube video.[24] In the middle of the video, at the mention of YouTube, she burst into song. It made me wonder: what is it about the Internet that makes you want to sing? Certainly YouTube with its cover-song culture frames these outbursts, but to address this question further, I'll turn to the example of net artist Igor Stromajer (figure 6.1).[25]

In the late 1990s, Igor Stromajer was driven to song by the Internet— more specifically, by its HTML code. I missed the live stream of his first Internet event, *Oppera Teorettikka Internettikka*, when Stromajer performed live for more than half an hour,[26] but I have watched the shorter documentation video on my computer several times. And every time I see it, I

Figure 6.1
Igor Stromajer, Oppera Teorettikka Internettikka Photo courtesy of Intima Virtual Base. Photo: Igor Delorenzo Omahen, 1999.

am immediately pulled in by his intense and intimate vocal performance; it compels me, despite the darkness of the small image. The video begins with Stromajer entering a fairly empty stage (a chair, a computer, a lectern) and moving around, with a headset microphone into which he gasps for breath, pants, groans, and stutters. It's unclear whether it's his voice that is driving the uncontrolled and dramatic movements within his body and around the stage, or whether his voice is enacting his bodily movements. Then a quiz-show-like buzzer sounds, and Stromajer moves to the lectern and starts reading the printed libretto—the HTML code—which he sings in a sort of mise-en-abyme gesture. Throughout the event, Stromajer's voice and improvisations are on the move, ranging from falsetto singing to drone-like chanting to raspy shouting—something between singing and speech. At some points, his voice dramatically breaks into autistic stuttering and at other times it exudes classic operatic emotion. Periodically during the performance, Stromajer's voice is also mixed with a range of sounds, including other very different voices, more or less processed or synthesized, including a female BBC-type voice informing us dryly about nuclear reactors, nuclear cores, navigational satellites, and so on. His "own" voice, too, is sometimes processed—distorted, pitch-shifted, speed-altered. During this exhausting and exhaustive performance—whether he is standing at the lectern or ranging across the stage, whether he is stuttering into the headset or speaking/singing into a handheld microphone—Stromajer's voice takes him, and us, through an extensive emotional range, an intense and intimate journey.

Stromajer's own journey to this work started in 1989 in experimental theater. He eventually became disillusioned with what he experienced as theater's failure to enable intimacy between performer and audience.[27] In order to perform intimacy, he began to improvise his *Oppera Internettikka* series in which he explored "the combination of classical opera tactics and strategies, together with singing HTML source code, text-to-speech software, Java scripts and applets."[28] Stromajer has described this trajectory of his practice thus:

Through [theatrical experiments] we studied relations between the body of the actor, dancer and spectator, physical energy, intimate plot, and the private examination of the actor in public (theatre) space. Since 1996 I've been working on the Internet. I started with so-called classical virtual net art, then I passed to multimedia emotional mobile and communicational projects, and at this moment I'm mostly working on inter-media guerrilla and political aspects of mobile intimate digital communication, which in other word means—net performance.[29]

Though Stromajer's more recent works perform their mobile intimacy often through location in ambiguously intimate spaces such as the public toilets of cultural institutions, his first work, *Oppera Teorettikka Internettikka*, plays particularly with the performativity of voice to evoke intimate connections. In *Oppera Teorettikka Internettikka*, as in all his Internet opera works, the fluidity and play in his voice performatively troubles a sense of a singular identity from which the voice emerges or which it expresses. And, listening to these works, we sense at an intimate level how voice is always/already performative and mediated.

Stromajer has called his studio "intima.org," which reflects his view of the particular intimate aesthetics of the Internet; it's significant that in *Oppera Teorettikka Internettikka* he realizes these aesthetics largely through voice—working with its potentials for intimacy without implying some singular identity.

There is no greater intimacy then the public and vice verse [sic]. When intimacy and the public are understood in their most radical, total form, they are only two performatives of the same fact, the same pleasure. That's why I think that the Internet is the most intimate media that ever existed. Exactly because of that quasi-total openness that reduced the public to complete intimacy and launched it to the public orbit.

. . . It's not television so that you have to be at the exact same time in front of the screen like "all the others." So we're not at the football stadium. No, we're in our room, in our intimacy, so that the "more or less same moment" is individualizing utopia, reducing the public, we can say that it's individualizing the public and creating exquisite pleasures.[30]

This play in the interstices of public/private is the "'impossibly intimate and necessarily distant'" aspect of the Internet that Theresa Senft also discussed in relation to camgirls.[31] With Stromajer's vocal performativity, we sense the Internet's paradoxically intimate distance.

Stromajer's voice is particularly inflected with a humor, which works through intensity and strangeness rather than a postmodern irony that would have a distancing effect contrary to the intimacy for which he strives. Further, his voice performs intimacy through a low-fi aesthetic, rather than sounding out in spectacular mode. This is not surprising, as the spectacular is not so easily an intimate mode. Indeed, the work is typical of the low-tech aesthetic that since the mid 2000s has been sweeping not just YouTube but much installation media art—a stuttering aesthetic that interrupts the smooth flow of (high) technology. It suggests that part of the appeal of low-tech aesthetics is that it does the work of art within a culture of digital perfection and big budgets, and, in particular, it provokes emotions, through an aesthetic that works through immediacy and intimacy—mirroring the uncanny immediacy and intimacy of the Internet with its distant connections. Aesthetically, Stromajer's performative voices disrupt and make thoughtful in part thanks to the intimacy of connection they produce. And, undoing the promise of digital code to be both abstract and pure signal, a voice singing code reminds us that the digital sounds out noisily as analog.

There are strong emotions at play in Stromajer's *Oppera Teorettikka Internettikka* as body and voice are driven into motion by emotion. We are left to wonder whether the emotions are somehow embedded in the code or a performative enactment of the code. In either case, the Internet makes Stromajer sing the Internet . . .

. . . and Stutter?

And it also causes him to emit stuttered speech, which seems to drive his stuttering movements—even his text stutters with its pp's, kk's and tt's.[32] His movements and gestures also stutter—they are uneven and feel unintentional, stuttering embodied with its frustrations and aesthetics or stuttering as the voice of a stuttering body? It is a stuttering that emphasizes the gap not just between sound and song and speech but also between the digital's ones and zeroes. It performatively reveals ambiguous, unexpected, and humorous qualities of digital code's potential in a way that smooth, transparent, clear-cut vocal performance would not (figures 6.2a and 6.2b).

Figures 6.2 a and 6.2b
Igor Stromajer, Oppera Teorettikka Internettikka Photo courtesy of Intima Virtual Base, 1999.

There is also a certain "cruelty" to Stromajer's stuttering and singing—in the Artaudian sense—to invoke another figure who voiced his disillusionment with theater. Certainly Stromajer's traumatized voice and body echo some very Artaudian emotion. For instance, there is a digitally induced glossalalia in this work, in the sense of a vocalization of/from the body—an excess beyond interpretation, meaning, and rationality. Glossalalia for both Artaud and Stromajer is a theatrically performative vocal undoing of classical theatrical performance—performative in the sense of both transformative and deformative. Artaud did not describe contradictory positions, from an ironic distance, but *inhabited* them. It is this sort of intimate inhabiting of the messiness of network connection that makes Stromajer's body and voice stutter and sing, running "out of control" and "to excess."[33]

With its play between stuttering and speaking and singing, Stromajer's first *Oppera* work also conveys the power of improvisation to contour a performative vocal mode: its energy, what Joan La Barbara calls "improvisatory energy," is palpable. Herself a master of improvisation (and of a voice that plays precisely and intriguingly between singing and speech), La Barbara understands "that level of immediacy, of intense stimulation that makes improvisation so dangerous and so rewarding."[34] I would add that it's not just the performer, but also the audience that is drawn in by the immediacy of the improvised voice and drawn with it to the edge of danger and uncertainty. As Stromajer sings the code, we have a sense that the medium is speaking through him, affecting his improvisations. Indeed, from the opening performance, Stromajer is as if a medium for the medium—performing the medium and performed by the medium.

Citing Voices from the Internet

In 2000, Yael Kanarek called out "Helloooo" on her *World of Awe: Hello* Internet work.[35] I remember that when I first looked at its archetypal virtual landscape and listened to Kanarek's amplified (and reverbed) voice, I also heard an "eww" that felt as if it was echoing my own surprised response. Accessing the work again recently, I was struck that it still produced such a powerful and uncanny effect, thanks to the voice. Kanarek's "hello" sounds like the call of virtual space itself, as the voice calls out to me in and from virtual space, pictured in the work as a (now classical) vast empty polygonal landscape. With its bravado, the "hello" makes our sense of the emptiness and loneliness of the landscape all the more vivid—it performs it. I wonder, is Kanarek making contact with me or is she making contact with the space itself? Or is it the virtual space that's calling out and calling me in? With this singular performative voicing of an Internet connection, I sense that Kanarek was dramatically and intimately enacting a networked performance of what Steven Connor has theorized as "vocalic space."[36]

Before Web 2.0, the main Internet sites of sociality and networking were chat rooms, bulletin boards, lists, and other public forums. These were spaces of real-time, text-based communication. With a renowned and often exhibited installation work, *Listening Post* (2001), Marc Hansen and Ben Rubin evoked a sense of these Internet spaces as a vast site of listening.[37] *Listening Post* works as a listening and sucking machine to pull voices out of noise and dark of the Internet by

cull[ing] text fragments in real time from thousands of unrestricted Internet chat rooms, bulletin boards and other public forums. The texts are read (or sung) by a voice synthesizer, and simultaneously displayed across a suspended grid of more than two hundred small electronic screens.[38]

Visually, the installation space of *Listening Post* is darkened and theatrical, though instead of a single screen (as it sometimes seems), it comprises 11 rows and 21 columns of small screens suspended before us in the proscenium space. Recalling the clackety-clack of typing fingers, the installation space resounds with a clackety-clack of shuffling text between sections, framing the voice and screen text that emerge from it (figure 6.3).[39]

The detached fragments of Internet text come to the audience in a detached voice. This cool, British-accented, synthesized voice funnels the diversity of Internet voices. Strangely, it does not neutralize or reduce those voices to sameness but somehow, paradoxically, gives us a sense of their variety—of so much excess and difference that the only way to deal with it is through this technique. This synthesized voice performs, metaphorically, a "blackness" of voice. As Sean Cubitt proffers, black "absorbs all visible wavelengths without emitting or reflecting any visible radiation itself."[40] For Cubitt, black is always virtual, potential, on the brink of becoming: absorbing all color, it has too much energy to *become* a color.[41] This is the quality that we feel in *Listening Post*—an excess of color and energy on the Internet that is too much for any familiar and conventional voice(s) to become it—so that the vocal performativity of the synthesized voice sounds just right.

Figure 6.3

Listening Post (2002) by Mark Hansen and Ben Rubin, shown here in the Whitney Museum, New York, March 2003 Photo by David Alison. Courtesy of Mark Hansen and Ben Rubin.

As with Stromajer's work, we can hear a certain performative vocalizing and channeling of the Internet's energy in this work. Thus, although the voice of *Listening Post* is "detached," the work nonetheless conveys intensity and emotion[42] parallel to the way Stromajer's vocal performativity produced intimacy in the dislocated, distant/proximate medium of the Internet.[43] In this case, however, unlike *Oppera Teorettikka Internettikka*'s singing of HTML code, it is the Internet at the level of a vast multiplicity of visual texts that the work vocalizes; this multiplicity seems to demand a synthesized voice to perform this work.

The voices in the work locate and dislocate us on the Internet. In a sense, the voice of *Listening Post* performatively connects us to the site of the Internet itself, the Internet as site, through which energy flows:

The sound-generating systems are constructed almost as wind chimes, where the wind in this case is not meteorological but human, and the particles that move are not air molecules but words. At some level, Listening Post is about harnessing the human energy that is carried by all of these words, and channelling that energy through the mechanisms of the piece.[44]

There is some technical-emotional variation to the synthesized voices—pitch, thickness, reverberance and the way they "compose" themselves—which makes the "one" synthesized voice sound as if it were multiple voices. These "voices" emerge thickly and thinly from the space and time of the Internet, in and out of focus in the installation space and time. The thickness of a single voice can be particularly intense and moving (especially in the "I am" scene, which I turn to shortly)—giving a sense of variety and depth of emotion, condensed in one fragment, filtering through that one thickened voice.

There is a strangely nourishing quality to the voices in this work, speaking of and from real-time data feeds. They answer our call for a sense of the materiality and diversity of the Internet and respond to the call, to us, from within the flow of the Internet. Within this flow are numerous individuals, whom the work doesn't reduce to identities or "presences" but gives a more fragmented sense, especially in the "I am" scene, which we overhear as if "I am the voice of the Internet." This scene starts with a blank screen, deepening the darkness of the room. The voices are sparser than in other scenes and accompanied by minimalist music and a regular beep, a bit like a heart monitor machine or submarine, sonar. A "litany" of "I am's," as Mark Hansen describes it, the "I am" scene came about because "I am" was one of the most common ways to start chat room conversations.[45] Like poetry, it works elliptically, calling out to us with intimate intensity yet also leaving room for us in its gaps and silences. It also reminds us of the performative power of the voice to call forth and to disrupt identity.

"I am not so god [sic] with English," "I am going," "I am hotgirl," "I am a professional killer dear," "I'm not really," "I'm good thanks." And on it goes, one after another, varying in real time and from real place but in the "as if" *same* voice. One of the striking aspects of this scene, and perhaps the reason it is commented on more than any other, is the way it performs this doing and undoing of identity in the space and time of the Internet. Although often "I am" denominates a stable identity, here it works differently. Partly it is the inexorable and contradictory excess of nouns, adjectives, prepositional phrases, gerunds that follow—grammatically and ungrammatically breaking apart the anticipated predication of grammar and, with it, stable identity and gender. Some form sentences; some are cut off before they can. And, as the text-to-speech-synthesized voice feeds us these morsels, it grows thick. Especially strange for me (in a recent listening to the documentation video in Australia) was to hear "I am in Victoria right now" echoing back to me through the Internet from elsewhere in Australia. It brought home the way that in this scene location is vocalized in the very moment of dislocation.[46]

There is a productive play between thickness and thinness of voice in this scene, and when the voice sounds forth on its own, it can easily sound intensely sad, or poignant. Ben Ruben explained,

Some things, I think, read as poignant that weren't necessarily typed that way. You might have this isolated fragment of a conversation where someone says "I am so lost"—but that sounds like, owww, that really gets you, but it could have been typed in a, you know, technical help forum or something.[47]

As Ruben's statement suggests, the voice in the "I am" scene often sounds *authentically* poignant and poignantly authentic. However, we might hear it instead as producing an authenticity effect, which is particularly uncanny as it is produced by an algorithm. In one way, a synthesized voice evokes the algorithm, yet in the lonely isolation of the darkened room we hear it as intimate, authentic, and poignant.

The thickened voices in the "I am" scene, framed by the musical sound-scape, are particularly effective in performatively evoking the weight of the Internet's time and space, which cumulatively pervades the rest of the work too. As Peter Eleey of *frieze* experienced it, "the timbre and tone of their sounds give one the feeling of being inside a tiny submarine, with the weight of an unspeakably vast ocean pushing in on the space where one sits listening."[48] The detached vocal quality also comes into play here, evoking the Internet's time and space as so weighty that no one recognizable voice could embody it.

Citing and siting voice on the Internet, *Listening Post* vocally works in a compelling and uncanny way. Though technically it is a work of "data sonification," its affect and effect are more understandable in the politically aesthetic mode that Jacques Rancière analyses, where artworks make the inaudible audible (and the invisible visible), rather than serving a scientific or political agenda—though of course the results throw light on the place of science and politics in digital culture.[49] In other words, the vocalized data sonification of *Listening Post* is not a display or expression of abstract beauty, nor does it directly serve to make politics or science "accessible." Rather, it offers an intimate and intense performative voicing of the Internet's chatter.

The Intense and Intimate Voices of Janet Cardiff

"Let's go outside. . . Try to walk with my footsteps so we can stay together . . . Stop . . . Listen . . . Close your eyes . . . Do you hear me . . . ? Do you see . . . ?"[50]

This feels like an intimate communication, just to me, performatively calling "me" into performative subjectivity—looking, listening, walking. It is the inimitable voice of Janet Cardiff in *Louisiana Walk*—one of her famous audio walks. From her first words, Cardiff draws me in with her story and especially with her storytelling voice, seamlessly punctuated with such invitations, directions, phatic communications. Sometimes whispering, sometimes speaking seductively, sometimes something in between, Cardiff's voice all the while performatively interpolates me and calls forth an intimate space—remembered and imagined, personal and mediated.

This inimitable voice of Janet Cardiff and her seminal audio walks provide a most fitting end to this chapter's discussion of voice, performativity, intimacy, media, and media art. As part of her larger media art opus—all deploying voice in provocative, pleasurable, and ever-surprising ways— Cardiff, in collaboration with George Bures Miller, constructed a number of audio walks around the world, where audiences could follow in her footsteps, listening through headphones to her voice guiding them physically, spatially, and emotionally. Cardiff produced her intimate and intense voice, the crucial element in the walks, by working in between script and improvisation, in performative relation to the space she traversed and evoked. Through digital binaural recordings of voices and sounds, she placed us in her head and herself in ours as we followed her on these walks through various urban environments (in actuality, if we are there, or imaginatively if we listen to the CD elsewhere).

Cardiff and Miller also deployed binaural recording techniques to shape her performative voice in their installation at the 2002 Sydney Biennale, *The Paradise Institute*—in this case to make and interrogate the space of a cinema audience. In this work, we put on headphones to become part of the audience of people just outside a miniature diorama-like cinema. In a sort of reversal of the usual cinema experience, we are the giants and the screen is Lilliputian, which sets the stage for uncanny events. Besides hearing the soundtrack of the film, which we can see, we hear conversations of people as if next to or behind us. The "shh" and whispered personal conversation startle us—performatively turned from a gallery goer into a cinema audience member, I turn around to see whom I have disturbed. In a way, through the performative voice, this work produces the intimate moment in the spectacle of cinema—the strange intimacy of being in the space with others, strangers, whom we mostly don't relate to because we are sutured into the screen, yet every once in a while . . . The piece is like an allegory for the uncanniness and intimacy of being a media audience with others. The work also makes us aware of the almost impossibility to unsuspend the suspension of disbelief once it has moved us bodily. No matter how much I know that the voice I hear behind me or next to me is actually binaurally in my headphones, I can't stop turning around. The voice compels me into the cinema space and to turn my head, just as it compels me to listen to Cardiff's stories in her audio walks.

Returning to Cardiff's soundtrack for the *Louisiana Walk*, listening, I enter a stream of consciousness, which streams through Cardiff's and our own unconscious. With her distinctive performance and recording of voice, Cardiff recalls her memory of places through intensely intimate and engaging storytelling. This walk, like the others in the series, intermixes an archive of her own poetic and elliptical memories of a place with snippets from that place's mediated and "historical" archive. And I am intermittently taken aback in the seductive flow of voice and story, whenever that storytelling voice of "personal" memory is disrupted by the media snippets, as, for instance, when cinematic scenes suddenly intervene—in one way constituting Cardiff's memory and in another disrupting it (texturally). With Cardiff I sense how the memories of media vocally inscribe themselves out of and into my own memory and my own story. At the same time, as she makes me think of the place of story's voice in memory and the cultural imaginary, Cardiff's work thus also has much to tell about how media and its voices performatively shape the way we know and remember a place.

There is a remarkable and palpable sense of bodily materiality in Cardiff's binaurally recorded storytelling voice, though its mediated and postproduced character undercuts any aura, authenticity, or essentialism. Her voice is seductive and intriguing—somewhere on the edge of neutral and viscerally intimate—sometimes on the edge of half-whisper and whisper. As she sniffs and breathes, I can feel in my own body the strain of her walking along a steep path. Using her performative voice to tell the story of a place—one I am in, one that she/I remember from her home and from her mediated past—Cardiff viscerally locates and uncannily dislocates me.

There's a chair here, that's where we're supposed to meet him . . . sometime in the future or the past, I'm not sure. He's with us trying to find that precise moment lost in the particles in the video tape. We're connected now. My breath, a part of yours. My thoughts, transferred to your mind. Please return the headset to the building. Press stop now.[51]

Press Stop Now

Through diverse examples, from installation art to machinima to YouTube "amateur" videos, I have argued that what seems to be a return to a pre-digital "authenticity" may be understood as an "authenticity effect." If we listen to the voices as performative, we can hear an embodiment that the voice brings forth in the making—rather than expressing some pregiven essential body. We hear, too, in these voices a desire for intimacy and intensity that the digital paradoxically enables. These performative voices from media and media art speak an intensity and intimacy that is neither nostalgic nor essential, but that happens in the making and listening to the work.

Acknowledgments

I would like to thank Maria Miranda for her insightful discussions as an artistic and intellectual collaborator. She has also generously shared many useful ideas from her forthcoming PhD that inform my thinking on media art and the Internet. Further, our joint artistic work, in particular on *Talking About the Weather* and *Searching for rue Simon-Crubellier* (http://www.out-of-sync.com) has been a site of practice as research where many of the ideas about voice presented here have developed.

Notes

1. Chris Salter, *Empyre*, July 7, 2005, https://mail.cofa.unsw.edu.au/pipermail/empyre/2005-July/msg00033.html (accessed November 8, 2005).

Butler is following Austin with this concept; see also J. L. Austin, "How to Do Things with Words: Lecture II," in Henry Bial (ed.), *The Performance Studies Reader* (London: Routledge, 2004); Judith Butler, "Performative Acts and Gender Constitution: An Essay in Phenomenology and Feminist Theory," ibid., and Andrew Parker and Eve Kosofsky Sedgwick, "Introduction to Performativity and Performance," ibid.

2. The title of J. L. Austin's seminal work, *How to Do Things with Words* (Cambridge, MA: Harvard University Press, 1962).

3. Parker and Sedgwick, "Introduction to Performativity and Performance."

4. Jacques Rancière, *The Politics of Aesthetics*, trans. by Gabriel Rockhill, (London: Continuum, 2004), passim, 12–34.

5. Brandon LaBelle, *Background Noise: Perspectives on Sound Art* (New York: Continuum, 2006), 63.

6. I discuss this in greater detail in the introduction.

7. John E. McGrath, *Loving Big Brother: Performance, Privacy and Surveillance Space* (London: Routledge, 2004), 142.

8. I elaborate on the paradoxical and uncanny qualities of voice in the introduction.

9. Mladen Dolar, *A Voice and Nothing More* (Cambridge, MA: MIT Press, 2006), passim, esp. 7–8, 70, 96.

10. Machinima are "filmmaking within a real-time, 3D virtual environment, often using 3D video-game technologies"; http://www.machinima.org/machinima-faq.html (accessed 02/01/09). See the chapter by Isabelle Arvers for extended discussion of machinima and voice.

11. Rebecca Cannon, *The Buff and the Brutal*, machinima.com., http://www.machinima.com/film/view&id=721 (accessed December 21, 2007).

12. Sheenagh Pugh, "The Erotic Space,"http://sheenagh.webs.com/theeroticspace.htm, 1–2 (accessed August 16, 2009).

13. Ibid.

14. Ibid.

15. Jeff Gertsmann, Quake III Arena (PC), *c|net reviews*, December 16, 1999, http://reviews.cnet.com/pc-games/quake-iii-arena-pc/4505-9696_7-30975976.html (accessed January 21, 2008).

16. Wayne Koestenbaum similarly discusses vocal qualities in relation to opera, in "The Queen's Throat: Or How to Sing," in *The Queen's Throat: Opera, Homosexuality, and the Mystery of Desire* (New York: Vintage Books, 1993), passim.

17. "The Lies Continue—Another YouTube Fraud: Marie Digby," Vlog Blog, http:// www.vlogblog.com/index.php/archives/2007/09/10/the-lies-continue-another-you-tube-fraud-marie-digby/ (accessed December 30, 2007). The article is a criticism of Marie Digby, another "lonelygirl15." "lonelygirl15 was an interactive web-based video series which began in June 2006, and ended on August 1, 2008. . . .The show focuses on the life of a fictional teenage girl named Bree, whose YouTube username is the eponymous "lonelygirl15", but the show does not reveal its fictional nature to its audience." http://en.wikipedia.org/wiki/Lonelygirl15 accessed August 13, 2009.

18. Teresa Rizzo argues convincingly against the commonplace reading of YouTube videos as narcissistic, proffering instead a reading as "exhibitionist" via Tom Gunning's theory of the cinema of attractions. Teresa Rizzo, "YouTube: The New Cinema of Attractions," Screenscapes Conference, University of Sydney, November 30, 2007.

19. Theresa M. Senft, *Camgirls: Webcams, LiveJournals and the Personal as Political in the Age of the Global Brand*. A dissertation submitted in partial fulfillment of the requirements for the degree of Doctor of Philosophy, Department of Performance Studies, New York University, January 2005, p. 16. According to Caroline Hamilton, Thomas de Zengotita makes a similar argument, understanding the new subject of such performances as "a new species of subject, what ... [he] calls 'the mediated person.'" This subject, as she summarizes it, "has their life transformed by representation, is shaped (and shapes themselves) using the tools provided by what Zengotita calls 'a culture of performance.'" Caroline Hamilton, "Autobiographic Disclosure in the Screen Age: 'Big Brother, This Is Your Life,'" Screenscapes Conference, University of Sydney, November 30, 2007. Author's draft, p. 2.

20. http://www.musicradar.com/news/guitars/blog-the-worst-cover-versions-on -youtube-146107 (accessed December 2, 2008).

21. See also Theresa Senft's discussion of camgirls, where she makes a similar point but counters the figure of voyeuristic gaze with a more digitally attuned figure of "a grab." Senft, *Camgirls*, passim, see especially pp. 65, 96–99, 284.

22. Ibid, 4, 12–14.

23. Ibid, 48.

24. "Follow an Oprah Show Producer Moments Before Show Time!" http://www. youtube.com/watch?v=tSW9UOE_3Ls (accessed December 21, 2008).

25. Johannes Birringer's insightful analysis of Stromajer's Ballettikka works on and off an Empyre list discussion in November 2007 brought Stromajer's work to my attention. Johannes Birringer, Empyre, November 23, 2007. -empyre—soft_skinned _space www.subtle.net/empyre/ See also Johannes Birringer, "The robot often cries.

Why shouldn't you?" http://body-bytes.de/02/?p=520&language=en (accessed November 24, 2007).

26. It was performed live at SeaFair, Skopje Museum for Contemporary Art, Macedonia, 1998; Transmediale, Cultural Center Podewill Berlin, Germany, 1999; and Opera SNG Ljubljana, Slovenia, 1999.

27. "Le Pavarotti du HTML," *La Liberation*, February 2, 2001, http://www.intima. org/liberation_01.html (accessed January 12, 2008).

28. "Operra Internettikka," Intima.org, http://www.intima.org/oppera/ (accessed March 5, 2008).

29. A. Vujanovic, "Love without Mercy: conversation/Ana Vujanovic with Igor Stromajer, Belgrade–Ljubljana, June–July," trans. by Maja Pelevic, *Performance Research Journal*, Autumn 2005, http://www.intima.org/tkh2.html (accessed January 5, 2008).

30. Ibid.

31. Senft, *Camgirls*, 116.

32. I discuss stuttered voice in more detail in the introduction.

33. Susan Buck-Morss, "Aesthetics and Anaesthetics: Walter Benjamin's Artwork Essay Reconsidered," *new formations* 20 (Summer 1993): 129–130.

34. Joan La Barbara, "Joan La Barbara," *Contemporary Music Review* 25, nos. 5–6 (October/December 2006): 407. (accessed January 10, 2009).

35. Yael Kanarek, *World of Awe: Hello*, http://www.hellobook.org/Hellocursor/html/ yael/hello.html.(accessed March 5, 2008).

36. Steven Connor, *Dumbstruck: A Cultural History of Ventriloquism* (Oxford, UK: Oxford University Press, 2000), 12.

37. The work has since been installed internationally many times, and video documentation is also available in fragments online; see "Listening Post-Part 1.mov," http://video.google.com/videoplay?docid=-1219120608081240028&q=&hl=en, "Listening Post—Part 2.mov," http://video.google.com/videoplay?docid=56172800 38634050895&q=&hl=en, and "Listening Post - Part 3.mov," http://video.google .com/videoplay?docid=1708581769160447056.

38. Mark Hansen and Ben Rubin, "Listening Post," *Ear Studio*, http://www.earstudio. com/projects/listeningpost.html (accessed January 10, 2008).

39. Some of these moments recall Jenny Holzer, as when, for instance, "I know the truth hearts" goes clacking across the screen in led lights. "Listening Post—Part 3.mov," http://video.google.com/videoplay?docid=1708581769160447056.

40. Sean Cubitt, "On the History of Black," *Scan Journal* 5, no. 1 (May 2008), http://scan.net.au/scan/journal/display.php?journal_id=106 (accessed May 10, 2008). This paper was originally presented at the Screenscapes Conference, University of Sydney, November 30, 2007.

41. Ibid.

42. At the time *Listening Post* was made, synthesized voices were not yet ubiquitous. Indeed as human voices at call centers became frustratingly more robotic in their "responses"—repeating set texts no matter what your question—they seemed to create a certain desire for a synthetic voice, which would produce less expectations and therefore be less annoying.

43. For a discussion of the Internet as a located/dislocated—"unsitely"—site of work for the viewer, see Maria Miranda's forthcoming PhD thesis, *Uncertain Practices Unsitely Aesthetics*, Macquarie University, 2009.

44. Hansen and Rubin, "Listening Post."

45. "Chat Room Art" *Here &Now*, WBUR, Thursday, February 12, 2004 http://www.hereandnow.org/2004/02/show-rundown-for-2122004 (accessed January 10, 2008).

46. "Listening Post-Part 1.mov," http://video.google.com/videoplay?docid=-1219120608081240028&q=&hl=en.

47. "Chat Room Art."

48. Peter Eleey, "Mark Hansen and Ben Rubin," *frieze* 75 (May 2003),

http://www.frieze.com/issue/review/mark_hansen_and_ben_rubin/.

49. Jacques Rancière, *The Politics of Aesthetics*, trans. by Gabriel Rockhill (London: Continuum, 2004), passim, esp. 9–10, 13.

50. The quote is from *Louisiana Walk*, which is on the CD in Christov-Bakargiev's 2002 catalog of Cardiff's works. Carolyn Christov-Bakargiev, *Janet Cardiff: A Survey of Works Including Collaborations with George Bures Miller* (New York: P.S.1 MoMa, 2002).

51. Ibid.

7 Voice, Dance, Process, and the "Predigital": Simone Forti and Yvonne Rainer in the Early 1960s

Meredith Morse

In this chapter, I will examine the work from the early 1960s of Simone Forti and Yvonne Rainer to ask how thinking about voice allows access to a history of conflated bodies and processes, the matrix that I will call the "predigital." The dancer's voice, ironized in speech and extending the body through dissonant sound, proved especially useful in countering the assumptions of dance forms that relied on the congruence and unity of interiority, expression, and movement. It was the expressive self, in its capacity to communicate feeling and the human condition, that Rainer would target, supplanted by her new model of the "neutral doer." The voice itself easily operated as both material and medium in the works I'll discuss, treated as the body's issue *and* a sonic marker of the new ordering and generative logic characteristic of the predigital. Attending to voice in these works leads me to the heart of the predigital paradox, revealing the oddities of process that could be simultaneously distinctly fleshly, resistant, *and* an order of equivalences and operations.

The Dancer's Voice and the Digital

In her recent memoirs, Yvonne Rainer wrote that "the finale of my solo, *Three Seascapes*, with its maniacal screaming and thrashing, [was] the last thing one would have expected of a modern dancer in those decorous times."[1] In this dance in early 1962, Rainer, wearing a coat, trotted in circles, fell down, and got back up; she walked jerkily to "the accompaniment of a number of tables and chairs moaning, scraping across the floor in the lobby," the sounds of La Monte Young's recent composition *Poem for Chairs, Tables, Benches, Etc. (or other sound sources)*;[2] then Rainer concluded the piece with "a beautiful fit of screaming in a flying mess of coat and gauze," as dance critic Jill Johnston described it.[3] In a later review, Johnston, who enthusiastically covered the new dance emerging from downtown New York for the *Village Voice*, described Rainer's scream in *Three Seascapes* as "an exciting abstraction."[4] Three weeks after Rainer's dance, Simone Forti, a dancer and friend of Rainer's, sang at the same venue. Comparing Forti's performance to what she saw as the tired theatrics of Happenings involving "naked girls" and faux "fertility rites," Johnston wrote in her review, "Speaking of the unspeakable, of signaling through the flames, Simone Morris [Forti] sounds like that when she sings. Wild, untamed noise from the center of a burning pit, the living gut."[5] In referring to Antonin Artaud's disparagement of "artistic dallying with forms" in favor of an art of "victims burnt at the stake, signaling through the flames," Johnston saw something in Forti that, she said, was not at all "symbolic," but approached "the real thing."[6]

In ballet and modern dance of the day, dancers were conventionally silent. As dance critic Edwin Denby had earlier written of George Balanchine's ballet, by 1960 not only mainstream but a "national style" that influenced dance in Broadway theater and Hollywood musicals,[7] "Ballet is the one form of theatre where nobody speaks a foolish word all evening— nobody on the stage at least."[8] And for Martha Graham, a dominating figure among the pioneers of modern dance who continued to perform and teach in the postwar period, the body never lied: the truths of human experience were communicated directly through the expressivity of the dancer's movement, not mediated through speech. If a dancer's utterance would have seemed unorthodox, Rainer rightly observes that a scream would have been the last thing an audience accustomed to ballet or modern dance might have expected. If Rainer's scream must have seemed doubly shocking, how could it have been regarded as "an abstraction"? If in Rainer Johnston had identified a "fresh wind" for dance, as she titled the review that covered *Three Seascapes*, what can be made of praise for what appears the polar opposite of abstraction, the heated "real" of Forti's "wild, untamed noise"? These two different voices, in fact, sounded a negotiation of the same question—not merely that of the role of the dancer and what might constitute dance at a time when canonical forms were ripe for challenge, but a larger refiguring of the moving body in terms of its productive work.

I'd like to suggest that considering Rainer's and Forti's early work through voice reveals a mediation of changing ideas not limited to concerns within dance or even New York's advanced art, with which the new dance was in close contact. This was a hinge moment in American culture—too early for the impact of information and communication theory emerging from the technological innovations of World War II to be felt in daily life, but certainly a time when new ideas about machines, systems, and processes had begun to circulate more widely. The earlier understanding of process was rather different from that of the present, when all forms are increasingly determined by and read against our own organizing and generative paradigm of the digital. Process without content, of the interchangeability of weightless informational units in an open-ended, combinatory circulation, would become central to the digital; however, as I'll suggest, the beginnings of the "Information Age" were anything but dematerialized. While being aware of the dangers of retrofitting contemporary modes to incommensurable pasts, I'd like to consider the body-space-time thinking of the very early 1960s as a historical antecedent to the conceptual framework that the digital would require. It is precisely its departures from present modes that make such a consideration useful now. Not least, recovering something of this earlier configuration by focusing on voice helps craft a past for dance in contemporary media arts.

If I were venturing to consider antecedents to digital thinking—the "predigital," to coin a handy anachronism—it would be useful to qualify what its attributes, at least as they might be understood in art forms, could be.

In the last decade, art and performance history have been mined for precursors to contemporary digital and media arts. In turn, this consideration has relied, sometimes unacknowledged, upon cultural histories of perceptual and representational technologies like Jonathan Crary's, and those forging links between turn-of-the-twentieth-century industrialization in the West and its figuration of the body's resources as energetic systems conceived in similar terms to mechanical process, as in Anson Rabinbach's discussion of the "human motor" and Mark Seltzer's analysis of the body-machine nexus of industry and its metaphors in contemporaneous literary fiction. More recent media histories, such as that of Siegfried Zielinski, have qualified the historiographic impulse to map the digital by clarifying the particularities of earlier formulations in order to shed light on their hidden cultural or political drivers.[9]

What have these treatments revealed of Western industrial and postindustrial thinking that may relate to, and have occasioned, the sea change called the digital? What, in other words, could be understood as the predigital? Oliver Grau, in discussing magic lanterns and phantasmagoria in relation to contemporary telepresence, cites a long-standing interest in sensory immersion in newly imaged worlds. Lev Manovich sees modularity, a form of the serial, as a precursor to digital process and its generative logic of rapid "remixability." Closer to the time of my topic, Peter Weibel reviews kinetic art, Fluxus events, and Happenings of the late 1950s and 1960s, contemporaneous with developments in early computer graphics and animation, as based on algorithmic principles: art practices that are audience-interactive and highly reliant on the instruction, the procedure, the task.[10]

Although I would qualify how the origins of the instructional or task ethos for dance at this time differ from those of forms Weibel considers, it is not unreasonable to add the new dance of Forti and Rainer (and much of the Judson Dance Theater) to "algorithmic" art forms. Looking at dance indicates, for example, what modularity and the algorithm might mean for the moving body. José Gil reinterprets Merce Cunningham's innovation as a Deleuzian series. Beneath the familiar litany of Cunningham's departures from the expressive conventions of modern dance—centrally, the clean break of movement from music, and the fragmentation of the dance phrase and movement "story" into segments, or modules, composed as a dance through sequencing by aleatory methods—Gil sees Cunningham's conception of the dance and the dancer as only constituting wholeness on a plane of immanence: Cunningham's dance is eminently *virtual*, its compositional logic that of an unrealized, heterogeneous multiplicity.[11] Seen this way, the recombinatory possibility of this dance reveals its relation to later digital process. In this chapter, I discuss Rainer's compositional logic similarly—as suggesting a never-ending, expansive virtuality. Later in this chapter, I associate Forti's dance with the experimental music composition and conceptual word pieces of La Monte Young. Indeed, there are clear connections between dance and the algorithmic, aleatory, conceptual, and serial practices of experimental and computer music composition of the larger American postwar period that would benefit from further explication than I can offer here.

Of greater importance than merely identifying further attributes to add to this list, though, is to recognize that it is through emergent time- and movement-based forms that the underlying logic of the predigital period can be discerned. Experimental music, the beginnings of conceptual art, and the new dance were guided by a common *processual paradox*. It is this paradox that I argue characterizes the *predigital*: the simultaneous privileging of the operational and the material. For dance, as I will discuss with regard to Forti's and Rainer's early 1960s works, this meant a highly functional approach to the body. In dance movement, this approach resulted in a new equivalence of body with objects, actions, and media themselves— all as elements held in play, modules selected from an array conceived as both virtual and spatial on the basis of external structuring agents such as chance, rules and instructions, or the physiological limits of the body.

Though I focus on the new dance to illustrate predigital process, I'd like to couch it within the broader frame of productive movement (and its rhetoric) in the American postwar period. I can only allude to its role within a larger theorizing of the moving body from the industrial revolution to that of the digital, but I will later set dance in parallel with the movement for which the body was trained under automation, the quintessence of American postwar productive process: both required an operational body constituted by its attentional capacities and endurance. Of historiographic significance, automation presents a transitional modality of productive process, at the same time material and dematerialized, that stands *between* the mechanical and the digital, models usually twinned in the history of industrialization.

Before I return to the role voice plays in this discussion, a few words qualifying my use of the term "process" in relation to its use within art are necessary here. By the end of the 1960s, process in visual art had come to designate a particular approach to performance art or installation related to conceptual strategies. Artist Robert Morris's view of process by the mid-to-late 1960s was to do with human action on materials, the outcomes of which would be determined over time in relation to their inherent natures. This sense of process comes closest to the broader scope for which I wish to use this term, as it refers to a system of productive change directly related to the unique properties of its constituent elements.

Though the use of voice in the works I'll treat here was indeed a political choice—opposing prevailing forms in dance and, for Rainer, asserting the agency of the dancer, as curator Catherine Wood has recently remarked[12]— I'll only mention, and not pursue, such readings. I'm also going to skirt the treatment in 1990s feminist analysis of women's voices in opera and in literature, where "voice" was to do with the question of woman's subjectivity as it was linked to expression. Voice in Simone Forti's and Yvonne Rainer's works, I suggest, is better understood not as a metaphor at all, but in deeply material terms.[13] Rainer and Forti used voice as if it were the dancer's body, itself subject to a new manipulation in performance. If the voice in their work suggested a new materiality, though, it was of a deeply paradoxical kind.

Rainer used voice from her earliest choreography, a radical move for American dance at the time. Rainer's vocalizations characterized strategies of repetition and fragmentation, in which she quoted her own earlier material and increasingly took up mediated effects. By the mid-1960s, Rainer had devised a task-based, uninflected movement as work linked to the visibility of the dancer's "energy distribution," as she put it. Movement became functional, related to task, within a narrative as series—its structures separable and nonlinear. Manovich's modularity, an attribute of organization and selection leading to the digital, can be recognized here—though distinguished in terms of the late postwar period's figuring of fundamental change.

Forti's early works used voice, often unanchored to a body, to mark space or trace pattern. For Forti, voice was the medium of an interiority recast in impersonal terms. Rainer, and others of the Judson Dance Theater, a loose group of dancer-choreographers based in Greenwich Village whose highly influential work set the scene for New York's dance for years to come, took up this impersonal use of the personal. For Forti, however, voice was also the preserve of pure content, an insistence in time. In performances structured by the physical limitations of props, rules, instructions, and tasks—what Weibel might see as algorithmic design—Forti, unseen, might sing.

The voice of Rainer's and Forti's work is not, however, clean, discrete, or tame. It is an ironic mediator, undercutting, distancing, and shaming emotion. It forces itself outward from the throat and emanates from the resonant torso, its dispersal at the same time enfolding space within the body. It emulates the body's rhythms and entwines itself with the pulse of the machine.

In this chapter, my discussion will move from the dancing body's immediate presence outward, toward dispersal. I'll first discuss the utility of voice for Rainer, in her generation of a new dance "narrative" grounded in disjunction, modularity, and fragmentation. I'll consider how Forti's dance, greatly influencing Rainer's serial structure and conception of the neutral performer, strove to reveal the body's capacities and limits through the voice in extremity. I'll then touch upon Forti's interest in sound-space and the mechanical drone in order to raise the spatial·and conceptual dispersion of the body through voice, and its immersion in newly imagined spaces of virtual community. Spreading the net outward still, I'll conclude with remarks on predigital process in postwar industrial production.

Disjunction, Serial Structure, and the Mediating Voice

As dissonant and surprising as Young's *Poem for Chairs, Tables, Benches, Etc. (or other sound sources)*, Rainer's scream in *Three Seascapes* articulated the insurmountable gap between the "new dance" and the expectations of the older style of modern dance that sought to express emotion and portray states of being. Of Rainer's performance in one of her earliest dances, filmmaker Hollis Frampton commented,

In the middle of *Three Satie Spoons* she started making *noises*: little mewing sounds, squeaks, bleats. I was electrified, because it was totally disjunctive within the situation. There she was in a black leotard, doing something that *looked like* a dance. ... What was important was not that she made the specific noises that she did, but that that single gesture broke open the whole decorum of dance.[14]

Frampton, like Rainer, remarked on the effectiveness of these unexpected sounds in overturning established norms. Rainer's animal sounds and phrases presented with stark immediacy a new ordering logic for dance— one based, as Frampton observed, on disjunction.

Rainer's early repertoire, which included prominent vocal sound, was seen as surreal, perhaps because options for young dancers then were limited. Rainer later said, "I guess a lot of it was a preference for surrealism over expressionism."[15] The surreal and the absurd seemed to offer antidotes to what was increasingly regarded as the trite inevitability of story and sentiment in modern dance. Dance critics comfortable with modern dance similarly looked for terms they could use to assimilate *noise* within dance, settling on the speaking voice as a novelty, as indicating avant-garde pretensions, or as evidence of inexperience in modern dance composition. "[T]hese 'off beat' symbolic dances," reviewer Lelia Telberg stated of new works by Rainer and Fred Herko in *Dance Observer*, a modern dance journal, "would stand out as Dada vignettes" if they "were to be incorporated into a work of scope and direction."[16]

Surrealism had mined the unconscious and forged links between imagery of different domains, such as the mechanical and the bodily, to form new and often disturbing associations; Rainer was actually interested in opportunities for discontinuity—precisely the severing of associational ties, in this first of many sallies in her career, in dance and later in film, against narrative. Framing her work as surreal constituted a strategy for the moment, allowing Rainer to use vocal and movement fragments to undertake a much more fundamental reorganization of dance structure.

In a 1961 letter, Rainer described the choreography of her first solos, *The Bells* and *Three Satie Spoons*, citing vocal passages from *The Bells*:

There is a lot of gesture in my stuff—also sounds and sentences—not necessarily related to the movements that accompany them. I imagine what comes across is incongruity, bizarre—maybe odd or eccentric—although I make no conscious attempts at humor. My image sometimes takes the form of a disoriented body in which one part doesn't know what the other part is doing. Examples: A movement in which my head looks at my moving feet, or my gaze follows the upward traveling of wiggling fingers; facing the audience, I walk slowly on half-toe while my fingers twiddle in front of my eyes and I say "I told you everything would be all right, Harry"; or in the middle of a long continuous phrase, I stop in a very convoluted posture, head upside down, and say "the grass is greener when the sun is yellower."[17]

Here, deracinated phrases of movement and utterance were equated in a work whose relational operations, if there were any at all, were almost exclusively situational. Vocal sound-objects were equivalent to movement-objects. "Meaning" was juxtaposition in performance, not an actualization of feeling inhering within a known storyline or theme.

Jill Johnston recognized in Rainer's work a very different logic from that of modern dance. In her review of Rainer's *Satie for Two* for the *Village Voice*, Johnston wrote, "We are not accustomed to looking at this kind of dance. . . . The phrases do not go any place; there is no connecting material, no climaxes, etc. It's a static dance and the phrases are repeated in whole or in fragments and new material occasionally appears that you see once and never again."[18] Rainer's structure was that of a series, completely unlike Martha Graham's or José Limón's mythological or literary narratives. Though Rainer was aware of Merce Cunningham's abstraction of dance phrases as movement qua movement, she had been impressed by the approach of her colleague Simone Forti. Forti stripped away "dancey" elements and, in a presentation of simple, task-based movements, suggested a sequencing and temporality drawn directly from the activities themselves. Rainer said, "What impressed me structurally about it was that she [Forti] made no effort to connect the events thematically in any way. . . . And one thing followed another. Whenever I am in doubt I think of that. One thing follows another."[19] Rainer's comments suggest her recognition of the utility of task in offering externally derived structure, like the algorithmic turn Weibel has observed in contemporary visual and other performance of Rainer's day. For Rainer, as for Merce Cunningham, the juxtaposition of movement fragments presented a powerful alternative to the thematic. As in José Gil's discussion of Cunningham, the "coherence" of Rainer's work as such would therefore lay outside the immediate spectatorial domain: fragments would be only the present instantiations of potentialities and the sequence offered a contingent one, sketching by its absence a virtual wholeness. Although Gil does not base his analysis on historical specificity, I'd suggest it was precisely due to the postwar dance audience's expectation for a narrative, gestural, and thematic coherence that its absence would not only be apparent, but glaring.

Rainer commented recently on the dangers of her earlier practices: "this mindset...can be seen as a refusal to differentiate events, thus running the risk of trapping the spectator in a chain of unlimited interchangeability."[20] Rainer's comments are highly suggestive of the distance of an earlier form of modularity from its present configuration within the digital. As Manovich puts it, "pre-computer modularity leads to repetition and reduction, post-computer modularity can produce unlimited diversity."[21] If Rainer's structuring was characterized by series and repetition, the problem of "unlimited interchangeability," or what Manovich calls "remixability," is more accurately one of contemporary combinatory process. Rainer inadvertently connects the two temporally distant forms of process by using the language of the present, the vantage point of her writing, in reviewing her past.

Rainer would retain a sequencing logic of "repetition and interruption," as she put it,[22] throughout her 1960s dance career. Rainer said of her 1965 work *Parts of Some Sextets*:

Its repetition of actions, its length, its relentless recitation, its inconsequential ebb and flow all combined to produce an effect of nothing happening. The dance "went nowhere," did not develop, progressed as though on a treadmill or like a 10-ton truck stuck on a hill: it shifts gears, groans, sweats, farts, but doesn't move an inch.[23]

Rainer's comical characterization of her dance as a stuck truck that stutters, groans, and sweats begs the question of the dancer's accommodation to this new progression. A narrative logic of repetition and task-like movement required a commensurate dancing body—one that was the antithesis of the artful, virtuosic ballerina or the modern dancer trained, as in the Graham method, for "the ordeal of expressiveness." Rainer's dancing body was impersonal, matter-of-fact. By the mid-1960s, Rainer's dancer was, she stated, a "neutral doer" producing "undynamic movement, no rhythm, no emphasis, no tension, no relaxation. You just *do* it, with the coordination of a pro and the non-definition of an amateur."[24] Rainer cultivated this movement in works of the mid-to-late 1960s, including *Parts of Some Sextets* (1965), *The Mind is a Muscle* (1966 and 1968), and her signature dance, *Trio A* (1966, then titled *The Mind is a Muscle, Part 1*).

Before the neutral doer, though, Rainer arrived at a similar solution in her early 1960s work by tackling the other side of the equation—by reconfiguring expression. Voice used to convey a decidedly neutral tone offered the most effective and immediate means. By removing the emotive themes that provided the rationale and motivation for modern dance narrative and by adopting a neutral posture for the moving body, Rainer opened feeling for irony and detachment. Using spoken textual material, she included in her dance what would otherwise have been emotional content, if not for its flat delivery. In a duet section of Rainer's 1963 evening-length work *Terrain*, performed within an early Judson Dance Theater concert, two performers traded lines including "I love you," and "I've always loved you" in a monotone while holding each other in romantic and sexualized poses, as Rainer described the dance in her choreography notes.[25] She likewise included autobiographical content in her dances, suggesting and undercutting the possibility of confession. In her 1962 *Ordinary Dance*, Rainer recited teachers' names and addresses where she had lived and uttered "atmospheric sounds" like "whack, whack" and "yes, yes, yes" while squatting, falling, and stamping her foot, her recitation, gesture, and sound equally unrevealing.[26] Later, Rainer performed a version of *Trio A* that she called *Convalescent Dance*, taking advantage of her shaky, uncertain movement while convalescing. During this period, Rainer suffered repeated bouts of illness. She taped her surgeon's letter while in hospital for use during a performance of

"Mat," a section of *The Mind is a Muscle*. Rainer taught her "watery-legged movement" to the two dancers performing "Mat," wryly remarking, "The absent choreographer was thus invoked in her diseased particulars while the robust dancers went through their athletic paces."[27] In both of these dances, a characteristically even, "undynamic" progression was inflected with Rainer's physical vulnerability, even where she was not present. This second-hand quality of movement was itself colored by Rainer's recorded reading voice. Was Rainer's voice more "Rainer" than her idiosyncratic movement performed as choreography by others? In what sense was the movement *hers*? These works offer tidy examples of the dual nature of process at this time that I am calling the predigital, simultaneously material and matrix. Both voice and movement were qualitative, uniquely associated with Rainer, while their dance context foregrounded their use-value, their *deployment* as mediation effects that fragmented presence.

These tactics drove a wedge between physical responsiveness to vocal expression—the visceral pull when one hears a scream, for example—and the signifying role of its utterance, the tacit knowledge that a scream conveys terror, and declarations of love enunciate romantic feeling. In performance such as the love duet in *Terrain*, emotion was referenced rather than pantomimed, Rainer's view of its portrayal in modern dance (and that of older, traditional ballet). Voice used this way sanitized emotion and the personal for contemporary consumption by undercutting the primacy of the authentic and the original. As visual artists such as Jasper Johns had done, Rainer separated meaning from media and questioned the sign. As a stuff of the body in uncertain alliance with the dancing body's presence, voice became split—its power lay in its presumed access to interiority, which was, through irony and disjunction, refused. (Similarly, Rainer has always cast a jaundiced eye on music, using none or choosing the most romantic passages in order to reveal them as bombast.) Recognizing this shift from a performance of felt emotion to a designation that was at the same time its own ironized portrayal, Johnston could describe Rainer's scream in *Three Seascapes*, even overacted as it was to ridicule modern dance's telegraphed cues, as "an exciting abstraction." Rainer would further explore vocal and visual quotation, reuse, and decoupling when she moved toward feature filmmaking in the early 1970s. In an interview given at the time, Rainer referred to a growing desire in her later performances for what she called a "tertiary" delivery, in which borrowed spoken material, such as quoted text, was performed "in a style completely different from or inappropriate to the known original."[28]

Voice, therefore, was a useful mediator, in ironized, quoted, or taped form. It was also the most obvious marker of a new kind of structure in which movement, verbal fragments, texts and objects, rendered equivalent, were arranged not according to the logic of a larger whole, but modularly, and parts could be reconfigured for other works, as Rainer often did with *Trio A*, offering it in multiple versions and situations.

The mediating voice could also manage and instruct to create spaces of work. In the large-scale *Carriage Discreteness* of 1966, Rainer signaled performers, including many nondancers, by walkie-talkie to pick up a wooden beam, plywood sheet, or other modular item and move it to another location. The audience could not hear Rainer's voice directing the action; Rainer herself was located well above the floor on a small balcony where she could not be seen. In this work, Rainer used voice to map an instructable space. The management of effects at a distance in *Carriage Discreteness* could be seen to herald Rainer's film direction work to come. It also linked electronics, instructions, and movement in a space of action not fully knowable to either audience or participants. The algorithmic nature of art and performance of the American postwar period remains to be theorized in relation to instruction in the contemporaneous sphere of work. As a start, I suggest that *Carriage Discreteness* borrowed not only the operational ethos of task, as did Forti, the Judson Dance Theater, and artist Robert Morris, among others, but also performed the management of dispersed activity characteristic of centralized postwar industrial production.

Voice and the Powers of the Body

When Rainer had remarked on Forti's approach that had so impressed her, "one thing follows another," she was referring to her performance in one of Forti's first New York works. Debuted in 1960 in an evening of Happenings, *See-Saw* involved Rainer's and artist Robert Morris's responses to each other's movements and shifts of balance while on a makeshift seesaw. Forti had Rainer perform a screaming fit that Rainer had earlier improvised; Morris read an art newspaper; and, at the end of the work, Forti sang a mournful song from her offstage position operating the lights. Unrelated thematically, these elements constituted the work through their sheer co-presence in an event unfolding over a time regulated by the seesaw's up-down motion. Rainer found *See-Saw*'s neutralizing of emotive content consistent with her developing interest in discontinuity and fragmentation, and it is likely that Rainer's involvement in *See-Saw* led to the screaming section in her 1962 *Three Seascapes*. For Forti, though, the use of voice in *See-Saw* was to do with an exploration of a new kind of movement drawn from the body's situational response.

In *Rollers*, a work Forti presented in the same performance evening as *See-Saw*, performers seated in shallow wheeled boxes were pulled faster and faster by audience members. The performers were instructed to sing as the boxes, outside their control, slewed wildly. Inverting roles of performer and audience, *Rollers* rendered the performers inert, object-like: the voice in song became their only active means of expression. Considering *Rollers* in relation to *See-Saw* suggests that in *See-Saw* Forti was, in effect, sampling different kinds of bodily response *as* voice, devised in relation to differing configurations of relational weight distribution and movement.

I've deliberately used "expression" here to lead to its new meaning for Forti. In *Cloths*, a later work, performers flipped layers of patterned fabric over frames that screened them from the audience. Unaccompanied, they sang folk songs that alternated with recorded song. Folk songs, as found materials, would have sat squarely within the category of the everyday, a rich source of movement inspiration for Rainer and the Judson Dance Theater choreographers. For Forti, though, the vernacular and the ordinary were useful chiefly in relation to unpremeditated performance. Forti collected her friends' favorite songs for *Cloths*' recordings, explaining, "I chose about eight that sounded the most like singing when you're hardly aware you're singing."[29] In their production of unpremeditated or uncontrolled "movement," *Rollers* and *Cloths* presented expression not as a revelation of the personal, but akin to the *other* meaning of "express" unrelated to emotion and volition: as a rendering forth. Forti wrote of *Rollers*, "For the singers in the boxes, this produces an excitement bordering on fear, which automatically becomes an element in their performance."[30] Just as voice quavering with excitement or fear would "automatically" become part of the performance, *Rollers* was, in a sense, geared to produce this "automated" reaction.

As Robert Morris wrote, Forti's use of external structures, as in *Rollers*, "effectively blocked the dancer's performing 'set' and reduced him to frantically attempting to respond to cues—reduced him from performance to action."[31] Movement in Forti's early dance was precisely that—the action required of a given situation, signaling a paradigm shift in which *work* became both dance's modality and its object. The apparent simplification of movement to necessary action—or reaction, as in *Rollers*—did not, however, mean that Forti's dance situations, which required the "algorithmic" constraints of built props, games, and rules, were uncontrived. Rather, their contrivances were, like those of Minimalist sculpture later in the decade, productive of ideas of objects and bodies in favor at the time. Morris saw Forti's dance constructions as salutary because they stripped away the inculcated stylization of modern dance training. In his performance work, Morris pursued a new strategic use of the performer's self in terms that blurred language operations and behavior: he referred to these (in the same article as he discussed Forti) as "syntactic." Forti, however, had other goals, to do with the revelation of the body's powers and limits. Voice could not only show this "unthought" domain of the body, but, as a bodily extraction itself, could ably perform it. It was the piercing, intense *quality* of the voice extended outside its accustomed bodily relation that Jill Johnston would call "the real thing."

Forti's "Five Dance Constructions and Some Other Things," an evening of her new works presented in a 1961 series of experimental composition and performance, structured performers into positions of tension or conflict. In *Slant Board*, performers held ropes to remain on a forty-five-degree incline for ten minutes; *Censor* was a sound competition pitting the din of nails shaken in a pan against voice. *From Instructions* provided contrary instructions to two performers, potentially resulting in a violent confrontation: "One man is told that he must lie on the floor during the entire piece. Another is told that he must tie the first man to the wall."[32] In *Hangers*, performers stood suspended in loops of rope attached to the ceiling. Their placement was calculated to impede passersby in the loft space; it was necessary to brush past, and thereby jostle, the hanging performers. During the first performance, Forti said, "a second 'Huddle' took place in another part of the room," creating conflicting demands on the audience's attention.[33] Forti's performance instructions for *Censor* stated, "One person shakes a pan full of nails very loudly, while another sings a song very loudly. The volume should be in perfect balance."[34] As a performer shook a pan of nails more vigorously in *Censor*, so the second performer's voice had to strain, to yell, in order to keep pace. The singing voice could no longer convey the song being sung: it could only signal its own conditions at the limits of utterance.

Forti's later *Throat Dance* participated in similar concerns, exploring the body's sensitivities and tolerances through voice. Forti described *Throat Dance* as a vocal improvisation consisting of "four types of vocal sounds":

One sound type was my very highest threshold of pitch. It is a matter of getting a great degree of constriction in the throat and increasing the air pressure very gradually until it just passes the threshold of being able to pass through the constriction. I can't keep this balance of pressure and constriction constant, but I do my best, producing a flutter of clear, piercing squeaks. Another type was a loud double sound achieved with a throat posture that must be close to purring. The third was rhythmic pitch leaps, and the fourth of a similar order.[35]

Referring to these four sounds, Forti stated that "[e]ach section had its own place in the room."[36] Thus set in the performance space, the sections of voice were "dancers," the work described in words normally associated with dance—"flutter," "posture," leaps." As well as the dancing vocal sounds, the work was constituted by the "dance" of Forti's subtle throat movements and moderation of air pressure, "accompanied" by the "music" of the voicing these produced. As in her dance constructions, Forti applied calculated stress to produce the portion of movement, or, rather, voice as "movement," normally hidden or assimilated.

Forti's interest in sustained, unusual vocalization, as in *Censor, Throat Dance*, even *Rollers*—and her vocal works with vacuum cleaner, which I will shortly discuss—shared affinities with composer La Monte Young's early works, to which she had been exposed when working with Young in dancer Ann Halprin's West Coast workshop before they independently moved to New York in 1959 and late 1960. These works, including *Poem for Chairs, Tables, Benches, Etc. (or other sound sources)*, which Rainer had usefully employed in *Three Seascapes*, involved sounds outside the musical canon "'such as gong on cement, gong on wood floor, metal on wall.'"[37] Young's view of the nature of sound was equally unorthodox. As Young had discussed in his landmark essay "Lecture 1960," a patient listener could "get inside a sound," a phrase he often used, rather than forcing sounds into acceptable, anthropocentric form. Forti appreciated Young's desire to approach sounds, even difficult ones, on their own terms. Forti wrote, "He was working with sustained tones: sound that had a lot of distinguishable parts within it, yet the parts were present all at once, and the sound didn't change very much in the course of its duration. The music had a sense of natural, untampered existence, and I was grateful to hear it."[38]

Young's "getting inside a sound" required extended exposure to held tones, often at amplified volumes. Because it exceeded sensory saturation, Young's listening was recreated as *experience*—a singular impress upon the body in a dilated moment of engagement. Similarly, Forti understood immersion as a bodily relation to space, expressed vocally, that could be shared with participants or onlookers. In her work, the body would produce itself as coextensive with space, or might become cavernous, a resonant chamber.

Voice and the Mechanical Drone

Before addressing Forti's use of voice to construct spaces that presage those of the virtual in media art that seek to share the body's properties and affects, I'd like to consider her attenuation of the performer's immediate presence in her works for voice with mechanical drone. Forti's interest in the drone was very likely related to Young's use of it from the early 1960s. Along with extended duration, harmonics, and protracted single tones, the drone characterized Young's mature practice from early on. Providing a sonic base line, the drone became so central to Young's composition and the performance of his group, the Theatre of Eternal Music, that it was regularized, and Young replaced the vocal drone with a mechanical one. As music scholar John Schaefer describes, "In fact, he [Young] turned the hum of an aquarium pump into one of his early sound sources, attaching microphones to the pump that filtered his pet turtle's water to create a continuous drone."[39]

Forti devised a vocal piece with a vacuum cleaner to accompany dancer Trisha Brown's 1962 solo dance *Trillium*. Brown described *Trillium* as "a kinesthetic piece, a serial composition where I involved myself in one movement after another accompanied by a tape by Simone Forti."[40] As her comments might indicate, Brown's use of Forti's vocal work seemed to acknowledge Forti's innovation of the modular, serial structure, "one movement after another," and a similarity of aim. *Trillium* featured "high energy movements involving a curious timing and with dumb silences like stopping dead in your tracks," according to Brown.[41] Brown's work with the effects of gravity, speed, and the body's own inertia and momentum would have been congenial to Forti's interest in the unseen of motion and the limits of the body's capacities revealed through stress. In the taped sound accompaniment to *Trillium*, Forti "sang in multiple pitches with a vacuum cleaner as a background drone,"[42] "a composite of all the different sounds that could come out of Forti's throat and mouth, including pitches, screeching, and scraping."[43] Forti's voice performed the effort, energy, and tempo of Brown's dance onstage. Similarly conflating the embodied voice, the dancing body, and the mediated body-as-voice, Forti provided vocal and droned sound for Brown's 1968 dance *Planes*, which involved dancers' traversal of a wall with concealed holes over which a film of aerial footage was projected. As dancers moved "in slow motion, giving the illusion of falling through space," Forti "vocalized the different pitches she could hear in the drone of the vacuum (taped)."[44]

The vacuum cleaner drone enhanced the visual and sonic mediation of these works, creating play between "bodies" (actual, mediated, vocal) that destabilized "presence." The drone also set the fragile body in relation to time. To describe *Trillium*'s quick transformations, Brown named the dance after a wildflower growing in her hometown that wilts soon after it is picked. Forti matched *Trillium*'s evanescence with voice that, in its difficult and strained extensions, exceeded the physical body and achieved a contingent state that was itself fleeting. Like Brown's movement, Forti's voice conveyed information about a "movement" that immediately disappeared, erased in the next moment—counterpointing the utter persistence of the vacuum-cleaner drone, which offered time as stasis and as an assurance of the continuity of the same. Forti's piece for *Planes* took advantage of this attribute of droned sound to arrest time. The static continuity of the drone and the no-time of taped sound presented the sonic equivalent of Brown's slowed movement in a counterintuitional space.

The drone was a human-machine nexus with attributes of both. Young first had Marian Zazeela perform the drone vocally in the Theatre of Eternal Music. Its predecessor was Young's sopranino saxophone, which he had in turn discarded for the voice, as it offered greater flexibility of pitch: Young said that "with the voice, I could sing anything I could hear."[45] Although Young's drone, emulated by Forti's use of the vacuum cleaner, may have been modeled on the voice, its origin for Young was the sound of electricity, the normally unnoticed hum in the background of modern life—that of the high-tension power lines and step-down transformers crossing the American countryside.[46] The drone, if voice, was a highly technologically mediated one. Reliant on electricity's omnipresence and continuous pulse, the voice of the drone was not subject to time in the same way as the human voice. The body would fatigue and—as for Young, who had famously lost a good portion of his hearing as a result of extensive experimentation with amplified, protracted sounds—become damaged, long before the electric drone would fail. (Indeed, Forti even made a drone piece in which Young performed where sound was to be moderated by fatigue.)[47] The drone represented the regulated voice *as* process, tireless and indifferent, far from the contingencies of the body.

As well as in the dance I have been discussing here, a blurring of forms and operations also characterized electronic and experimental music of the late postwar period in America, marking a shift from music as thematic continuity to a series of discrete sound events. The logic of this new structure was that of a spatial array. Just as the visual art world would soon focus its critical concerns on the dematerialization of the art object (to use art writer Lucy Lippard's well-known phrase), experimental music was, in the wake of John Cage and *contra* Cage, creating spatialized sound forms that might equally be physical emplacements, notations, or series. Composer Richard Maxwell, one of Young's circle, for example, regarded his works as "essentially process objects," according to artist Henry Flynt: "The only thing that mattered to him [Maxwell] was the series of transformations to which he subjected the tape. (He was renowned for cutting a tape up, dropping the pieces into a salad bowl, and ordering the pieces by the depth to which they fell in the bowl.) Playing the tape after it was finished was of no importance."[48] The term "process object" conveys the implications of this emergent aesthetic of the predigital: a composition was now multiple and virtual, as Rainer would later allude with regard to her own work. (Magnetic tape was itself a quintessential process object, the central medium, and often subject, of experimental music of the postwar period.) Like the newly modular, serial structure for dance, a work's form at any moment was a matter only of its current arrangement in a (conceptual) space, and its obedience to external rules, instructions, or imposed constraints. Later digital sound and visual composition, of exponentially greater speed, combination, and output, would operate according to similar generative and organizing principles.

Forms of Dispersal and Immersion: Voice-Body-Spaces, Notation, Conceptual Spaces

The spatializing of composition took shape in Forti's work as the congruence of qualities of body and voice with space—an immersive approach not dissimilar to Young's. It should by now be clear that Forti imagined the dancer's body in her early works as drawn from, but not necessarily identical to, the physical body of muscle and bone. Voice was the perfect medium for spatial investigation, because it was both sound, which readily expanded out or resonated within, and the body's more mobile, flexible counterpart. As such, her use of voice did not simply extend the dancer's body, but attenuated and multiplied it in diverse and complex spaces. In intent, these spaces foreshadow those of later mediated live performance that link virtual and actual loci.

Forti's dance construction *Platforms* set up micro- and macro-environments of vocal sound. *Platforms* was "a dance construction and a duet for whistling" in which a male and a female performer lay underneath two elongated wooden boxes of slightly different sizes, and whistled a tune for a period of time; the audience could only hear the performers' whistling. Forti's instructions state, "It is important that the performers listen to each other." As they "gently whistle," they notice that "the boxes act as resonating chambers, making the sound clear and penetrating." Performers should be aware of their breathing and sound production. "Their whistling should come from the easy breathing of a relaxed state of easy communion. Each inhalation should be silent, and as long as in normal breathing." Voice in *Throat Dance* was produced by the muscles of the throat; here, voice began in the chest as the inverse of breath. In *Platforms*, voice was the shared communication between performers, and between performers and audience in the larger performance arena. The quiet resonance of the intertwined whistles offered the delicate body of rhythm and susurration.[49]

Forti first trialed this relation of voice, performer, and space in *See-Saw*, and later in *Cloths*, where frames hid the singers. From the performer's perspective the space of *Platforms* was that of the resonating chamber of the wooden box, itself a metaphoric structure for the dancer's sonorous inner cavities and for the envisioned performance space in which the audience sat. It is not inconsequential that the performer's physical body was occluded in these works. The occlusion of the performer's immediate presence heightened emphasis on the body's issue, its effects, and the spaces these created.

Only Forti as choreographer was in a position to appreciate the duality of the work's spaces-of-body and body-of-spaces created by voice. The total work, in other words, existed only as instructions and as its always-partial actualization, much as for the conceptual text artworks developing in the same New York milieu of the late 1950s and early 1960s. George Brecht's event scores, Young's word pieces (which he composed concurrently with his early sound works), and Yoko Ono's instruction pieces described poetic or paradoxical actions or moments that may or may not be realized.

Similarly conceptual in nature, an informal work that Forti simply called an "elevation tune" existed as both score and performance. Forti recorded her travels over a two-week period, up and down stairs, in the subway, and across the city, during a time when, she said, she was sick in bed and her relationship with artist Robert Morris was ending. Forti charted her movements over time, inflected by physical debility and strong emotions, on a musical staff. The score, quantifying Forti's travels, translated movement into a textual pattern; Forti imagined its second "generation," translation into vocal sound, as a reconstitution. Forti wrote, "One day I handed the elevation tune to La Monte [Young] to hear what it sounded like. He whistled it to me, and in a palpable sense it had very much the feeling of those two weeks. It seemed to me that it was their ghost."[50] For Forti, Young's whistle articulated both the informational content of her urban traversals and the homelessness and dislocation that lay between the lines of the notational text.

In *Platforms*, the elevation tune, and other works in which she separated voice from the visible body, Forti created dispersed spaces associated with the body and a layered temporality that were no longer reliant on the immediacy of the dancer's physicality. Performative presence could be multiple, diffuse, and at-a-distance, principles upon which later mediated dance practice, such as telematic dance, would be based.

Conclusion: Voice, Inner Voice, Automation

For a dancer in the early 1960s to sing, or worse, to utter nonsense phrases or noises, was a shock to the system: there was no better tool than voice to explosively undermine dance's established terms for narrative, expression, and the dancer. Voice, cultural historian Walter J. Ong remarked in the 1960s, was understood to bear a unique relationship to interiority due to the interiority of human consciousness and communication.[51] Manipulating the voice in performance exploited the understanding that the voice offered unique access to the self. For these reasons, when a dancer spoke or sang or screeched, she necessarily estranged the voice and drew attention to the body from which it emanated. Voice was therefore an exceptionally effective medium for the transformation of the dancer's body from the expressive self to a "doer" grounded in neutrality. The dancer was now seen in material terms, as a body that would behave according to its own "properties." Forti's extremities of voice can be understood with regard to this notion of intrinsic properties—not as emotion as such, but as an extraction of the body.

But what of the strangely penetrating quality of Forti's voice, the "real" upon which Johnston had remarked? As well as participating in a circulation of objects, spaces, and actions, the refigured interior was plumbed to elicit its inner "voice." Many experimental musicians of the postwar period, including Cage, used contact microphones to amplify otherwise imperceptible sounds drawn from objects and human beings. David Tudor sought to hear the unique resonations of objects and, like Pauline Oliveros, the sounds of systems themselves. Young's sonic immersion similarly sought the otherwise inaccessible world of a sound. These approaches, including Forti's, presumed the elusive inner voice as an index of the vital truths of things: in effect, a kind of metaphysics through the back door when metaphysical claims in visual art, music, and dance were highly suspect. Voice in Forti's work therefore was allied to the larger mystery of the real, cleansed of self.[52]

It's useful to note that this new body within dance bore a close similarity to the body envisioned within a concurrent context, that of late postwar industrial production. Just as I've been discussing the particularly material nature of process as it was seen in the arts, so, I suggest, it was in industry. American industry at this time was characterized by the incursion of automation. Articles on automation featured prominently in business journals of the late 1950s, and by the early 1960s the impact of automation on the nature of work was of significant public concern in America, England, and elsewhere. Social anxieties about work under automation, specific to this period, were figured through the body and its double, the machine.

As aptly observed in a 1964 series of public lectures by Sir Leon Bagrit, "the father-figure of British automation," ordinary people feared automation would mean not only the loss of a job but the obsolescence of their own skills, and thus their superfluity in society; that the machine would take over the work of human beings; and that, conversely, workers who were left would become machine-like.[53] In short, automation exceeded its business origins to filter through to the common culture.

Rather than a smooth transition from work based on muscle to that of mind, as the standard history of the "information economy" would have it, automation, I suggest, was a transitional form. It involved the integration of a diffuse body to do with *attention* rather than physical strength into productive process that, importantly, occurred *out of sight*. More and more jobs involved the dynamic survey and collection of information on systems that operated outside the worker's immediate scope of vision. The new work involved the monitoring of dials, readouts, and other numerical displays, or the preprocessing of information to be fed into mainframe computers, such as punch-card preparation or data entry.

The beginnings of the dispersal of body and process that would culminate in the information economy were effected through this earlier economy of automation, which linked attention, signs, and mechanized machinery in a spatial field. Significantly, the body that managed this array was now one of affect, of endurance and psychological fitness, ideally resistant to what management journals of the day termed "mental fatigue." In short, automation figured a productive body similar to that which Rainer and Forti explored, a body of operations and intensities. The pervasiveness of this model in industry and in the broader social imaginary assists to explain why the new paradigm for productivities of all kinds in the late postwar period became that of *work*.

Manovich includes automation in *The Language of New Media*'s attributes of the digital, which he discusses within the narrower scope of operations on media. Though Manovich's interest in the history of visual representation is genealogical, looking for forms that coincide with and have created our own, I find greater utility in clarifying what automation, considered historically, reveals of the understory of the digital. If it is valuable to analyze automation as a superceded technology of thought, my larger discussion here is an archeology.

The mark of the distance of this past from our present is its insistent and reflexive materiality. Attending to voice has revealed earlier forms of movement and body that, as in Forti's elevation tune, haunt digital thinking and contemporary mediated dance, which has rejected their paradoxes. The voice, in essence, sounds the digital's contingent past.

Acknowledgments

My thanks to Yuji Sone and Norie Neumark for their insightful comments, and to Nola McMillan and Peter Gallagher.

Notes

1. Yvonne Rainer, *Feelings Are Facts: A Life* (Cambridge, MA.: MIT Press, 2006), 221.

2. The title of this piece can vary in reports. I've used the version in Keith Potter's account as it conveys its open-ended nature—that it may be of any length and include the sound of any activity. Potter quotes Young's remark that *Poem* was the "forerunner of [his] 1960 conceptual word pieces," thus connecting composition and sound performance to conceptual practice. See Keith Potter, *Four Musical Minimalists: La Monte Young, Terry Riley, Steve Reich, Philip Glass* (Cambridge: Cambridge University Press, 2000), 46.

3. Jill Johnston, "Fresh Winds," *Village Voice*, March 15, 1962, in Jill Johnston, *Marmalade Me* (Hanover and London: Wesleyan University Press/University Press of New England, 1971 and 1998), 32.

4. Jill Johnston, "Pain, Pleasure, Process," *Village Voice*, February 27, 1964, in Johnston, *Marmalade Me*, 45.

5. Jill Johnston, "Boiler Room," *Village Voice*, March 29, 1962, in Johnston, *Marmalade Me*, 33.

6. Ibid.

7. Gay Morris, *A Game for Dancers: Performing Modernism in the Postwar Years, 1945–1960* (Middletown, CT.: Wesleyan University Press, 2006), 59.

8. Edwin Denby, "Ballet: The American Position," in Edwin Denby, *Dance Writings*, Robert Cornfield and William McKay (eds.) (Miami: University Press of Florida, 1986), 507.

9. I refer to Jonathan Crary, *Techniques of the Observer: On Vision and Modernity in the Nineteenth Century* (Cambridge, MA.: MIT Press, 1990) and Crary, *Suspensions of Perception: Attention, Spectacle, and Modern Culture* (Cambridge, MA: MIT Press, 1999);

Anson Rabinbach, *The Human Motor: Energy, Fatigue, and the Origins of Modernity* (Berkeley: University of California Press, 1990); Mark Seltzer, *Bodies and Machines* (London: Routledge, 1992); and Siegfried Zielinski (trans. Gloria Custance), *Deep Time of the Media: Toward an Archaeology of Hearing and Seeing by Technical Means* (Cambridge, MA: MIT Press, 2006).

10. The following, for example: Oliver Grau, "Remember the Phantasmagoria! Illusion Politics of the Eighteenth Century and its Multimedial Afterlife," in Oliver Grau (ed.), *MediaArtHistories* (Cambridge, MA: MIT Press, 2007); Peter Weibel, "It Is Forbidden Not to Touch: Some Remarks on the (Forgotten Parts of the) History of Interactivity and Virtuality," in Grau, *MediaArtHistories*; also Steve Dixon, *Digital Performance: A History of New Media in Theater, Dance, Performance Art, and Installation* (Cambridge, MA: MIT Press, 2007).

11. José Gil, "The Dancer's Body," in Brian Massumi (ed.), *A Shock to Thought: Expression after Deleuze and Guattari* (New York: Routledge, 2002).

12. Catherine Wood, *Yvonne Rainer: The Mind is a Muscle* (London: Afterall Books, 2007), 33.

13. I do not wish to dismiss the relevance of a feminist reading of Rainer's and Forti's early work, which was situated in the overlap of dance, with its own gender politics, and New York's visual arts, the culture of which has been described by many art historians as particularly unfavorable to women artists. Such a reading would, however, need to proceed from a historically nuanced understanding of subjectivity and the uses of the personal or autobiographical (in relation to gender, the focus of much feminist scholarship of the 1980s and 1990s), which I cannot treat here.

14. Hollis Frampton quoted in Sally Banes, *Democracy's Body: Judson Dance Theater 1962–1964* (Durham, NC: Duke University Press, 1993), 109–110.

15. Nicholas Zurbrugg and Yvonne Rainer, "Yvonne Rainer," in Nicholas Zurbrugg (ed.), *Art, Performance, Media: 31 Interviews* (Minneapolis: University of Minnesota Press, 2004), 296.

16. Lelia K. Telberg, "Yvonne Rainer and Fred Herko, Maidman Playhouse, March 5, 1962," *Dance Observer*, May 1962: 72–73.

17. Yvonne Rainer, letter to Ivan and Belle Rainer dated August 25, 1961, in Rainer, *Feelings Are Facts*, 204-205, and Yvonne Rainer, *Work 1961–73* (New York: New York University Press and Halifax: Press of the Nova Scotia College of Art and Design, 1974), 285.

18. Johnston, "Fresh Winds," 31.

19. Yvonne Rainer with Liza Béar and Willoughby Sharp, "The Performer as a Persona: An Interview with Yvonne Rainer," *Avalanche* 5 (Summer 1972): 54.

20. Rainer, *Feelings Are Facts*, 398.

21. Lev Manovich, "Remixability and Modularity," 2005, http://www.manovich .net (accessed February 14, 2008).

22. Yvonne Rainer, "Some retrospective notes on a dance for 10 people and 12 mattresses called 'Parts of Some Sextets,' performed at the Wadsworth Atheneum, Hartford, Connecticut, and Judson Memorial Church, New York, in March, 1965," *Tulane Drama Review* 10, no. 2 (Winter 1965): 172.

23. Ibid., 178.

24. Ibid., 170.

25. Rainer, *Work 1961–73*, 40.

26. Banes, *Democracy's Body*, 66.

27. Rainer, *Feelings are Facts*, 297–298.

28. Yvonne Rainer, "Excerpt from a Letter to Performers, January 28, 1970," in Rainer with Béar and Sharp, *The Performer as a Persona*, 24.

29. Simone Forti, *Handbook in Motion* (Vermont: self-published, 1998, first published by Halifax: The Press of the Nova Scotia College of Art and Design, 1974), 80.

30. Ibid., 44.

31. Robert Morris, "Notes on Dance," *Tulane Drama Review* 10, no. 2 (Winter 1965): 179.

32. Forti, *Handbook in Motion*, 66.

33. Ibid.

34. Ibid.

35. Ibid., 92.

36. Ibid.

37. Young quoted in Potter, *Four Musical Minimalists*, 46.

38. Forti, *Handbook in Motion*, 34–35.

39. John Schaefer, "Who Is La Monte Young?" in William Duckworth and Richard Fleming (eds.), *Sound and Light: La Monte Young and Marian Zazeela* (Lewisburg, PA: Bucknell University Press and London: Associated University Presses, 1996), 28.

40. Brown quoted in Ramsay Burt, *Judson Dance Theater: Performative Traces* (London: Routledge, 2006), 67.

41. Hendel Teicher, "Chronology of Dances 1961–1979," in Hendel Teicher (ed.), *Trisha Brown: Dance and Art in Dialogue, 1961–2001* (Andover, MA: The Addison Gallery of American Art, Phillips Academy, 2002), 299.

42. Burt, *Judson Dance Theater*, 70.

43. Teicher, "Chronology of Dances," 299.

44. Brown quoted in Teicher, "Chronology of Dances," 302.

45. Potter, *Four Musical Minimalists*, 64.

46. Young titled compositions accordingly: *The First Dream of the High-Tension Line Stepdown Transformer* and *The Second Dream of the High-Tension Line Stepdown Transformer*. Another, perhaps apocryphal, tale of environmental influence is to do with the whistling of the wind through chinks in the cabin where Young grew up in rural America.

47. A work Forti created in 1968 used the vacuum cleaner juxtaposed with vocal sounds and visuals, very likely involving vocals by La Monte Young ("L.Y.") and Marian Zazeela ("M.Z.") as well as Forti's own ("S.F."). *Bottom* included four slides of landscapes, the fourth showing a buffalo grazing, "together with four sections of sound." These were, first, "drumming as frenetic and constant as possible, varied by fatigue," then a "constant chord held by three voices—L.Y., M.Z. and S.F.," third, "vacum [sic] cleaner," and fourth, a "melodic line whisteled [sic] repeatedly and feelingfully." See Forti, *Handbook in Motion*, 85.

48. Henry Flynt, "La Monte Young in New York, 1960–62," in Duckworth and Fleming, *Sound and Light*, 59. Art historian Liz Kotz has explored the relationship between language in visual art practices in early 1960s New York and the changed nature of the score and the "event," relating these in turn to the effects of new sound technologies emerging from wartime scientific innovations. See Kotz, *Words to Be Looked At: Language in 1960s Art* (Cambridge, MA.: MIT Press, 2007), and her earlier essay "Post-Cagean Aesthetics and the 'Event' Score," *October* 95 (Winter 2001). I am interested in the implications for movement practices of these works' concern with "a different kind of materiality, one structured from the outset by repetition, temporality, and delay," for which Kotz sees language as a model. See *Words to Be Looked At*, 98.

49. Forti, *Handbook in Motion*, 62.

50. Ibid., 71.

51. Walter J. Ong, *Orality and Literacy: The Technologizing of the Word* (London: Routledge, 1982, 2002), 70. Here, Ong discusses oral sound's negotiation of bodily interior and exterior, and refers the reader to his 1967 *The Presence of the Word* for a more detailed treatment of consciousness and communication.

52. To say this is to raise the question of the anthropomorphism that Michael Fried saw in Minimalist sculpture, or literalist work, as he put it, in his well-known essay "Art and Objecthood," published in the June 1967 issue of *Artforum* and widely anthologized since. Fried observed that contemporary commentators had remarked

approvingly that works such as Robert Morris's have an "inner, even secret life," supporting his suspicion that they are meant to be read as hollow, that is, possessed of an interior. Fried stated he wasn't troubled by this so much as the theatricality of the hidden anthropomorphism—thus returning to his central thesis concerning the distinction between work that is theatrical (Minimalist sculpture) and work that is not (modernist painting and sculpture that contests its objecthood, rendering an apprehension of wholeness outside time and circumstance, a state of "presentness"). I agree with W. J. T. Mitchell that Fried's remarks were, in fact, "insufficiently literal," as Morris's phenomenological posture would necessitate the demonstration of this very hollowness, an "antihermeneutic openness about the hidden interior": the works' insistence that "they have 'nothing to hide' and (as Cage might have said) that 'they are hiding it.'" (See Mitchell's "Wall Labels: Word, Image, and Object in the Work of Robert Morris," in Rosalind Krauss and Thomas Krens [eds.], *Robert Morris: The Mind/Body Problem* [New York: The Solomon R. Guggenheim Foundation, 1994], 78 n43.) However, that the time-based work I have been discussing here relied in both direct and oblique ways upon the stuff of the body—and that its temporality did not, I feel, *necessarily* cohere with the "real time" of Minimalism, the well-rehearsed argument of Annette Michelson and others to this effect notwithstanding—requires an explanation of this late postwar materialism beyond the demands of its contemporaneous art-world polemics. I speculate that the history of this hidden interior, which intersected with the requirements of the moment to present the impersonal object/body shared by dance and Minimalist sculpture, can be related to an older scientism of the body concurrent with turn-of-the-century modernization. This central aspect of Forti's work can be traced from her New York experiences to her years of training with dancer Ann (later Anna) Halprin, and to Halprin's influential teacher, Margaret H'Doubler, whose dance pedagogy, formulated in the first decades of the twentieth century, operated through the body's kinesthetic and anatomical possibilities.

53. Sir Leon Bagrit, *The Age of Automation* (Harmondsworth, Middlesex, England: Penguin Books, 1965). This volume contains Bagrit's six Reith lectures on the social, educational, and political challenges posed by automation. Beginning with the McLuhanesque view that automation "extends man's faculties," Bagrit presented the common argument of business management and technology journals of the day, when they paid limited attention to "human" questions, that the purpose of automation "is to help us to become full human beings" (23). Automation and its related technologies would enrich work and increase leisure time and prosperity. The "father-figure" appellation appears on the inside cover.

8 Raw Orality: Sound Poetry and Live Bodies

Brandon LaBelle

I talk a new language. You will understand.
—Brion Gysin, 1960

Shifts in technology bring with them new configurations of embodiment, and in addition, resituate how voicing comes to make incarnate a sense of self. For instance, the analogical fragmentation and doubling of the body initiated with radiophony and telephony set momentum to refiguring the individual in modern times, throwing the voice into frenzied arrangement. From radios to telephones, phonautographs to speaking machines, modernity opened up a space for a range of vocal coordinates defined by the electronic imagination. The specter of transmission was generative of an entire avant-garde poetics, manifest in early sound and concrete poetry. Works by Hugo Ball, F. T. Marinetti, Giacomo Balla, V. Khlebnikov, Arthur Pétronio, Hans Arp, Richard Huelsenbeck, and Tristan Tzara and further paralleled in modernist literature (Gertrude Stein being exemplary) all tussle to reinvent the structures, grammars, typographies, and verbalizations of the word. The productions of sound poetry, continuing into the 1940s and 1950s with movements such as Lettrism and the activities of the Vienna Group and into the 1960s with Ultra-Lettrism and the Text-Sound projects in Sweden, continued to explode and reinvent words and voicing through electronic manipulations that also distend and tear subjectivity. Yet sound poetry also signals an attempt to recover the embodied energies of the voice from modern technologies of reproduction. As sound poet Bob Cobbing writes:

Two lines of development in concrete sound poetry seem to be complementary. One, the attempt to come to terms with scientific and technological development in order to enable man to continue to be at home in his world, the humanisation of the machine, the marrying of human warmth to the coldness of much electronically generated sound. The other, the return to the primitive, to incantation and ritual, to the coming together again of music and poetry, the amalgamation with movement and dance, the growth of the voice to its full physical powers again as part of the body, the body as language.[1]

Sound poetry thus oscillates between these two threads, between an appropriation of electronics and a recuperation of a primal, original voicing. It offers insight into the interlacing of individuals and electronic machines, drawing out the tensions and consequences of their integration. In doing so, sound poetry literally amplifies these embedded tensions through an agitation of words and breaths.

The advent of digital technologies resituates this understanding of embodiment, foreclosing routes toward "original" voicing through intensifications of simulated, virtual presence and the language of coding; the conditions of the digital replace the fantasies of primary beginnings with a dissolution of the original—though the fragmentation and doubling of analog technology may refer to a presumed notion of origin, to the "real" voice, the digital ruptures such a link. In doing so, it stimulates not only other forms of artistic experimentation (which I will explore at the end of this text) but also modes of hearing the voice. The digital voice might be heard not just as a poetical revolution tied to subjectivity, but more as a signaling of its current pluralization and post-human future.

Though an eclectic and heterogeneous practice spanning the twentieth century, at its core sound poetry aims to embody literary and musical forms through an insistence on the materiality of speech.[2] Following the early avant-garde projects of experimental poetics (Dada, Italian Futurism, Russian *zaum*), sound poetry would emerge in postwar Europe as an interweaving of performance, voice, and electronics. In the early 1940s, the Lettrism movement launched an extension of the Dadaist project by breaking down concrete utterance to an extended minimalism focusing on the letter. Isidore Isou, who founded the movement along with Gabriel Pomerand (later joined by Maurice Lemaitre, Jean-Louis Brau, Gil J. Wolman, and Serge Berna), theorized Lettrism through an understanding of the history of poetry, seeing the movement as the next phase toward revitalizing the poetic tradition. Poetic tradition for Isou held within its center a dynamic relation to vocality and the actions of spoken words. With the further introduction of the tape recorder in the 1950s, the question of restoring the letter to the poetical center shifts toward one of breaths and the construction of brute utterance. The appropriation and incorporation of electronic technology gave new dynamic to the potentiality glimpsed within the letter, granting poets the means for manipulating the phonemic—for literally capturing the granular and tactile intensities found within every movement of the mouth. Importantly, such manipulations extend the vocabulary not only of language but also of the entire vocalic body: electronic manipulation went hand in hand with contortions of the uttering, breathing body. This shift toward the vocalic body as a sounding cavity prior to even the letter resulted in the development of Ultra-Lettrism, with Jean-Louis Brau, François Dufrêne, and Wolman breaking from Isou in 1958. Ultra-Lettrism draws out the single letter as a radical constellation of oral, phonemic, and guttural movements, capturing and prolonging utterance through an extended expressiveness that incorporates all the spit and spasm of the mouth.[3]

Overlapping with concrete poetry, early multimedia projects, mail art, spoken word, and hypertextual and algorithmic poetics, the legacy of sound poetry unfolds into what Nicholas Zurbrugg would describe as "multimediated hybrids" by integrating avant-garde tendencies into an experimental poetics prescient of cyber-cultural and transverbal conditions.[4] Sound poetry opens up not only a general itinerary of the performing body within the twentieth century avant-garde project, but also exposes the ongoing intensities and ruptures found in voices and their electronic manipulation.

Voice

The voice comes to us as an expressive signal announcing the presence of a body and an individual—it proceeds by echoing forward away from the body while also granting that body a sense of individuation, marking vocality with a measurable paradox. The voice is the very core of an ontology that balances presence and absence, life and death, upon an unsteady and transformative axis. The voice comes to signify through a slippery and unforgettable semantics the movements of consciousness, desire, presence, while also riveting language with bodily materiality. The voice is sense and substance, mind and body, cohering in a flux of words that imparts more than singular impression or meaning. It carries words through a cavity that in turn resonates with many uncertainties, excesses, and impulses, making communication and vocality distinct yet interlocked categories.

Such a relation might be said to reside at the core of the practice of sound poetry and related poetical projects, for sound poetry recognizes the paradoxical and productive gaps at the base of what it means to speak. As Steve McCaffery proposes, sound poetry's primary goal is "the liberation and promotion of phonetic and sub-phonetic features to language to the state of a *materia prima* for creative, subversive endeavors."[5] Attempting to free orality from the constraints of linguistic meaning, sound poetry edges against tensions inherent in subjectivity and its related codifications. Because sound poetry may partially be heard as a nonsensical adventure into solipsistic conditions, it poignantly reveals a locatable conflict of the subject in relation to the swirl of language. We might identify sound poetry as a cultural arena granting witness to the movements of certain bodies on the way in and out of communicative acts. It seeks to rivet language with new sonorous materiality and in doing so refashions the self's relation to vocality and processes of signification. Thus, sound poetry stages a curious performative: in seeking other relations to speech, it retools the mouth by incorporating an oral calisthenics, concocting conditions for other linguistic acts, literally seeking to bypass the regular movements of orality for new configurations, and turning the mouth into the site of production for other semantics. That is, sound poetry yearns for language by rupturing the very coherence of it. To cultivate such work, sound poets develop a variety of methods and approaches, such as mounting idiosyncratic language and notational systems for recital, performing spontaneous and improvised poetical oralities, or appropriating electronics and technological devices so as to fragment and montage utterance; sound poets fool with their bodies, rupturing the ordered movements of vocality so as to produce abstracted, viscous and vertiginous oralities.

The voice, in carrying forward notions of self-presence and embodiment, stages a complex performance when such a voice aims to undo or unravel the signifying weave that comes to define its resonating reach. Such voices can be heard to refer back to prelinguistic origins—that primary bond initiated in relation of mother and infant. As Kaja Silverman proposes, "Since the child's economy is organized around incorporation, and since what is incorporated is the auditory field articulated by the maternal voice, the child could be said to hear itself initially through that voice—to first 'recognize' itself in the vocal 'mirror' supplied by the mother."[6] The voice then retains a primary link to an embedded sonority prior to speech proper, which surrounds the child in a nurturing and active bath of sound. The rhythmic, the pulsional, the musicalizing of language as performed by sound poets counter the order of speech and might be heard as a ritualistic celebration and restaging of the primal (maternal) scene, making of language a sonorous excess so as to unsettle subjectivity and its reliance on linguistic coding. "In other words, man in the age of writing is relatively unhappy, having renounced a part of his libido in order to subject himself to a series of restrictions which deprive him of the pleasure connected with the vocal act."[7] Poetical verbalizations seem to attempt to restore this primal happiness.

Investigating the long-standing tension between orality and writing, Adriana Cavarero further examines how the logocentric, metaphysical tradition (inaugurated by Plato) shuns the mouth and the "uniqueness of being" in favor of an all-encompassing eye. Traditionally, metaphysics silenced the *saying* for the *said*, binding speech to the power of the signified and the properties of semantic meaning. In doing so, it relegated the dynamics of the voice, of orality, to a narrow performance, obliging the individual to follow the written word as a directing medium. "In other words, logocentrism radically denies to the voice a meaning of its own that is not always already destined to speech."[8] Cavarero strives to remind us of the pleasures and potentiality inherent to the voice, as not solely a medium for arriving at an idealized notion of truth, but vitally as a relational, performative, and social sound. As she explores, the work of the voice partially seeks to remember or rediscover the pleasures and power of the uniqueness of being by restaging the voice as a movement toward others. Such could be said for sound poetry, and its legacy throughout the twentieth century. It hinges itself on remembering a lost voice, an origin, defined by Khlebnikov as the "predawn of the soul,"[9] which, following Cavarero, is precisely an anti-metaphysical and ontological beginning, before the voice and the pleasures of speech were heard to counter the design of meaning.[10] Sound poetry's seeming nostalgia for a primal voice is thus a voyage back to what we might call an "oral imagination"—a sense of how the voice operates *alongside* language without necessarily always arriving at words as the main oral target. Following sound poetry's charge against writing—as Bernhard Heidsieck articulates, against the "written law"[11]—orality appears as an attempt to return to the live moment, of a personalized and embodied action that returns the voice to language while also nurturing an extended orality for the future. The poetical is thus a material act occupying the mouth, throat, and internal cavities rather than the page only.[12] Sound poetry reunifies sound and subject by realigning sensorial coordinates toward a sonifying poetics, echoing Bachelard's own sonorous epistemology captured in his statement: "Man is a 'sound chamber.'"[13]

Following such thinking, sound poetry sculpts this future orality by working with language *as* sound, weaving together an experimental vocal praxis with the very linguistic matter by which meaning is made. In doing so, it might also be said to envelope Roland Barthes's call to multiply or pluralize the signified—to stagger on the way to meaning and to prolong that voluptuous gap. Yet for sound poetry, the sonic itself, not only language, carries an array of signifying substance according to the phonological features of voicing—that is to say, one does not leave behind signification simply by speaking nonsense, or by turning the mouth into a noise machine. As Roman Jakobson has shown, the phonemic feature of language—that is, the "system of sounds considered as elements which serve to distinguish the meaning of words"[14]—significantly impart meaning to the act of speech and radically feature as generative differences to the comprehension and use of language. Sound poetry attempts to recuperate the embedded phonological and sonorous matter inherent to voicing by unmarking the voice from the coding of a social linguistics. From this perspective, sound poetry disregards the notion of the arbitrariness of the signifier/signified relation, grasping instead the sonic specificity embedded in acts of speech that lace sound with meaning.[15] Rather than dissipate into meaningless, much sound poetry then occupies phonological territories by performing on the level of the phonemic, and further to the oral energy of the glottal, multiplying and pluralizing meaning by disintegrating words into sonic gesturing, into a prolongation and amplification of the ruptured sign. It then might be said to give an answer to the dichotomy of meaning/nonmeaning, symbolic/semiotic, or language/body often appearing in Barthes's (and related cultural/literary theory, such as Julia Kristeva's) works by infusing language with sonic materiality, making excessive the already embodied act of speech. Yet sound poetry often does so by unwittingly following such dichotomy, believing in the power of the body and the thrust of word play to fully escape the constraints of linguistic meaning.[16] In doing so, might sound poetry's obsession with the voice then signal a further iteration of the (technological) reworking of the body spanning modern history?

Such performativity is wed to the potential found in electronic machines, marking the history of sound poetry with the appearance of electronic bodies. Its legacy of works since the beginning of the twentieth century offers a glimpse onto predigital manipulations of the voice that point toward a digital future in which the voice is more firmly wed to its surrogate avatars. In doing so, it continues a deeper legacy related to the technological figuring of disembodied voices and their transmogrified presence in the form of speaking machines, robots, and radio voices, where the voice is replicated through the construction of wooden boxes and rubber valves as well as circuits. In staging this bodily tension of self and sound, unfixing and amplifying the dangling coordinates of subjectivity, sound poetry is a vital underground to the ongoing question of language.

Machinic Oralities

The questions of language, the rupturing of self, and modernity's technological future circle in and around information theory and the question of communication mounted in the surge of cybernetics in the 1940s and 1950s. In order to come to grips with the movement of information made possible through electronic networking, the equation "transmission—message—reception" breaks down the act of communication, seeing the importance of the medium by which communication flows. Working at Bell Laboratories in the late 1940s, Claude Shannon defined information through applying mathematical principles, turning the question of communication into a technical one.[17] Information in this sense was not necessarily equated with communication, placing it instead within a larger structure and task of computing. Such theories and subsequent work leads to an understanding that what one ultimately receives as information is contoured by the mechanics at work that make possible the movement of messages.

Against the early cybernetic formulations of communication and information theory, which supply the industrial and military complex of production in the early 1950s with advances in computing and statistics, sound poetry's desire to rupture signifying channels seem to both arise out of this atmosphere of technological coding while pitting itself against its industrial thrust. For instance, François Dufrêne's Ultra-Lettrist works eliminate the remaining particles of language in favor of a corporeal, spasmodic performance, where noise is drawn out of the mouth through an exaggerated communicational thrust. His *Triptycrirythme* from 1966 consists of a series of superimposed guttural retching bringing forward a body of phlegmatic exuberance. The work is a voyage into the throat, an oral spasmodic cacophony captured on the way in and out of the body. It wheezes, it spits, it moans, it pants, and it chokes, forcing out the many movements of the entire vocalic mechanism into a reverberant noisescape that pushes the body against the listener. Paralleling such approaches, the works of Gil J. Wolman equally leave behind the word and the letter in favor of a hyper expression focused on breath. His "La Mémoire" (under his general concept of *Mégapneumes*) from 1967 captures the artist exhaling and inhaling into a microphone to a point of tactile abrasiveness. The single drawn breath comes to reveal the individual body moving in and out of itself—a wheezing vessel full of animating energies that also exults a primary poetical matter, that of the breath behind every utterance. As Dufrêne would state of Wolman in 1965, "the BREATH alone founds the poem—rhythm and outcry, that cry, content contained, until now, of the poem: of joy, of love, of anguish, of horror, of hate, but a cry."[18] This essential, anguishing matter of breath exemplifies sound poetry's return to primary origins, breaking down language to the core of bodily actions. As Bachelard would further iterate, "In its simple, natural, primitive form, far from any aesthetic ambition or any metaphysics, poetry is an exhalation of joy, the outward expression of the joy of breathing."[19]

Such actions find echo in performance practices that would emerge within Fluxus, Actionism, and performance art, charging the live body with social and transformative energy. Seeking to exceed the limits of representation and what we might recognize as the informational apparatus of media theorized by thinkers such as Herbert Marcuse and Hans Magnus Enzensberger as the basis for social control, these practices form a vital and aggressive production for redrawing the lines of embodied presence and social participation.[20] Sound poetry's ongoing appropriation of technical devices, and its breathing, hissing spirit, alongside related actions such as Nam June Paik smashing violins or George Brecht's conceptual audio-miniatures, may all be heard to supplement information theory by explicitly cultivating noise as vital to communication. Though "transmission—message—reception" sought clear channels, the neo-Dada, phonetic, and sonic agitations of artists and poets at this time were filling such channels with spit, silence, cracked electronics, and broken music.

Against much of the idealism surrounding electronic media and the mechanistic and technical language of information theory, Jean Baudrillard's further critique in the late 1970s aimed to reassert questions of specific forms of exchange. For Baudrillard, "it is not as vehicles of content, but in their form and very operation, that media induce a social relation," turning McLuhan's "medium is the message" into a platform for critical examination. If electronic media contour the shape of messages through their very formal operations, then for Baudrillard they radically shut down the potential for response by relegating meaning to "sign form" which is "articulated into models and administered by the code." The production of social relations through electronic media then shifts the exchange of messages, as forms of "speech," from the symbolic to the orders of the sign and representation.[21] Baudrillard's counterargument against the strictly mechanistic and technical rhetoric of information theory opens up the question of language, messages, machines, and speech, which can be located throughout literary and oral experimentations occurring alongside these technological advances. We might follow the development of sound poetry—from early Dadaist and Futurist projects that sought to rupture and recapture a primary link to language through embodied oralities, and further, to the works of Lettrism and Ultra-Lettrism that broke wording down to brut performances of breath and glottal movement, and into contemporary work infused with digital tools—parallel to the development of audio technologies and the surge of a general technological milieu. In parallel, the work of William Burroughs prefigures Baudrillard's critique and poignantly shows that the systems of technology are entangled with the transmission of messages, shifting the coordinates of exterior and interior into viral proximity. His work mobilizes the radical potentiality of words to act as raw matter infused with larger apparatuses of control and infection. "He views Western culture as ruled by a system of mass ventriloquy in which disembodied voices invade and occupy each individual."[22]

As N. Katherine Hayles has chronicled, Burroughs's work in the late 1950s and throughout the 1960s remarkably performs in and against the presence of electronic media. McLuhan would coin the electronic age a form of "global embrace";[23] Burroughs would see it as the confrontation between the Nova Mob and the Nova Police, a science fiction bringing machines and bodies together in difficult union. The global embrace for Burroughs is viral warfare in which language occupies every mind and turns the self into a host for word parasites. Contagion, language, body, and technology intertwine to form a vertiginous constellation of references and characters, part human and part animal, a medley of organisms awash in a maze of detective stories and orgies of bacteria and word. In doing so, his work signals a futuristic figuring that undoes the coding of fixed identity, and its related languages, extending modernist literary and oral experimentations.

For Burroughs, the tape recorder was to play a significant influence upon his unique writing and related ideas of language. As Hayles proposes, "Burroughs was drawn to both aspects of the technology. The inscription of sound in a durable medium suited his belief that the word is material, while its malleability meant that interventions were possible that could radically change or eradicate the record."[24] Such processes are already at work in Burroughs' use of the cutup as a literary operation. Cutting up news stories, literary works, and other texts, and pasting together fragments, the cutup produces a form of Surrealist collage. Yet significantly, for Burroughs, notions of the unconscious were not solely individualized productions of fantastical images, but a complex link between the subject and the disciplinary force of language. The method of the cutup utilized by Burroughs comes to mirror the viral infection of language mobilized by the technological as well as potential to counter the disciplinary function embedded in thought. In short, the cutup is both analysis of the operations of language found in media and a potential short-circuiting of its ability to make psychic inscriptions that draw lines around the imagination. By extension, the tape recorder allows for certain recognition of the workings at play in technology while also granting access to an appropriative conduct.

"Get it out of your head and into the machines," Burroughs writes. "A tape recorder is an externalized section of the human nervous system"[25] and can be used to expunge the habitual patterning inscribed by language. If language is already a technology, further mediatized by the advent of radio, television, and related broadcasting operations, then literary mechanisms and strategies are appropriative interventions into such technology—they begin to function as forms of hacking that aim for the mechanics at work. The cutup is one extended series of associative and random links that neither cohere nor totally disjoin but rather signal a prolongation of signification, as with Brion Gysin's *Poem of Poems*, a cutup text recorded on tape in 1958 at the Beat Hotel in Paris. *Poem of Poems* is a hypnotic recital that splinters time and space, with Gysin's reading voice clipped by the start and stop of the tape machine, a slurping and hiccupping of words that leaves one dangling on the edge of understanding. Incorporating works by T. S. Eliot, Shakespeare, St. John Perse, and Aldous Huxley, *Poem of Poems* is a medley of literature filtered through and amalgamated by the mechanics of the cutup. The gesture creates a form of sonified text in which words are punctuated by the recording process, leaving traces of sound that add to and subtract from the voice and its connection to the related text.

Gysin's and Burroughs's work gives us the text as a concrete, material, and infectious matter brought forward in the act of the cutup—a *voicing over* that introduces another form of iteration and spacing made possible by the electronic machine. This spacing is the space of the cut itself, the jag or hiccup that produces an alternative rhythm to the flow of reading, where "The scriptive warranty of lexical autonomy may then frequently be breached, words rent by jostling divergences, syntax itself unravelled in the slippage of difference."[26] The *voicing over* is an act of splicing together—with Shakespeare voiced over St. John Perse, interrupting the flow of the logic of text—forming a textual architecture that allows another mode of inhabiting and of being inhabited by language. One is placed on the periphery through an intertwining of voicing, enabling or enforcing reflection upon how signification comes to bear down on the matter of language and the process of reading. As Robin Lydenberg proposes, "But while the sound poets (such as Chopin) seem to celebrate this language of the body as opposed to the artificial limits of the page, Burroughs perceives the body itself as a prerecorded script, a prewritten 'ticket' to be exploded."[27] Burroughs's work stages the mechanics of a subincorporation and infiltration at the level of the cellular and phonemic: word and body are intertwined in a viral relation that disciplines the imagination while also exposing potentiality, turning the modernist question of phonemes into one of code.[28]

Noise-Praxis

Sound poets' embrace of electronic machines, like Burroughs's, signals attempts to disturb and release the individual body through acts of doubling, decentering, replicating, and transmitting beyond its perceived limits. Wolman's embodied sputtering or Dufrêne's rabid exhalations gain intensity through electronic machines—they are partially conceivable by the promise and provocation of electrification. The artist Henri Chopin in particular was to embrace the potentiality of the tape recorder to push sound poetry to an extreme form of multiplicity. His "poésie sonore" multiplies the singular voice through performative verbalizations and their superimposition onto tape media. Instances of sputtering, sucking, or snorting are recorded and composed as contortions of the mouth and vocalic cavities, revealing an extensive audible palette. Drawing out these micro-movements, his poésie sonore is a sonic vocality amplifying the elaborate yet generally sublimated oral leftovers of everyday speech.

I started in '55 with sound . . . the date is academic . . . I wrote some poems . . . not like traditional poetry . . . but avant-garde . . . [. . .] I listened to my voice on a tape recorder . . . and my voice is very good . . . the timbre is very good too . . . so I put my finger between the head and the tape on the tape recorder . . . and . . . the sound was different! Distortion! After that I changed with my finger the speed of the tape on a very simple tape recorder and again the sound was different . . . [. . .] And it was absolutely incredible to find a sound like ahgggggg . . . subjected to different speeds . . . it was like an orchestra.[29]

These initial revelations led Chopin to incorporate the possibilities of audio recording and manipulation into his poetic project. Yet the tape recorder, in allowing new forms of poetical utterance to take shape, also instigates an examination of the very spirit of language as it comes to fill the individual. Pushing the microphone against the lips and into the mouth lays open not only the sonic viscosity of the oral but also the threshold of the individual, amplifying the hole of the mouth and all the linguistic trembling taking place there.

Following his observations of using tape recorders, Chopin envisioned the possibility of multiplying the voice in live performance: "And in 1957 I imagined that it would be possible to produce with one voice ten or fifteen or twenty voices. . . . I started with that idea."[30] With extended layers of amplified vocal actions turning into oscillating tones, punctuated chanting, exhalations, and respiratory cacophony split across the stereo channels, Chopin's work *La Peur* (1958/1969) is an elaborate example. Running at thirty-three minutes, *La Peur* is an elongated clamor of sonic oral matter, with broken whistling cascading into harsh echoing electronic feedback or frictions resulting in distorted yet controlled sheets of noise that fly in and out of audibility. *La Peur* captures "the possibility of going beyond the conventional poetic systems" by turning the body into a "factory for all sounds."[31] The artist performed the work in Stockholm at the Text-Sound festival in 1970, appearing on stage naked. As he stated in the program notes for the event: "This long poem is an incantation against FEAR, that I have come to know between 1942–1950 in camps, prisons, war, etc. I have accepted to liberate myself from this poem, one of the first six I made before 1960, where after I threw my past into the sounding waves. Well, thanks to this trauma poem I again found my laughter and my lightness."[32]

Chopin performs as a live pantomime; often pretending to utter sounds heard from audiotapes, he becomes his own ventriloquist, extending and displacing his own presence on stage while punctuating through live additions the prepared materials. As with his colleague Bernard Heidsieck, whose literary practice would lead to the incorporation of recorded spoken texts played as accompaniment to his live "poésie action," Chopin would liberate poetic expression through the use of microphones, tape machines, and loudspeakers. In doing so, the superimpositions of words and voice build up into a physical material, creating a theater of the *body-mouth*. What might this theater ultimately convey if not the attempts to negotiate the territory of signification, as a fooling that unsettles the subject to exalt the fevers of the poetical? Or a radical recuperation of the primary ties between self and sound found at the heart of speech? Chopin's "trauma poem" might extend beyond his personal sounding waves to filter through the cultural arena of sound poetry in general, defining it as a transformative operation onto the very site of language's infective penetration.

The Ultra-Lettristes' works stand out as the culmination of sound poetry's project to usurp and undo the pressures of the semantic in favor of a raw orality. Whether Dufrêne's rough reduction of speech to the glottal and guttural, or Chopin's maximalized tape constructions that amplify the very movements of the jaw and mouth, Ultra-Lettrism abandons the word overall. In its place, we might hear the mechanics of an embodied drive at the base of subjectivity directed by fantasies of a primal oral-aural coupling—seeking the uniqueness of being by turning up the volume on the self's ability to make a noise. Making audible such drives locates sound poetry at the edge of musical and poetical cultures—the sonic actions force the listener to witness the rending and restitching of the relation of body and language. Such emancipatory acts, though, rely upon an existing language that sees in the body a performative means toward release. We might witness in the works of Chopin or Dufrêne in particular then an action that weds a manipulation of vocality with an imaginary center defined by the body *as* natural. In this regard, sound poetry oscillates unevenly between sound as formal matter and voice as cultural meaning. In doing so, their projects mirror much of modernism's thrust toward an emancipation of the subject as well as an overt formalism that supposed a suspension of direct cultural reference.[33]

Digital Expressivity

The incorporation of electronics, machinic oralities, and the analogical doubling of the self come to radically infuse the work of sound poetry with performative energy, echoing the earlier avant-garde's fascination with the phantasmic, ghostly potentialities of radiophony to leave the material plane. This fascination finds articulation not only in Dadaist rituals of noise or Futurists' technological chaos, but also in a larger technological history of voice reproduction found in the legacy of speaking machines and synthetic voice fabrication. The early inventions of Wolfgang von Kempelen in the eighteenth century in Austria is but one instance of trying to recreate the human voice, to channel it away from the body and into other materials. Consisting of bellows that simulated the lungs, a wind-box and a mouth made of rubber all housed in a wooden box, Kempelen's speaking machine is a mechanistic model of the human larynx and vocal instrument duplicating the action of speech. It divests the voice from the human body, recreating words through an alien machine.

The ability to recreate the human body as an artificial mechanism appears as an ontological subtext throughout modernity, prefigured in the haunting tale of Dr. Frankenstein, whose creation turns into a monstrous inhuman body, and further contorted in a variety of Surrealist practices and works, such as Hans Bellmer's disjointed doll constructions. Though Frankenstein begins to give narrative to the darker possibility of modern artificial intelligence, early sound poetry, in redistributing the coordinates of self and voice for poetical ends, suggests new forms of expressivity. For instance, Hugo Ball's "jolifanto bambla o falli bambla" provides a route back to the primary voice, that prelinguistic, primal force of voicing, while Kurt Scwhitters's "dll rrrrrr beeeee bö / dll rrrrrr beeeee bö fümms bö / rrrrrr beeeee bö fümms bö wö / beeeee bö fümms bö wö tää / bö fümms bö wö tää zää / fümms bö wö tää zää Uu" of the *Ursonate* operates according to what Renato Barilli terms "electrolysis," in which "the material of expression, freed of semantic adhesives (lexemes and morphemes), is pronounced letter by letter, each of its various minimal components exploding in the acoustical space."[34] These predigital voicings hint at a displacement and ultimate networked condition of the human subject, rerouting the expressive self through an alterity that turns one's own body into a speaking machine.

Modernist notions and experiences of the disembodied voice find a new set of conditions within the digital era. Voice recognition and voice activation programs rely upon our own sense of displacement and duplication, in which the demands of interacting with voices of unknown origin, or placing our own onto various media, is an everyday experience. Speech synthesis extends from the deeper history of speaking machines and gathers momentum with early electrical engineering, resulting in numerous machines that could produce vocal sounds, such as Homer Dudley's "Voder" from 1939 or Frank Cooper's "Pattern Playback" from 1950. Such legacy takes a bold step with the work of Max Matthews in 1961. Rendering the song "Daisy Bell" through computer synthesis at the Bell Labs introduced the digital voice into the fields of radiophony, and has led to the implementation of computerized voice programming to appear within a variety of electronic appliances, vehicles, and other networked systems. With the advent of computer technologies, the synthetic voice brings a twist to the poetical by introducing a voice that has no origin in a given body: the disembodied, radiophonic, and electronically manipulated voice is emptied of psychology, spirit, or granularity with the synthetic voice.[35] Leaving both life and death behind, the synthetic voice is a digital shadow, no longer a ghost without a name but a signal circulating among everyday experiences. From ATM machines to voice-activated messenger services, the digital synthetic voice is "enabling audio technology to have further impact on the already vague provenance of the disembodied voice."[36]

The digital, as both a tool and importantly, what Tiziana Terranova refers to as an "informational milieu,"[37] seems to empty out the embedded nostalgia of sound poetry and the attempt to remember or rediscover a primary orality, delineating another form of psychology according to an absence of origin and the potential of connectivity. Sound poetry from the 1950s, 1960s, and 1970s, at times sounds marked by a lingering modernism haunted by a belief in the possibility of unmarking the voice, of dissolving the body so as to arrive at the remembered imaginary plateau of voice as pure action. In attempting to strip the voice from its cultural integration, Chopin and others dramatized the oral cavity as a primary site of expression. With digital technology, the possibility of remembering or rediscovering shifts in the wake of networked, informational, and immaterial dynamics. The copy and paste culture of the postmodern hears the electronically manipulated voice as one but many already existing within the everyday landscape, where the synthetic voice hovers upon every bus or train, inside each machine or telephone call, as one but a series of informational signals that already sounds misplaced, unsettled, and machinic.

The intensification of network culture has amplified the sense of the self as being made up of extensive input that is not entirely one's own, leading Steven Shaviro to claim: "My selfhood is an information pattern, rather than a material substance"[38] echoing Burroughs's earlier statement that "a symbiotic relationship has been established and the virus is now built into the host which sees the virus as a useful part of itself."[39] The "terror of the code" observed by Baudrillard is based on recognizing that the conditions of the information society rewire the previous channels of relations so as to turn the material world into a question of computation. With the apparatus of the network in place, "power is no longer faceless and invisible," rather "it operates in plain sight. . . . It does not need to put us under surveillance, because we belong to it, we exist for it, already."[40] As the digital era has demonstrated, such an entanglement is a kind of co-production of radical individuation *and* mass surveillance.

The legacy of sound poetry as I've been discussing here integrates a handling of electronic machines and articulates a distributed sense of subjectivity. Thus it stands within a larger legacy bent on manufacturing a sonorous body—to harness the body's ability to make noise into the production of an amplified poetics. In following the voice on this course of rupture and rapture, of flayed subjectivity and raw orality, I'm interested in lending an ear to not only the granularity of a broken voice, in all its aesthetic intensity, but to take notice of the specificity of a body seeking a renewed and reinvigorated language. While extending a larger history of voice productions, sound poetry hints at future voices acclimated to media and their refiguring of the self. With sound poetry, we might already hear the digital voice, that voice defined both by intensified hybridity and dynamic dispersal. Such a combination can be glimpsed in a number of contemporary artistic projects that put to use the voice, as medium and as an expressive signaling of new forms of poetical connectivity.

The work *The Giver of Names* (1990 to present) by media-artist David Rokeby melds computer intelligence with the material sphere of objects to generate a series of mediated translations. Essentially, the work functions as a computer system, which includes a video camera, a series of objects, and an empty pedestal. Visitors to the installation are allowed to choose one of the given objects and place it on the empty pedestal. In response, the computer system (via the camera) observes the object and makes a series of calculations as to its color, size, texture, and component parts, resulting in an array of visual analyses that are projected on a screen in the space, turning the objects into a series of mediated images. Finally, the computer attempts to describe in words its analyses, forming a series of expressions metaphorically linked to a database of other objects, information, and ideas. As the artist describes, "the results of the analytical processes are then 'radiated' through a metaphorically-linked associative database of known objects, ideas, sensations, etc. The words and ideas stimulated by the object(s) appear in the background of the computer screen, showing what could very loosely be described as a 'state of mind'. From the words and ideas that resonate most with the perceptions of the object, a phrase or sentence in correct English is constructed and then spoken aloud by the computer."[41] The computer system is a form of "alien mind" having to interface with the material world, resulting in an associative language that gives voice to another form of subjectivity, for the computer is not simply randomly selecting phrases to produce a jumbled mess of words, but rather actively seeking to impart meaning—the object's name—and in doing so, as the artist suggests, gives a picture of an expressive state of mind.

Rokeby's project examines the conditions of a digital mind by also extending the scene as an interface between computer and object, database and digital translation, perception and verbalization. The space of the interface then is an interweaving of multiple perspectives and opportunities, and finds further articulation in Susan Härtig's project *Marionette* (2002). Presented as an interactive video installation, the work consists of a projection made up of three video sequences each the part of a single body, from the head, torso, and finally, to the legs. In addition, a microphone and computer are presented in front of the projection, and visitors are invited to use their voice to interact with and manipulate the figure. "The visitor controls the movement of the marionette by using the microphone. This happens for each of the three body sections separately, because the parts of the body react to different frequency domains. While the head reacts rather to higher frequencies, the legs of the marionette move themselves to lower frequencies and the torso to center frequencies," weaving one form of intelligence with another, one body with its digital avatar.[42] The interfacing of these two planes is choreographed by a visitor's voice, creating a platform of interaction that in turn stimulates an imaginative verbal trajectory—the dancing figure is literally broken and reconfigured by the vocal range, aligning personal sonority with a cyber-figure.

The interaction and integration of bodies and voices, material and immaterial intelligences, flesh and digital expression may open up to a sound poetry occupying the territory defined by the interface. Max Neuhaus's project *Auracle* further elaborates this territory by proposing an extensive global online installation. Currently housed at http://www.auracle.org, Neuhaus's project is designed as an instrument for voice. Users access the site and perform with others, forming ensembles and contributing to the ongoing evolution of the system. Importantly, the work does not function through live streaming of vocal expressions in real-time, but rather it collects the voice as information and makes a series of analyses. This information results in synthesized sound responses, turning the voice, as with *Marionette*, into a partner. Transmitting over the Internet then for Neuhaus creates a form of architecture by which users/performers come to communicate, yet generated through a musical, poetical production or language. This in turn stimulates an appreciation for the ongoing feedback between speech and audition, between one's voice and the simultaneous listening that occurs with every utterance. The dynamics of the audible range intrinsic to the voice are given a virtual stage, with the *Auracle* operating as an experimental chorus.

Fissures

In following these works, what stands out is the production of an interface that relies upon or stimulates an integration of body and digital effect—this coupling functions as an instrumental potential, making possible performative actions that in turn retain levels of compositional structure and poetical production. Yet such experience is fully wed to the making of an electronic self that seems to leave behind a sense of uniqueness or primary origins. What such contemporary works may point to is a sense of informational relations, where media open up to conditions of exchange. For the voice, it may still retain that primary sonorous pleasure Cavarero seeks to unearth, not only through a singular vocal act found at the center of the unique self, but also importantly through its sense of distribution and dispersion. Whereas modernist notions of disembodiment led to a sense of fragmentation or rupture, the digital voice seems to find a new sense of agency (and pleasure) within networked conditions.

As forms of representation fragment under the fluid weight of digitality and unfold into a myriad of potential connections and exchanges, the voice must be heard not only as the direct communication of meaning (even below the line of the semantic) but also as an audible signal that surrounds or demarcates an arena where meaning may be found as well as distorted through forms of live actions or digital manipulation. Such meaning may well be ahead or behind of signification, according to an auditory range that is always already disappearing or being affected by its connection to other signals. As Bruce Andrews proposes, "the challenge . . . is to simultaneously cut the ties that bind sound to traditions of lyric harmony and speech or autonomous, inward-absorbing form *and*, through drastic and emancipated construction, to highlight what we can call its 'social tone' or its 'semantic music'—*in praxis*."[43] This may resound as a pertinent description of sound poetry and the related vocal practices following that search for routes in and out of the signifying self, while also remaining tied to a sense of *making connection*—to cut the ties while remaining in tune with given social relations, even those built from extreme forms of sonic production and listening. What Andrews pinpoints is a recognition of sound poetry's potential withdrawal into strict formalism or "fetishism," where vocality becomes just another sonorous matter spinning into amplified internal monologues. His "semantic music" is an attempt to rescue vocal sonority from such a dead end by hanging onto notions of signification yet determined by a "polylogic"—"a free or athematic sound 'prose' or permanent transition and motivic fragmentation, a 'becoming' of constant subdividing and particularizing where even disruption comes to seem developmental because of the flurry of tangible connection."[44] What such polylogic opens onto for Andrews is noise, yet noise as a "manic relationalism" in which an indeterminate, forceful, and propositional matter circulates in and among levels of meaning and sharing. Noise may then stand as a "counter-contagion" or productive supplement to the directive of semantics, giving us an auditory drive that seeks so many possible connections.

What may mark this shift in sound poetry (at least as I am defining here) from a search from primary origins (modernism) to an engagement with noise as a point along so many connections (postmodernity) is a cultural shift in the milieu where the voice, listening, and meaning have altered their location—where a "polylogic" seems already at play. Within the frame of a culture of digitality, Rokeby's project does not register a subject in the throes of seeking an outside to language, nor do Neuhaus's virtual architectures aim for an original core of orality. Rather, they enter a space of productions where the voice as sonic matter is fully recuperated while never being obligated to signify. Such performative actions incite the individual body, yet within the expanded field of contemporary audition defined by network cultures, such notions perform alongside a general recognition of the body as masquerade, as hybrid, as marked by so many scripts, making notions of origin or returns unstable.

The continual integration of electronics with vocality marks a history that not only produces an electronic aesthetic but stages electronics as a general social and psychological framework—of fragmentation, multiplication, and dissipation. Sound poetry manifests such interweaving, pitting the voice against or within the ruptures of modernity. This legacy of sound poetry then leads to hearing words *on the run* that also have a destination in mind determined or molded by psychological and metaphysical beliefs in interior states, glossolalic rants, and bodily figurations that nonetheless have signifying bearing. In short, although sound poetry seeks to leave behind or undo semantic meaning, it can be heard to relocate or reorient meaning through a poetical and musical performativity fully wed to electronic machines and conditions. In this sense, it seems important to understand sound poetry not as a free-floating catharsis that steps outside of language, but an attempt to dislocate language and interpretation onto the level of vocalic sonority. Its project *produces* a tension between linguistic and sonorous meaning, and it is my view that sound poetry is best appreciated through such tension, recognizing in what way it manipulates speech so as to generate other itineraries for language, while granting us an unfurled or unsteady picture of subjectivity. Such work integrates the technological, readily incorporating the decentering potential of electronics and laying the groundwork for alternative routes toward "words in freedom" that both announce a postlinguistic future and reinforce existing notions of embodied performance. In short, sound poetry takes pleasure and generates means for undermining the metaphysical legacy of essences, while also reproducing the notion that freedom lies *through* the body. In doing so, it may be said to choreograph a "relational" body: defining this space between a return to the body and its absolute decentered sonic other, sound poetry figures an unsteady constellation of coordinates for the body to occupy. Attempting to redefine the links and ties that bind one to signification, the excessive agitations enacted onto speaking seems to lay open possibilities for new forms of relating. This work is undertaken by fully investing in the auditory as a means to split the subject from a totalizing semantics, lacing speech through the erotic potentiality of sound and amplifying the tension at the heart of what it means to speak (and to be spoken to). In doing so, it necessarily falls in and out of what Chopin terms "major languages," producing sonic projects that generate provocative instances of the human body *as* process. Sound poetry might be said to have participated in opening up a space through which we learn to inhabit our current relational and networked geographies by an auditory fissuring and extension of voicing.

Notes

1. Bob Cobbing, quoted in Teddy Hultberg, "A Few Points of Departure," in *Literally Speaking: Sound Poetry and Text-Sound Composition* (Göteborg: Bo Ejeby Edition, 1993), 10.

2. It is worth noting that Steve McCaffery and others point toward sound poetry's larger historical sweep, from the "vast, intractable area of archaic and primitive poetries" to a second phase in spanning the turn of the twentieth century, and leading to the third, more contemporary phase, inflected by the use of electronics. In this sense, the project of sound poetry is but an extension of a greater oral and poetical history. See Steve McCaffery's introduction to *Sound Poetry: A Catalogue*, eds. Steve McCaffery and bpNichol (Toronto: Underwhich Editions, 1978).

3. This historical thread is certainly incomplete, and should include many additional names and projects, such as the important work of the Vienna Group. Surfacing following the devastations of the Second World War, Gerhard Rühm, Konrad Bayer, H. C. Artmann, and others gathered together around a general recuperation of the avant-garde project. This quickly splintered into various groups and developed into a significant array of practitioners leading to an extremely rich and fruitful cultural movement that further evolved into early media work in Austria. The Vienna Group in particular embraced the poetical and the materiality of language, resulting in works of concrete poetry, and what Rühm called "dialect poetry,"

including performances of spoken word, actions, and related visual-sound happenings which were to intersect with Lettrism and Ultra-Lettrism. For further details, see the important publication *Die Wiener Gruppe: A Moment of Modernity, 1954–1960*, ed. Peter Weibel (Vienna: Springer-Verlag, 1997).

4. See Nicholas Zurbrugg, "Programming Paradise: Haraldo de Campos, Concrete Poetry, and the Postmodern Multimedia Avant-Garde," in *Writing Aloud: The Sonics of Language*, eds. Brandon LaBelle and Christof Migone (Los Angeles: Errant Bodies Press, 2001).

5. Steve McCaffery, "Voice in Extremis," in *Close Listening: Poetry and the Performed Word*, ed. Charles Bernstein (Oxford: Oxford University Press, 1998), 163.

6. Kaja Silverman, *The Acoustic Mirror: The Female Voice in Psychoanalysis and Cinema* (Bloomington: Indiana University Press, 1988), 80.

7. Renato Barilli, liner notes to *Futura: Poesia Sonora* (Milano: Cramps Records, 1989), 4.

8. Adriana Cavarero, *For More Than One Voice: Toward a Philosophy of Vocal Expression* (Stanford: Stanford University Press, 2005), 13.

9. Velimir Khlebnikov locates notions of the essential sound in relation to what he called "beyonsense": "Its strange wisdom may be broken down into the truths contained in separate sounds: *sh, m, v*, etc. We do not yet understand these sounds. We confess that honestly. But there is no doubt that these sound sequences constitute a series of universal truths passing before the predawn of our soul. If we think of the soul as split between the government of intellect and a stormy population of feelings, then incantations and beyonsense language are appeals over the head of the government straight to the population of feelings, a direct cry to the predawn of the soul or a supreme example of the rule of the masses in the life of language and intellect, a lawful device reserved for rare occasions." Velimir Khlebnikov, "On Poetry," in *The King of Time: Selected Writings of the Russian Futurism*, ed. Charlotte Douglas (Cambridge, MA: Harvard University Press, 1985), 152–153.

10. As Caravero points out, the voice was heard to threaten the ability to behold truth in the mind's eye, often appearing as the embodied, sensual (and often, feminine) material matter.

11. For an insightful source, see the interview with Bernhard Heidsieck in *Stereo Headphones* 8–10 (1982), 20–21.

12. I might point to works of concrete poetry that in employing methods of linguistic game-playing, turn the page into a performative space. For instance, the Brazilian concrete poetry of Augusto de Campos is but one example, with his LUXO poem from 1965, which consists of the single word "Lixo" (meaning "garbage" in Portuguese) made up of tiny images of the word "Luxo" (meaning "luxury"). In mixing these two words and their meanings, literally integrating the one inside the other,

de Campos performs a simple yet effective concrete poetical effect. This method is found in numerous other works, and echoes how I'm positioning Burroughs's work.

13. Gaston Bachelard, *Air and Dreams: An Essay on the Imagination of Movement* (Dallas: Dallas Institute Publications, 1988), 240.

14. Roman Jakobson, *Six Lectures on Sound and Meaning* (Sussex: The Harvester Press, 1978), 32.

15. For an extremely insightful work on this subject, see Allen S. Weiss, *Varieties of Audio Mimesis: Musical Evocations of Landscape* (Berlin: Errant Bodies Press, 2008).

16. Although I cannot delve into the following question in depth here, I would like to raise the issue of whether in unsettling the territory around subjectivity sound poetry has particular implications for masculine subjectivity. Is it possible to further query the issues opened up by sound poetry by specifically hearing in many of its works a particularly refined set of actions aimed at unleashing a new condition for male subjectivity? As Kaja Silverman examines in her study of masculinity, *Male Subjectivity at the Margins*, theories of psychoanalysis underscore the acquisition of language as generally forming the individual around a central lack—language comes to wound subjectivity by removing one from the co-mingling of self and world experienced as a child. Through the acquisition of language subjectivity is essentially inaugurated, fixing identity around a social coding and locating expressions of sexuality and desire onto a gendered body, thereby separating one off from a prelinguistic plenitude. Silverman points out that masculinity forms the site for the perpetuation of a certain "dominant fiction"—patriarchal society rotates around the symbolic and productive assertion of masculinity as bearer of language, and thereby power. Onto the site of masculinity then is placed not only the privileging of maleness, but the pressure to uphold what language defines as masculine. Following Freud and Lacan, Silverman underscores that at the core of male identity, the figure of castration threatens to radically undo not only the single individual male, but the larger, dominant fiction which supplies social values with a repertoire of representations (family, home, etc.). Generally, the dominant fiction comes to "indicate that conventional masculinity can best be understood as the denial of castration." Kaja Silverman, *Male Subjectivity at the Margins* (New York/London: Routledge, 1992), 46. In light of this, I would ask whether the incorporation of a seeming glossolalic breakdown of subjectivity found within sound poetry might also be understood as performing a particular self-imposed cut onto masculinity.

17. His 1948 article "A Mathematical Theory of Communication" set the stage for the burgeoning of information theory.

18. François Dufrêne, "Pragmatic of Crirythme" in *OU—Cinquième Saison*, CD box set, ed. Emanuele Carcano (Milan: Alga Marghen, 2002), 47.

19. Bachelard, *Air and Dreams*, 239.

20. See Herbert Marcuse, *One Dimensional Man: Studies in the Ideology of Advanced Industrial Society* (London: Routledge, 2002), and Herbert Magnus Enzensberger, *The Consciousness Industry: On Literature, Politics and the Media* (New York: Continuum, 1974).

21. Jean Baudrillard, *For a Critique of the Political Economy of the Sign* (Telos Press, 1981), 169, 175–176.

22. Robin Lydenberg, "Sound Identity Fading Out: William Burroughs' Tape Experiments," in *Wireless Imagination: Sound, Radio and the Avant-Garde*, eds. Douglas Kahn and Gregory Whitehead (Cambridge, MA: MIT Press, 1992), 411.

23. Marshall McLuhan, *Understanding Media* (London: Routledge, 2001 [1964]).

24. N. Katherine Hayles, "Voices out of Bodies, Bodies out of Voices: Audiotape and the Production of Subjectivity" in *Sound States: Innovative Poetics and Acoustical Technologies*, ed. Adalaide Morris (Chapel Hill: University of North Carolina Press, 1997), 91.

25. William S. Burroughs, *The Ticket That Exploded* (London: Paladin Grafton Books, 1987 [1967]), 123.

26. Garrett Stewart, *Reading Voices: Literature and the Phonotext* (Berkeley: University of California Press, 1990), 106.

27. Robin Lydenberg, "Sound Identity Fading Out: William Burroughs' Tape Experiments," 423.

28. Burroughs's literary project finds interesting parallel in the work of the group Oulipo. Formed around Raymond Queneau in Paris in 1960, Oulipo was an experimental laboratory focused on new forms of writing and text projects that employed specific and strict conceptual methods. For instance, the "lipogram" is the practice of excluding one or more letters from a text, the most pronounced example being Georges Perec's *A Void* (1969), a novel written without using the letter "e." As the story unfolds, it becomes apparent that the letter is in fact caught up in the very narrative of detective work to locate a missing person. Or another method is writing the same narrative multiple times yet according to different styles. For example, Queneau's own *Exercises in Style* (1947) describes a man on a bus witnessing an incident yet written 99 different ways. Their exercises hint at leaving behind aspects of psychology and the unconscious, turning literature into an architectural and algorithmic process, which would find its ultimate expression in the establishment of ALAMO (Atelier de Littérature assistée par la Mathématique et les Ordinateurs/Literature Workshop aided by Mathematics and Computers). Initiated by the Oulipian member Jacques Roubaud in 1981, along with Paul Baffort, the project was based on the the use of computers to generate textual works. Their investigations into algorithmic systems would lead to the production of text-generating computer programs (such as the language APL), which comes to figure in Baudrillard's earlier announcement

that the problem for a leftist, revolutionary critique of media is not in redistributing content but in working on the level of the media's formal apparatus.

29. Henri Chopin, *Stereo Headphones* 8–10 (1982): 12.

30. Ibid.

31. Teddy Hultberg, "Sound Poetry and Text-Sound Composition—the Swedish Story," *Text-Sound Compositions: A Stockholm Festival* CD boxed set (Stockholm: Fylkingen Records, 2005), 6.

32. Ibid., liner notes, trans. by Maria LaBelle.

33. Such productions parallel Clement Greenberg's influential writings and ideas from the 1940s and 1950s. Championing the "essential" features of art objects and their making, Greenberg defined art according to its intrinsic formal elements. For instance, modern painting gave expression—through an abstraction defined by color, movement, pictorial space, and related plasticity—to a set of surface effects. Such reductions enacted by Greenberg sought to embrace what he perceived as art's historical drive away from representational or illusionistic space and toward a material purity, which modernism seemed to promise. Lettrism and Ultra-Lettrism sound poetry seem to unwittingly mirror much of this project by seeking to transcend or overcome the cultural parameters that make one subject to language.

34. Renato Barilli, *Futura* (Milan: Cramps Records), 9.

35. For more on the history of speaking machines, see the exhibition catalog, *Phonorama: Eine Kulturgeshichte der Stimme als Medium* (Karlsruhe: ZKM, 2005).

36. Paul Elliman, "Guided by Voices," *Pages #4: Voice* (July 2005): 104.

37. See Tiziana Terranova, *Network Culture: Politics for the Information Age* (London and Ann Arbor, MI: Pluto Press, 2004).

38. Steven Shaviro, *Connected, or what it means to live in the network society* (Minneapolis: University of Minnesota Press, 2003), 13.

39. William S. Burroughs, *Electronic Revolution* (Bonn: Expanded Media Editions, 2001), 8.

40. Steven Shaviro, *Connected*, 31.

41. See the artist's website: http://homepage.mac.com/davidrokeby/home.html.

42. See the artist's website: http://www.verdaechtig.at.

43. Bruce Andrews, "Praxis: A Political Economy of Noise and Information," in *Close Listening: Poetry and the Performed Word*, ed. Charles Bernstein (Oxford: Oxford University Press, 1998), 73–74.

44. Ibid. 79.

9 Vocal Textures

Amanda Stewart

I work as a poet, writer, and vocal artist, spanning many forms and themes. Some of my texts utilize more traditional literary devices, and others aim to make an intervention at the level of the materiality of language itself: to crack open oral and written signs and strike at the basis of our listening and reading processes and the cultural assumptions that they embody. Most of my publications and performances utilize analog media. For some years I have worked within literary, new music, and sound poetry scenes in Australia, Europe, the United States, and Japan. Although I still choose to work predominantly with analog technology, I also contribute to new media environments[1] and my activities have been progressively informed and influenced by the emergence of digital technologies and their attendant cultural forms and practices. I will focus, here, on discussing several of my aural works for voice. These stem largely from my writing practice, but they also reveal a strange trajectory of engagement that has implications for digital forms, despite—and perhaps precisely because of—their absence. So, though I may take some time to speak here of my engagement with digital forms, I ask the reader to follow the tale of my education, because my slow comprehension of several modes of vocalization needs to be outlined first so I can show how digital technologies can be understood anew through my own particular vocal and acoustic processes.

Over the years, I have become increasingly interested in the distinct but linked properties of different oral, written, and electronic forms of language and the "modes of memory" or mnemonic states that they engender. Part of my interest has been to engage with these different modes in order to experience, often intuitively, some of their diverse implications for how language, body, memory, and subjectivity can be constituted and organized. Whereas my written works tend to be fixed in form, many of my vocal works utilize a mixture of scored and spontaneous systems that change function over time. These works generate interactive environments of voiced and written texts, which become so multilayered and complex that they create a disorientating effect. I become "lost for words," strategically "confounded," and this becomes a revelatory process that can ignite a return to our earliest and most vital engagements with language. On a related note, I have become interested in how different analog and digital media engender different *pneumonic* as well as mnemonic states. Digital technology has created new possibilities for exploring and articulating some of this complexity, creating new discourses which continue to profoundly affect and alter both our pneumonic and mnemonic systems, even when we don't use that technology. Although most of my solo works have been quite prudent and minimal in their engagement with new media technologies, as I was exposed to these forms, over time, they inevitably influenced my analog and printed poetry pieces.

Since the 1960s, I have been writing poetry, prose, plays, and scripts, and since the 1980s, I have worked also as a composer/performer for voice. In a sense, my life spans a period that encompassed the shift from analog to digital forms. In some ways, this shift is analogous to the technological innovations that developed and influenced all art throughout the twentieth century. My work began on the page and in performance without amplification. I was then exposed to amplification and various analog recording technologies, and over the past twenty-five years I have been exposed to a variety of digital forms. As my work has unfolded, I've learned—often implicitly more than explicitly—how language in its multifarious feedback loops with the voice is perhaps the most fundamental and complex of all human technologies. The ability to speak involves a level of virtuosity that we may never fully understand. It is the link between use and being. "Voice" reconstitutes "me" and in dialog or declaration makes "us." We assume each other's voices. We internalize the phonemes, pitches, rhythms, speeds, dynamics, nonverbal vocal sounds, songs and discourses of "others." Everyday speech utilizes a range of complex, extended vocal techniques and musicalities that we often take for granted. Voice forms us by embodying the "other." It is ethos incarnate.

I've learned also that where the voice is present, so is language, even if no "words" are used. Our bodies are fundamentally mapped in this presence. We are haunted by voice from our beginnings in the womb. Voice is the first home of self and no self, of form, logic, feeling, song, and all the modes of cultural assumption that we embody through our time and place. It is a multireferential chameleon. It structures our bodies so that all these forms coexist simultaneously as potential, with varying degrees of latency and utterance. All these potentials are present at every moment. Voice makes us present. As the Australian poet and historian Barry Hill has observed, because of its vocal origins, language is "a somatic act before it is anything else: it goes into the ear before anything else and all our attempts to understand its speaker are bound up with bodies in space together, with a form approaching intimacy."[2] The voice modulates us: our breathing patterns and blood flow. Different vocal and linguistic structures affect our brains, our bodily functions, our memory systems, our possible subjectivities and our ability for grammatical recombination, our ability to synthesize semantic, musical, analytical, and emotional structures.

Part of my interest, as an artist, has been to play with some of these notions. In some of my vocal works, I have done this largely as an intuitive exercise to subject myself to different linguistic and vocal forms in order to see how this affects my subjectivity—my own memory systems, my body constitution, and my modes of listening and being. In doing so, I have been influenced by ideas from philosophy, linguistics, psychoanalysis, and science, but if I'm totally honest, my earliest influences were by far the most significant and have formed the substructure for all future development in my work. Learning oral language as a child is the most profound technology and influence I have engaged with and informs everything I have done subsequently. The second major influence was from my mother, who taught me to read when I was two without me noticing what she was doing. This deeply affected my relationship to the English language. The third most important influence was learning to sing and to whistle through listening. I am recounting these trite, autobiographical details (yes—let's kill the author!) because I believe that this part of the human trajectory is often assumed or ignored in discussions of new media. Our first encounters with learning language remain fundamental and involve a level of virtuosity and complexity that still defies adequate description or definition.

In the late 1970s and early 1980s, in addition to writing poetry for print, I began to experiment with unamplified vocal techniques based on language structures. I became interested in the difference between the oral and written forms of the English language. When the unamplified voice is presented in live performance, some of the inherent virtuosity in everyday speech is formalized, as it frequently involves projecting the voice in extended ways to deliver "texts" or "songs."

When I started performing, I had no experience with sound poetry or even the earlier literary works of Dadaism or Futurism,[3] but I had been very interested in the history of twentieth-century visual art since my school days, and I began to incorporate concepts from visual art into my poetry. My poetry began to utilize more truncation, collage, and nonlinear composition methods. At this time I also became involved in making works for radio, video, and film as a student at the University of Technology in Sydney. In 1979 I was involved in the establishment of 2SER FM (Sydney Educational Radio) and then went on to ABC (Australian Broadcasting Corporation) Radio, where I worked full-time until the mid-1990s.

My involvement in radio made me increasingly interested in how musico-poetic systems work within discourse.[4] I researched particular discourses to try and see how they were articulated by various individuals and institutions. What specific syntax, vocabulary, and mythic structures were they using? What nonverbal and musical architectures—with their particular intonational, rhythmic, timbral, dynamic, and pitch systems—shaped these discourses? I wanted to hear what sort of subject a specific mode of address assumed, the paradigms it was capable of invoking, and how it set up its connections. I became interested in the complexity of oral grammars, which function, at different levels simultaneously, within language and in our use of the voice. In particular, I was interested in the mesh of systems at work within Australian speech. I made a series of experimental radio documentaries that analyzed political language, nuclear language, and the language of genetics, as well as making poetry, drama, features, and audio arts programs. Filmmaker Nicolette Freeman and I cowrote and directed an experimental documentary film called *Eclipse of the Man-Made Sun*, which analyzed the development of nuclear language between 1945 and 1990. The film examined how this new technology was assimilated into our language structures over this period.

Radio had a huge impact on my poetry. When you are slowing down, processing, mixing, and cutting up voices all day long, you become inevitably attuned to the materiality of speech in all its dimensions. I gained many valuable insights into speech patterns and our often unconscious use of extended vocals. When working with radio and tape, the natural speaking voice is amplified and removed from the body that produced it. This act changes the ontology, materiality, and presence of voice as well as the way we listen to speech. It seems that the moment the body is removed is the very moment that it "returns" with reinvigorated power and intimacy. Amplifying the voice, putting it through speakers or headphones, and subjecting it to editing and other treatments transforms it into a new materiality and also affords a greater intimacy with and awareness of the embodied, unamplified voice. Every fluctuation of breath, pitch, timbre, and volume is revealed at the edge of the speaking subject: stutters, slips of the tongue, strange timbral fluctuations, squeaks, rasps, clicks, size and consistency of lip smacks, rhythm of speech, and length and functions of pauses. The complexities of discourse as it regulates our pneumonic systems are revealed, as well as where and how vocal sounds are resonated through the body. One of the most obvious examples is if someone is put "on the spot" in an interview. Hesitations, stutters, truncated speech rhythms, increased breath depth and dynamics, and sharper articulation are some of the effects that often result.

Radio and recording have fundamentally changed our listening structures and how we use and manipulate voice. The fluidity and complexity of the extended vocal systems that form speech are truly impressive. We take much of this virtuosity for granted and focus on the signifying aspects of these "fluctuations," but the incredible range and diversity of structures that speech employs can also be analyzed for the brilliance of its extended vocal techniques.

As I became increasingly attuned to how different our oral grammars are from our written ones, I began to mix codes within my poems and started to try to develop new notation systems to represent these graphically. In 1984, composer Richard Vella offered me brief use of the New South Wales State Conservatorium of Music's computer and its notation software as a means of exploring notation systems. The computer accurately notated a number of oral patterns in one of my poems. The score was detailed and ugly and I began to question what my motivations actually were in producing such an object. If I wanted people to slavishly perform my work "accurately," I would be better off providing a recording that would be the most precise form of notation for such a purpose. I decided that I had no further interest in using the computer for this task. I instead began to focus on emphasizing the distinctions between the oral and written forms of the

English language. Although I rejected the computer as a means of extending my poetry in this way, it directly facilitated my passage into other means of writing. For example, I became interested in making an intervention at the basis of our listening and reading systems: how text met the eye, and voice the ear. On the page, I began to include more language fragmentation and conflation techniques in my written poetry and to experiment with amplified voice in oral works. I found the muscles and processes involved in developing amplified voice techniques to be very different from unamplified forms. The public address (PA) system blew up speech in such a way that one could produce very fast flows of phonemes without projection and also allowed me to use all sorts of tiny vocal sounds that would normally be inaudible and to extend these as compositional tools.

In the late 1980s, I started to explore live, stereo vocal techniques. I would use two microphones, which were patched left and right into a stereo PA. This was a very different system from using one microphone. With one mono microphone, even abstract vocal sounds still held the unity of "the voice" intact. It referenced "singing," "extended vocal performance," "speeches," radio, and other contemporary amplified voice forms.

Figure 9.1
Amanda Stewart. Solo performance at club zho, Perth, July 24, 2006, for Tura New Music and De Quincey Co. Photographer: Jon Green. Image courtesy of Jon Green.

Using two microphones gave the voice a rich, spatialized plasticity and ambiguity that hadn't been present in my work before. The voice was materialized as a shifting, sculptural entity. Two microphones also changed my own relationship to my voice. It became a split entity that in one way was more disassociated from me, as a subject, and on the other hand allowed a far greater intimacy and specificity in listening to different substructures in my voice that I hadn't been aware of before.

Most of the sounds I explored were enlargements or abstractions of speech. I could break speech down into different categories of use and quickly shift between them, creating a disorientating effect. I experimented with fragmenting the vocal technology that springs automatically into action in speech. I incorporated stutters, lip smacks, croaks, and squeaks as well as a diversity of renderings of text spoken at different speeds and subjected to various abstraction techniques, so that residues of semantic content would flicker into the mix.

In the early 1990s, I extended these ideas into amplified, stereo works that also utilized tape and the analog recording studio. A piece called " ≠ " was commissioned by Larry Wendt for *Leonardo Music Journal* in 1993. It was the first in a series of works that explored subject/object relations in language. As various versions of a subject-verb-object structure were prevalent in western languages, I was interested in composing texts that explored some of the phenomenological implications of this structure. In " ≠ " I composed two parallel, written texts in which the word orders were set but the oral realization of these words was to be manipulated by the voice in live improvisation to tape. I recorded the first (subject) text onto the left channel and then recorded the second (object) text on the right channel, which overhears and comments on the first. The third and fourth layers are stereo vocal improvisations, which make occasional interjections and comments.

The texts use a diversity of references and constructions from schizoid operatic personal pronouns to mercurial tirades, fractured English, phonemes, calls, statements, stutters, outbursts, mouth sounds, and parallel speech so that modes of listening are constantly switching between different fields. The four layers were recorded consecutively and then mixed to two tracks without processing or editing. As I had no access to postproduction facilities, it was crucial to get the work done in four eight-minute takes. This was very demanding for me, as a performer, as the piece involved sharp shifts and tight, syncopated passages. The sheer degree of difficulty caused me to enter a strange, abstract mental state, which I found very interesting. Even though the analog tape technology was extremely constraining, in that predigital era, I could discern benefits in the challenges it presented. In retrospect, I can see now that I was developing techniques that would become more widespread as digital technologies became more available. For example, in this series of analog subject/object works, I utilize various systems of language fragmentation, nonlinear real-time text generation, kinesis, intertextuality, and nonlinear access forms. Each performance of a work is unique and unrepeatable. Modulated through context, the "work" becomes the work of a process of engagement with overlapping fields of notation. The multiple simultaneous texts create a dynamic, heterogeneous, interactive, immersive environment that is contiguous with some contemporary digital approaches to hypertext, kinetic poetry, and interactive web-based and installation works. As is often the case, aesthetic and performative needs and abilities preceded and to some extent demanded the arrival of a new technology.

" ≠ " was a studio work, originally, but the strange mental state I entered while making it caused me to begin to think about how I could work with the piece in live performance. I decided to use two microphones so that my live stereo voice became the "verb" moving between the subject and object texts, which were split left and right. I also created another layer of written ideas and texts with the idea of simultaneously subjecting myself to multiple aural and written signs, which I would have to make sense of in real time. Performing with tape tends to be a very boring medium for live performance, as the tape is fixed and immutable, but the difficulty of negotiating the parallel processes of both reading multiple textual scores and listening to the aural ones simultaneously seemed to ignite a very complicated series of mental processes from simple elements. When I performed the piece, it was as if my brain was completely overloaded, as it attempted to quickly make decisions and shifted between reading and listening to all these parallel "texts." It felt like I was lost in an immersive chaos of oral and written signs, subject to multiple fields of engagement, as different dimensions of inscription and notation were ignited and overlaid. I was suddenly at the edge of myself and of my presumptions about the function of different linguistic signs. The process also revealed some of the complexity of our listening processes and how we categorize different sequences of voice sounds.

I tried to analyze what was actually happening to me during this performance. I took some of the sounds and put them back "under the microscope," stripping them down to stereo voice with no tape. I found, for example, that if I made a high pitched "aghh" in the right channel followed by a "t" sound in the left channel, the fragmentation technique threw into question the exact use of these two sounds. They could be read according to the relation of their pitch, rhythm, envelope, dynamics, or as expressive nonverbal sounds that functioned semantically or they could be heard as an abstraction of the word "at." It was as if during performance, my brain was doing multiple feedback loops trying to classify the sounds according to some cultural category or to filter the sounds into some clear notion of "use."

Multiplying these ambiguous stereo vocal signs and speeding them up created a barrage of signs, which would overwhelm me, as a subject, trying to form sense from it all. I found this fascinating. What happens when the process of classifying vocal sounds is confounded? The vocalist must generate her/his performance from a multiparadigmatic reference field of notations (written and oral) and implied utterances. Many of these potential utterances remain unarticulated, so that the piece is as much about what is not uttered as what is. For every emergent sound there are innumerable defining absences, transmissions, lacks. In such an environment, "knowing" is not possible or relevant. Fragments of use interweave. The coexistence of multiple potential fields of use ignites a rich simultaneity of listening processes. This is a multicausal structure that remains ultimately inarticulatable. It seemed analogous to some sort of wave/particle duality theory or uncertainty principle in which the observation system is itself constantly on the verge of collapse, bending under its own weight with its inability to absorb the potential multiverses that lurk beneath, somewhere in-between, at the edge of something else.

Over the past fifteen years, I have developed an ongoing series of pieces exploring these ideas. In some ways, they serve as a metaphor for how we, as children, as subjects, are born into the world and are articulated through the discourses of our time and culture and the associated mnemonic and pneumonic states that they engender. Breath and how it passes through the body is the fuel and fundamental means by which language is formed and resonated. It is also the primary fuel for the body and all its organs. Different discourses and uses of the voice reconfigure our breathing patterns in varying ways and these breathing forms then integrally affect the body and its processes.

Apart from affecting pacing, depth, and quality of breath, this discourse affects the entire pneumonic, vocal, and organic system. Where and how the breath passes through the body, the vocal tract, the larynx, the mouth, and so on integrally affects how the voice signifies and how it constitutes and reveals the subject. Different distributions of air affect the timbre, dynamics, pitch, articulation, and envelope of different forms of language, and our listening processes are finely tuned to the nuances of this system. For example, as I discovered in the context of editing interviews for radio, hesitations, truncated rhythms, and fluctuations in dynamics and pitch revealed the emotional and thinking processes of the subject and all these signifiers return to the body in a complex multiverse of feedback loops. The tongue, the hand, the ear, and the eye are closely connected with this structure.

This relation between language, listening, voice, and our pneumonic systems is also fundamental to our mnemonic systems. By this, I mean the different memory storage systems or "discourses" of memory that are constantly at work within the body. Memory, itself, is the primary form of notation. A simple example is the fascinating complexities of sound and how we process it. As soon as we hear a voice, multiple potential associations are triggered, and the ways in which these simultaneous systems interrelate are staggeringly intricate. They operate at every level of language and being. The subject internalizes the vocal and linguistic patterns that surround it, learns to mimic and reproduce the signs in the body, the memory, the ear, the eye. The body is articulated through the signs that it internalizes. We are used by language and it is through use that we intervene in this system. When I perform my subject/object works, I become very aware of the effects of different breathing structures and their relation to various modes of language and vocalization. I sometimes feel like a child, lost for words, hovering at the edge of learning language for the first time.

Although many of these pieces use simple analog techniques, some of the effects they produce are analogous to those created digitally in new media works that are composed of elements integrated or disintegrated at the behest of a governing code. For example, when I perform these subject/object works, they create an immersive field that engenders different mental and physical states or discourses of consciousness. In some senses, I am constantly being deconstructed and reconstructed at the edge of "composed" subjectivity. As a performer, it makes me very vulnerable. Sometimes I have no idea what has occurred. To place myself at the edge of uncertainty where I cannot know or control outcomes remains exciting, addictive and impenetrable. Strategic "disorientation" becomes a revelatory process.

The later works that I produced in this series have used several simple digital techniques and although these have not altered the general direction underpinning the pieces, they have affected the way I treat voice and the subsequent performing states I enter into. "IT .·. I" was commissioned by Donaueschinger Musiktage in 2002. Thematically, the piece was, in some senses, an homage to some of the great, progressive developments in the early twentieth century in the areas of art, science, and literature with some dark reflections on how many of these ideas had been assimilated or lost later in the century. Once again I used a parallel texts technique, both on tape and on paper, but I increased the number to six. The difference between this and other works is that I composed the piece using Session software on a computer. Shortly afterward, I was able to buy Pro Tools.

Having access to home editing, mixing, and multitracking was a luxury that I was a little scared of at first. Since I'd left the ABC, I hadn't been able to afford to do much postproduction on my tape works, and this had caused me to develop a clear, sharp discipline about producing works straight to tape without mixing or editing. With Pro Tools, I had virtually unlimited postproduction options. I was worried that I would become obsessed with new trivialities afforded by the possibilities of the system and lose touch with the raw vulnerability of my previous disciplines.

Digital editing allowed me to go into the sound material and extract tiny micro phonemes from speech sounds. I could also use multitracking to create overlays, which I could never have produced live in an analog recording studio. This whole postproduction environment created a different dreaming space for making work. I would spend hours lost in the material, disappearing into the intricacies of the process. The number of long hours I worked would also alter my consciousness. As I became more and more exhausted, strange coincidences and accidents would also shape the material. The faster transport of Pro Tools and the ability to save multiple versions of ideas also changed the mental processes of composition. I could be more spontaneous. I could store multiple versions simply and try out ideas quickly, which allowed a fluidity of thinking and a more intuitive response to the material. The immediacy of digital editing means that you stay focused on the one idea and instantly realize it. Then comes learning how to re-embody and perform what has been learnt from this process.

In my most recent series of vocal works, instead of investigating the complexities of a subject traversed by a plethora of written and oral signs, I have tried to strip signification from the voice. This interest came about, in part, because of changes of uses in technology in the music scene over the past ten to fifteen years. Over this period, many of my friends and colleagues in this field started to use interesting configurations of new digital and analog techniques.[5]

I began to develop new vocal techniques that initially aimed at mimicking some of the sound structures being produced by artists using new digital processing systems and programs like Max/MSP. I wanted to strip the voice of its semantic power and make a voice that is no voice. As always, I used no processing, except for extreme stereo amplification. I developed new microphone techniques and vocal sounds that referenced electronic glitches, scratches, scrapes, pops, buzzes, hisses, bumps, and high-pitched tones.

In some of the music performances I did, in which I worked with these techniques, I found it exciting that in several cases, people were unaware that there was even a vocalist in the group or thought that I had to be using digital processing. I myself found that sometimes I was confused as to whether I had made a sound or whether it was a collaborator's computer. Sometimes I would spontaneously produce a new vocal sound that I had never made or heard before in response to what someone else had done. I found this exhilarating. It was as if an inherent language facility was internalizing and reshaping a new syntax of vocal sounds, which was performing me. It felt like this was some other sort of return to our earliest engagements with language.

I then developed a series of new solo, multitrack works to explore these processes further. In "As If," I recorded different sets of vocal sounds, which made the voice unrecognizable as voice. I then took the files home and composed the piece on Pro Tools, overlaying subsets of sounds to make a work that proceeds in three sections. As with most of my multitrack works, I never rehearsed with the piece but waited until my first public performance to see what would happen. I found the piece very demanding, physically and mentally. It involved a completely different way of breathing and micro lip, mouth, throat, and stomach control. At the end of this five-minute piece, I was disorientated, exhausted, and on edge. I felt like I'd been out surfing a rough swell and had little memory of what had just occurred. It was a most peculiar experience. I then produced another work, which is simply a live-to-tape mono recording, so that the voice is nakedly revealed grappling with these vocabularies of utterances. The choice to *not* use real-time digital signal processing in these pieces reveals an analog voice that is aware of digital possibilities but is embracing them in a different form.

It was not until 1998 that I made a collection of my solo work publicly available in a nonperformed medium. I released a CD and book box set of my selected poetry and vocal works from the period 1980–1996. I designed the set as a sort of extended book concept. It unfolds rather than opens. I wanted to be able to represent both the visual and oral versions of the work in one collection. "I/T" (a pun on Information Technology and a conflation of the words "I" and "it") integrates a range of different poetic forms. As well as more traditional poetry, it includes conceptual poems, visual poems, oral poems, and poems that have both written and aural forms.

On opening the box set, one finds a series of visual poems, a book, and a CD. The book and the CD can be regarded separately or experienced as one entity. The CD follows the book with the same sequence of poetry so that one can experience both the written and aural forms of the poems simultaneously, if desired. However, the aural versions of these poems are not simply performances dictated by the page (or vice versa). The two forms (written and aural) exist in parallel, integrally related but also distinct from each other.

The book also contains visual and conceptual poems, which have no aural identity and the CD includes oral poems, which do not have a written form. These electroacoustic pieces vary in their conception and production. In "mt," miniature, abstract poems that incorporate nonverbal vocal sounds, extended vocals, and text were recorded onto a MiniDisc player and then played on random shuffle to form a new text, which the performer had to negotiate in performance. "residue" explored residues of tuning systems in speech in a live stereo improvisation to multitrack tape in three layers.

Part of the purpose of "I/T" was to highlight the distinct but linked properties of oral, written, and electronic forms of language and the "forms of inscription" or "modes of memory" that they engender. Many of the works use techniques that are similar to those employed in some digital and new media works. For example, they utilize nonlinear composition methods, various graphic dislocations of reading systems, truncation, collage, and parallel reading and listening systems. However, all the works were produced using analog technologies. Some of the most profound influences from new media poetries have been conceptual. We still do not fully understand the potentials of new media in relation to the voice. This is what makes the area so vital. Festivals like Proposta in Barcelona,[6] Kri Kri in Gent, and organisations like literaturWERKstatt[7] in Berlin, the EBU Ars Acoustica group, or the Kunsttempel in Kassel offer opportunities for the rich, multilayered possibilities of contemporary poetic and vocal forms to flourish.

I have discussed only a few of my vocal works here; however, my written texts and poetry have also inevitably been influenced by digital modes, even those that use more traditional literary forms. Each field of inscription—printed, amplified, digital, analog, unamplified—interinforms and illuminates the other and provides further insights into the endless recombinant potentials of language and voice. As I discovered in these vocal works, various disassociations of the voice from the body not only fundamentally transformed its materiality, but also revealed various complexities of the embodied voice and its systems that I hadn't been aware of before. I am still learning from this process. These pieces create an interactive environment of signs that I find so complex and multilayered that it remains ultimately beyond "understanding," inducing "disorientation" as a revelatory process. Digital forms frequently produce similar insights, and in an age where the richness and prolific duplication and transaction inherent to this culture have made filtering, distilling, and discarding increasingly important, the implications of certain technologies can sometimes be more clearly discerned through their strategic absence. Absence and disassociation can—often unexpectedly—facilitate new forms of intimacy and also reveal some of the intricacies of the interplay between conceptual and technological manifestations and their effects on our bodies, language, memory, and listening systems and the ethos that emerges.

The trajectory of development in the vocal works that I have traced here moves from the unamplified to the amplified speaking voice to the amplified split-stereo voice in various configurations. Although I have attempted to identify some of the outcomes of these explorations, these series of works remain, for me, ultimately confounding. This is why they are still of interest to me. Through an intuitive exploration of the different effects of these voiced environments I have entered different bodily states, consciousness states, and triggered varied linguistic, pneumonic, and mnemonic patterns. This process is somehow analogous to the cumulative etymology of forms that underpin the richness of the voice as it moves through the history of technologies and forms and how these are accommodated into codings, language, the body, and the subject.

Voice-based art forms will continue to be profoundly affected by digital technologies as they evolve, regardless of whether they literally use that technology. Digital technology has revolutionized possibilities for production, distribution, collaboration, and interdisciplinary synthesis in ways that were not possible previously. The voice has been extended into new discourses and sign systems that also shed new light on those that came before (for example, the way hypertext reposits early notions of intertextuality). In some ways, digital technology has been able to rematerialize many of the concerns of twentieth-century avant-garde traditions that sought to extend the unlimited semiotic potentials of language and voice.

The voice-based arts have perhaps never been so rich and multifarious in diversity and affectivity as they are now. As computer-generated voice and speech synthesis becomes more sophisticated, there will be more fluidity in voice-activated processes replacing printed interfaces. As this becomes more prevalent, it too will have a huge affect on how we use, imagine, and listen to voice. In a sense, the computer itself is an adjunct of the language impulse, and its feedback loop with nondigital forms has greatly enriched the potentials of all our semiotic systems, analog or otherwise.

Notes

1. Gerhard Johann Lischika and Peter Weibel, *Im Netz Der Systeme—Fur eine interaktive Kunst: Ars Electronica Linz, Amanda Stewart: Kollaborationen, Kunstforum, Bd. 103*, Cologne, September/October 1989, 272–274.

Nicholas Zurbrugg, "Electronic Arts in Australia," *Continuum* 8, no.1 (1994), 83–90.

Since the mid-1980s, I have collaborated with a diversity of fascinating artists who work with digital forms, including Warren Burt, Rosie Dennis, Rainer Linz, Chris Mann, Ikue Mori, Maria Miranda, Norie Neumark, and Jon Rose.

2. Barry Hill, *Broken Song: T.G.H. Strehlow and Aboriginal Possession* (Sydney: Random House, 2002), 3.

3. The UbuWeb website (http://www.ubu.com) contains much interesting material in these areas from early in the twentieth century to the present.

4. Roland Barthes, *Image, Music, Text* (London: Fontana, 1977; Henri Chopin, *Poesie Sonore Internationale* (Paris: Jean-Michel Place, 1979); Julia Kristeva, *Desire in Language: A Semiotic Approach to Literature and Art* (Oxford: Blackwell, 1980) (English translation of *Séméiôtiké: recherches pour une sémanalyse* [Paris: Edition du Seuil, 1969]); Benjamin Boretz, *language, as a music: six marginal pretexts for composition* (Iowa City: lingua press, 1980); Kenneth Gaburo, *Allos: "Other" Language* (Iowa City: lingua press, 1980); Noel Sanders, "Notes on Photoportraiture," *Photo-discourse* (Sydney: Sydney College of the Arts, 1981), 116–121; Paul Chilton, "Nukespeak: Nuclear Language, Culture and Propaganda" in C. Aubrey (ed.), *Nukespeak: The Media and the Bomb* (London: Comedia Publishing Group, 1982), 94–112; Max Atkinson, *Our Masters' Voices: Language and Body Language of Politics* (London: Routledge, 1984).

5. For example, for more than twenty years I have collaborated with the Australian musician/composer Jim Denley in many contexts, including as a duo and in the Australian electroacoustic ensemble, Machine For Making Sense (which was cofounded with Chris Mann, Rik Rue, and Stevie Wishart in 1989). More recently, our duo work has been radically extended through Jim's innovative use of wind instruments, throat mic, and hand-crafted electronics using GRM software (as evidenced at his recent solo concert at the Melbourne International Biennale of Exploratory Music, 2008, at the ABC Iwaki Auditorium March 30, 2008 (recording available from ABC Radio). Another musician using breath and voice as part of her music making is Natasha Anderson, with whom I have worked in a duo and in other contexts over the past three years. Natasha interfaces her acoustic playing with the digital signal-processing software Max/MSP via a multi sensor environment attached to the vast real estate of a Paetzold contrabass recorder. This set up allows her to exert immediate and more organic control over the real time processing, enabling, in particular, rapid shifts between digital and acoustic sound and abject and processed gestures. Given the unfamiliar nature of her instrument and her anomalous approach to playing it, these constant shifts often result in the source of her sounds and gestures, whether electronic, instrumental or bodily, becoming tangled and confused. This sensors/computer/instrument nexus also allows her to exploit the semantics of her particular library of playing gestures (particularly in audio/visual works). Thus, for instance, the light sensor is placed on the labium of the instrument, whereby the inflection of an acoustic shriek or low frequency guttural articulation becomes linked to the visibility of a particular physical gesture and/or projected image. When activated by violent key slaps, pressure sensors under particular keys trigger certain sounds and/or images, and a slide sensor placed along the side enables suggestive sweeps of this palpably phallic instrument to be linked to specific visual and/or sonic outcomes. (Personal correspondence with Anderson, June 17, 2008.)

6. There is a good DVD set of performances by contemporary poets and voice artists who appeared at the Proposta Festival, edited by Eduard Escoffet, *Proposta 2000–2004, festival internacional de poesies+polipoesies* (Barcelona: Proposta, 2006).

7. literaturWERKstatt, http://www.literaturwerkstatt.org, organized a very interesting digital poetry exhibition in Berlin in 2004 with an accompanying book by Friedrich W. Block, Christiane Heibach, and Karin Wenz, *poesis: The Aesthetics of Digital Poetry* (Ostfildern-Ruit: Hatje-Cantz Verlag, 2004).

10   Professor VJ's Big Blog Mashup

Mark Amerika

The Performer

Remix this, remix that

We've heard it all before

It doesn't take long for buzzwords
to lose their usefulness as reference points
especially when challenged by an activist
new media intelligentsia

But what happens when the new media artist
becomes a kind of "mashup filter"
sampling data from a variety of sources
who then via their unconscious readiness potential
manipulates this data with their own
signature-style effects
and the experiential residue of a life
lived on Planet Oblivion?

When it comes to translating your own
experience as part of a larger relational aesthetic
is there an implicit politics involved in
the act of remixing?

Who controls the experiential opacity
the crunchy altertones

the asynchronous assemblages
that tremble at the touch of a keyboard?

Anecdote:

While she was visiting Boulder in the mid-90s
Kathy Acker and I were invited for an interview
on the local public radio station KGNU
and the show's host though very sweet
was quite unfamiliar with Acker's work
and so asked a very general question

"Where do you find your voice?"

which is a joke for a pirate hacker
like Kathy Acker
who published books with titles
like *Don Quixote: Which Was a Dream*
Blood and Guts in High School
and *Pussy, King of the Pirates*

and so without being rude she replied
"What voice? I just steal shit"

which was kind of funny given the fact
that *shit* is one of the seven words
the comedian George Carlin made fun of
when talking about the Seven Dirty Words
the Federal Communications Commission
ruled you can *never* say over the airwaves

(KGNU did not lose their license over this)

remixologically inhabit -- / -- the social voice -- / -- signature style

For the live A/V artist who is continually
remixing found footage with personal video data

with computer-generated imagery
with memories of various location shoots
with metempsychotic flashbacks of
images never rendered before

meaning has a way of smudging
into the experiential event itself
and is as difficult to cherrypick
as it is to waft through endless
tracks of performance writing
and locate the artist's voice

Where is the artist's voice?

("What voice? I just steal shit.")

I first came into contact with my so-called voice
when I was in an experimental sound art ensemble
whose name said it all:

Dogma Hum

Dogma Hum had a rotating crew of
about five or six members of which
I was considered the group's lead vocalist

although back in the day
we may have referred to my role
as *performance poet* or *spoken word artist*
but these terms do not adequately describe
my contribution either since I was also
resident novelist and theory-slut
as well as budding net artist (soon to bloom)
always sampling from and mixing in ideas
at times exact words and phrases
from other artists who were influencing me
while in the midst of performing my improvisational talking

I say *talking* because I could not sing
not in the way Frank Sinatra or Ella Fitzgerald
or John and Paul and George could sing
(Ringo could never sing either, could he?)
and so this talk-rock sound art ensemble
that was embodied in the group dynamic
known to some (not many) as Dogma Hum
was not really being *led* by my vocals

My so-called voice was just more data
more live and totally ready-for-manipulation
source material awaiting digital effects processing
and whether it was the grain of the sound
or the gram of the potential meaning
or the rhetorical quality of grain and gram
remixed in *the measure of my delivery*
no longer mattered

What mattered was *the matter itself*
(that trajectory of nervous energy
where the source of unconscious readiness potential
encountered the physiological *matériel*
and the persuasive quality of grain and gram
spasmodically improvising
method over madness
would project my unconscious buzzing
even as the madness would break through
porous metaphors of structure
and deliver the occasional prophetic illumination
in its stead)

My fascination at the time was not words
although I needed some data to play with
and had endless scraps of paper
with anarcho-existentialist markings on them
somehow capturing the lossy bits of
what Acker once referred to as

this other world within the dream
that my body language was circulating in

(these almost hieroglyphic drawings
masquerading as meaning-laden words
could trigger unexpected noise performances
including the most popular track we composed
the title of which referred to these mental jottings
as "Somnambulistic Chickenscratch")

My real fascination was with the digital effects processor
that would change the so-called grain of my voice
into something other than I knew it to be
and that when remixed with my own supposed voice
the one that we would generally call "natural"
but that is really a *pigment* of our imagination
(one instrumental data stream among many
ready for instantaneous postproduction)
created a new processual version of "me"
just like writing my novels created
new processual versions of "me"

which then led me to unexpected questions
like "What am I when writing my fictions?
Some kind of digital effects processor?"

(Maybe the remixologist is a contemporary
version of Whitman's "body electric"
but loaded with customized artist-apparatus filters
never quite put into use before now)

Especially given the fact that my *forte*
if you can call this sort of a thing a *forte*
is my ability to selectively sample
from the sea of source material
I am biologically swimming in
and spontaneously discovering new uses for

in my on-the-fly remixes no matter what medium
I happen to be working in (fiction, photography,
cinema/video, dance, performance art, spoken word, etc.)

Keeping this in mind
could it be said that my voice
has nothing to do with the sounds
I make while vocalizing
but rather has *everything* to do with
the unique way I remixologically inhabit
the source material I sample from
while unconsciously projecting
the next version of "me"
in whatever new performance event
I happen to be activated in?

No—you'll never hear my digital voice

You'll feel it as it finds its way
into your own body language
in hopes of unconsciously triggering
the next version of "you"

In fact I look back at my relationship
to voice *per se* and realize that
there is *no voice to speak of*
and must self-reflexively point out
that even this semi-rant wanting to be
poetry narrative philosophy theory memoir
is really a conversational mix sampling heavily
from the styles of many other artists
like David Antin Frank O'Hara Spaulding Gray

i.e. the so-called talk-poets
or *performativity-inclined*
processual agents of projective verse
whose "authority" (loose term used

by poet Michael Davidson)
"derives from an ability to instantiate
physiological and psychological states
through highly gestural lineation
and by the treatment of the page
as a 'field' for action"[1]

Remixologists move off of the page *per se*
and reconfigure what we used to call *the poet*
into an affective agent of live A/V performance
whom on (unconsciously) becoming a postproduction medium
intersubjectively jams within the autohallucinatory mix of
the artificial intelligentsia they *play-to-play* in

(without even thinking about it
I just co-produced that last line
with the avant-garde jazz artist Ornette Coleman
who recently said "I didn't know you had to learn
to play, I thought you had to *play* to play")[2]

[Artist's aside: Can one perform an (anti-authorial? creative? remixological?) function within an optimum *economy of motion*, one that wastes no
time-movement? I ask this because sometimes writing out an artist's poetics
itself feels like wasted motion as it takes away from the more primary bursts
of creativity immersed in its own potential. What's a digital artist/avant-
writer/live A/V performer to do?

Sustaining my optimum *economy of motion*—something athletes, particularly runners, are aware of, as is Kung Fu legend Bruce Lee—is part of a life-
long practice. Interestingly enough, it's damn near impossible to physically
train yourself to perform with optimum economy of motion (unless you're
Lance Armstrong, in which case you can improve your efficiency one percent a year over seven years). In general, fluid economy of motion is most
likely something that you are born with, the *with* in this case being not
just physical advantage but possibly intuitive or unconscious advantage
too (though that's just my projection—there is no scientific data available
to prove the point).]

The Philosopher

In his book *Artist of Life*, Bruce Lee writes that his martial arts practice is driven by an ECONOMY OF FORM in relation to an ECONOMY OF MOTION (all caps are his):

The less confident we are in ourselves, the less we are in touch with ourselves and the world, the more we want to control.

NOW = EXPERIENCE = AWARENESS = REALITY

Gestalt therapy = phenomenological approach (awareness of what is) + behavioral approach (behavior in the now)[3]

Lee tells us that we need to initiate progressive, harmonious forward motion that minimizes wasted movement while perfecting technique (*embodying praxis*) but that we still must "use variety" (or, in the terminology of this artist essay, we must develop multiple and hybridized styles of remixological practice).

In his handwritten notes on Gestalt Therapy, the martial artist Lee writes:

Once you have a character, you have developed a rigid SYSTEM. Your behavior becomes petrified, predictable, and you lose your ability to cope freely with the world with all your resources. You are predetermined just to cope with events in one way, namely, as your character prescribes. So it seems a paradox when I say that the richest person, the most productive, creative person, is a person who has NO CHARACTER.

If I were to remixologically inhabit the "voice" of Lee while writing out his martial arts theory, I would say:

Once you have a voice, you have developed a rigid SYSTEM. Your behavior becomes repetitive, predictable, and you lose your ability to sample freely from and interact with the world with all of your resources. You are predetermined just to act within social networking and performance events in one way, namely, as your predetermined voice prescribes. So it seems a paradox when I say that the most interesting artist, the most productive, creative persona, is one who has NO VOICE.

My sense is that the reasons why many artists, novelists, poets, and performers still take on the role of philosopher or timely rhetorician are many, but none of them have to do with refining their voice. To be clear, this is not an attempt to over-academicize types of artistic practice, or if it is coming across as that, then please, stop me right now before it's too late. Rather, this kind of autocannibalizing discourse generally evolves as a way to pragmatically take into account why our shared and primary bursts of creativity immersed in their own aesthetic potential exist in the first place and how they may relate to the intuitive discovery of new forms of knowledge that grow out of what has been remixologically inhabited in the past as part of the Renewable Tradition. If this sounds similar to a zen-like remix of Alfred North Whitehead's *process theory of organisms* while bringing to mind his introduction of the word (and idea/theory behind) *creativity* into the philosophical lexicon, then so be it.[4]

Now like Bruce Lee who advises us
that the most creative person imaginable
is one who has absolutely NO CHARACTER
(and in my remix consequently NO VOICE)
I have never been one who invests much
in concepts of self or character per se
opting for *flux personas* or even
the idea of an erotically charged
fictional decharacterization of said self
(said who?)

fictional decharacterization --/-- novel consequent --/-- freedom to compose

"An intense experience is an aesthetic fact,"
writes Whitehead in *Process and Reality*
and then he begins to lay down
some "categoreal conditions" as he calls them
that are to be generalized "from aesthetic laws
in particular arts"

He samples from *Religion in the Making*
two of these conditions / aesthetic laws
and remixes them into *Process and Reality*:

1. *The novel consequent must be graded in relevance so as to preserve some identity of the character with the ground.*

2. *The novel consequent must be graded in relevance so as to preserve some contrast with the ground in respect to that same ground of character.* [5]

These two principles (he goes on to say)
are derived from the doctrine (what doctrine?) that
"an actual fact is a fact of aesthetic experience.
All aesthetic experience is feeling arising
out of the realization of contrast under identity."[6]

Looking back at my possible reading of this excerpt
when I first encountered it as a teenager
during the late '70s and into the early '80s
I can see where I would have been attracted
to Whitehead's focus on intense aesthetic experiences
and his high valuation of novelty as a way to generate
fluctuating forms of identity/characterization
that would morph the "actual entity" into pools of
differential feelings sinking and swimming
with the flow of whatever life rhythm
they may have been inventing as part of their
ongoing aesthetic practice (he would call this
a "religion in the making" but I would not buy into it
and thought of it as something more akin to
the freedom to compose a Life Style Practice
even as I started using my body as an it-thing
to be guinea-pigged for an ongoing research project
lending itself to all manner of future observation and data collection)

Remixologically speaking
"Religion in the Making"
circa 1979–1980
became for me something like
"Art in the Making"

How was I to become an artist
acting on whatever ground was available
unless I made it up from scratch?

Vito Acconci once wrote:

if I specialize in a medium, then I would be fixing a ground for myself, a ground I
would have to be digging myself out of, constantly, as one medium was substituted

or another—so, then instead of turning toward 'ground' I would shift my attention and turn to 'instrument,' I would focus on myself as the instrument that acted whatever ground was, from time to time, available.[7]

Is this what we mean by "grounding out"?

What is the relationship between the instrument
acting on whatever ground is available
and the novelty generator arising out of
the realization of contrast under identity?

Even today this "Art in the Making"
becomes something different yet again
let's call it (for lack of better)
"Life in the Making"
(a total cliché for sure, one I adore
especially after having pursued a Life Style Practice
for almost three decades across ten planets
and forty galaxies and seventy blood transfusions)

Given all of the above
would it not make utter sense that the biosphere
would be the next best place for me to unravel
my free flow sensations of intense aesthetic experience
especially since the "actual entity" of the it-thing body
moonlighting as a "novelty generator" hacking the Real
is always operating in *asynchronous realtime*?

Remixing Whitehead's "categoreal conditions"
with Acconci's instrumental quote above
a novel version of the aesthetic law
for "New Media Artists in the Making" would read:

1. The novelty generator must be valued in relation to their ability to position the energy [source material] they create with the ground they act on while performing their latest remix.

2. The novelty generator must be valued in relation to their ability to position some contrasting energy [source material] with the ground in respect to the already existing energy [source material] they are sampling from while performing their latest remix.

novelty generator — / — creative momentum — / — perpetual postproduction

Remixology samples from Whitehead when he says
"Creativity is the principle of *novelty*"
a *conditioned* indetermination
that morphs into a *real* potentiality
spurring on the further advance of
our ongoing creative momentum
via an applied aesthetics that both manipulates
and is unquestionably manipulated *by*
the environment that each novel situation
presents to us in its state of immediacy

This "advance" garde of Creativity itself
in pursuit of transmuting aesthetic moments
creates a physical momentum
formally felt as an ongoing satisfaction
within an optimum *economy of motion*
and is triggered by the intensity of experience
which in itself becomes an aesthetic fact
and informs "the production of novel togetherness"

The "production of novel togetherness"
(as Whitehead refers to it)
is the ultimate notion embodied in
the term *concrescence* (where the many
become one and are increased by one)

An artist role-playing a mathematician
who aligns his avant-garde practice
with the entrepreneurial spirit of an antiacademic
looking to hurdle impenetrable institutions
in a series of single bounds (still binding)
might formulate it as such:

M = Many
One = Fluid Singularity

1 = Remix-in-Process

and conclude

M = One + 1 (always becoming)

The casual dropping of the parenthetical
"always becoming" signals a break away
from what others might call "total togetherness"
and instead highlights how Whitehead's
"production of novel togetherness"
advancing into the future of now
is really what it means for artist-mediums
to live in perpetual postproduction
(a non-totalizing experience)

Always becoming a postproduction medium
is what it means to be aesthetically networked
(to tweak synaptic knobs while spinning)
(to customize artist-apparatus filters
as part of an hallucinatory achievement)
(to embody creative synthesis *in praxis*
while intersubjectively jamming with the autopoietic
environment I call the *artificial intelligentsia)*

In my book *META/DATA*[8] I suggest that we are all *born*
avant-garde (that it is our natural birthright)
but that one of the cruel ironies of being
a living breathing postproduction medium
in an age of super-late turbocharged capitalism
is that the environment that produces innovation
is now also the environment that kills creativity

This sets up an epic struggle for artist-mediums
whose ongoing satisfaction of formally felt experience
is co-dependent on their being able to intuitively
generate emergent forms of novelty ("Creativity itself")

The Professor

And where is Professor VJ in
all of this remixological role-playing?

Does The Professor even have
a voice worth sharing here?

 "I am losing my voice"

(something says)

(writes)

(transcribes)

(codifies)

(autogenerates)

"and loving every minute of it
because as I lose it
I find more connectivity
to what shapes my intuition"

This is the voice of intuition
improvising its presence
in states of perpetual postproduction
(perpetually perishing while "making it new")

How does the voice of intuition manifest itself?

Professor VJ[9] sees and hears it everywhere
even though it's not necessarily something
that you can literally see or hear
maybe it would be better to say
he has felt it form inside of him
and has become intimate with the rhythm of

its projections as he acts on
whatever ground is available

"I have watched it [*intuition*] change shape
a kind of embodied yet amorphous shape-shifting
vector (a magnitude with *direction*)
that has metamediumistically stimulated me
to tap into my ongoing processual relayerings
forming a pattern of energetic transmissions
between all of the intense aesthetic experiences
I have mutated myself through as
a *just-in-time* postproduction medium
(the creative advance of novelty *embodied*)
and so it seems only right that
I would [temporarily] end this advance into
novel forms of creative remixology
by turning to Whitehead again
feeding off of his word flesh
stealing his voice
('What voice? I just steal shit')
as would any hungry parasite so ravenous
they can no longer speak for themselves
and are hoping to locate renewable energy sources
in the production of novel togetherness."

Thus the "production of novel togetherness" is the ultimate notion embodied in the term concrescence. These ultimate notions of "production of novelty" and "concrete togetherness" are inexplicable either in terms of higher universals or in terms of the components participating in the concrescence. The analysis of the components abstracts from the concrescence. The sole appeal is to intuition.[10]

Notes

1. Hazel Smith, *Hyperscapes in the Poetry of Frank O'Hara: Difference, Homosexuality, Topography* (Liverpool: Liverpool University Press, 2000), 141.

2. Andrew Purcell, "Free Radical," *The Guardian*, June 29, 2007. http://www.guardian.co.uk/music/2007/jun/29/jazz.urban. Accessed June 30, 2009.

3. Bruce Lee, *Artist of Life* (North Clarendon: Tuttle Publishing, 2001), 80.

4. Alfred North Whitehead, *Process and Reality: An Essay in Cosmology* (New York: Simon and Schuster, 1979, revised edition).

5. Alfred North Whitehead, *Religion in the Making: Lowell Lectures 1926* (New York: Fordham University Press, 1996, revised edition), 115.

6. Ibid.

7. Vito Acconci, in *Theories and Documents of Contemporary Art: A Sourcebook of Artists' Writings*, edited by Kristine Stiles and Peter Howard Selz (Berkeley: University of California Press, 1996), 759.

8. Mark Amerika, *META/DATA: A Digital Poetics* (Cambridge, A: MIT Press, 2007).

9. *Professor VJ* blog, http://professorvj.blogspot.com.

10. Whitehead, *Process and Reality,* 21–22.

III   Reanimating VOICE

This section focuses on mainstream media such as recorded music, films and computer games. In this context, voice as "character" reappears, and the voice is often seen as reintroducing an element of authentic humanity in a world cluttered with machine-born artifacts and animations.

Ross Gibson starts by showing that, to some extent, Jamaican music prefigured the digital, making copious use of remixing, sound "sweetening," and modular compositional techniques that rely on relational databases. But the Jamaican producers routinely abjured the clean sound that digital recording affords; indeed, they tended to deliberately introduce gramophonic "crackle" and "analog decay." However, once the Jamaican studios were refitted with digital gear, the "processed" voice was usually rejected: the voice had to sound "real," meaning that it had to sound like a traditional analog recording of a real-time event. The voice had to "bounce untrammeled across a digital environment composed of shining surfaces and slippery circuits." Gibson then goes on to discuss artists such as Kode 9, representatives of the next generation in this tradition, those who were "born digital."

Isabelle Arvers provides an historically, technically, and theoretically informative introduction to the world of machinima, already briefly encountered in Neumark's chapter. In this context, too, the voice is deployed to "give an as if not digital feel to the digital world," in fictional as well as in nonfictional genres, such as documentaries, in which the sound of interviews can be lip-synched to game characters. Discussing the machinima makers' production techniques as well as the content of a range of machinima, Arvers explores voice as "the human side of the virtual game environment," working both in tension with and to expand the possibilities of game worlds.

Helen Macallan, a film scholar, and Andrew Plain, a film sound designer, explore the use of new voice technologies in film sound design, using a wealth of examples, for some of which Plain was the sound designer. They show that it is only in computer animation that the affordances of 3D sound are fully used, allowing voices to travel to space. In other films, 3D technology is used more sparingly, and always narratively motivated—for instance, to signify "disorientation" or "unreality." The same applies to voice processing technology. It too is used relatively sparingly and always motivated in terms of characterization, or in terms of some interpretation of the dramatic action. The chapter's approach to voice provides important new understandings of film sound.

Mark Ward's chapter discusses similar themes in relation to computer games, including an engaging interview with computer game sound designer Emily Ridgway. He examines how games use voices to coach players through the game ("Finish him!" or "You're awesome!") and how computer game sound designers (as also signaled in Arvers's chapter) prefer voices to insinuate and integrate emotions familiar from the world that prevails nearby the game's world.

Axel Stockburger's chapter further elaborates these points, with reference to a wide range of games. Stressing the different functions of the voice in games (and paying attention also to multiple-player games) he also signals the prevalence of nonlinguistic sounds—screams, gurgles, sighs, and so on—enriching a theme in the work of many of the artists described in the preceding section.

11   Carbon and Silicon

Ross Gibson

This chapter examines some shifts in the representation of the human voice—that most studied and palpable of noises—in digitally designed music during the past thirty years. With producers and engineers now using precise digital technology to select, separate, copy, and conjoin all the portions of their compositions, it stands to reason that the capture, processing, and placement of the human voice must have undergone significant change since the introduction of the computer-based systems. For example, one presumes that vocal scoring and performance must have been affected by the fact that a theoretically endless number of subtracks and partial phrases can now be finessed, linked, and layered using postproduction programs that cause no inherent deterioration of sound fidelity from copy to copy. Indeed, it is valid to ask: with digital technology now enabling entire soundscapes to be constructed without any living person actually addressing a microphone in a habitable space, what use is the voice? Or more exactly, what use is the vocal performer?

Against the tide of this quandary, however, there has been no diminution of voice-based compositions in all forms of music, from avant garde through to popular. So, the questions keep pushing forward. In the myriad compositions that use voice tracks, what qualities of utterance are typically emphasized or altered as producers drag and drop vocal recordings and samples into a sonic matrix that is predisposed to be machine-accurate, "lossless," "dirt-free," and susceptible to endless polish? In short, after more than twenty years of widespread digital audio productions, what have we learned about the voice, about the technology, and about music?

For reasons that will become apparent soon enough, I want to start addressing these questions by examining a 1975 composition called "Version

Dub."[1] Created with analog gear but prescient about how the digital future could sound, "Version Dub" is just one example from the thousands of compositions that were issued by the studio of King Tubby, who was one of the four or five Jamaican artists who have unarguably shaped global music during the past forty years. My contention is that in Tubby's aesthetic, we can find guidance about the structure of music, about the organics of nature, about the mechanics of technologized culture.

In less than three minutes, "Version Dub" builds a world, sets a stage, and on that stage arrays a set of powerful feelings and propounds a subtle argument about history and art and the place of subjects (be they vociferous or voiceless) within the legacy of colonialism and slavery. The song propounds these arguments and then, to the extent that it is a *version*, it is offered to the audience, thereby inviting an engaged response, a new iteration that will motivate the next invocation of the tune in an interactive feedback system of reception, criticism, appropriation, and new creation.

Herein lies one other reason for starting the chapter with this example: 1970s Jamaican music culture was behaving "digitally" well before the digital technology became readily available. It worked like this. Across Jamaica every week, popular dances were blasted with competing sound systems purveying new tunes in a high-churn commerce that encouraged the rapid turnover of songs and answer-songs, to the extent that a dozen versions of a tune might get issued by several producers over a cycle encompassing a testy few weeks of sound clashes and record-releases. In these social and commercial conditions, we have a small, highly productive industry constantly replenishing, accessing, iterating, and reiterating its assets with reference to a "database" of component and convergent information. Prescient of the "plunderphonics" and Creative Commons movements that have swept through Western culture in the past decade, the Jamaican system treated songs as resources that were practically communal, malleable, and "open source" in their provenance. Accordingly, producers had little reticence about pulling apart the constituent elements of recordings— voices included—then copying and effects-treating them prior to recombining the "purloined" details into new iterations that would themselves be cannibalized by the next interactive respondents. Indeed, producers would happily plunder their own back catalog as well, taking the opportunity to assemble musical hotrods out of previous tracks, mutating existing artifacts in a rapidly evolving bloom of productivity that, in retrospect, is dizzying to comprehend. Tubby worked this way, prodigiously, for more than a decade of invention and innovation.

Cueing Tubby's "Version Dub," we hear the tune commence with a quiet cymbal stutter that sounds like wind agitating seedy gourds hanging off jungle vines. This dry rattle lasts exactly one second before it gets settled by electric guitar that is highly reverberant, almost pedal steel, but more peppy, with jazz tonics that stretch singing over a sonic bed of crackly distortion pushing up through the top registers. This crackle is no accident or problem in the mix. It is meant to be there. It might be the inserted sound of a stylus grooving on degraded vinyl or it might be grain in the ferrous oxide of magnetic tape that has been deliberately dubbed and overdubbed and amplified a dozen times or more until the producer has heard and logged the "trouble" he has in mind. There is wow and flutter in there, too—purposefully included. As soon as we have understood all this, we get a few beats more of the grit, and then we hear some drawly, massed brass instruments blowing underneath the guitar, pushing between the plucked strings and the crackle. And now a bass line settles in—solid, dry, no reverb in this last burr of the sound.

Thus with the tune only twenty seconds old, Tubby has already sketched out a space for us: the reverb accords this sonic world dimensions with audible boundaries, the crackle puts a dirty ground under our feet, the bass gives a dependable schedule and encourages trust that this ground will hold, while now and then the cymbals agitate and the horns blow a flitting breeze to measure the atmospheric pressure. This world is an aural island of some kind, with edges, resonance, humidity, and a localized sense of time and tone.

But is the island populated? Yes! There it is at the thirty-second mark: a little falsetto vocal gulp. An emotional utterance rather than a semantic statement, this gulp anticipates Michael Jackson's yelps in "Billie Jean" but also harks way back to African singing techniques as well as Caribbean church music and early American R&B crooners like Sonny Til from the Orioles.[2] Clearly, the human voice has a place in Tubby's world. Into his ever-thickening soundscape, he has dropped this startling ululation by Yabby You, a vocalist renowned for silky melodies that smuggle politically and spiritually "conscious" messages across to the local "sufferahs." The sound might be anguish or it might be rapture. Of course, in Tubby's world it is both; it is complementary as well as contradictory.

Then, as if in response to Yabby's call, we get a barely audible and deliberately thin and degraded skerrick of choral singing—perhaps it is an ensemble of singers, or perhaps it is one voice copied multiple times upon itself to form a slightly outphased harmonic. This sound is not words you can decipher; rather it is a vocalized, aestheticized echo that has been conjured and shaped in response to the first voice. These "answering" voices are a long way back in the mix, as if coming from across a river, off in a valley yonder, or drifting over the sea from out past the horizon. The distant call wafts a couple more times and then Tubby pulls all the environing sound down almost to zero for a moment; in this lull, he lets the faraway voices register unchallenged, as if they are carried on a pushing breeze or in a momentary wave of radio transmission.

Only fifty seconds into the song now, we have an aesthetic model of Jamaica—not just the geography, ecology, and atmosphere of the island but also its history and ideology. We have a model of this place where absence is a defining feature, where influences drift in partially and perennially over the horizon, where radio programs come and go from Florida, Cuba, and the coast of Texas. In this place of traces, the ancient indigenes have long been obliterated and the contemporary inhabitants are migrants always searching for orientation, always harking back in memory to some elsewhere in their heads even as they know that *this place here* is their lot now, that they have no other home to make but here.

With the aesthetics of seepage and submergence that define dub music, we hear a testament to the silence, exile, and cunning that often define a migrant's life. In his perceptive study of "soundscapes and shattered songs in Jamaican reggae," Michael Veal offers a different, arresting way to understand this same idea, proposing that we think of dub as a strain of magical realism. "The otherworldly strain in dub partially evokes an idealized, precolonial African utopia," Veal declares.[3] As for the reverberating calls and echoic bounces, he adds, we can hear in them "the intertwined experiences of exile and nostalgia."[4] Certainly these experiences are audible in "Version Dub." One and a half minutes into the song, the "sound weather" that Tubby has been conjuring finds its full, stealthy shape. And straight away the song begins to form its finish. The distant voices are quickly engulfed again by the drums and horns, louder than ever, making a swell of larger elements washing over and obscuring the human presence in this world of restless sound.

Bringing the tune home now, Tubby waits for the symphonics to lull once more, wavelike, before cueing the humanity one last time. The voice resurfaces and the guitar, horns, and drums slowly ebb with the diminishing vocals until the entire composition goes down to a kind of sun-setting silence.

What strengthens, as the song lopes toward its conclusion, is the sense of a sonic island, so closely and sensually modeled on an actual island. From the reverb, we can estimate the scope of the world. From the crackle, we get a haptic sense of how that world might grip. From the emerging and submerging insinuations of the different melodies, we get a sense of the dynamics flushing through the world that Tubby is witnessing. The impact of the human voice is light but emphatic in this interlaced environment. Enveloping the human timbre with manufactured sound, the steady bass, the plangent brass, and the syncopated drums, all commingle and grow, as does the crackle, signal distortion, and static. It's as if we're left hearing an exquisite abstraction of the geography and fecundity of Tubby's kingdom.

In this way, "Version Dub" is a summation of an insular Rastafarian ontology. But to the extent that the song refers to the drift and decay of radio transmissions emanating from Florida and Cuba, it's also a quick lesson in international pragmatics. Like a condensed guide to survival in a postcolonial world, the tune offers a sensory commentary on the memory waste and institutional forces that abrade any migrant's attempt to find a home or a voice in any place, new or old, where one might establish an identity founded not on origins but on ingenuity and persistence.

Bringing our attention back to the waning music of "Version Dub," we understand somewhere in our feelings (rather than immediately in our intellection) that we have been hearing a gorgeous thesis about how the immigrant consciousness is inevitably a variable work in progress, something that has to be asserted and endlessly earned and performed moment by moment in negotiation with prevailing conditions. Not autochthonous or "grounded" in a homeland, the immigrant cannot rely on myths that celebrate how people can *arise* from the new, hosting soil; instead the immigrant must *arrive* and *survive* in a place where no birthright is ready-made. Hence the defining sense of erasure and incompletion in dub, the sense of a musical form in which utterance competes with voicelessness, where agency contends with anonymity. And hence the "x-ray" quality of this music, the way it is built from traces and underlying hints, the way it features wastage, submergence, removal and "cysted" fragments in its composition, the way it is the sound of the spaces left when a place is purged of all but its most basic reference points.[5]

Finally, having gathered all these sonic ideas and structural relationships in the form of aesthetical sensations rather than as grammatical disquisition, Tubby lets the magical island of "Version Dub" float away from us. But we carry impressions of it with us, as the sound abates while the crackle and bass persist to the last beat. We realize that the "dirt" in the sound is strangely comforting, because it is grounding, because it gives the music some organic thickness, something to touch and inhabit, spare as it is.

In summary, therefore, two factors help "Version Dub" feel connected to our lived experience: (a) the crackle or dirt in the production and (b) the presence of the voices struggling to be registered amidst the tune's sonic bluster. These factors affect the listener's holistic, multisensory interpretation of the recording, appealing not only to the head but also to the heart and skin, giving the listener an aesthetic feeling rather than a spelled out message. Tropical and topical, the music generates a felt impression of the conditions of migrancy in the aftermath of the slave economy that initiated modern Jamaica. More than an abstract thesis, the music is an *aesthetic* proposition (something *perceptible by the several senses*) concerning Jamaica and all that the island represents as a postcolonial locale.

The startling thing about Tubby's productions is how he was practicing digital culture even before the technology was readily available. Tubby understood that the composition and appreciation of music is a process of assemblage—iteration after iteration—of endlessly negotiable elements drawn momentarily from relational repositories; on a customized mixing desk that remains legendary, Tubby conjoined all his elements in experimental versions of compositions so that he could ascertain their effect, and then he could disintegrate that version so that another could then be essayed and offered to critically responsive audiences whose appetite and sophistication are prodigious, schooled as the people are in sound clashes and dances that get staged several nights every week. Thinking digitally before the world was digital, Tubby accepted that his analog gear could not achieve "lossless" multiple copying, but undeterred, he compiled his databases of ever-iterating possibilities anyway. Each painstaking new copy introduced a degradation into the substrate sound of each newly iterated track. Dirt built upon dirt, in a situation that you would think unworkable.

But Tubby found a way to give this degradation great aesthetic and seman-tic value. Conceptually digital as Tubby's dubs were in his mind, the analog technology in his studio guaranteed that Tubby's momentous composi-tions were built on dirt. It would take a while for younger producers to understand the value of this degradation, how this dirt could be gold.

Even though computer encoding and compositing would eventually make the copy-and-layer processes of dub exponentially easier than it had been in the 1970s when Tubby was in his prime, the new "born-digital" generation of "first-world" producers who came after Tubby would need several years to understand how effective it was to sully the shiny sound of the ones and zeroes. More slowly than in Jamaica, this creative evolution would happen at digital desks in different parts of the "developed" world, especially in Germany and Britain during the late 1980s. Fans espouse their own favorites, but in Germany it was the musicians, engineers, and pro-ducers in Kraftwerk and Can who changed the sound of popular music. In Britain, there were innovators like Trevor Horn and Brian Eno.

Meanwhile, years ahead of these more famous trendsetters, back in the poverty-struck sheds and yards of Kingston, the next wave of Jamaican pro-ducers were working in the aftermath of Tubby's great innovations to make yet another set of breakthroughs, this time using the first generation of low-fi digital equipment, particularly the Casio keyboard. And this time, with computers now available to them, it was the startling decisions that the Jamaican producers made concerning the treatment of their singers' voices that showed the world the next phase of the future.

Jamaican producers "went digital," famously, with the creation of *the* definitive "digital rhythm," a basic track that revolutionized reggae exactly when it needed an upheaval—during the gloomy paralysis after Bob Mar-ley's death. In 1985 a record came out of Prince Jammy's studio. Called "Under Me Sleng Teng," the song features the rapid fire voice of Wayne Smith intoning over a slowed and treated rhythm track extracted from a Casio MT-40 keyboard. The rhythm—locally this basic track is always called a "riddim"—is all machine. It is robotic and bloodless but driving and intriguingly alien, full of the allure of an other world. (This robot sound is part of a history of science fiction and outer-space fantasies that have ener-gized African-American music for at least half a century. But the sci-fi sound is a topic for another book.[6]) The *voice* on "Sleng Teng," in contrast to the song's inorganic *rhythm*, has been recorded so that it sounds immediate, like a perfect analog of a singer toasting in a yard or a dancehall, not tampered by any obvious studio machining other than some slight, old-style reverb. At the time, this approach was a surprise. As computers were starting to turn up in Kingston studios, commentators had presumed that the producers would apply the new digital processes to the *singers*, to work some magic on the element that seemed to be so grievously missing now that Marley was gone. Thus while everyone expected the Jamaican music scene to work to its strength by continuing to rely on the musical dexterity of the supremely accomplished studio musicians who were abounding in Kingston, Jammy reversed the logic and completely digitized the environment that the voice rode over, thereby leaving the singers untreated by the digital innovations.

In retrospect, it makes good economic sense for a producer to curtail the salaries of so many session employees and to let a tireless machine deliver the mass of the work while a single paycheck goes out to the singer at the microphone. But there was another insight that Jammy snared immediately: the voice can bring humanity to a machine world that needs the comfort of blood-warmth. By parlaying a relationship between the "organic" voice track and the electronic rhythm, Jammy could offer a triumphant version of everyday experience in an increasingly coded world of global informatics and economics. In the overlay of warm voice on cool machine, of carbon on silicon, listeners could hear their own contemporary world being offered to them—upbeat, aesthetically considered, and refined. Audiences could sense the relevance and the consolation of the new sound.

Whereas Tubby's dubs sound like the sonic model of a postcolonial island, Jammy's songs let the Kingston singers ride on the digital sound waves so that they sound like what they usually were—hustlers from the street who have learned how to make their way in a boundless global network, doing good business by virtue of their peculiar bodily energy allied to the intellectual resilience and ingenuity that sounded through their voices. We hear Jamaica in both songs—in "Version Dub" and "Sleng Teng," ten years apart—but the engulfing world is radically transformed in the later song. In "Version Dub," Yabby You's mostly submerged voice inkles through an environing soundscape that is tangled and organic. In "Sleng Teng," Wayne Smith's unremitting voice bounces untrammeled across a different world, across a digital environment composed of shiny surfaces and slippery circuits. For Tubby, the dirt is in the world and the voice rubs into it, living with the grit; for Jammy, the world is a cool metallic circuit board that has to be warmed up by the voice of a living and breathing yard-boy improvising his way over quick flows of pressure delivered as information. Tubby's world is magic realist; Jammy's is pragmatic fantasist.

The voice in "Sleng Teng" is still that of a migrant. But whereas Yabby You is inside a Caribbean jungle singing an exile's call and yearning for Mother Africa, Smith is a footloose urban trickster who lives by the pulsing quickness of his wits and his smart mouth as he negotiates a vast world of replicants that have been dumped out of some new mothership of global commerce. Both voices have a pronounced *yearning* in them, a yearning to be composed, to be well accommodated in the environment where the singer can render himself functional, where the singer can make a hostile world habitable by lulling it with his voice. Both times, the yearning touches the listener's heart. The voice in each track has been recorded so that you think: "someone was here, completely embodied, warm and breathing; someone prevailed in this world, and this song remembers him."[7] So, for all their radical differences, for all the changes in the intricately produced environment that hosts each voice, these two songs rely on and celebrate the bodily presence of the singer, the minimally effected and directly *recorded* presence of the singer.

This word "record" is a key to understanding the status of the voice in any musical composition, especially when the voice is placed within a digital soundscape. "To record" means literally "to bring back to the heart." It is from the root that makes "cardiac" and "coronary" in English, makes "corazon" in Spanish, and makes "coeur" in French. A recorded voice—particularly if it is processed without any emphasized special effects—sounds as if it comes from the flesh of the utterer and goes into and through the flesh of the listener. This is not to insist that there is anything ineffably organic about something so machine-processed as a recorded voice, regardless of whether the voice has been captured on analog or digital machinery. However, notwithstanding all the artificial manipulations that actually cause a recording to vibrate out of the cones and diaphragms of a loudspeaker, the voice can be made to sound "natural." If the voice is offered up as plausibly "present" in this way, as if it has come from a real, habitable space, then it brings strong connotations of direct, embodied access to experience. By replaying a seemingly uneffected voice, a producer can offer a phenomenological bass line: the voice can "say" that someone stood in front of a microphone, someone who was somewhat composed and bore witness to an aspect of lived experience in real space and time. One might gain access to the world through such a body. Hearing the recorded voice, the listener might project his or her own body into the constructed soundscape, thereby grasping some of the proposed world's dimensions and dynamics, thereby imagining personally and precisely how one could be "placed" in the world and how one might go through that particular world willingly.

While the digital innovations were sweeping through the Jamaican scene during the 1980s, the dub aesthetic was being transplanted and mutated in England so that versions of the music were spliced into a production scene that was radically different. Migration upon migration produced new cultural versions. In Great Britain, there were no yard dances; rather, there were pubs and clubs. And the business of music production and sales was emphatically more industrial and stratified, relying on record companies, marketing campaigns, television and radio schedules, and heavily invested recording and postproduction studios. This meant that anyone who could snag a record deal was then shunted into studios that were equipped with up-to-the-minute gear (as opposed to the low-fi and spot-soldered technologies that were stuffed into most of the Kingston studios).

Such comparative opulence had its advantages and disadvantages. Confronted with the utter "cleanliness" that is the "default standard" of digital sound programs, many musicians and producers shied away from the dirt-free aesthetic. In the standard computational sound, there was a kind of "weightlessness" that many artists wanted to counteract. Whereas the Jamaican producers simply allowed the "organic-sounding" voice to float over the robot world, thus making the singer into a sign of transcendence and triumph, the British producers tried to bed the voice down more into the gloom, thus making the singer a sign of some torpor or drugged-out disrhythmia and alienation within mother England.

During the early 1990s, a loose consortium of music performers, producers, and sound designers based in Bristol came to prominence partly by revamping the sound of 1970s Jamaican popular music. Sensing the polyglot jumble of their port town to be consonant with the plush multicultural blends in Jamaican music, Bristol producers such as Nellee Hooper and Tricky revisited the "versioning" strategies that had been pioneered by King Tubby, the original dub-reggae master. Finessing the music of contemporary artists such as Massive Attack and Portishead, the producers used digital equipment rather than the fabled analog contraptions that Tubby had originally invented in his Kingston workshop.

Simultaneously quoting and superseding the 1970s sound, but ignoring the digital approach of Kingston's "sleng teng generation," the Bristol artists found they were challenged as well as excited by the easy operability of the new digital equipment that filled their studios. Striving to replicate and intensify the emotions that oozed out of the old dub tracks, the Bristol crews needed to add something like digital dirt, decay, and sonic frailty to flavor the pristine sound, to encourage people to *care* somewhat about the noise environing the singers' voices. They discovered that their productions needed to refer to a world that listeners recognized as "real," a world that sounded as if it were suffused with human history, with chance, with inhabited spaces, with accidents and the right dose of chaos. Hence the famous stylus-in-the-groove paste that gets laid down at the start of a typical Portishead track; hence the smoky tang in the background "atmos" of most Massive Attack tracks.

This need for something other than digital clarity and all its manageable precision became especially pressing when the producers brought the human voice into the mix. It was in these moments that the dirty world really grounded the song. For example, when Beth Gibbons from Portishead leans toward the microphone and utters her near-traumatized but gorgeous tremolo, you hear someone just barely negotiating (rather than transcending) the globalizing world of preponderant technology. (So different, this, from the braggadocio blasting out of the Kingston dancehalls.) The "Bristol aesthetic" of the immersed voice persisted from late 1990s, when Portishead burst on the scene with two utterly distinctive albums, right up until a decade later when they returned with their third album.[8] The most telling track on that release is "Machine Gun," which features a riddim as robotic as the "sleng teng" juggernaut, but Gibbons still refuses Prince Jammy's and Wayne Smith's triumphalist strategy. Instead, she pushes her voice around, through and sometimes under the riddim. Yet again: silence, exile, cunning. And moments of exhaustion and melancholy. Here in Britain, where she should feel her birthright, Gibbons vocalizes a spiritual homelessness amidst a world gone digital, a world no longer organic or native in any way she was born to.

This dyad of "native" vs. "migrant" has mutated remarkably in the digital era. It is now completely valid to distinguish those who had the digital world come down upon them, from those who were "born digital." On the first side, we have Tubby, Jammy, Nellee Hooper and Portishead, all of them seeking to adapt the newly arrived digital world to their particular encounters with displacement even as they alter that world; on the other side, we have artists like the "post-grime" impresario Kode 9, who has grown up assuming that the digital sound and all its segmentable components are merely a part of the nature that he was born into.[9] Picking up the digital gear, the born-analog generations have sought out ways to accommodate their vocal carbon to an encompassing world of digital silicon, sometimes giving the voice a lighter, more slippery ascendancy (which is the "sleng teng" approach) and other times commingling the two elements in a conglomerate sound that speaks of withdrawal or lethargy or stealth (which is the approach of Portishead and Massive Attack and a hundred other blunted Blair-gen artists.) And then there are the younger, born-digital crews, who have tended to trust and incorporate the silicon, mostly behaving as if they believe that they have some computational element inside them along with carbon, that their voices are some alchemical alloy of both, that they are made of a new man-machine matter.

Kode 9's track "Sine," for example, is a startling testimony to how the grandchildren of King Tubby have mutated and evolved.[10] Like so many of Tubby's great works that came before it, "Sine" is a version song. It even commences with a showy mutation of one of Tubby's trademark echoic chords before rolling ominously along to remake Prince's "Sign of the Times" by cooking it in a transponder that alters its base elements, and particularly alters the voice (intoned by Daddi Gee), which is to say that Kode 9 seems to be from a generation that is finally prepared to use digital segmenting, compositing, and processing to get inside the human voice and make it sound *other* than organic, to give it the timbre of silicon without completely expunging the carbon. "Sine" slows down the Prince song to an extent where you almost swear you can hear the ones and zeroes computing, almost hear some otherworldly grain in the atmospherics that stand for the music out of which granular and electromagnetic-sounding vocal tones intermittently arise. And that's the main point: the voice *comes from* the digital ground. The voice and sound are digitally autochthonous. The "singer" sounds as if he was born digital, with a birthright of lossless migrancy in a world where everything can be copied and transposed, where the old definitions of homeland and exile, origin and trace are no longer relevant.

When this voice first turns up in "Sine," it has some human "mois-
ture" to it, but it also has machine in it. It is strung with digital interlacing
and drop-out that make the utterances equal with the "air" from which it
emerges. It is a voice that is all bits within quotes. Prince's original lyrics
get clipped and erased and granulated down to about thirty percent of their
original heft and flow. The language and the voice become immaterial,
which means that the utterances are *digital* and *embedded* in a silicon-based
world that Kode 9 has been born into, a world that is *natural* for him. This
bottomless place is home for Kode 9, and this reconfiguarable world is all
ground, all air, and all voice, potentially.

It has taken well-nigh thirty years to get the recorded voice to this juncture, where the avatar at the microphone is prepared to admit to being a
replicant, or more accurately a morphant, like the shiny T2 in James Cam-
eron's great sequel to *The Terminator*. No longer obliged to fly the flag for
analog citizens, the singer can ooze into the world and shift shape as the
need or urge arises. One can hear similar kinds of mutations in R&B "singing," such as the bravura performances that get constructed by producers
like Timbaland, from the vocals of artists like Missy Elliott.

But before heralding the dawn of the new age of the digital singer, we
should pause to note that for every Kode 9 or Missy Elliott, there are still
a thousand crooners purveying voices whose recorded qualities have persisted unchanged for one hundred years. In other words, at this moment,
barely a decade into the new millennium, there is still an overwhelming
craving for carbon-voiced singers who can reassure us that silicon life is still
subservient to a planet full of harmonic apes.

But the sines are everywhere, that the times are at last changing. And
copying. And versioning.

Notes

1. King Tubby with Yabby You, "Version Dub," *King Tubby's Prophecy of Dub* (Audio
CD, Blood and Fire Label, 2000, ASIN B000008481). "Version Dub" was first issued
in 1975.

2. Listen especially to Sonny Til's keening in "It's Too Soon to Know," *Sonny Til and
the Orioles, Greatest Hits* (Audio CD, Collectables Label, 1991).

3. Michael E. Veal, *Dub: Soundscapes and Shattered Songs in Jamaican Reggae* (Middletown, Conn.: Wesleyan University Press, 2007), 197.

4. Veal, *Dub*, 199.

5. Michael Veal acknowledges Luke Erlich and Lee Perry as the sources of the "x-ray" description. See Veal, *Dub*, 196.

6. For an introduction to this theme, see Kodwo Eshun, *More Brilliant than the Sun: Adventures in Sonic Fiction* (London: Quartet Books, 1998). See also Kevin Holm-Hudson, "Apocalyptic Otherness: Black Music and Extraterrestrial Identity in the Music of Magma," *Popular Music and Society* (26), 2003: 481–495.

7. Perhaps the most striking example of the "uneffected" voice remaining the reference tone in the Jamaican digital aesthetic is found in the opening of the song "Like Mountain" (1998) by the dancehall superstar Sizzla. To start the track, four times before the digital riddim kicks in, Sizzla intones a long, unadorned "Ohmmmmn." He's establishing his primacy and his priorities before all the circuitry fires up and makes an unholy racket until his own thundering and astonishing voice brings the righteous Jah message into and over all the iniquitous noise: "Like mountains round about Jerusalem/So is Emperor Selassie I/Around I and I, I and I, higher than/ Higher than high."

8. The first Portishead album, *Dummy*, was released in 1994, to be followed by the equally influential *Portishead* in 1997. *Third* was issued in early 2008.

9. Kode 9 is a Scotsman named Steve Goodman, who was born in the mid-1970s, when King Tubby was defining the "version dub" aesthetic by bending his analog gear to futuristic tasks. By the time Goodman was old enough to be DJ-ing and producing, the digital sound was already incumbent.

10. "Sine" is also known as "Sine of the Dub," featuring highly treated vocals from Daddi Gee. See Kode 9's album "Memories of the Future" (Hyperdub Label, 2006).

12   Cheats or Glitch?: Voice as a Game Modification in Machinima

Isabelle Arvers

Machinima is defined by Hugh Hancock (a machinima director and, more recently, the author of *Machinima for Dummies*) as "a technique of making films inside virtual realities." The word *machinima* mixes the idea of cinema, machine, and animation. It is the encounter between a film and a game, in which gamers become film directors. As a technique to produce films, machinima is a new cinematographic genre.

Voices in machinima appear as the human side of the virtual game environment. Behind the gamer's performance that produces characters' actions, dialogs create the sense and drama of the movie. Voices, through dialogs, songs, or voice-overs, also become game modifications, as they transform the original game function and offer a new set of meanings to the virtual realities initially created by game developers.

Background: Games and Machinima

A videogame is a means by which we learn to control the 21st century. By playing, we situate and understand ourselves as citizens of hyperactive electronic space.
—Justin Hall

Video and computer games are the major entertainment industry in the twenty-first century, more popular than cinema and the music industries. For the new generation, this interaction between a machine and a human body even takes the place of another powerful mass medium—television. Michael Stora, a French psychoanalyst who uses video games to treat autistic patients, says: "Playing time is a pleasure time. It is a time where we can take a revenge on the images and manipulate them as they manipulated us before."[3] However, although games do involve interaction, there is still an element of passive consumption, entertainment, and passing time in these digital media. During play, one often loses the notion of time: we wander in a virtual world fighting against each other or building worlds endlessly. Therefore, I would argue that games may be more usefully analyzed as objects of mass consumption rather than as sites of interaction, action, or even perhaps, play in its fullest sense.

While playing games, the gamer's body is mainly immobile—except, at the time of this writing, with the new Wii console. The body is like a statue, but the hands and the eyes move nervously and in a compulsive way. What is happening with the gamer's own voice is outside the province of this chapter, though it does come to the fore in machinima—perhaps suggesting something of what goes on among game players.

In the art world, works making games, modifying games, and using games for machinima can be seen as following in the footsteps of Dadaism and Surrealism, which saw play and entertainment as the most subversive and also as the ultimate forms of art. Even outside of an art context, it is important to remember that as soon as the first personal computer was created, MIT computer scientists hacked the computer code to conceive the first digital creation: *Spacewar!* And *Spacewar!* was a computer game. So, if computer game history is related to the roots of digital creation and to digital code hacking, machinima can be understood to follow this tradition.

Machinima represents the particular moment when gamers begin to produce content and where games become tools of expression. These movies are mostly narrative, but they can also be experimental, artistic, or related to music, documentaries, ads, and feature films. They can be seen as a new way of representation in the digital age, along with 3D animation, digital cinema, or video.

It is interesting that the word "machinima" came about in a way similar to the origins of the term "net.art."[4] Both were born in the mid-1990s and have a relationship with an e-mail exchange and a misspelling. The original name was "machinema," which merged machine and cinema, but the "e" disappeared, misspelled by Hugh Hancock, who replaced it with an "i": the word "machinima" sounded better and was used from then on.

The machinima movement began in the mid-1990s when game developers created the functionality to record game action in real time, like in the game *Doom*, released in 1994. This allowed gamers to show each other their gaming skills, by exchanging demos of their actions. What were called "speedruns" appeared and consisted in the best-timed performances of the gamers to finish *Doom* levels.

Although it is not possible to delve too deeply here into the history of machinima, it is relevant to mention what the demoscene is and how it can be seen as the early roots of machinima. The demoscene is part of the hacker scene. It began in the 1980s when developers hacked games and then created some credits titles, putting their signatures on the cracked game. A major community was born, exchanging these "intros"; then the game-hacking culture grew up by developing audiovisuals to improve their skills in sound, image, and computer code development. The demoscene was huge in Europe and meetings often happened in stadiums. These audiovisuals were rarely narratives, but as the technology evolved they became real digital animations.

As Hugh Hancock writes of machinima's history:

Machinima grew out of hacks made to the game *Quake*, which allowed players to edit recordings of their gameplay into real movies. And while most of these movies were the equivalent of hip-hop songs explaining how tough and macho the game player was …, some filmmakers were using these *Quake* hacks to make real films.[5]

From death matches to fan demos, some "real" films emerged and were put online by the gamers on websites. Teams called "clans" were created. One of them, the Rangers, are known as the first directors of a narrative *Quake* movie, *The Diary of a Camper*, released in 1996, which added dialog on the screen. A new cinematographic genre had emerged and continued to evolve with new technologies: new game engines (*Quake II*, *Quake III Arena*, *Unreal Tournament*), graphic rendering, and real-time video capture tools like FRAPS (which comes from frames per second), and others. Within a few years, the movement became popular and received quite positive recognition from the media. In 2000, the website machinima.com was launched by Hugh Hancock and allowed the community to put their movies online and also to find tips, tutorials and all the resources they needed to create their own machinima.

As machinima developed, makers made use of new tools to work with a wider range of games, including massively multiplayer games. In the first version of one of the most popular games, *The Sims*, the developers discovered that some players used this community building game to create stories told in photographs. In 2004, the second version of the game was created with a complete series of tools for movie making. This is the easiest way to create machinima. And with this type of game, machinima makers emerged as people who weren't just hard-core gamers or 3D animation directors, but those who found it cool to express themselves by using *The Sims* to tell stories. This is how in 2005, April G. Hoffmann, a sports trainer in her normal life, became famous with her serial *The Awakening*. Made with *The Sims 2*, her movies tell the story of people who awake in a place they didn't know and where strange things are happening. For one of the first times, the movie wasn't so much related to the themes developed inside the game; thus from fan movies, or game fan communities, the machinima movies became more diverse in terms of content, stories, or genres.

During the riots in Paris in 2005, Alex Chan, a graphic designer based in the northern suburbs of Paris, directed the short film *The French Democracy* using *The Movies* game engine, from a game created by Peter Molyneux. This was the first political machinima. It explained how and why the riots began. Alex Chan had never made a movie before, but faced with the media coverage of the riots, which was massively biased against the youngsters, he decided to give them a voice by the means of a game. He directed the movie in one week, subtitled it in English, and posted it on *The Movies* website. Alex Chan's movie was downloaded more than a million times.

This brief history demonstrates that machinima can be a means of political, social, or artistic expression and open to a wider audience than the games were initially designed for. The main question for this chapter, to which I will now turn, is concerned with the role of voice within machinima and the complex ways voice can relate to image. I will begin by looking at the technical process of recording and editing voice performances.

Recording and Editing Voice in Machinima

There are many different techniques for directing machinima: human action, scripting, and artificial intelligence. Paul Marino explains:

Character control in Machinima production can be approached from two different directions: scripting based (or algorithmic) or human controlled (or interactive). The scripted approach is much like animation and the human-controlled approach is more akin to puppeteering/acting . . . the person triggers the character's actions as needed, either to pre-recorded dialogue or dialogue performed in the moment. From here, you can see this technique's affiliation with live-action filmmaking.[6]

Game actions are recorded in real time, thanks to tools like FRAPS for the video capture and then edited with some specific editing tools like Keygrip.

Most times, the sets, the designs, and the games characters are used without any computer code modification. But for "serious" machinima productions, some directors modify the game characters and environments, as the German artist Friedrich Kirschner did for *The Photographer* and *Person 2184*, using *Unreal Tournament* and the Ill Clan respectively, with Quake. For the first-person shooter games, the game is often modified in order to hide the weapon of the character controlling the camera—otherwise, there would be always a weapon in the foreground of the image. The dialogs are mostly done in real time, recording the actor's performance live. For that purpose, machinima makers use microphones and headsets to communicate during the action.

Hugh Hancock also discusses the possibilities of recording dialogs from different locations; however, in his view, it is always better for a director to communicate live and directly with his actors. Nevertheless, there are some makers who do record dialogs separately and then edit to the images after the shooting. It mostly depends on whether the dialogs are scripted. Some machinima movies are subtitled, rather than using recorded sound, to make it easier and faster to create them. Subtitles may also deal with language hegemony. Alex Chan chose to subtitle "The French democracy" in English to be able to post it on *The Movies* website, but also because he wanted it to be watched by the international machinima community. As Cillian Lyons, resident machinima artist and producer for Machinimasia (The Asian Machinima Festival), also explains, voice is something they specially discussed for Asian movies because the majority of the machinima community is English-speaking.[7]

Editing voices in machinima is a bit like in traditional filmmaking, except for the fact that you are actually monitoring puppets. Also, unlike traditional animation, you don't have all the facial animations at your disposal. Tones and expressions of voices make the difference between each character. As Hugh Hancock reminds us:

Unlike a live film director, you can't really just let an actor's performance carry the moment. Your audience will get bored watching your characters, even in the tensest of verbal confrontations. Cut to a wide shot or a reaction shot as needed.[8]

Voice in machinima isn't limited to narrative movies with dialogs, but also appears in songs for video clips directed in game engines. Since 2003, machinima have also been used to make video clips, called Video Mods, played initially on MTV. One of the most famous Video Mods is *I'm Still*

Seeing Breen. Paul Marino, directing in the game engine of *Half Life 2*, used the software Face Poser for the lip-synching. He explains his work with Face Poser:

In *Still Seeing Breen*, I used the *Half-Life 2* SDK (software development kit) & Face Poser, which uses voice analysis software to automatically lip sync the characters to spoken text. This represents a large leap in productivity, as animators are no longer required to spend time creating the lip sync by hand. As a result, this allows for more experimentation, as the workload doesn't factor so much into the effort. Seeing this, I decided to attempt a music video, with a lead character singing the lead track.

However there was an additional challenge in that the music was already mixed down—with the vocals and instruments together in the same file. This causes a problem with the voice analysis software in FacePoser, as it can only analyse a clean vocal track in order to create the lip sync automatically. What I did to get around this was to sing the song myself and record that as a WAV file. Then use FacePoser to analyse that file for the lip sync. Once the lip sync character worked correctly, I captured the character to video, deleted the audio of my singing and then merged the character video with original song file. It was a creative work around of sorts, but worked extremely well.[9]

Relation of Voice to Image

Apart from the gamer's performance that creates the action in the movies, voices are the human side of machinima. As machinima are entirely shot in 3D environments of games, they are made of digital images. These images are part of already existing worlds, and even if machinima directors modify them, they remain digital and mostly unchanged. Each of these worlds bring their own visual imaginary: a fantasy world with *World of Warcraft*, an urban modern life with *The Sims*, futuristic landscapes with *Halo*, or a violent suburban atmosphere with *Grand Theft Auto*, for instance.

More than an aesthetic, it is a 3D vision of the world—a digital representation of it. And in these environments, voices transform the meaning of the scenes. Originally imagined by hard-core gamers, machinima are a way to come back to the virtual universes with which they feel so comfortable. Voices are a tool to appropriate these worlds by adding their own stories, thanks to dialogs between characters. Voices bring sensitivity, a sense of humor, or an absurd touch to these virtual spaces. In *366 Days*, a one-hour, twenty-minute video created by the French artists Ultralab, *Unreal Tournament* landscapes are mixed to video and graphic design. This video is a fiction telling the story of an intelligent agent born inside a video game that wants now to take the control of the world. The agent talks through a voice-over in a poetic monologue that creates a dichotomy between the emotion held in the text and the violence of the fights from the games images.

Games are created to be fun, rather than to make you laugh or cry—even though this sometimes happens. Nevertheless, machinima voices offer a new set of emotions and allow us to perceive images in a different manner by getting closer to game characters and landscapes. It also brings an "as if analog" feeling to the machinima—a counterpoint to the digital. There is a sort of uncanny feel here, as the voice and image are out of phase with the warmth of the voice and the coolness of the image. The performed and scripted quality of the voice gives a not-digital feel to this very digital world. Polygons and avatars take a new dimension, a new personality—as if a human body would fill them up and breathe inside them.

Furthermore, the voice works to bring about a reverse engineering of a mass consumerist object into a tool of narrative and artistic expression. With machinima, we can talk about an emerging game play: an unsuspected use of a game for an artistic objective. Here play operates in the fullest, most artistic sense of the word. Even though, of course, now ads are also created using the machinima techniques—for commercial purposes—nevertheless, machinima remains a tool that is available to anybody who has a game engine at home and who wants to express himself or herself by combining voice with the games' visuals.

Voices in Machinima as a Situationist Détournement of Video and Computer Games

By using virtual spaces and changing the perspective as an artistic strategy, machinima allow a distanced critique of a simulated world. They tend to erase the boundaries between reality and fiction and redefine the transgressive power of the game. "When the real world is transformed into mere images, mere images become real beings—dynamic figments that provide the direct motivations for a hypnotic behavior."[10] They reactualize the Situationist concept of cinema, in which images, voices in dialogs or interviews or voice over, act as different layers of content. Guy Debord and Gil J. Wolman, in a joint text written in 1956, added to the Situationist theory of détournement[11] the point that cinema is the most efficient method of détournement where détournement tends to pure beauty. It doesn't need to be a parody or a critique of a movie. In this text, both authors argue for the strategy of diverting a movie like the racist one *Birth of a Nation* by D. W. Griffith by just changing the soundtrack in order to denounce the horrors of the war and the KKK's activities.

Some machinima, like *This Spartan Life* (TSL) by Chris Burke, or *Landlord Vigilante*, written by artist Eddo Stern and writer Jessica Hutchins, could, I would argue, be compared to Situationist movies. *This Spartan Life* is a talk show about digital and gaming culture directed in the virtual space of the network game *Halo 2*. Chris Burke, aka Damian Lacaedemion, has special guests in the game: for instance, he interviewed Bob Stein on the future of the book and Malcolm McLaren about 8-bit music and the roots of punk music. As the talk show is filmed, players are fighting around Lacaedemion and his guests. Sometimes, other gamers, who don't realize that a talk show is happening live in the game, actually kill the guests. For instance, while Damian Lacaedemion was defending Malcolm McLaren against futuristic monsters, we could follow McLaren walking through the digital landscape, in the shape of a strange purple animal, talking about "magnificent failures better than little successes."[12]

Landlord Vigilante combines the visuals of a car chase with the musings of a cab driver about the economy. It allows a second level of reading the images. Based on a true story about their ex-landlady, *Landlord Vigilante* is an artistic monologue of a women cab driver (figure 12.1) directed in the game *Grand Theft Auto*, according to its makers,

because of its gritty depiction of Los Angeles and prospective violence, and the Sims, which is property/real-estate oriented. Each game presents a "world" or narrative arena confined by a set of prescribed "rules"—we wanted to stretch and play with those rules to tell our own post-traumatic story.[13]

Why do I compare these machinimas to Situationist movies? Because, thanks to the voices, they add an artistic or a theoretical content to the images of violent games, and for that reason they are close to a Situationist film like *Can Dialectics Break Bricks?* This movie, produced in 1973 by the French director René Viénet used a martial arts film—*The Crush* by Doo Kwang Gee—overdubbed with French revolutionary philosophic ideas. It was a radical critique of cultural hegemony designed to entertain and amuse, while demonstrating a number of artistic and political points.

With machinima, the images come from a video or a computer game but are then transformed into short films. Though the Situationists had the idea

Figure 12.1
Landlord Vigilante 1, the woman cab driver in action, excerpt of a machinima created by Jessica Hutchins and Eddo Stern, 2006 Image courtesy of Eddo Stern.

of using a movie as the most efficient détournement because of cinema's capacity to reach a popular audience, new kinds of audience encounters are now possible with the extensive games audiences. Machinima began in the gamers' community, but it has expanded very quickly. The audience tends to be quite young and movies are often downloaded millions of times on websites such as Machinima.com or *The Movies*. You Tube and Dailymotion also distribute these films widely. Among the varying kinds of machinima, some like TSL or others mentioned earlier offer an alternative vision of the world. And it is voice, in particular, which gives the detourned edge to these machinima.

The Influence of Theater and Improvization in Machinima Performance

As Roland Barthes wrote, the grain of the voice is an "erotic mix between the language and the tone."[14] In the human voice, the body travels from thought to its expression as language. Joseph Beuys once said during a conference given at the Dokumenta VI in 1977, that voice is a sculpture of the thought.[15] It is the information sculpted by the air through the organs. It transforms the immateriality of thinking into materiality by bringing the body inside the sound.

Voice reflects the idea of alterity and the relationship to another person. Voice is the simultaneous presence and absence of human corporeality. Voice is the content and the meaning in language but also the sound of a person and their body through time and space. With recorded voices in cinema, the grain of the voice takes another dimension: it is the "anonymous body of the actor in my ear."[16] As we move into the digital domain, this materiality of voice is essential to machinima and their virtual game spaces. Besides the narrative in the dialog writing, the voice over represents a huge part of machinima. Paul Marino talks about it as the "humanness that is otherwise missing from the digital package":

Without the vocal performance, we lose all connection to relationship—between characters, between creator and audience and between audience and the narrative. The vocal work in a Machinima piece grounds the work in reality. It makes it not only digestible, which is paramount, but also makes the piece much more enjoyable.[17]

That is why the machinima Film Festival, which Marino founded in New York City, has a Voice-Over Performance prize. Voice represents more than half of the work of making machinima. As Burnie Burns, one of the author of the serial *Red vs Blue*, points out:

We spend most of our production time on the audio and voice work. In a 40 hour work week, 25 of it is spent in the writing and recording of the audio. I feel that the only way to differentiate a character from the others is through the voice. Since the videos are made in another medium, typically a "borrowed" medium, the actor's voice can make the project stand out.[18]

The voices of actors in machinima "animate" the virtual spaces. They give life and personality to digital puppets, which were not a priori conceived by the game developers to have dialogs with each other. And as machinima directors cannot play with the facial expressions of their digital puppets in the way cinema does with live actors, or in traditional animation, they need to work very precisely on the voice-over. As Matt Dominianni, cofounder of the ILL Clan explains:

I think good voice-over work is a very important part of Machinima, since in most Machinima the characters are not very expressive. Traditionally, animation is an art form that allows for an unlimited degree of expression, and in particular when we think of animated characters we think of exaggerated facial expressions. But Machinima is different because the game assets don't usually allow for much more than a static face, or in some cases a helmet with a mask covers the face. So it's really key that the voice-over work be as good as possible, giving the characters distinct, recognizable voices.[19]

The Ill Clan is one of the most famous in the machinima world. In 1998, they directed *Apartment Huntin'*, a great success in the *Quake* movie community. They are also known as the first to have performed a machinima live before an audience, in 2003 at the Florida Film Festival. In that performance, they improvised dialogs with the audience who were reacting to the story that Ill Clan were developing and filming live. The Ill Clan came from improvisational comedy and this has greatly influenced the way they make machinima and also explains how they managed to bring machinima to the live stage. Thanks to their theater experience, their work with dialogs is a wild mix between improvisation and scripted segments:

When we started doing the voice-over work for machinima, we improvised most of the dialogue. We would write an outline, based on the action we knew we wanted to happen, and then improvise dialogue to help get us from point a to point b. Later, with *TrashTalk* the scripts became more refined and most of the lines of dialogue were written in advance. Being improvisers though, we often would stray from the script. Also with *TrashTalk*, we recorded the dialogue at the same time that we controlled the characters, which makes it easy to go off on an unscripted tangent, and in my opinion gave the show an unpredictable nature that I really like.[20]

For Matt Dominianni, the main difference between improvisation on stage and with machinima is the absence of the body and its physicality. That's why the voice performance is so important, as it needs to give a personality and a clear intention to each character and be very expressive. Each character has to get its personal style, a special tone of voice, a certain type of reaction, vocal twitches, and a particular rhythm. To handle this kind of performance, the French directors of the award-winning film *Bill & John: Danger Attacks at Dawn*, appealed to a theater teacher to learn to act and to understand the main principles of theater. Bertrand Le Cabec explains:

Given our lack of talent and inexperience as actors, it was necessary to make these characters credible through their responses . . . to find the tone of voice, the vocal tics, to differentiate between characters and to play/act them as well as possible.[21]

Bill & John tells the story of two advanced pilots inside a military flight simulation game: *Lock On: Modern Air Combat*. The directors tried to counter the cold atmosphere of the game by the use of hilarious and absurd dialogs between the two pilots. The first scene begins with two military flight aircrafts on the ground, and one of the pilots amazed by the beauty of a flight aircraft yells:

"What-the-fuck, mo-ther fu-cker, that's fucking beautiful! Hey John! See, even after all these years, I'll never get tired of it . . . That's when I think to myself . . . " "Bill!

You piss me off! You've been pissing me off for ages! But now you're really pissing me off! You yell, you yell! It pisses me off hearing you yelling from the minute you get up . . . and you, you, and you yell, You never shut up." "Well, You're in a great mood this morning . . . we're gonna have a great day." "But do you realize that because of you . . . we are stuck in these shit wrecks!"

As they try to take off, the more foolish of the two pilots has forgotten how to begin and launches a missile instead: "All right, now, let me see, slowly give it some gas . . . and ease up on the brakes. Wrong switch. So, brake, switch . . . and releasing brakes. Wrong switch again. Oh right . . . there it is . . . and let up on the brakes."

The authors played with the rhythm of each scene during the editing:

The silences in the sound track were moreover a way to give life to characters we do not see but whose gestural presence we can sense. . . . The succession of uncontrolled events provoked by the two protagonists creates a distance effect which puts the spectator in the skin of an accessory witness.[22]

In a game, the imagination of players is driven by the actions of the play, scripts, and maps. In machinimas, our imagination can fill the empty spaces between the dialogs and, as with books, we can imagine what is happening in between. As in traditional cinema, we find elliptic narration in machinima, which allows us to take an active part in the story and to go back to a more personal perception of what the images mean.

Bill & John reminds us of Beckett's absurd theater, where clownish characters hold discussions in strange spaces—cold and mostly empty. This confrontation between humorously edged and warmly human dialogs and "cold" digital spaces is also prominent in the voice performances of the famous machinima series *Red vs Blue*. Shot in the futuristic game *Halo 2*, it tells the story of the battle between Red and Blue. These two characters seem to be lost in the game space, talking endlessly about the meaning of life and death. The dialogs' script and its deep sense of humor is what made the series enormously successful and allowed machinima in general to achieve significant success.

Interviewed about the link between the dialogs written for the serial *Red vs Blue* and the Theater of the Absurd, Burnie Burns agrees: "Yes, especially the early episodes. We wanted to know what would happen to videogame characters after the games were turned off. It's funny to think that these guys would have a life where they wait for someone to come along and play their game."[23]

This shift in meaning isn't only used for comic effect in machinima. To create a fictional effect and an artistic work by a détournement of game images, Eddo Stern and Jessica Hutchins worked differently with voice. *Landlord Vigilante* is a monologue and the tone of the voice is monotonous. Based on a true story that happened to the authors with their ex-landlady who tried to dupe them, as mentioned previously, we follow the thoughts of a woman cab driver. The authors chose third-person narration because it "gives the whole (first-person) monologue a disembodied, artificial feeling. Maybe these qualities allow it to be perceived as a subjective work of fiction, instead of blatant slander!"[24] Watching *Landlord Vigilante* is like traveling constantly from the text of the voice to the images, as if sometimes they couldn't be connected to each other, operating on different levels of perception.

To create their character, Stern and Hutchins hacked three different games: *The Movies, The Sims,* and *GTA San Andreas.* (figure 12.2) They also used images from the Net to make the fourth one, but for the voice they kept one young woman's voice:

We decided to conflate the disparate Leslies into one character by use of one voice for her monologue. To make the voice of the narrative more obviously disjointed and unnatural, we recorded the voice of the writer (an obviously younger female voice) as Leslie's voice. . . . We think the use of an unnatural voice for the character persistently disturbs audience immersion in the narrative and doesn't allow for suspension of disbelief. We're not sure if that's effective or not, but you could say the technique refers to the social atmospheres created in online role-playing games, or internet chat rooms, where the actual people behind the avatars you're interacting with aren't necessarily who they appear to be onscreen.[25]

This unnatural voice deals with the complexity of human identity and the boundaries between the fake and the real. We are lost, because we'd like to believe in 3D images, but we know that it's a fiction, and the monologue reinforces this feeling, because it doesn't seem to take any side. It doesn't entirely reveal the identity of this woman.

Natural Voice versus Special Effects

Unlike in the fictional machinima I've been discussing, the work on voices in interviews done with machinima has to sound as natural as possible, because the people are real. However these, too, create a strange sensation.

Figure 12.2
Landlord Vigilante 2, one of the faces created for the cab driver character, excerpt of
a machinima created by Jessica Hutchins and Eddo Stern, 2006. Image courtesy of
Eddo Stern.

The voices of the people are real, they are talking about very diverse subjects related to reality, but their visual representations in the game—as digital puppets—make the whole thing funny, although strangely so. During
the French presidential elections, Alex Chan transformed voters' interviews
into short machinima. During the day, he went out onto the streets in
order to interview people about French identity, left or right wing, and
then during the night, he replayed these interviews in the game *The Movies*, keeping the voices as he had recorded them. The result is very bizarre,
because the characters in *The Movies* are created to move and follow a series
of actions and not to stand up as in an interview. So as the "voters" played
in the game move like jumping jacks, this creates a distortion between the
meaning of what is said, the reality of natural voices and the images on the
screen.

In *This Spartan Life*, Chris Burke, alias Damian Lacaedemion—the host of
the show—also interviews real people while they are playing the network
game *Halo*. During the interview, the host and his guests move through
the game landscapes as discussed earlier. Because they are real people, the
voices must sound as natural as possible. Chris Burke, a sound engineer,
invites his guests to his New York Studio Bong + Dern, where their voices
are recorded before being edited on the videos. He explains,

Our goal with TSL audio is to reinforce the fact that the "characters" are actually real people in the real world who are making the show on Xbox Live, inside *Halo*.

Since we cheat in order to get a clean recording in the interviews, we then go back and dirty the audio up again in the mix. This is to put the voices into the XBox Live space. If they are left dry, we feel they sound like they exist outside of that sonic space. I have experimented with several variations, even playing the audio back through the Xbox Live headset to add the streaming sound. We have settled on a series of audio plug-ins that overdrive the audio a bit and add a slight distortion and EQ to approximate the Xbox Live headset sound. . . . We avoid panning and spatializing with reverb, etc. because our goal is to not interfere with the fact that these are real people operating avatars in an online game. The audio should sound like the game experience. Infrequently we break that rule and add echo or other effects if it is dramatically justified or just funny.[26]

Burnie Burns also relates that initially they recorded voices with a very cheap speaker on a telephone but now use very expensive software to achieve the same effects.[27]

Conclusion

Even though there are some machinima that are not dubbed with voice for technical or linguistic reasons, I have tried to demonstrate that voice in general constitutes the major game modification in machinima. Following the hacking tradition, voice gives another dimension to the use of games, transforming them into a form of expression. Voices in machinima provoke a shift in meaning similar to the way that Pascal Bonitzer discusses in relation to voice-over in cinema—they reopen the doors of our imagination as we watch preexisting digital images.

"To bring the focus to the off screen space, as another screen space," writes Pascal Bonitzer, "is to displace the focus from the gaze onto the voice, to release the voice from the dictates of the reality of the image."[28] Voices move our mind to another range of perception, diverting us to immerse totally in digital images and allowing us to keep a critical distance while getting closer to characters.

Notes

1. Hugh Hancock and Johnnie Ingram, *Machinima for Dummies* (Indianapolis, Indiana: Wiley Publishing Inc, 2007) 10.

2. In Justin Hall's official website http://interactive.usc.edu/members/jhall/ (accessed August 15, 2009).

3. Interviewed by Isabelle Arvers by email in 2002 while preparing the exhibition Playtime—the gaming room for the Festival Villette Numérique in Paris.

4. The legend says that one day, the artist Vuk Cosic received an anonymous e-mail with this sentence: "Everything is possible with the emergence of the Net. Art becomes obsolete." But because of a bug, the only word readable was net.art.

5. Hancock and Ingram, *Machinima for Dummies*,12.

6. Paul Marino, *The Art of Machinima* (Arizona, Paraglyph Press, 2004), 26–27.

7. Cillian Lyons, "The voice matter is something we have discussed previously for machinima and more so how it relates to Asia and as a foreign language as the majority of the community would be English speaking. Then also depending on the software of choice for the production would also depend on the voice or audio." E-mail message to the author, February 24, 2008.

8. Hancock and Ingram, *Machinima for Dummies*, 165.

9. Interview by Isabelle Arvers with Paul Marino, major figure in the machinima world, a maker, and founder of the Machinima Film Festival, January 2008.

10. Guy Debord, *La Société du spectacle*, 1967, (Editions champ libre, Paris, 1971). "Là où le monde réel se change en simples images, les simples images deviennent des êtres réels, et les motivations efficientes d'un comportement hypnotique." Translated by Ken Knabb, *Bureau of Public Secrets*, http://www.bopsecrets.org/SI/debord/1.htm (accessed August 19, 2009).

11. Guy Ernest Debord and Gil J. Wolman, *Mode d'emploi du détournement*, initially published in *Les lèvres nues,* no. 8 (May 1956).(See translation in K.Knab, A User's Guide to Détournement, in *Bureau of Public Secrets*, http://www.bopsecrets.org/SI/detourn.htm#1 (accessed August 19, 2009).

12. Malcolm McLaren interviewed in the machinima *This Spartan Life,* episode 3, directed by Chris Burke, 2006.

13. Email interview by Isabelle Arvers with Eddo Stern, one of the first game artists to produce a thirty-minute art machinima, *Landlord Vigilante*, and author Jessica Hutchins, who wrote the *Landlord Vigilante* text, January 2008.

14. Roland Barthes, "Le grain de la voix," in *l'Obvie et l'obtus* (Paris: Seuil, 1982), 238- 243, first published in *Musique en jeu,* no. 9 (1972) as "Le grain est un mixte érotique de timbre et de langage."

15. Joseph Beuys, "L'entrée dans un être vivant," conference at Free International University, documenta 6, Kassel (1977), "Il (l'homme) doit, par la force qui est der-rière la corporalité, mouvoir aussi la corporalité de son environnement, avec le flot d'air qui est mû à travers la trachée artère, qui est pressé à travers le larynx, et qui

entre dans d'autres organes du langage (la langue, le palais, les dents, l'espace de la bouche). Il doit 'sculpturer' quelque chose à l'intérieur de ce flot d'air. Le récepteur doit 'exformer' cette sculpture." [He (man) must through his own corporeal energy move the corporeal energy of his environment, using the stream of air that moves through the trachea, that presses through the larynx, and that enters the other organs of speech (the tongue, the palate, the teeth, the cavity of the mouth). He must "sculpt" something inside this stream of air. And the one who receives it must unmake this sculpture.]

16. Roland Barthes, "Le grain de la voix," 1982.

17. Arvers interview of Marino, January 2008.

18. Interview by Isabelle Arvers in March 2008 of Burnie Burns, founder of the machinima company Rooster Teeth and author of the famous machinima serial *Red vs. Blue* .

19. Interview by Isabelle Arvers of Matt Dominianni, January 2008. Matt has been directing machinima since 1997 and did voice-overs for many characters, including Lenny Lumberjack in their award-winning *Hardly Workin'*, and more recently, the voice of ILL Will, host of the gaming and news comedy talk show *Tra5hTa1k*. He performed improvisational comedy throughout the 1990s in New York City.

20. Ibid.

21. E-mail interview by Isabelle Arvers of Bertrand Le Cabec, December 2007. "Il fallait, avec nos faibles talents de comédiens et notre inexpérience en la matière, rendre crédible ces personnages a travers leurs répliques. Trouver des tonalités de voix, des tics de langages, bien différencier les personnages entre eux et jouer le plus juste possible."

22. E-mail interview by Isabelle Arvers of Bertrand Le Cabec, December 2007. "Les plages de silence dans la bande son ont été d'ailleurs capitales pour donner vie à des personnages qu'on ne voit pas à l'image mais dont on devine la gestuelle. . . . La succession des péripéties incontrôlées provoquées par les protagonistes donne cet effet distancié qui met le spectateur dans la peau d'un témoin complice."

23. Arvers interview of Burns, March 2008.

24. Arvers interview of Stern and Hutchins, January 2008.

25. Ibid.

26. Interview by Isabelle Arvers of Chris Burke, December 2007. *This Spartan Life*, a talk show directed inside the network game Halo 2 with real guests who are invited to speak about digital or gaming culture while playing and fighting inside the futuristic game.

27. Ibid.

28. Pascal Bonitzer, *Le regard et la voix* (Union Générale d'Editions, Paris, 1976), quoted in "Le bercail de la voix," a text written by Johanne Villeneuve, (Montréal, Presses de l'Université de Montréal, 2003), vol. 39, no1. "Porter l'accent sur le hors champs, comme autre espace champ, . . . c'est déplacer l'accent du regard vers la voix, libérer la voix de son asservissement à la scène réaliste de l'oeil."

13 Filmic Voices

Helen Macallan and Andrew Plain

The following chapter is a synthesis of theoretical and practical perspectives on the subject of the digital voice in cinema and is the product of an (ongoing) collaboration between professional sound designer Andrew Plain and film academic Helen Macallan. The analyses and reference to Catch a Fire, In the Cut, *and* Candy *are based on Andrew's direct involvement with the films.*

In a discussion of the process of the digital remastering of *Apocalypse Now*, sound designer and picture editor Walter Murch describes the new treatment of the voice-over narration of the character Willard (Martin Sheen): "In the final mix we took the single soundtrack of his voice and spread it across all three speakers behind the screen, so there's just a soft wall of this intimate sound enveloping the audience." He notes that the establishment of difference between the narrating voice and the dialog of the characters in the film, which continues to issue only from the central speaker results in a "distinct shape to the sound [voice-over] as it hits the screen."[1]

The notion that film can be conceptualized and discussed in terms of its geometric properties is not new. In 1959 Eric Rohmer wrote an essay on the underlying geometric form in Hitchcock's visuals; a decade later Jean-Luc Godard analyzed Alexandre Astruc's work in similar terms.[2] But not until the advent of digital technology was such an argument feasible in relation to sound.

A reconceptualization of film sound in general and the filmic voice in particular is taking place in the contemporary era of digital culture. The shift from cutting to clicking, from a technique of sound editing based on a hands-on process to an electronic one whereby a digital audio file is manipulated on a computer screen, has brought with it a new perception of sound. In its translated graphic state as a digitized configuration of sound waves, the concept that sound possesses a spatial as well as a temporal dimensions is emphasized.

That sound has the function of establishing a sense of spatial "reality" to film scenes has long been noted; Rick Altman's description of it as a material "event" in which the various stages of "attack, sustain and decay" constitute a "sound envelope" makes clear its dual dimensions.[3] And it is evident that there are many instances in which filmmakers have used sound to demonstrate that beyond its traditional function of supporting the image, it has its own value.

Now, in the context of several interrelated digital developments, mainstream cinema is beginning to exploit the potential of the new technology to reconceptualize sound in general and the voice in particular. The major innovations that have affected the voice include changes to the mode of delivery, more complex layering techniques (which are inseparable from the expansion of the dynamic range), and various new means of treating the voice. These developments have also meant a blurring of former hierarchical distinctions between the voice and other sounds.

Changes to the Mode of Delivery

When used in relation to cinema, the term "digital sound" refers in the most precise sense to the technical systems of delivery into the theater: Dolby Digital, SDDS (Sony Dynamic Digital Sound), and DTS (Digital Theater Systems).[4]

In the predigital period, any attempt to send the voice to the three speakers in the manner described by Walter Murch would have courted almost certain failure. The inability of the encoding and decoding analog system of delivery (Dolby Stereo) to discriminate precisely between signals would have resulted in the voice collapsing into the one center channel rather than emerging from all three with the desired "merging" effect. Consequently, neither a full sound nor a sense of its "shape" because of its distinct identity would have been achieved.

The lack of precision in sound delivery in the analog era meant that there was a reluctance (with a few notable exceptions) to use the "surrounds" other than to spread the atmospheres and music through the auditorium. In addition, because of the continued dominance of the front speakers, the sound that went to the surround speakers was experienced as little more than a wash that flowed from the screen, across the audience.

But although the digital sound replay system means that now all speakers in the theater are capable of discretely replaying the sound with the same clarity and dynamic range, apart from the occasional movement of voices from left to right speakers, the practice of sending the voices of principal characters to the center speaker continues to hold sway.

The longevity of this practice is attributable to historical reasons. John Belton points out that attempts to move the voice in the 1950s were resisted by exhibitors, audiences, reviewers, and even industry personnel, on the grounds of the perceived artificiality of the "traveling" voice.[5] And, to a large extent, the rule that the voice should come from the center speaker (a rule analogous to "crossing the line" in cinematography) has its roots in that concern—the fear that the voice will be perceived as floating free of the body, hence rupturing the film's narrative. So, unless there is very strong narrative-related motivation, the convention has prevailed.

If mainstream feature film has clung to this practice, in contrast, the makers of computer-animated movies have been radical in seizing the opportunity to relocate its position. For example, since *Toy Story* (1995) the dialog in Pixar films has "followed" the characters.

But the conditions of making a live-action feature and an animation film differ substantially. The panning of voices in animation films has been greatly facilitated by the fact that the voice is always recorded in a studio environment and is unencumbered by the extraneous and uncontrollable noise ("dirt") of live-action film production dialog. In contrast, voices recorded on location cannot be panned, because the background sounds accompanying them would move as well.

A consequence of the ease with which the technique of "gluing" of the voice to the body has been taken up in animation may be that voice panning will be increasingly identified as a defining characteristic of animation, its particular "reality effect" throwing into relief the conventional nature of the live-action feature-film voice, which (at least to date) in contradistinction gains its "reality" from the way it issues from the center speaker.

If the panning of principal voices so far remains a marginal practice, nonetheless film makers and sound designers are beginning to exploit the possibilities of the new delivery system in terms of deployment of the voice to the surrounds.[6] The brief second scene of the sequence in Phillip Noyce's *Catch a Fire* (2006) in which the character Patrick Chamusso (Derek Luke) is subjected to torture by the South African secret police is such an example.

In the scene, the torturers' voices do not issue from the center speaker but are spread around the left, right, and surround speakers. And while the victim's breath comes from the central speaker—the site of the "real," the "present," and, in this film, a vital signifier of life—his screams and moans, like the voices of the torturers, issue from the surrounds, finally climaxing over the latter and morphing into the cry of a blue crane, a national symbol already seen encaged in the torturers' compound.

The unconventional deployment of the voices constructs a space that possesses a temporal dimension but also functions as a "space in the head," representing the subjective hearing of the victim. Even his own screams, it is suggested, are part of his terrifying environment, functioning like auditory hallucinations, while our apprehension that we are experiencing Patrick's point of audition is made clear by the way only certain words spoken by the torturers are heard. Over-determined "incriminating" words such as "Communist," "ANC," "collaborators," are intelligible, while others are difficult to decipher because they have been deliberately overlapped and given a distancing "reverb."

The technique uses the same principle that Hitchcock employed in the famous knife scene in *Blackmail* (1929), although in *Catch a Fire* digital tools now allow for the treatment of the dialog so that there is greater refinement of the distinction between intelligible and unintelligible words than in *Blackmail*. The impact is thus subtler and better suited to the naturalistic (rather than expressionistic) effect required by the director Phillip Noyce.

Digital tools were also used to treat the sounds of the torture instruments, the water and rope, in the same way as the torturers' voices, so that they are abstracted, extended, and heard against a tonal background that continually slides between all the speakers. And the correspondences established between the voices and the dematerialized objects contribute to the lack of a "real" space, reinforcing our sense of Patrick Chamusso's disorientation.

The scene illustrates one of the ways in which when the voice is placed differently (in this case, conceptualized as producing an oppressive "encircling" effect), it can function to transmit a sense of the mental state of a character.

Katherine Bigelow's *Strange Days* (1995) is of interest in this respect, because of its extensive use of the surrounds in order to render "virtual experience" (a concept emblematic of early digital culture). A thriller/

noir, the film centers on a former cop, Lenny Nero (Ralph Fiennes), who is involved in the circulation of bootleg clips that graphically depict people's emotional and sensory experience of violent or sexual events. These events have been recorded directly by means of a head-fitting net device called a "SQUID" through which Lenny's customers are able to "experience" virtual reality through playback.[7]

Although there have been numerous commentaries on the film's perceived radical aesthetic, there has been minimal discussion of the significant role that sound has played in its production.[8] In fact, though camera and picture editing techniques (analog and digital) are essential to the construction of the virtual experience, equally important is the deployment of the voice to the surround speakers and the particular interplay with the image that occurs as a consequence.

Gary Rydstrom, the film's sound designer, notes that the decision to place in the voice in the surrounds was made on the grounds that it was in accord with the film's logic, its concern with the "point of view of someone captured on this futuristic technology that can capture experience, and so part of the experience of life is that things happen around us, including dialogue."[9]

The transmission of the subjective experience of "immersion" involves a high degree of defamiliarization of the customary relationship between sound, image, and audience. At times, for example, there is an uncanny perception that the sound is pushing toward the screen, a reversal of its usual outward-bound trajectory. At other times, there seems to be a genuine equality between the sound originating from "behind" the screen and the image on the screen. It is as if the sound draws the image out, making the audience the center point at which all sound and images meet.

The strange oscillating relationship between sound and image is most effective in the first sequence, when we watch a "clip" made by a man participating in a violent robbery and take his point of audition as well as his point of view. As he rushes forward away from the police, agitated voices associated with the people he approaches—those who pass in front of the SQUID's lens and whose bodies are often truncated because of the limited perspective—are heard from the surrounding space (the surrounds). The sound seems to form a phalanx across the theater, pushing toward the screen with the recordist/viewer of the SQUID. Thus the voices race toward the screen, trying to catch the image that remains elusively out of reach.

The operational logic is the same as that in Robert Montgomery's *Lady in the Lake* (1946), in which events are enacted from the first-person point of view and there is a similar withholding of the "agent." But there the subjective experience is achieved through camera and picture editing and the monophonic sound is conventional, with voice, effects, and ambience issuing from the center speaker. Far from authenticating the first-person point of view, the position of the voice "in the frame" points to the absence of the main character (Robert Montgomery) in an unsettling and unrealistic manner, in that he seems to drift uncannily in the auditorium, appearing only in mirrors and windows—a vampire in reverse. By contrast, in *Strange Days*, the push-and-pull thrust of the sound, and its possession of a spatial as well as a temporal dimension, produces a mimetic effect, one based on "immersion" in the character's panic and directionless real-time flight.

Catch a Fire and *Strange Days* both make use of the then-new ability to place the voice precisely in the surrounds in order to produce a sense of immediacy and the first-person perspective. But although placing the voice in this manner can create a novel sense of subjectivity, the technique is still dependent for its effect on its difference (the point that Walter Murch makes in relation to the spreading of the sound of the narration in *Apocalypse Redux* through the front three speakers). And so the knowledge, or memory, of the place of issue of the "objective'" voice is part of its effectiveness. In addition, other digital techniques—in particular those to do with the placement of the voice in relation to other sound elements and the image and its treatment—are important.

Layering and the Highly Treated Voice

If the defining feature of digital film sound is the new system of delivery, the by-products of this delivery are the greatly increased clarity, dynamic range, and potential for placement. In the main, these developments have their roots in Dolby Stereo, but they have been highly refined by digital technology. And one of the most striking outcomes of the refinements is that sound can now be "layered" in ways not previously possible.

In *The Voice in Cinema* (1988), Michel Chion uses the term "voco-centrism" to describe the privileged place of the filmic voice in relation to other elements of film soundtrack. The centrality of the voice is, he suggests, a natural phenomenon, in that "the presence of a human voice immediately

sets up a hierarchy of perception." Yet he describes this hierarchy as it functions in film as dependent upon technology: "The level and presence of the
voice have to be artificially enhanced over the sounds, in order to compen-
sate for the absence of landmarks that in live binaural conditions allow us
to isolate the voice from ambient sounds." Thus, he concludes, "production mixing is really the taking of voices in most cases and other noises are
reduced as far as possible."[10]

Chion raises—albeit with the exaggeration that accompanies any
polemic—the important issue of the order of the elements of the soundtrack
in feature films. In the predigital era, the overriding concern of most films
was that dialog be intelligible; this meant that the voice had to be protected
against the intrusion of other sounds—atmospheres, effects, and music and
even other voices—because of their potential to distract or, more seriously,
to destroy the clarity of the dialog. A careful balancing act was required to
bring the voice and other elements of the soundtrack into play with each
other while maintaining the right amount of atmosphere (for example,
crowd babble or music in a restaurant) to maintain a perception of spa-
tial-temporal coherence and continuity. This balance was achieved mainly
through the use of fade-ups and pre- and post-lapping techniques.

Now digital layering techniques allow the filmic voice to break free of the
constraints caused by its compartmentalization. Each sound, including the
voice, can retain its own integrity yet simultaneously interact with other
sounds in a manner not unlike the traditional dialectic between sound and
image. Sounds can now interpret, confirm, comment on, or contradict one
another while occupying the same time zone. In addition, their ability to
coexist extends the sense of sound's spatiality.

Jonathon Glazier's *Sexy Beast* (2000) offers an example of the innovative
use of digital technique to place the voice. It pays homage to the traditional
British gangster film, just as the great neo-noirs of the 1970s—*Chinatown*,
Night Moves, and *Three Days of the Condor*—were tributes to an historical era
in cinema. Above all, it returns us to the pre-1980 films, to a time when
there was an emphasis on and level of sophistication to the dialog that
assumed an adult audience. The use of language in *Sexy Beast*—its wit,
robustness, and energy—ensures that the film doesn't fall into the trap of
affect-less pastiche that Fredric Jameson describes as characterizing so many
contemporary films. And it eschews the "no-place" transatlantic or Hollywood "global" voice, instead drawing attention to the accent, pitch, timbre,

and the rhythm of the voice of the British gangster, the loving reproduction of which is now possible because of the new clarity and dynamic range afforded by digital tools and exhibition.[11]

If the act of storytelling is fundamental to narrative cinema, there is no better illustration of the way in which digital technology can emphasize the performative dimension of the voice than in the film's montage sequence in which Don (Ben Kingsley) attempts to persuade "Gal" Dove (Ray Winstone) to be part of a planned heist through his storytelling prowess.

Although montage has always been used as an efficient mode of transmitting information, the sequence has an astonishing compactness, imparting—in a very short space of time—an enormous amount of information about the genesis of the planned robbery and its major players, including their foibles and status within the gang.

The act of telling is inseparable from the act of listening. We are drawn into Don's story by the simplest and oldest of devices—he says, "Let me tell you a story"—and to make it perfectly clear that it is not just Gal but us to whom he is directing this story, he turns his chair away from Gal toward us, the audience, and he begins. But, although he appears to initiate the story, his words occur at the same time as a telephone rings, and this simultaneity and equality of sounds, made possible by layering, suggests that the story has its own dynamic beyond the control of its individual storyteller.

Before and after he recounts the story, Don is portrayed as a bully whose aggressive bullet-like delivery of language (often obscene) is the most visible aspect of his malevolent persona. But, as he slips into storytelling mode and takes on the persuasive mien of the storyteller, his voice is modified, becoming, if not benign, at least more neutral. And what is striking about his narrating voice is that its tone, pitch, and volume are shared by all the other voices that participate in the story (the main distinguishing factor is their specific class accents, which range from East End cockney to upper-middle-class).

The highly stylized use of sound in the sequence includes the exclusion of ambient sound even at the times of a return to Don and Gal sitting at the table on the terrace. Although shots like this apparently take us back to "reality," the absence of the sound of crickets that we hear earlier in association with the Spanish villa and the close-ups of the two characters emphasizes the notion that storytelling is an artifact—a form with its own time and space.

Techniques of placement and more complex layering and the related expansion of the dynamic range allow for new expressive possibilities in terms of the delineation of character. For example, in the scene in which the character Teddy (Ian McShane) is introduced—a scene twice repeated— he is seen striding up and down in his bathrobe as he combs his hair. The sound is layered so that we hear a voice announcing his name, "Teddy," while we hear, in synchronism with the music, the sound of the comb as he runs it through his hair. The simultaneity of these sounds and the ability for us to hear a normally unheard sound sets up unusual correspondences, allowing us to associate a seemingly insignificant mannerism (hair-combing), a name, and the owner of that name's narcissism.

There is a confusion of "who speaks" in the sequence. This occurs, in part, because of the uniformity of the voices, but also because the obvious markers of enunciation are removed or subverted through the play with film syntax—the constant slippage of aural and visual point of view and rapid shifts between synchronized and unsynchronized sound. Although obviously premeditated, these devices produce a sense of the digressions and energy that make real-life storytelling so pleasurable.

A striking contrast occurs between the highly constructed scenes and the one in which Teddy and Harry converse as they walk through the foyer of the bank into the street. There is a shift from the time of the story to a perception that the voice is being heard in a real time and in a real context. The scene has clearly been shot on location, and the inevitable dirt attached to the voice makes it the only instance in the episode when digital technology is not employed to separate sounds. As such, it has an anti-illusionist, destabilizing effect, one that comes very close to breaking the spell of the story. But its coherency holds because of the return to the storytelling voice in the car scene that follows: a voice which, as before this break, has been recorded in postproduction through the technique of automatic dialog replacement (ADR) and sustituted for the original "dirty" location dialog.[12]

Stripped of the usual accompaniment of atmosphere, the voice provides the necessary binding element for the intricate movement between rapidly changing contexts. In this sense, the sequence is structured by a string of voices, the uniformity of which has been achieved through digital technique. The leveling of the participants' voices functions, as Eisenstein notes of tone, to provide a level of rhythm. And the rhythmic unity and sense of intimacy it engenders ensures that the whole (the story) is more important than its individual parts, its participants. What is heard is an "ur-voice," the timeless voice of the storyteller.

One of digital editing's important features is its flexibility. Now the various options for a relatively unorthodox sequence—as in *Sexy Beast*—can be rehearsed without penalty, because decisions can be made offline. And the speed and precision of digital editing also means, as sound editor Larry Blake points out, "minute edits and cross-fades," which contribute to a sense of seamless picture and sound, can be quickly achieved.[13]

And just as the sound designer can now map the delivery of the voice in the theater so that it has a shape and layer it so that it acquires "thickness" through its simultaneous engagement with other sounds, it is also now possible for the sound of the voice to be radically reshaped by digital tools. It can be made similar to other voices, or other sound elements (as in the examples of *Catch a Fire* and *Sexy Beast*) or it can be reconfigured to express difference—to emphasize or exaggerate a character's idiosyncratic identity. Tomlinson Holman, for instance, describes the postproduction technique of adding artificial "reflections" by use of "digital delay" to Darth Vader's voice in the remastered version of *Star Wars* to give it a mechanical "sound in a barrel quality."[14]

Although such processes have their roots in analog technology, as increasingly the sound of the voice is regarded as raw material that can be manipulated—elongated, contracted, thickened, and fragmented and thus given its own fictional coloration and shape—questions to do with the "real" and the "perfect" have become more acute.

Whereas once the authenticity of the work of certain filmmakers, such as Rohmer, Altman, and Straub, and documentarians, such as Jean Rouch, was signified by voices in which there was a perceptible presence of dirt, in an age in which high production values rule, both producer and public have been conditioned to expect first and foremost not just an intelligible voice, but one with exceptional clarity.

Director Christopher Coppola's comment that, "kids are growing up with the hyper-real look of video. It's what's normal for them" *is* equally applicable to sound.[15] The highly treated, hyper-real voice has rapidly been absorbed, not just into obvious genres such as science fiction and the horror, but into mainstream cinema and television in general.

Now, the most "authentic" voice may be the most constructed, and the voice only mediated by the microphone and left untreated may transmit as "bad" or "poor," or even—in an ironic turn—as simply "unreal." And the inability of even sound designers to always be able to discern the difference between a fabricated and a untreated voice indicates that sound has arrived at the same ambiguous position that William J. Mitchell noted of electronic photography in 1992, when he argued that the digital image "shakes our faith" in the truth of the image.[16]

The Quest for a Perfect Voice

As digital film sound becomes standard practice, numerous web blogs have appeared echoing the criticism made of the digitization of music. Thus it is argued that the digital treatment of filmic sound results in brittle, sharp, clinical, and unnatural sound, and though to an extent this is true (as we will show), in general, the advantages of digital techniques outweigh the advantages of analog.

Equally, there are those who assume that digital brings with it a qualitative leap. Many actors, for example, are unaware of the extensive work done on their voices in postproduction, believing that the new technology renders their voices perfectly. But the proposition of a perfect voice is a utopian one for several reasons, not the least because the sound designer, director, and audiences may have all have different ideas as to what constitutes such a voice.[17]

For one thing, the conditions under which the voice is heard are seldom "perfect." Just as there is a "sweet spot" in a mixing theater where the sound is exactly as intended, there is also a counterpart "best seat" in the auditorium where the film is exhibited (usually in the center section, about halfway back). All other seats are an approximation of this perfect position. For instance, if a member of the audience is sitting on the right-hand side of the theater directly in line with the right speaker and under a right surround, then that approximation is fairly slim. For another, though there is a new ability to treat and place the voice does not mean that that sound problems that occur at the level of the location shoot can be magically remedied.

When the director Jane Campion required a realistic effect for the *In the Cut* restaurant scene, she shot it in an extremely busy section of New York, and the production dialog was difficult to understand. The first instinct of the sound team was to replace it through ADR, on the grounds that the noise of the city attached to the production recordings worked against the projection of a sense of intimacy between the main characters Frannie (Meg Ryan) and her sister Pauline (Jennifer Jason Leigh). But the director and producer were adamant that it was precisely through the way the street sounds intruded into the café, functioning like an assault upon the senses (the subtext is the brutal "masculinity" of the city), that the audience would understand Frannie's retreat into her own world. The sounds of the environment and their effect were therefore viewed as important as—and inseparable from—the scripted words and the voices of the actors.

The final outcome of discussions as to how to achieve the desired realism and yet still allow for a comprehensible conversation between Frannie and Pauline was a compromise. When the characters struggle to hear each other, the audience is involved in a similar struggle, although, in fact, "lost" lines have been replaced by "cleaner" takes to make the performances intelligible. Clearly, this "verité effect" is highly constructed at the postproduction level and its realism can be perceived as of a very different order to that of films where the voice captured on location retains its own integrity.

Although the retention of street sounds in *In the Cut*'s restaurant scene are viewed as providing the rationale for Frannie's withdrawal, in contrast, any perception of an outer sensory environment is completely eliminated in the subway scenes that follow.

Campion had emphasized in her brief to the sound team that these scenes should transmit a sense of the "bubble" Frannie had constructed herself, the perception that while she was in the world, she was not really partaking of it.

At various times, Frannie reads musingly aloud the poems that are displayed on the walls of subway trains on which she is traveling. The original synchronized dialog recorded on location was not used for these scenes, because—quite apart from the fact that it was unintelligible under the real sounds of the New York subway—there is a deliberate stylization through the absence of real train sounds and therefore the synchronized voice.

To get a "clean" version of the lines, Meg Ryan's voice was rerecorded in a studio on the same brand of modern microphones used on the location shoot, with her rhythm and performance matched against the original sound. These lines were then further fitted by an ADR editor to match the original dialog precisely. The procedure followed standard dialog editing procedure: marrying the voice to the body in accordance with the assumption that, with some exceptions, the performance of the voice and the body form a unity that should not be violated.

But the conventional treatment of the voice, the exactness of the perfect match between the voice and the body, mitigated the "bubble effect," the dreamlike feeling that had been achieved through the way the scenes were shot and the stylized nature of the soundscape as a whole. After several abortive experiments to remedy this, it was realized that the problem was happening because the realism of the recording—the perfect fit between voice and body—did not capture the absorbed yet abstracted state of mind of the character.

Meg Ryan recorded the lines again, and this time a 1950s ribbon "Larry King" microphone, renowned for its warmth and smoothness, was used. And, instead of the "before and after" recordings being fitted precisely, they were laid roughly in synchronism but allowed to drift slightly in relation to the location recordings—not enough to be perceived on a conscious level, but enough to have a subliminal disconcerting effect. Thus, while it is clear that Frannie's lips are saying the words that are heard, the abandonment of the attempt to produce a precise fit of sound and image, and the substitution instead of a floating, dream-like voice, allows for a different kind of connection, a sense of access to Frannie's inner self.

The use of the 1950s Larry King microphone rather than a modern one, brings a particular grain to Frannie's voice, but without the inevitable dirt that would have attached to it if it had been recorded in the 1950s. The voice is, of course, still a mediated one and it is perhaps not without significance that this particular microphone was principally used for radio broadcasting, the medium where the ultimate separation of the voice from the body occurs.

So both old and new tools and technique played a part in allowing Frannie's voice in the subway to be soft, dreamy, familiar, floating free yet still attached, intimate but impersonal—at the same time.

The Voice-Body Relationship and a New Mode of Performance

One of the reasons why the voice-body relationship has received considerable attention in the digital era is that an essential part of the new layering

techniques is the expansion of the dynamic range, which enables the reproduction and hearing of very loud and very soft sounds without the kind of
audible distortion previously experienced.

However, an unsought outcome of the technology's increased dynamic
range is that now all the sounds that previously would have been lost in
the "noise floor"—especially breathing and mouth noises such as swallows
and "lip smacks"—have become audible. On the one hand, this means that
certain "tics" can be left in place so that they function as vocal leitmotifs. In
this case, the voice is tied closely to the body and this, in turn, gives "body"
to the voice. On the other hand, clearing the voice of such sounds, though
labor-intensive, can yield benefits and in some instances the removal of a
disruptive, nonverbal sound—for example, a melodramatic sigh—can have
a potent after-effect, because traces of the melancholy will almost certainly
remain as affect in the tone of the voice.

The new ability to achieve a seamless imbrication of sound and image
raises the question of where the line should be drawn between voice and
body. For example, is a character's personality manifested by the way she
or he breathes? The increased allocation of breathing to Foley (studio-
manufactured effects), ADR, and dubbing, whereby the "breathing" of
major characters is performed by others in the postproduction studio, further complicates the already problematic notion of "organic" or "natural"
performance.

It is within the context of such issues that the question of a new style
of acting arises. In 1988, three years before the release of *Batman Returns*
(the first all-digital sound, live-action film), Charles Eidsvik noted a change:
"Actors such as Robert DeNiro now often just mumble their lines on location, and depend on ADR sessions to get the right intonation and subtextual subtlety into the final film."[18]

The strategy of actors deliberately underplaying their lines has a long
history. Famously exploited by Marlon Brando in the era of "looping" that
preceded more modern ADR techniques, a low-key style of acting is now
gaining general acceptance. The sound designer Tomlinson Holman attributes its ascendancy to the "intimacy" of contemporary cameras, and this
and other factors related to digital technology can be identified as contributing to the trend.[19]

In the analog era, the "stage whisper"—which was delivered to the audience rather than the diegetic characters—was a necessary convention. It

had to be loud enough to survive the extra noise that the various stages of processing on analog tape added, while still appearing to be a whisper. Now actors can dispense with the time-honored theatrical tradition of projecting the voice. They can whisper as they would in everyday life and the recording will be audible.

An example of the "digital" acting approach is Heath Ledger's performance in *Candy*, in which, because of his very soft delivery, his voice becomes a lure, drawing the audience into the space of the screen with the kind of binding effect usually reserved for visual devices such as the shot-reverse-shot editing figure. However, the new style of acting has provoked a varied reception, as an article, "Menace of the Mumblers," in the English newspaper, *The Guardian*, indicates.[20]

The hyper-intimate style of performance made possible by digital technology has revived old sound-image relationships and generated new ones. To some extent, there has been a return of the close-up, which is now used in conjunction with close-up sound, but the camera also has the option of staying "wide," because low-level, intimate dialog can now be embedded in a noisy milieu. The wide shot can therefore provide the geography, or context, and the body language and voice, the sense of closeness.

The Digital Voice and the "Two-Suitcase Film"

Any argument that digital technology has contributed to the democratization of film should be tempered by the fact that the twentieth century saw several significant technology-related innovations—notably, in the late 1950s, 16mm cameras that operated in synchronism with tape recorders, and in the 1970s, Super 8 technology, which facilitated low budget film-making. But one of digital technology's unique contributions is that both economically and technologically, it has been equally available to independent filmmaking and high-budget productions.[21]

In an interview in 2000, Jean-Luc Godard expressed optimism about film's future: "Rohmer is preparing to shoot a film for 60 million francs in digital and with costumes. We will always be able to make films. When I saw *Voyage in Italy*, I knew you could shoot a two-hour film with a couple in an automobile. I've never done it but I've kept it as security."[22]

Several years after the Godard interview, the internationally renowned Iranian filmmaker Abbas Kiarostami realized just such a project with an all-digital film *10*, a "defiantly 'small,' ultra-low-budget film set almost entirely within the confines of one car, and made with two digital cameras and a handful of nonprofessional actors."[23]

10 is a minimalist film with an episodic structure based on conversations that a woman driver, Mania Akban (Mania Akban), has with her son, Amin (Amin Maher), and various women passengers as she drives around the streets of Tehran.

The employment of just two stationary digital cameras mounted on the dashboard inside a car along with counterpart microphones allowed Kiarostami to make a film that is virtually "directorless"—one, as he says, that departs from conventional storytelling.[24] In the absence of obvious spectacle and action, the audience is asked to pay the same attention to what is said as the film's driver and her passenger characters require of each other. There is no third person narrator, no plot, or any of the usual mise-en-scène props. Tension is generated through the interaction of the car's driver and her passengers.[25]

The focus of the film's long takes is simple; the faces, gestures, and the dialog between the driver and her passengers who come and go, often simply disappearing into the flux of the city. As in his other films, Kiarostami uses the Bressonian technique of sometimes withholding the image, and at others, the sound, in order to let the audience's imagination supply what is missing.

But it is *10*'s emphasis on dialog that calls to mind Gilles Deleuze's comment, "What cinema invented was the sound conversation," at the same time offering a refutation of Deleuze's (qualifying) caveat against cinema being drawn into a "dead-end: filmed dialogue."[26] Rather, as Rolando Caputo notes, "Kiarostami uses digital technology as a means to return cinema to a degree zero, to wipe the slate clean, and thus renew the terms of dialogue between spectator and screen."[27] And it is no mean feat that through what is "voiced" in the interchanges that take place in the car, we are given, "an image of Iran as a complex living culture and society, not one [...] totally silenced, subjugated, or ruined by the backward ruling mullahs."[28]

10 and the genre film *Sexy Beast* provide examples of the way in which digital technology allows for the coexistence of very different "filmic voices." In *Sexy Beast* there is a complex integration of sound and image that is dependent on a premeditated screenplay. The voice has been highly treated and at times functions as a major structuring device, but it also shares a place with the film's dramatic events. In comparison, in *10* much of the dialog is improvised; the sound is low-tech and it is unlikely that it has received much postproduction treatment.[29]

In the storytelling montage in *Sexy Beast*, there are no atmospheres in order to focus on the voice which functions as the sequence's connective thread. *10*, on the other hand, offers an example of how ambience—once the most lowly of lowly elements of the soundtrack—is no longer a filler to be faded when the voice makes its entrance, but can function as an essential part of its grain, becoming an integrated element in the storytelling. The voice in *10* is thus inseparable from the sounds of the streets. And the low drone of the city—punctuated by sirens, street voices, and tooting cars—not only constructs a constant environment to the episodic structure, providing the "glue" that holds the episodes together, but also functions as a metonymic device replacing images of the city (which we barely glimpse) with its sounds.

The Voice of the Future

From the ability to record unimpeded, "messy" conversations in a traveling vehicle in *10* to the stripped-back, highly stylized use of the voice in *In the Cut* and *Sexy Beast*, it is clear that digital technology has made possible a wide range of combinations of the voice and body. Not only is there a greatly increased ability to clarify, distort, disguise, and transform the voice on its journey to the audience, but there is also a much greater ability to capture the voice in context in the world. And the wide spectrum that the digital voice occupies also includes its various manifestations within the public sphere of communications—for example, cell phone and YouTube "movies."

The advent of digital sound technology has brought a slow redistribution of the weight and value of the various components of the soundtrack; it has also released the potential for redistribution within that component that we refer to as the voice, the possibility of a continuum from the "perfect" to the "real" to the extremely degraded voice (the highly compressed sound of much Internet distribution).

The Return of 3D

It is tempting to argue that because of the exploratory nature of much contemporary digital multimedia, there is likely to be a shift of the order of that which occurred when the techniques of New Wave film-makers began to make their impact on a new Hollywood generation. But two major impending changes suggest an even more dramatic shift—one that will have a number of ramifications for the filmic voice.

The return of old technology—3D, for three-dimensional—in digital form (*Beowulf, Avatar*) as a serious contender to 2D cinema, marks an attempt to fill the space that has until now been defined by sound: the auditorium, as the "playground" of both sound and image.[30]

It is too simple to view the return of 3D as a contest for the attention of those who belong to the "net" generation, given the self-interest of all those involved in the intermeshing of global digital media. Nor is it likely that the return of the old technology is a direct response to the threat posed by digital sound, given Dolby's investment in both technologies. Nonetheless, it is clear that surround sound has the potential to, and sometimes does, distract from the "sacred" bond in mainstream cinema between the body of the film (the screen) and the voice of the film (the soundtrack).

So there is some argument for saying that 3D films like *Beowulf* are an "answer" to digital sound and its potential disruptiveness. If the foreground action of the film—the body of the film—is shifted out into the theater, it would seem that it regains its rightful place, once again becoming the centerpiece. But such a notion is conceptually misleading, because it privileges the image, when in fact once the image leaves the screen, the relationship between it and sound is changed. No longer a slave to the flattened image, digital surround sound has the possibility of finally getting its own identity, of cooperating with the image on its own terms.

Filming in 3D thus makes it evident that sound and image are equivalent, not competing, entities. Although the audience remains positioned to face a rectangular screen, and the image continues to exert its magnetic pull, even when (or especially when) it leaves the screen—an adjustment occurs to our received viewing and listening habits. Though audiences may initially experience the proximity of the image with something of the visceral shock reputedly felt by the viewers in the late nineteenth century when the Lumière train appeared to be heading directly toward them, it is also apparent that film sound's acquisition of new dimensions has substantially increased its affective power.[31]

When sound—especially the voice—is sent to the surrounds, its most striking feature is that, unmediated by the screen, it can simultaneously cooperate with the image and function in an abstract manner, taking the form of clouds or bubbles that envelope the listener (or, as in the example of *Strange Days*, pushing or pulling). Sounds cannot have the same physical dimensions as the body—the image—but they are shapes just the same. It is this conception of sound as shape that is a distinguishing mark of digital cinema and that comes sharply into focus in 3D films.

A New Digital Continuum

Apart from the possibility of 3D replacing 2D formats, the other significant imminent change concerns the increasingly close relationship between sound and image. In 1999, Walter Murch noted the new seamless flow of sound and image in cinema and attributed it to the "mathematical commonality" between digital media. Predicting that in the future both picture and sound editing would be under the control of one person, he remarked, "I can see this already happening in the sound-mixing work that I do, where the borders between sound editing and mixing have begun to blur. And it is about to happen in the further integration of film editing and visual effects."[32]

As Murch foresaw, a decade later the borders between picture and sound editing have become increasingly blurred. A technical manifestation of this is the introduction of an adjunct to the picture editing program, Final Cut Pro. This addition, Soundtrack Pro, is a sound-editing program that gives the picture editor (the viability of this title now comes under scrutiny) the same control over the sound as the previously separate sound department.

The ramifications of the convergence of the two systems of editing for the voice cannot be predicted with certainty. Sound editor Gary Rydstrom believes that, "When digital editing systems both for picture and sound begin talking to each other and sharing files that are compatible, that will be very exciting. You'll do the basic sound editing and begin to swap sound and pictures back and forth. It will allow us to create better films."[33]

But if this kind of conversation between sound and picture edits turns out to be an interim phase before the development of a single unified system of editing—a digital continuum—it seems likely that picture will function as the host and sound will be assimilated. If that happens, just as the line between sound editing and mixing has blurred, the digital manipulation of both picture and sound will blur all distinctions, including the present confused line between voice and body.

The outcome of such assimilation could be that sound editing issues will receive attention earlier in the postproduction process, in contrast to their present situation at its end point. Although we have shown that the shift from analog to digital editing has involved new attention to the voice during postproduction, if in the future greater value is again placed on location performance—on the original dialog track—there could be a return of emphasis on the notion of the inseparability of voice and body.

In the contemporary era, digital sound technology has not only been out of step with image technology but also, especially at the level of exhibition, ahead of it, so it has finally gained an undeniable value of its own. As we have indicated, film sound designers have the newly acquired ability to identify and experiment with points of connection between voice and body in the cinema space. So, to a large extent, the freeing up of technical constraints has been accompanied a loosening of the ties of the "forced marriage"—as Michel Chion terms it—between sound and image. Now, there is a possibility of the voice being viewed once again as being wedded to the body, thus foreclosing or stifling any imaginative exchange between the two.

This possibility returns focus to the question of just how the voice functions for the audience. It is salutary to recall Altman's comment that each generation has its own sound.[34] One of the ironies that occurs at the very moment that the voice has achieved a clarity impossible in the past is that, in terms of the net generation, there is a good chance that it will be experienced in an extremely degraded condition, either through the media of a bootleg copy on a blog or a cell phone.[35]

In addition, the acceleration of technology has been accompanied by a changing public apprehension of its role in mediating the world. Film has been demystified by the availability of cheap digital cameras and the presence in many households of desktop computers equipped with picture- and sound-editing tools that are used to assembly all manner of narratives. Many film and film sound theories have assumed an innocent audience whose mystifcation has been perpetuated by conventional modes of representation, but now a large proportion of the cinema-going public is literate as never before.

An Epistemic Shift?

To a certain extent, the issue of the place of the voice can now be viewed as much as one of historical contingency, as it has been of conservatism. And if the imperative to protect it has previously resulted in the kind of mono-logism that Bakhtin identifies with the nineteenth-century realist novel, its democratization and the more easily obtained separation (and synthesis) of voice and body may simply indicate the arrival of a new digital-related aesthetic. Thus, although *Strange Days* has wonderfully inventive sound and is radical in its freeing of the voice from the fixed center that it has tradition-ally occupied, neither this nor the film's intelligent direction are sufficient measures to overcome the banality of the script that underpins its narra-tive. The potential radicality of the digital aesthetic cannot be conflated with the radicality of a film as a whole, and James Lastra's warning that the "lure of the simulation argument and the pull to generalize the ideal of perceptual simulation to the point of aesthetic rule" is timely.[36]

The ongoing shift in technology has been accompanied by the aware-ness that film, as such, may soon be consigned to the media and memory archive. But as the term "film" is replaced by "image," there is a strong perception that even when total digitalization of the industry occurs, any resulting stability will only be provisional. Thus it seems likely that a por-table and even disposable vocabulary will evolve with a rapidly changing praxis. It will need to be matched by a flexible mode of theorization, one that acknowledges—and is thus able to critique—significant innovations.[37]

There is already a need for such a reconceptualization. For example, much attention has been given to the voice-off, because in monophonic and Dolby Stereo films, it is one of the few times that the voice-body nexus is disrupted or broken. In the past, such ruptures have been seen to dem-onstrate the conventional union of voice and body (the supposition of a unified subject) to be no more than an ideological fabrication. But it now seems the epistemic and ideological—as opposed to aesthetic—stake in the separation of voice and body requires reconsideration. As sound and image move (albeit temporarily) toward a genuine equality, there is also a need for an integrated framework of inquiry, one in which the past theory contests over sound and image—in particular, those waged for good reason against sound's marginalization within film studies—may have to be put aside. That meaning is generated by the interrelationship of all components has never been so evident as at this time, the second moment of the Dolby era.

Notes

1. Michael Ondaatje, *The Conversations: Walter Murch and the Art of Editing Film* (London: Bloomsbury Publications, 2002), 65.

2. Eric Rohmer, "L'helice et l'idée," *Cahiers du Cinema* 93 (March, 1959), 50, and Jean-Luc Godard, "Review of Astruc's UNE VIE," in Peter Graham (ed.), *The New Wave* (Garden City, N.Y. Doubleday & Co., Inc., 1968), 81–83. For commentary on these analyses in relation to Platonism, see George Lellis, *Bertolt Brecht Cahiers du Cinéma and Contemporary Film Theory* (Ann Arbor: UMI Research Press, 1982), 18–21.

3. Rick Altman, "Material Heterogeneity of Recorded Sound," in Rick Altman (ed.), *Sound Theory: Sound Practice* (London: Routledge, 1992), 18.

4. For a description of digital theater systems, see Thomas A. Ohanian and Michael E. Phillips, *Digital Filmmaking: The Changing Art and Craft of Making Motion Pictures,* 2nd ed. (Woburn, MA: Focal Press, 2000), 212–213. For an account of the various stages of the film sound "Dolby Era," including the digital phase, see Gianluca Sergi, *The Dolby Era: Film Sound in Contemporary Hollywood* (Manchester, :Manchester University Press, 2004), 3–35, and Mark Kerins, "Narration in the Cinema of Digital Sound," *The Velvet Light Trap* 58, no.1 (2006): 41–54.

5. John Belton, "1950s Magnetic Sound: The Frozen Revolution," in Altman, *Sound Theory: Sound Practice*, 161–164.

6. John Belton, *Widescreen Cinema* (Cambridge, MA: Harvard University Press, 1992), 205.

7. For Bigelow's description of the technology, see the Alan Jones interview, "Strange Days," *Cinefantastique* 27, no. 9 (1996): 53.

8. See for example, Romi Stepovich, " Strange Days: A Case History of Production and Distribution Practices in Hollywood," Deborah Jermyn and Sean Redmond (eds.), *The Cinema of Kathryn Bigelow Hollywood Transgressor* (London: Wallflower Press, 2003), 154–156, where discussion of "the soundtrack" is almost exclusively confined to the music track, while the focus of articles on the image in *Strange Days* is indicated by their titles. For example, Laura Rascaroli, "Scopic Drive, Time Travel and Film Spectatorship," *Kinema,* no. 15 (April 2001): 9–41.

9. Sergi, *The Dolby Era*, 170.

10. Michel Chion, *The Voice in Cinema*, ed. and trans. by Claudia Gorbman (New York: Columbia University Press, 1999), 5.

11. See Sarah Kozloff, "Genre Talk," for a description of the (different) vernacular of the Hollywood gangster, in Philip Brophy (ed.), *The World of Sound in Film* (North Ryde, Australia: Australian Film, Television and Radio School, 1999), 116.

12. For a description of ADR, see Elizabeth Weis, "Sync Tanks: The Art and Technique of Postproduction Sound," *Cineaste* 21, no. 1–2 (1995): 57.

13. Ohanian and Phillips, *Digital Filmmaking*, 172.

14. Tomlinson Holman, *Sound for Film and Television*, 2nd ed. (Boston: Focal Press, 2002), 20.

15. Skip Ferderber interview with Christopher Coppola, "A Filmmaker's Odyssey," *Digital Cinema* 4, no. 2 (April 2004): 24.

16. William J. Mitchell, *The Reconfigured Eye: Visual truth in the Post-Photographic Era* (Cambridge, MA: MIT Press, 1992), 60. See also Stephen Prince, "Perceptual Realism, Digital Images and Film Theory," in *Cineaste* 49, no. 3 (Spring 1999): 27–37.

17. See Gary Rydstrom's amusing anecdote about Barbet Schroeder's comment on his "David Lynch-Alan Splet-like" sound in *Single White Female*, in Sergi, *The Dolby Era*, 168.

18. Charles Eidsvik, "Machines of the Invisible: Changes in Film Technology in the Age of Video," *Film Quarterly* 42, no. 2 (December 1988/January 1989): 21.

19. Elizabeth Weis notes that Marlon Brando's "mumbling" was a delay strategy because "he doesn't like to freeze a performance until he knows its final context." Weis, "Sync Tanks," 57.

20. Jenkins, "Menace of the Mumblers," *The Guardian* (February 21, 2008): 35.

21. The "two-suitcase film" is said to be the term used by Mike Figgis to describe his ideal (digital) film (Ondaatje, *The Conversations*, 214).

22. Jean-Luc Godard, "Jean-Luc Godard, interview by Emmanuel and Charles Tesson," *The Future(s) of Film Three Interviews*, trans. by John O'Toole (Berlin: Verlag Gachnang & Springer, 2000/2001), 42–43.

23. Geoff Andrew, *10* (London: BFI Publishing, 2005), 10. See also Adam Ganz and Lina Khatib, "Digital Cinema: The Transformation of Film Practice and Aesthetics," *New Cinemas: Journal of Contemporary Film* 4, no. 1 (2006): 21–36.

24. Abbas Kiarostami interview, quoted in Andrew, *10,* 35.

25. The serial form of the "leader" leads nowhere, requiring us to furnish our own conclusions.

26. Gilles Deleuze, *Cinema 2: the Time Image* (London: Athlone, Minneapolis: University of Minneapolis Press, 1989), 231.

27. Rolando Caputo, "Five to *Ten*: Five Reflections on Abbas Kiarostami's *10*,"http://www.synoptique.ca/core/en/articles/kiarsostami_interview28. Kiarostami, quoted by Hamid Naficy, "Receiving/Retrieving Third (World) Cinema," in Anthony R. Guneratne and Wimal Dissanayake (eds.), *Rethinking Third Cinema* (London: Routledge, 2003), 198.

29. Abbas Kiarostami has said, "I never think of sound during the editing stage. There may be some minor changes during the editing, but sounds are finalized before that stage." Interview by Shahin Parhami, "A Talk with the Artist: Abbas Kiarostami in Conversation," *Synoptique*, http://www.synoptique.ca/core/en/articles/kiarostami_interview.

30. Because the technology has been streamlined to suit distribution and exhibition and a large part of the public is habituated to interactive video games players for which a device is required as an aid, the technology will be a serious contender for theater space, not to mention, as Dolby publicly maintains, for home theater space.

31. Louis Lumière, *L'arrivée d'un train engare de La Ciotat* (1895; the reaction is described as a myth by Tom Gunning, James Lastra, and Martin Loiperdingerpoint).

32. Walter Murch, "A Digital Cinema of the Mind? By 2099, It's Possible" in "Summer Films section," *New York Times* (2 May 1999), 1.

33. Ohanian and Phillips, *Digital Filmmaking*, 170.

34. Rick Altman, "The Sound of Sound—A Brief History of the Reproduction of Sound in Movie Theatres," *Cineaste* 21, nos. 1–2 (1995): 68.

35. This begs the question as to whether "perfect clarity" should be the ultimate goal of cinema: an issue made concrete in the split between "D-Cinema," the high-quality, tightly controlled exhibition format being extolled by Digital Cinema Initiatives (DCI), a product of the major Hollywood studios, and "E-Cinema," a looser and more flexible format being embraced by the developing world and independent film-makers.

36. James Lastra, *Sound Technology and the American Cinema: Perception, Representation, Modernity* (New York: Columbia University Press, 2000), 221.

37. For example, the arrival of the "Red" camera signals a major shift from time-based editing to one conceptualized on spatial logic. See also Murch, "A Digital of the Mind," in which the enormity of possible future developments is clear.

14   Voice, Videogames, and the Technologies of Immersion

Mark Ward

Introduction: Videogames Find a Voice?

In this chapter, I consider the technologies of voice within videogames. I investigate the use of the voice both as an extension of the principles underpinning cinematic sound design and, importantly, as an extension of gameplay and game design. Crucially, videogames reinvigorate the principles of sound design for the screen arts by transcending the limitations placed upon them by the technical apparatus of cinema. I propose that the digital technologies and audiovisual designs of videogames seek to immerse and engage the human perceptual and emotion systems, by creating an "emotion-machine" (to use a term originally coined by Ed Tan[1] for analyzing some aspects of cinema) that intensifies the player's sense of involvement and implication in the scenes under negotiation. To explore these ideas, I conducted an interview with Emily Ridgway, the Audio Lead[2] of the game *BioShock*.[3] Released into the Xbox 360 market in 2007 to critical and financial success, *BioShock* remains a breakthrough project that has highlighted a number of important developments in the landscape of commercial videogaming, and for the purposes of exploring the interplay between sound design, vocalization, game mechanics, and narrative, it will serve as the focus text for this discussion.

The Case of *BioShock*

Aside from the genre hallmarks of the first-person shooter, *BioShock* is notable in its attempt to engage its audience in ways familiar to the natural audience of the cinema, that is, through psychological and perceptual immersion and emotional salience. However, it is the feature of gameplay, as the game industry website *Gamasutra* noted in its review of *BioShock*, that sets the game apart:

Like many of the *BioShock* reviews compiled at Metacritic, Andrew Pfister's at 1UP. com is scored at a perfect 10 out of 10. "By the time [*BioShock*] ends," he says, "you'll likely feel quite different about how you interact with games, and more importantly, how they interact with you."

BioShock's organic gameplay approach is its most intriguing aspect, according to Pfister. "As much as anything, *BioShock* is a conversation," he posits. "The game speaks to you in the usual 'go here, shoot this' language, but it also expects you to provide the answers to some relevant and surprisingly personal questions."[4]

Before detailing the function of voice in *BioShock's* "organic" and "intriguing" gameplay, it is important to return briefly to the so-called ludology/narratology debate, as it is the context within which Ridgway has developed her distinctive strategy. Gonzalo Frasca[5] and Janet Murray[6] have each noted with some irony that the gameplay versus narrative argument never really took place, as there remains no clear differential between the two groups' positions, only a spectrum that privileges either game-mechanics at one end or narrative at the other.

However, the fact that gameplay affords a unique selling point to paying customers has not been lost upon the videogame industry. If videogames have historically tended to favor gameplay over narrative, then the success of this formula seems to be supported by the global uptake of console videogaming when examined against a backdrop of plateauing movie box office sales.[7] In an oft-cited and much-debated comparison,[8] *Halo 2* surpassed the gross take of *Spider-Man*,[9] Hollywood's box office contender, by selling US$125 million in the first twenty-four-hour period in North America.[10] Although this cannot be taken as evidence outright that gameplay trumps narrative in the digital game arena, it does provoke questions. The skirmishes within the academy between the primacy of gameplay versus narrative are firefights that continue to erupt sporadically across the contested terrain of videogames, suggesting that something remains unsettled in the understanding of the mechanisms driving audience consumption and enjoyment of videogame content.

By way of response to this conceptual tension, Deborah Todd, screenwriter turned game-designer and game-educator, contends that videogames do not easily lend themselves to behaving like previous artforms. Videogames resist the superimposition of the tropes of literature, theater, and cinema, and particularly the concepts of Aristotelian drama, requiring instead a reconsideration of the definition of "content."

We've heard today that "Story is not King" ... and I'm a writer, and I'm here to tell you that that's true, I'm sad to say. However, I like to say that "Content is King" and Content and Story are not the same thing. In the games world, Content means: Story, Characters, Game-Mechanic, Sound . . . and [visual] Art is part of that equation.[11]

If Todd is correct in that we do indeed need to understand the affordances of games in their own terms and not in terms of older media, what would it mean for content to be reconfigured as "story, characters, game-mechanic, sound and [visual] art"? Does voice have a new role to play in this new configuration?

This [*BioShock*] is a game about story and everything in it is meant to get you through that story in the most exciting and (more importantly) immersing way possible. It IS much like reading a good novel while playing through it's [sic] pages. Never before with a game have I been so unconscious I was even playing at all. I don't see how that's anything but revolutionary. Though no one technical part of this game (except the sound design) are [sic] perfect, the presentation makes this game far greater than the sum of it's [sic] parts.[12]

Although this review by SliderFury describes the game in terms of the traditional medium of literature, I would argue that *BioShock* is a useful vehicle by which to explore a reconfigured notion of content, to trace the new lines of meaning created between gameplay, narrative, and vocal and visual design strategies. For Sliderfury, *BioShock* achieved a "revolutionary" state by providing an optimum balance between the difficulty of goal-tasking and the ease of execution in what Csikszentmihalyi[13] calls "flow." For the player, when in this state, awareness of the technical apparatus recedes to allow immersion into the world of the game. Immersion, as McMahan lays out in her metastudy, is comprised of a slippery set of concepts.[14] Immersion, however, is central to the reconfigured relationship of "content."

Another striking aspect of the previous review is its explicit reference to *BioShock's* sound design. In the reviewer's opinion, the sound design was "perfect," and "the presentation makes this game far greater than the sum of it's [sic] parts." But what, precisely, are we to make of this "perfection"? Perfection measured against which norms? And how exactly does this function within the gestalt of the game experience?

Emily Ridgway, *BioShock's* innovative Audio Lead, orchestrated a number of sound design strategies to integrate the spheres of perceptual and psychological immersion to create a unique sonic signature for the game. Voice design was key in her attempt to dissolve the historical fault line between gameplay and narrative. Conscripting her to the theme of this chapter, I asked a series of questions about the theories and reflections that informed her practical decisions pertaining to the use of voice in *BioShock*. For example, given that she was first trained in music and sound design for mostly linear media, I asked her what she thinks is special about the deployment of voices in computer-based games:

When considering voices in-game I think you're basically considering everything you do in film and TV but with the added factor of gameplay and interactivity.

I'll focus on how gameplay affects voice because that's the defining factor.

In my experience, understanding the designers' goals for the gameplay experience has been crucial. If the designers said to me, "ok, we're making the next *Mortal Kombat*" then immediately I would understand that the gameplay experience is all about amazing one-on-one fights that probably would last no more than a couple of minutes each. So I'd say the primary role of the voice in such a game would be to feed back and enhance the combat experience for the player, and the secondary goal might be story and character.

One of the many things *Mortal Kombat* is famous for is having an invisible narrator comment on the fight as it progresses. The classic lines "Finish Him!" for when the other player is close to death but not dead, and "Flawless Victory!" for when one player defeats another without even getting hit once, are great examples of how voice is used to make the player feel satisfied about the combat experience. The game is literally saying to you "You're awesome, I saw you kick that guy's ass." So the interesting thing is, *BioShock* also had the goal of creating a satisfying moment-to-moment combat experience. And yet to have an unseen voice comment on the blow-by-blow results during a fight would have been fairly inappropriate. This is because the primary gameplay goals of *BioShock* are considerably different to the gameplay of *Mortal Kombat*.

Aside from the obvious differences in genre, *BioShock* was all about immersion. We really wanted to lure the player as much as possible into thinking they were actually in an underwater city full of deranged citizens. Knowing this goal, it's easy to see how an invisible voice commenting "Multiple Kill!" or "Finish Him!" as you fight your way through would have broken immersion. In *BioShock* it was crucial that all voices were explained and given a narrative context.

The issue of balancing story and gameplay seems to be a really hot topic, especially recently. In a lot of games you can see that the "gameplay" (the player's story) and the "story" (the game's story) are two separate things that move in parallel. Like the player will start with a little movie story, then go and play the game, then another little movie plays which develops the story more. The most satisfying games I have played have been where the player's story and the game's story are the same thing. Case in point is *Portal*. Hopefully this merging between the player's story and the game's story will become more prevalent.

However, in *BioShock*, we faced the traditional battle between gameplay and story. Early on Ken Levine [creative director and chief writer of *BioShock*] and the design team decided that they did not want to use cut-scenes (little movies that deliver story) because they believed cut-scenes broke immersion and made it harder for the player's story and the game's story to be as close as possible. This forced Ken and the designers to be more creative about how they integrated story. They decided to use "audio logs/diaries" to convey the back-story and broadcast radio messages to convey the game's present story and tell the player what to do. (They got this idea from *SystemShock2*—a cult game they made back in 1998.) They also tried to say as much as possible without voice, such as posters, writing on the wall, artwork, carefully planned scenes and environments.[15]

Historically, the role of game audio has been primarily understood in terms of feedback to the player, signaling to the player the game-state and how well he or she is doing. Ridgway's goal, however, was to facilitate uninterrupted perceptual and narrative immersion, always careful to observe that genre also cued which form the audio feedback was expected to take. Ironically, a device made popular in the novels of the eighteenth century, epistles, was employed in the form of the "audio diaries" to supply back-story or to reveal new information to drive plot.

Eventually, however, the player bumps up against the aesthetic constraints and gameplay limitations determined by the needs of the game's AI:

I remember one point of internal debate in particular was with the voices of the AI themselves. Originally Design wanted the AI (the on-screen enemies) to just clearly state what they were doing and no more. Such as, "I'm coming to get you!," "I'm running away from you!," "I'm looking for you!," "I'm dying!," etc.

The reason for this is that game developers do not have control over the viewer's camera during game play, and thus cannot force the player to focus on the enemy running away behind a wall like a camera would do for the viewer in a Hollywood film. This means that there is a chance that the player could completely miss the crucial information that their enemy has run and hid behind the wall. The main way game developers solve this is to make the AI state what they're doing at all times. Hence the "I'm running away from you!" etc. I think is the primary reason why a lot of combat dialog in games sounds very poorly written, when in fact it is bound by the constraints of the gameplay.

On *BioShock* I was granted the privilege to try something different. I understood that the designers needed the AIs to exclaim their actions and why, so I decided to convey this information through the emotional performance of the voice, and not so much the words themselves. This freed me up to write completely weird and abstract dialog and yet still help the player figure out if the AI is attacking them, or hiding from them or something else. So for example, if we take the line "my daughter is dead, my daughter is dead" as it stands it doesn't really tell the player anything about what the AI is actually doing. Yet if we make the AI scream this line at the top of their lungs, like they're swearing and yelling it at you whilst running at you with a lead pipe, "MY DAUGHTER IS DEAD! MY DAUGHTER IS DEAD!" it becomes very clear that you're in trouble. It also adds back-story to the AI, it appears she's blaming you for her daughter being dead, which in turn could incite an emotional reaction from the player toward the AI.[16]

Not only does Ridgway's technique employ voice performance as a form of metadata to be used by the player to monitor the state of gameplay, but, by using the player's own faculty for social cognition, Ridgway is able to fold backstory into contextualized information for immediate use by the player. In this way, emotion, gameplay, and narrative are understood concurrently, thus sustaining immersion.

By making NPC[17] dialog carry emotional content and not just the semantic content required by the AI, Ridgway invokes Barthes's notion of the "grain of the voice":

Listen to a Russian bass . . . : something is there, manifest and stubborn . . . : something which is directly the cantor's body, brought to your ears in one and the same movement from deep down in the cavities, the muscles, the membranes, the cartilages, and from deep down in the Slavonic language, as though a single skin lined the inner flesh of the performer and the music he sings.

. . . The "grain" is that: the materiality of the body speaking its mother tongue; perhaps the letter, almost certainly *significance*.[18]

Barthes's concept of the voice calling up an absent body takes on special significance in the context of videogames. When considering the materiality of the voice during voice casting, performance, and recording, Ridgway leverages the cross-modal link between the perception of vocal affect and the perception of facial expression, particularly in an environment where visual facial data in games has historically been impoverished:

I think it's still challenging to sell a subtle performance and so voices in games still tend to be very over-exaggerated. I think this is because traditionally game developers couldn't rely on animation and cinematography to sell the necessary details of facial expressions and body language at least to the degrees film and TV can with actors and camera control. Perhaps if every game developer had the technology and talent of Pixar then this might not be the case, but alas most game companies don't have this resource and so the emotion in the voice really has to hit players over the head [. . .] For games, I predict that as animation and AI gets better then voice performances will be free to become less over-exaggerated and more realistic, and I think we're already starting to see this happen in games like *GTAIV*,[19] *BioShock* and *Brütal Legend*.[20]

As far as voice casting goes, on *BioShock* I was really looking for a super-realistic, un-gamey, natural performance. Sometimes you get a better performance if you tell the actors that they're auditioning for an "interactive film" instead of a video game. Otherwise some assume that because it's a "game voice", that you're making a kid's toy and it has to be cliché and cartoony. This might seem contrary to my paragraph above but I think it's important that an actor can still deliver a very emotional performance without being hammy about it. This was the balance I was searching for in *BioShock*.[21]

Interestingly, the affective vocal content Ridgway created using this technique also triggered a cultural taboo:

I rallied against most forms of post processing, apart from the environmental reverb that gets applied in-game, and of course the logs and radio fx. I was strongly against the processing on the voice of the Little Sisters and of Frank Fontaine. I felt they were too cliché and cartoony. Originally we had an amazing actor as the Little Sister, she was actually a young girl, 11 years old. . . . Her performance was so real and tragic because she was pretty much a real little girl. However, during development the designers and publishers became increasingly aware of the possible controversy of being able to harm little girls in our game and the potential negative press that would get. So the solution was to make the Little Sisters "more like monsters than little girls." So we hired a woman to re-record all the Little Sister lines, pitch-shifted her performance, and added a bunch of post processing to make her sound like a monster.[22]

Ridgway also employed cinematic sound design techniques when creating NPC vocalizations, such as the physical modeling and emotional tagging of the Big Daddy characters. Contrary to her approach to the Little Sisters and Fontaine, Ridgway used heavy postproduction techniques to create the desired affective vocal performance and sense of presence for the player:

I did enjoy the processing on the Big Daddy, however. My concept for that was fairly simple and I was really trying to give the player a sense of what they would really sound like in real life. I wanted the Big Daddies to sound like whales due to their huge lumbering, endearing nature. So we got a guy in to moan and scream in a deep tonal kind of way. Then I pitch shifted his performance down 18 semitones. Then I added some "metal helmet" reverb to his voice and that was it. The Big Daddy is probably good case in point for an AI that doesn't speak words yet is able to effectively communicate what they're feeling/doing to the player.[23]

Though the communication of vocal affect is one of the central strategies Ridgway employed to create meaning within the game, spatialization is another. Axel Stockburger also foregrounds spatialization. Quoting Brenda Laurel, he suggests the essential difference between cinema and videogames is the latter's creation of immersion through the "[t]ight linkage between visual, kinaesthetic, and auditory modalities." Stockburger amplifies Laurel's insight by arguing that game narrative is anchored in spatialization: "[The game environment] can be understood as a collection of sound elements organised as culturally coded representations of space."[24] Ridgway's work confirms the significance of spatialization in videogames.

For a game like *BioShock* the spatialisation is very important. It was used as a way to distinguish different voices and their function for the player. All logs and radios were "2D." 2D means that a .wav file will play without a 3D location in the [game] world. 2D voices don't pan from left speaker to right speaker as you move around and they don't get quieter as you move away. 2D sounds basically "follow" the player as they move as they are "stuck" to the camera. 2D is mostly used for gameplay direction because it grants the player the freedom to move around and perform actions and the player won't have to worry about missing an order or direction from the game. 2D voices usually duck [reduce] subtly the volume of the rest of the game while they're playing so they don't get drowned out by combat SFX [sound effects].

The problem with 2D lines [dialogue], though, is that they're fairly unnatural. We only really have a couple of 2D sounds in real life, i.e., your own inner monologue, and perhaps headphones that come from a portable music device, or cellphone. Games that have rich story lines often have to explain where the 2D voice is coming from.

In *BioShock* one of the first things you do is pick up a radio which you carry around with you for the rest of the game so that's how our 2D voice was explained. In a lot of military combat games and spy games your character comes with a headset. *Halo* and the Master Chief has "Cortana," the "AI" that sits in the player's head and chimes in when necessary. These are examples of ways which designers have justified the game's 2D voice in a narrative context.

On the other hand you have 3D dialog. 3D dialog means that the voice is positioned in the [game] world, it pans from left speaker to right speaker as you move around, and can also fade out the further the player moves away from the source. It's for this reason that 3D voices are most often not as critical for the player as the 2D voices. If a voice is marked as being 3D it means the designer/game is saying, "it's OK if you don't hear this all the time." As such 3D voice tends to be AI vo [voiceover], ambient chatter, grunts and oophs of combat, and other non-critical dialog.

The parameters given to 3D voice are derived from the goal to sound as natural as possible. However, sometimes 3D voice parameters will become unrealistic to suit the needs of the game design. For example, in *BioShock*, being able to hear your enemy AI well before you see it was critical in establishing a sense of tension and fear. So often times, you'd be able to hear someone muttering a couple of rooms away, when in real life you wouldn't hear them from that far away at all.[25]

Ridgway's use of 3D dialog functions as an aid to perceptual immersion for the player, simulating audition of real-world spatial characteristics, while the interplay between 2D and 3D can be understood to actively construct narrative point of view. Significantly, Ridgway's final observation regarding the tactical breaking of the rules of acoustic simulation to support gameplay underscores the function of sound design, first and foremost, as *design*.

Voice, Embodiment, and Barthes's Concept of Grain

As we have heard, in the case of *BioShock*, Ridgway contends that the current hot-spot in game sound development is not only the tussle between gameplay and narrative, but also in communicating emotional content through the voice.

Contemporary videogame practice deploys voice as prerendered audio files and therefore remains an extension of the old filmic process, that is, pre-scripted and unable to be influenced by the player once the audio file has been triggered. This practice is contrary to game sound's greatest success—the development of audio-engines such as FMOD,[26] Unreal Engine 3,[27] and Wwise[28] to facilitate interaction with music, sound effects, and atmospheres. Voice is frozen out of the fluidity offered by these game sound systems, relying instead upon predetermined and prerecorded audio files, and so representing something of a semiclosed system.

The underutilization of voice as an element of gameplay, however, is under challenge within massively multiplayer online games (MMOs). It is now commonplace within MMOs for a player's own voice to be used in an extra-diegetic sense; that is, game-playing peers use VoIP chat in the style of a walkie-talkie to comment on in-game action during gameplay. This is a complex issue, as the use of the player's own voice risks his or her removal from deep immersion within the fictional world, but it has been observed that VoIP chat appears to more strongly bond the player to peers who are also playing within the same fictional world.[29] In opposition, group cohesion and interaction can be adversely affected by poor media environments.[30]

It would seem, then, that the next zone for game sound development is in the real-time generation of emotionally charged dialog in true interaction with the totality of the game environment. Although such AI-controlled, synthetically generated voice is some way off in a technical sense, it can be said that this is already happening, but in a way that has more to do with Web 2.0 aesthetics and a systems-based architecture allowing user participation. Emerging voice technologies for networked games, such as DICE,[31] Vivox,[32] and Dolby Axon[33] point toward scalable, real-time, and spatialized in-game voice interaction. It is expected that these environments will support deep levels of perceptual immersion, situating the player via his or her voice within a high-resolution, dynamically modeled simulation of an aural environment.

From the development consortium's media release for DICE:

The software [DICE] will enable players to hear a spatially-accurate rendering of the voices of others in their virtual vicinity as they happen. The voices are adjusted based on orientation and distance from the listener, as well as their loudness (whispering versus shouting). This is expected to significantly enhance the player experience and create new opportunities to improve the game.[34]

It is clear that the developers of such systems expect to not only create greater perceptual immersion by modeling more "accurate" architectural acoustics, but desire to directly influence and shape gameplay as a result of player voice interaction by means of these acoustics.

Going hand in hand with the rise of these simulated aural environments is the emergence of sound-design tools that support deeper narrative immersion through roleplay. Through a suite of selectable parameters, VoiceThing![35] and Dolby Axon's "voice font" feature modify the player's voice in real time to create an aural signature more in keeping with the player's assumed in-game persona. Vocal design of this sort is reminiscent of Barthes' idea that the nonsemantic meaning of the voice is rooted in the body, or, in this case, the grain of the voice is perceived as a function of the virtual body located in virtual space.

If the impulse of sound technology as a medium is toward transparency, it could be said that its greater goal is to render the voice so fully that the body is not only recalled but reconstituted in the listening. The effect of this massively multiplayer voice technology is to allow the player to sense the body that generated the voice, not to hear the technology rendering it. By recalling an absent body, or by projecting an absent body onto a digital stand-in, an enhanced perceptual immersion is created, and, through the communication of subtle emotion markers contained within voice timbre and breath, so is emotional engagement.

Conclusion: Voice, Videogames, and the Technologies of Immersion

Looking to the future of videogaming, what role might there be for the human voice? Will there be more prerendered performance in the form Emily Ridgway does battle with in her strategies to bring emotional content into *BioShock*? Most likely not. The clearest glimpse of the future role for the human voice appears to be in the emerging voice technologies for MMOs and their affordance of participatory aesthetics.

The distributed networks of modern videogames reconfigure the human voice in exceptional ways. Voice has become a significant factor within gameplay, offering more than just game-state feedback; it allows the player's own performance to configure the fictional space. Recent innovations in immersive and real-time voice, such as Dolby Axion and similar tools, create a previously unexplored way in which spatialization and voice grain may construct an absent body. This supports a greater sense of embodiment in the game for the player; clearly, the next step in this evolution is player engagement via natural language with a synthetic agent in true dialog with game AI.

The human voice has taken some time to make its way meaningfully into the mediated world of interactive and spatialized sound, but its arrival completes the trinity of dialogue-music-effects identified in early cine-sound. Maybe this time, it will be heard for what it is.

Notes

1. Eduard S. Tan, *Emotion and the Structure of Narrative Film: Film as an Emotion Machine*, trans. Barbara Fasting, Lea's Communication Series. (Mahwah, N.J.: Erlbaum, 1996).

2. The game sound role of Audio Lead is equivalent to the cinematic role of Supervising Sound Editor or Sound Designer.

3. BioShock, 2K Games. Released August 21, 2007

4. Danny Cowan, "Critical Reception: 2K Games'/Irrational Games' BioShock," *Gamasutra* (2007), http://www.gamasutra.com/php-bin/column_index.php?story=8734.

5. Gonzalo Frasca, "Ludologists Love Stories, Too: Notes from a Debate That Never Took Place" (paper presented at the DiGRA Conference, Utrecht, 2003).

6. Janet H. Murray, "The Last Word on Ludology v. Narratology in Game Studies," (keynote presented at the DiGRA Conference, Vancouver, 2005).

7. Eric Bangeman, "Growth of Gaming in 2007 Far Outpaces Movies, Music," *Ars Technica* (2008), http://arstechnica.com/news.ars/post/20080124-growth-of-gaming -in-2007-far-outpaces-movies-music.html.

8. Halo 2, Microsoft Game Studios. Released November 9, 2004

9. Sam Raimi (director), *Spider-Man* (Columbia Pictures, 2002).

10. David Becker, "'Halo 2' Clears Record $125 Million in First Day," *CNET News* (2004), http://news.cnet.com/Halo-2-clears-record-125-million-in-first-day/2100-1043 _3-5447379.html.

11. Deborah Todd, "Living the Story," ed. Gary Hayes (LAMP [Sydney, Laboratory of Advanced Media], AFTRS, 2007). http://lamp.edu.au/podcast-from-blue-sky-to -green-light/

12. SliderFury, "BioShock—the Big Daddy of Video Games," IGN, http://rr.pc.ign. com/rrview/pc/bioshock/707, 40/69348/.

13. Mihaly Csikszentmihalyi, *Flow: The Psychology of Optimal Experience* (New York: Harper Collins, 1991).

14. Alison McMahan, "Immersion, Engagement, and Presence: A Method for Ana- lyzing 3-D Video Games," in Bernard Perron and Mark J. P. Wolf (eds.), *The Video Game Theory Reader* (New York: Routledge, 2003).

15. Emily Ridgway and Mark Ward, email, May 5, 2008.

16. Ibid.

17. A nonplayer character, or NPC, is a character controlled by the videogame's AI.

18. Roland Barthes, "The Grain of the Voice," in *Image, Music, Text* (London: Fon- tana Press, 1977).

19. Grand Theft Auto IV, Rockstar Games. Released April 29, 2008.

20. Brütal Legend, Sierra Entertainment. Released October 13, 2009.

21. Ridgway and Ward, email.

22. Ibid.

23. Ibid.

24. Axel Stockburger, "The Game Environment from an Auditive Perspective," in *DIGRA Level Up Conference (2003)* (University of Utrecht, Holland: 2003).

25. Ridgway and Ward, email.

26. FMOD, Firelight Technologies. http://www.fmod.org/

27. Unreal Engine 3, Epic Games, Inc. http://www.unrealtechnology.com/technology.php

28. Wwise, Audiokinetic Inc. http://www.audiokinetic.com/4105/wwise-introduction.asp

29. Dmitri Williams, Scott Caplan, and Li Xiong, "Can You Hear Me Now? The Impact of Voice in an Online Gaming Community," *Human Communication Research* 33, no. 4 (2007), 427–449.

30. Kevin Hew, Martin R. Gibbs, and Greg Wadley, "Usability and Sociability of the Xbox Live Voice Channel," paper presented at IE2004 *Australian Workshop on Interactive Entertainment* (Sydney, Australia: 2004).

31. P. Boustead, F. Safaei, and M. Dowlatshahi, "DICE: Internet Delivery of Immersive Voice Communication for Crowded Virtual Spaces" (paper presented at the IEEE Virtual Reality 2005 Proceedings (VR2005), March 12–16, 2005).

32. Vivox Precision Studio, Vivox, http://www.vivox.com.

33. "Dolby Axon—Better Voice. Better Game," Dolby Laboratories, Inc., http://www.dolby.com/professional/game_development/technologies/dolby-axon.html.

34. "Real Sound | CRC Association," CRCA, http://www.crca.asn.au/media/real-sound.

35. Voice Thing!, Antares Audio Technologies, http://www.antaresvox.com/voicething.html

15 The Play of the Voice: The Role of the Voice in Contemporary Video and Computer Games

Axel Stockburger

Introduction

In recent years, there has been a slow awakening of scholarly interest in issues related to sound and sound production in digital games. The majority of writers have focused on the differences between game audio and sound in other media such as film and TV[1] or on the musical aspects of game audio.[2] Interestingly, the human voice and its specific role in video and computer games did not feature very prominently in any of those accounts. If it was addressed at all, the voice was mainly regarded as the carrier of narrative structures in games. If other aspects, such as the communication among players, were addressed, this was usually undertaken from a purely technological perspective, not one that attempted to address other important aspects of this phenomenon such as, for example, the problematic relationship between the avatar and the playing subject's voice.

The voice is undoubtedly among our oldest and most immediate forms of shaping cultural relations among individuals, even if we avoid the conflation of speech and voice. In media systems characterized by digital signals, processing the sound of the voice is increasingly part of a wider matrix of sounds that are all affected by a myriad of potential transformations within a dynamic system. Nonetheless, the specificity of the voice within this system is capable of providing numerous unique and important functions in digital games.

This chapter aims to engage with the voice as part of the game audio or narrative system, as a function for character generation, as integral element of the gameplay, but also with the voices of the players themselves. Thus one is already confronted with informational and affective qualities of the voice. Specific games that use the player's voice as a means of interaction will be addressed and the intriguing role of the player's voice in multiplayer online games will be scrutinized. This discussion of the voice in digital games not only aims to better our understanding of internal game structures, which might be of interest for the field of game studies, but sets out to provide insights for the discussion of the wider implications of the shifting impact of the voice in the realm of digital technology. There are numerous issues at stake that separate the role of the voice in interactive environments from that in more traditional media systems such as radio, film, and television, and a discussion of the shifts this implies for the role of the subjects involved from the perspective of contemporary game environments can provide valuable insights into this phenomenon.

However, before delving deeper into this subject, it might be useful to establish a few basic parameters that will help to define our playing field throughout this text. As Theo van Leeuwen has pointed out very precisely, "sound never just 'expresses' or 'represents,' it always also, and at the same time, affects us. There is always both the social and personal, both meaning and pleasure—or displeasure. The difference lies in how we value the social and the personal. Or meaning and pleasure, and in the degree to which we acknowledge, their unavoidable interconnections."[3] This acceptance of the affective, material, and social aspects of sound that clearly also affect the voice is very important for the analysis and understanding of different forms of the voice's impact in game environments. On the one hand, the voice (even in the form of player metacommunication) is part of an affective mix, a dynamic soundscape that always provides an emotional link to the players of the game; on the other hand, it can simultaneously carry out diverse functional, expressive, and at times representational operations. Furthermore, in many cases it is precisely the material side of the voice that greatly enhances the depth and believability of simulated bodies. Although one has to differentiate between voice as sound and voice as speech, these two domains have to be regarded as opposite sides of one coin and the border separating them as fluid. It is important to keep in mind that a sound that might be recognizable as voice but not as a speech act can still convey meaning within a given context and simultaneously affect the player. For example, in many situations in contemporary 3D games, it is up to the player to transform voice as mumbling undecipherable sound into voice as meaningful speech by actively navigating closer to the location of the speech act. Thus, in such cases the shift between voice as sound and voice as speech becomes part of the gameplay itself. It can be present in the background and the foreground, it can switch between presentation and representation, and it carries out numerous tasks that cannot be delivered by other sound elements.

As a first movement of delineation, it is necessary to define two interconnected territorial domains, namely that of the players and that of the game. In other words, there are voices heard during gameplay that either emerge from the players or have been programmed or recorded into the game. In this context, the different Voice over Internet Protocol (VoIP) systems used in multiplayer online games represent a specific case of the userspace, namely a multiplication of individual auditory userspaces that intersect through the game software. This conception allows for a distinction between prerecorded, selected, or designed voices and the live voices emanating from human players during gameplay. This distinction, although based on a spatial metaphor, coincides with Folmann's view, which separates internal vocalization, speech, and voice sounds in the game from external vocalization, the communication between players.[4] In this context, these two categories of auditory space will be referred to as "user environment" and "game environment."[5] The subsequent discussion will first address the voice in the game environment and then move on to the user environment.

The Voice in the Game Environment

Although intelligible speech does play an important role in digital games, it is crucial to bear in mind that voice always designates a much broader range of sonic possibilities, including a wide array of emotionally affecting sounds, some of which are universally understood. In the context of digital games, voice also stands for all the possible sounds that might accompany actions of characters or even objects that either originate in the human voice or are explicitly aimed at simulating it (voice synthesis).

Similar to the voiceless period in film, games, due to the technological limitations of the early hardware, had to evolve until the recorded human voice fully entered the medium. During this time, voices of game characters were exclusively synthesized by the computer, which often resulted in the well-known "robot speech" effect, a general lack of emphasis and tonal range that could, up until very recently, easily be distinguished from a "real" human voice. Interestingly, in this context, Mark Grimshaw observes that there exists a gap between the achievements of visual realism and the quality of voice or speech synthesis, and points out that "it may be that humans are more prepared to perceptually paper over visual cracks than sonic anomalies in the animation given the sensitivity of the human auditory system."[6] This is indeed a crucial point, as it affects the production of speech elements for digital games. At present, recorded speech is much more prevalent in games than any synthesized forms. In general, it can be stated that voices emerging from the game environment are either synthesized or recorded (and potentially transformed subsequently). Thus the voice is either part of the classical regime of reproduction/representation or part of the regime of simulation. In this sense, spoken voice recordings belong to a much older tradition that can be traced back to the phonograph via radio and film; speech synthesis is still being developed in line with a specific idea of realism that aims for the "human" qualities of the synthesized voice. Early attempts to integrate voice recordings were based on using synchronized external technologies:

AutomataUK's ambitious 1984 release *Deus Ex Machina*, for example, featured a tape that you played along with the game. This tape consisted of a full soundtrack with music, sound effects and voice narration by John Pertwee, Ian Dury, Donna Bailey, Frankie Howerd, E. P. Thompson and Mel Croucher. This is more along the lines of a progressive rock concept album than a video game of the time, and represented a glimpse into the future; albeit rather more abstract in its nature than a Hollywood action movie.[7]

In 1982, the arcade game *Dragon's Lair* introduced human voices— namely, those of the animators themselves—for the first time. The first recorded samples of human voice snippets became possible with the advent of the Nintendo Entertainment System (NES) and Amiga and evolved further with the introduction of CD-ROM disks that enabled higher production and reproduction values due to the increased amount of data storage.

At present, the increasing synergy between film and game franchises— especially in conjunction with the Hollywood mainstream—has led studios to recognize the value of parallel voice acting for film and game projects. Furthermore, as Bridgett clarifies, "A qualitative production element to consider is the fact that voice-over recording is starting to become entrenched as part of motion capture shoots (and vice versa), and is therefore bringing together the artistic disciplines of both physical visual performance and audio performance."[8] Voice acting for video and computer games is also gaining in significance because the studios have realized the marketing value of well known Hollywood actors. Very good recent game examples of this are *Grand Theft Auto: Vice City*, in which Dennis Hopper, Ray Liota, Debbie Harry, and Burt Reynolds appeared as voice actors, or *The Godfather*, whose voice was spoken by none other than Marlon Brando. In terms of production, voice acting for games is very similar to the traditional "mickey mousing," namely voice generation for animations and cartoons. In these cases, the human voice provides a spark of life for the often fictional game characters. Douglas Kahn writes about Sergei Eisenstein, who was deeply affected by early Disney cartoon films, such as the famous Steamboat Willy (1928), "[w]hereas Eisenstein sought to find an auditive equivalent to his visually derived montage, Disney extended the elements of silent cinema into sound under the actuality (not metaphoricity) of music in such a way that the music and sound performed the visual elements of the film—its characters, objects and actions."[9] It is precisely in this sense that voices in games literally perform the visual game characters, such as avatars, and thus provide them with a meaningful existence in the fictional game universe. This, however, does not mean that the characters necessarily have to speak at all. Grunts, sighs, laughs, and so on are of a similar importance in relation to the creation of a believable character as intelligible speech. As game designer Steve Meretzky writes,

Voice characterization is a fantastic way to get a lot of bang for your buck. Even if you line up some very talented professional voice talent, you'll be spending a fraction on vocals than you will be on graphics. And the human brain is equally attuned to audio and visual signals, so voice characterization is an excellent and not very expensive way to telegraph personality to the player. Voice characterization is particularly important if your main character is a first-person character, and is rarely or never seen.[10]

The observation that the voice is important for first-person avatars, which do not generate strong visual identification, is particularly significant, because here it—rather than the visual object—is the foundation for the necessary link between player and avatar. Here the voice indeed delivers its grain in the Barthian sense in order to produce the phantasm of a body. In addition to this generative process, it can also function as a signal system that provides feedback about changes of "avatar states" such as low health, pain, joy, exhaustion, and so on, which adds an indexical dimension to the affective, emotional one. Although the kinesthetic bond between player and avatar creates the first layer of identification based on the interaction system, the voice immediately plays an important role in this respect— even more so in games that deliberately attempt to recreate elements from film. Because the identification of the player with the avatar lies at the core of most digital games, the way in which the voice is connected with the avatar and its potential actions is of crucial importance for the suture of the player into the fictional game universe. In order to explore the player/ avatar relation further, it makes sense to turn toward this process of identification with an acousmatic voice in the context of film.

Michel Chion asserts that in order for an acousmatic voice to become "the pivot of identification, resonating in us as if it were our own voice," a kind of voice he terms the "I-voice," two criteria have to be met.[11] He writes, "First, close miking, as close as possible, creates a feeling of intimacy with the voice, such that we sense no distance between it and our ear. We experience this closeness via the surefire audio qualities of vocal presence and definition, which manage to remain perceivable even in the worst conditions of reception and reproduction, even through the low-fidelity medium of the telephone."[12] Chion defines "dryness" as the second important issue, pointing out that "it's as if, in order for the I-voice to resonate in us as our own, it can't be inscribed in a concrete identifiable space, it must be its own space unto itself."[13] The game *Max Payne* is a very good example of this technique at work, as it extensively deploys a Chandler-inspired first-person voiceover narration in the style of classic film noir. Here, the voiceover dialog very precisely demonstrates the qualities that Michel Chion introduced in relationship to the I-voice, namely, close miking and dryness. In *Max Payne*, the player floats in the timbre of the acousmatic voice that provides the background narrative for the gameplay. The game designers have successfully transferred a film sound principle to the game universe, as the qualities of the voice recording lead to a strong link between player and avatar. This specific use of the voice has to be regarded as a core element that enhances the identification between player and avatar, especially in first- and third-person-perspective games.

Furthermore, the narrative in *Max Payne* is a very good example of the implementation of storytelling qua intelligible speech in contemporary digital games, because it serves several functions: it uncovers the background story, which leads into a noir revenge plot; it orients, leads, and at times steers the player through the game space; and it delivers hints and warnings at important moments in the game. Thus we are confronted with avatar identification, information, spatial guidance, and general status feedback, all delivered via voice. These operations are very common, even across different game types, and it can be argued that this is because voice communication adds an independent layer of information to the visual elements on screen. In certain types of games—for example, *Tom Clancy's Ghost Recon*—simulated military radio communication is used to inform the player and add to the realistic feeling of commanding a team of soldiers. Very limited use of voice samples in order to inform players about the current event status (number of kills, weapons used, players entering the game, flag status) is also very common in first-person shooter (FPS) games and is often provided in the form of simulated radio communication. This has been well documented by Mark Grimshaw, who writes about *Quake III Arena* that

The feedback/directory contains mainly speech samples indicating, for example, how much time is left in a game, samples praising the player who has managed to "frag" several opponents in a short specified time span, and, a particular favourite, the derisive Humiliation! sample that is played whenever a player's character has been splattered by the gauntlet, a close-quarters and difficult to wield weapon.[14]

A very interesting special case is the use of voice communication in the *Metal Gear Solid* and *Resident Evil* series, in which load and save functions as well as additional guidance in the game are often wrapped up in the communication with an in-game character that speaks via radio. This usage is significant, because it hides the necessary feedback, load, and save operations, which are usually nondiegetic elements within the narrative structure of the game. Rather than interrupting the fictional universe by presenting the player with a save button, saving and loading game states become part of a conversation that refers to actions within the game.

The previous examples demonstrate very clearly how voice can surpass intelligible speech and give rise to an affective dimension that enables player identification, the construction of the link between playing subject and avatar, as well as an emotional dimension. Yet the voice is also capable of simultaneously maintaining narrative and feedback functions that are important for the gameplay.

Once language appears as intelligible speech, games have to be translated or localized for different national markets, adding to the production costs.

This is clearly not the case with voices that do not utter intelligible text-based content. This might partly explain the interesting fact that a lot of game characters avoid intelligible speech but have a voice that laughs, murmurs, emits angry noises, and so on. The game *Oddworld: Abe's Oddyssey*, for example, invented an entire original language termed "gamespeak" for the main character, Abe, that includes bodily noises such as farting alongside shouts and whistles. The player can control the use of this "language" of sounds in order to affect and control game characters and the environment. Another excellent example for the generation and integration of nonhuman speech is the odd language spoken by the covenant aliens in the *Halo* series. Here the player can listen in to conversations that are usually a series of high-pitched noises, screams, shouts, murmuring, and, very occasionally, intelligible English words woven into this web of alien sounds (such as the word "run" when a panic breaks out among the aliens).

The screams and sighs uttered by the zombies in the first level of *Resident Evil 4* display another important feature: the affective register of the voice. Here, we are mainly confronted with the scream, which is curiously semiotically based in a field between language, information, and very deeply rooted animal affection. Douglas Kahn highlights how the issue that screams

> are resolutely communicative and meant for others is demonstrated by the fact that people who have been in a life threatening situation often must be told by others that they have been screaming. Although screaming does not engage language, we are still attuned to its signals. A parent knows when a child's scream at play becomes a true call of alarm or when an infant's fever has taken a dangerous turn, and people regularly walk by the screams coming from whiteknuckle rides at carnival comfortable in the knowledge that they are not heartless.[15]

The screams of terror that emanate from the peasant zombies in *Resident Evil* are on the one hand a means of information about the state of rage the creatures are in, telling the player when they will attack, and, on the other hand, simultaneously enhance the eerie atmosphere of horror that characterizes this particular part of the game. Although these screams, or "war cries" give evidence of an enemy's position if it is offscreen and consequently invisible, screams of pain deliver information about whether an enemy has been hit or hurt. In this sense, such screams can become an important element of a game's information and feedback system, while at the same time aiming to trigger ancient fears embedded in the players.

However, apart from narrative, informational, and affective functions, the voice can become even more central for digital games, up to the point of becoming an integral part of the gameplay itself.

The Voice as Part of the Gameplay

As pointed out in the previous section, voices in gameplay can be separated into those that are part of the game environment, where one might play in order to be able to understand a specific conversation, or those that belong to the user environment, where the human voice is used to interact with the game.

At this point, it is useful to highlight a crucial difference between the film medium and most instances of digital games. While in film the score is produced in advance during the sound edit, in 3D games the players can often decide themselves what they want to hear by actively navigating through the gamespace in order to listen in and identify the sources of sounds. This means that the kind of speech that Michel Chion has introduced as the rare case of emanation speech in film, "where speech is not necessarily completely heard and understood,"[16] is possibly the prevalent mode of speech in games with territorial 3D audio. He writes that in these cases, "speech becomes . . . an emanation of the characters, an aspect of themselves, like their silhouette: significant but not essential for the mise-en-scène."[17] In a sense, the link between recorded speech samples and in-game characters that is provided by the game engine is captured very well if one thinks about sound as the silhouette of the game character. Due to the interactive nature of computer games, the power to turn a speech event from being in the background to being in focus is, in many instances, in the hands of the players. This represents one of the most significant, and most often overlooked, issues regarding the interplay between visual elements and sounds in digital games. As opposed to film or TV, where the soundtrack is predefined during the edit, the player can deliberately create temporary connections between visual events and sound events. To give an example, the speech of game characters in the 3D game *Deus Ex* can be fully understood only if the player's avatar is moved into their vicinity; otherwise the speech remains part of an unintelligible atmospheric background sound. Some games even turn this active focusing on the intelligibility of speech into a game principle in its own right. This is the case with the directional microphone feature that can be used in particular parts of *Metal Gear Solid 2*. In a short episode of the game (Oil Rig Shell 2, Core 1, Air Purification Room), a directional microphone is used to listen to a conversation that takes place behind a wall. Because the source of the voice is moving, the player has to move the directional microphone in exactly the right directions to overhear the conversation. This situation generates a complex spatial setup that dynamically links the user action of moving the microphone in the right direction with the possibility of making speech intelligible. The idea of the directional microphone has since also been used in the game *Tom Clancy's Splinter Cell: Pandora Tomorrow*. Here the player has to point a directional microphone at a moving elevator in order to listen to a significant conversation taking place inside an embassy building. If the player moves slightly too far away from the target, the speech is rendered unintelligible.

In these cases, as an element of the game environment, the voice becomes an integral part of the gameplay rather than being merely an atmospheric addition to the general soundscape of the game. Furthermore, the player's spatial operations in the game environment are directed by the locations of speech events, which adds a dimension of realism to the game, because it relates to our everyday experience in sonic environments. Thus, as film plays with the viewer/listener by hiding and showing sources of sounds (which is an essential element in the generation of film space), games often leave the decision whether to link the source of a sound with a visual event up to the player. In these types of games, the player takes over the role of the sound editor as he or she judges during gameplay which sounds should remain acousmatic and which should be connected to a visual object. There are a lot of situations in which players can hear character's voices in separate rooms or from around the corner and subsequently deliberately identify those voices with visible characters by turning around the corner, or by avoiding doing so. This process has a strong impact on the way players are drawn into the game, because the domain of avatar movement is dynamically linked to the sonic environment. In other words, a continuous sonic feedback to spatial actions of the avatar exists that, most importantly, can become meaningful within the narrative setting of the game whenever voices are transformed from mere sound into intelligible speech.

In other types of games, the active use of the players' voices becomes part of the game principle as the system of interaction. On a technological level, these games depend on a microphone as well as the implementation of live sound analysis. One of the earliest games that employed the use of the human voice as a means of controlling in-game action was *Hey You Pikachu!*, developed by Nintendo in 2000. According to Norman Chan, "it introduced players to the idea of controlling the character with one's voice. *Hey You Pikachu!* came with a microphone and a voice recognition pad; the aim was to guide Pikachu through endless mini-quests with one's voice."[18] Nintendo has followed up on this original idea by implementing a microphone in their Nintendo DS device. The experimental music tool *Electroplankton* developed by the Japanese media artist Toshio Iwai in 2005 for the Nintendo DS employs this microphone to enable voice interaction. However, the most famous example of a game principle based on the human voice acted out in the user environment is the immensely successful karaoke game *SingStar*. Here the player's singing is analyzed and evaluated, leading to a number of subgames based on principles such as rhythmic or melodic accuracy. The game follows in the tradition of classic party games, in the sense that it is usually played by groups of people, which means that they are not only singing for the computer evaluation but simultaneously in a real-life situation for the other players in the user environment. In *SingStar,* digital technology affects the voices of the players dynamically via a visual feedback system that allows the players to adapt their intonation and tonality to chosen pop songs.

The Player's Voice

Language-based communication is an important aspect in a wide range of multiplayer Internet games. These games generally provide the means for different levels of communication among the players, whether in textual form or via chat or other operations in the game, such as specific signs, gestures, and so on. This communication serves numerous purposes, ranging from social exchange outside of the actual gameplay, the discussion of or introduction to the rules, specific strategic issues, or the exchange between players during gameplay. With the spectacular growth of multiplayer online games, the implementation and use of voice-based communication instead of chat- or text-based forms has increased significantly. In 2001 Sony introduced their Network adapter for the Sony PlayStation 2, which allowed voice communication in specific games. Microsoft followed suit with the Xbox Live system in 2002. Third-party companies like the add-on VoIP solutions TeamSpeak and Ventrilo were increasingly taken up by players of FPS games. A number of large massively multiplayer online role-playing games (MMORPGs), such as *World of Warcraft*, have recently started to integrate voice chat options into their client software. And even *Second Life* has gone into a beta test phase with the "second talk" voice chat system. In the light of these developments, it is important not to overlook the fact that speech-based communication between players is as old as games themselves. So it is useful to differentiate between online and offline multiplayer games and between players' voices in the user environment and in the game environment. Subsequently, I will be addressing the difference between the voice in online multiplayer games and in shared physical environments.

As Newman points out, "Even ostensibly single-player games are frequently played by more than one person. There are a number of ways this might be seen to happen. For example, players may play in turns—perhaps taking responsibility for one level or one life each before swapping over, or perhaps comparing completion times, number of items collected and so on."[19] In addition to this practice of taking turns, which can be referred to as "relay play,"[20] people often play single-player games in teams made up of the game-player and active advisors. In these cases, specific roles within the team, such as "map reading/making co-pilot," "puzzle solver," and "lookout" are assigned. All of these different styles of play are necessarily based on continuous communication in the user environment, which is in these cases the living room or the game arcade.

Rather than sharing one physical space, online multiplayer games have as many user environments as there are players; however, the voices come together in only one place: the game environment. It can be argued that this complex spatial situation directs the player's voice toward a very specific function, which, among other things, affects the physical spatial gap between the player and the game space. Besides the perspective that communication among the players is necessary in order to coordinate actions or agree on rule changes in subgames, there is another relevant aspect to this form of exchange: in online games that represent simulated spatial environments used by players who are not physically present, the player's voices provide a kind of bridge that reaches from their private subjective spaces into the shared game space. The act of enunciation posits the player as a subject and "person" in the simulated environment. In other words, the immediacy of the player's voice anchors him or her in the representational space and thereby suppresses the feeling of disjunction that might arise, especially during phases of the game that are not characterized by intense action. I will refer to this phenomenon as "anchor function" and discuss the unique and at times contradictory implications it introduces. For example, this anchor function can at times become highly problematic in that it provides a great deal of information about the persons playing that they might not want to disclose. Most importantly, the characteristics of this anchoring differ in accordance with the kind of communication as well as the type of game. In games that are heavily dependent on character development and presentation, such as role-playing games (RPGs), the anchor function can pose problems that are not as relevant in strategy games and shooters.

However, before this point can be focused on in more detail, it is necessary to have a brief overview of the major motivation behind this kind of communication.

As Tony Manninen points out,

Language-based communication forms a strategic backbone within games and game communities that support and value the communication aspects of playing (e.g., RPGs). However there are several examples of this strategy in fast-paced shooting games, too. Bluffing the opposite team by using false status reports, or distracting the enemy by delivering irritating taunts indicate the use of this interaction class. In addition to these, the strategic manoeuvres are generally executed based on the spoken (or written) dialogue between the team members.[21]

This can be witnessed in team-based games like *Counter Strike*, where the teams often develop highly specialized coded language that allows them to switch quickly between prearranged tactical maneuvers. During fast-paced action sequences, voice communication is an advantage, because the players have their hands free. Additionally, in clan- or team-based games, the players who talk to each other are usually part of a group of individuals who know each other, and voice communication adopts a similar role to that in team based sports, such as football or basketball. In these types of games, the anchor function allows players to identify their team members quickly and opens up a realm of social interaction that reaches beyond the game. In this context, it is also important to consider that the fictional aspects of the game universe, especially in relation to character development, are usually of no great importance in FPS and strategy games.

This situation changes in the case of online RPGs and MMORPGs, which present fictional universes that are maintained by the players' willingness to actively perform their roles. Furthermore, in large game universes, players are often confronted with strangers. In such a situation, it can be argued that the anchor function can have a negative impact on the player's relationship with the game universe. Information about the speaker's gender, age, and location can be inferred by listening to the voice, which potentially leads to a suspension of the illusion in these types of games. In order to highlight this point, it is necessary to consider that RPGs are dependent to a large extent on what Roger Caillois has termed "mimicry," that is, the performance of fictional identities. Caillois is convinced that

All play presupposes the temporary acceptance, if not of an illusion (indeed this last word means nothing less than beginning a game: in-lusio), then at least of a closed, and, in certain respects, conventional universe. Play can consist not only of deploying actions or submitting to one's fate in an imaginary milieu, but of becoming an illusory character oneself, and of so behaving. One is thus confronted with a diverse series of manifestations, the common element of which is that the subject makes believe or makes others believe that he is someone other than himself. He forgets, disguises, or temporarily sheds his personality in order to feign another. I prefer to designate these phenomena by the term mimicry, the English word for mimetism.[22]

It can be argued that in the case of RPGs, the anchor function provided by voice chat can disrupt the state of mimicry that is essential for such games not only because the player hears his or her own voice as well as that of the others, but also because other sounds from the user environment, such as car sounds, machines, or telephones, can enter the fictional world via the microphone. Even more importantly, voices offer information about the player's identities outside of the game that they might want to leave in the dark, such as their gender, age, upbringing, or locality, as well as their emotional state during gameplay.

Thus the believability of the fictional character is endangered precisely because the anchor chain of the subject's voice leads outside of the game universe.

One just has to imagine a meeting with a mighty Tauren warrior in *World of Warcraft* and then hear it speak with a lisp or in an odd dialect. In such a situation, the voice can turn into a crack of the real in the matrix. As Brandon LaBelle notes, "The voice, or the speaking subject, is . . . embroiled in a performative tension whereby speaking is always already enacting an uncertain and tenuous connection to the real—one speaks in and out of oneself, fixed and unfixed at the same instant to the parameters of being, of social interaction, enacting the essential paradox of the voice, identified by Steven Connor, in which the voice must leave itself in order to return, so as 'to move from me to the world, and to move me into the world.'"[23] This is a very important point that reverberates strongly with the anchor function mentioned previously, as it is precisely this capability of the voice to move from me to the world that also moves that "me" into the game. This "movement of the me" into the game world holds the power to break the magic circle in those types of games that maintain their pleasure from the illusion of a fictional "me" in an imaginary scenario. In this sense, the anchor function poses a specific problem for female players with male avatars and vice versa, because it denies them the option to leave their real-life gender identities behind. This problem might lead to the further development and use of live voice modulators or filters that are not commonly used at present.

Notwithstanding all of these issues, the drive toward voice chat in online games seems to be very strong at present, which could be due to a number of reasons. Voice-based communication allows people who are not used to typing text to interact easily with each other, and in fast action games, it is simply impractical to have to use prepared keys in order to trigger signs. Especially team-based games and those that depend on complex group tactics gain significantly in complexity with the option of voice communication. After all, as we could witness with one of the most fascinating and transformative technologies, the telephone, "the voice appears to lend itself to hallucination, in particular the hallucination of power over space effected by an extension or restructuration of the body. Thus, as Lacan points out, our mass media and our technology, as mechanical extensions of the body, result in 'planeterizing' or 'stratospherizing' of the body."[24] It is in this sense that the voice allows the players' bodies to reach out and colonize fictional online universes, and because these universes are inherently spatial structures and the operations in them are of a spatial nature, this amounts very directly to a kind of "hallucination of power over space." At this point, it is possible to draw conclusions about the impact of digital technologies on the voice. As we have seen, voice chat systems allow the subjects to anchor themselves further in simulated spatial environments, which entails the construction of "stratospherized" bodies that cross the borders between physical and simulated spaces. On the one hand, this enables much more complex social interaction with subjects spread out across the globe, while on the other it can lead to the suspension of mimicry, the play with imagined identities that lies at the heart of many online games and communities. If this thought is taken a little further, it also touches upon an intrinsically political issue, namely the slow erosion of privacy that can be witnessed in the current developments regarding policies regulating the use of the Internet. Because the individual voice continues to be a unique signifier of the subject, voice chat systems ultimately enable the identification of subjects in a mediated universe that until the present was widely characterized by the promise of a certain degree of anonymity.

Conclusion

The point of departure for this text was the claim that the voice provides a range of different unique functions in digital games and that an analysis of these functions enables us to see the role of sound in those games in a different light, beyond the overt focus on music and functionality, especially in relation to the players themselves. It has been argued that an important impact of the voice is on the generation of believable game characters, and pointed out that the voice can perform the visual game characters and thus provide them with a meaningful existence in the fictional game universe. It can be concluded that the voice is a key element in the functioning of first-person-perspective avatars, which do not afford strong visual identification, because here they—rather than the visual object—are the foundation for the necessary link between player and avatar.

In numerous digital games, as opposed to film or TV, the players deliberately connect sounds with visual elements and can thus transform voices from sound into intelligible speech, which can even become a specific category of gameplay. Most important, it has been argued earlier that this phenomenon strongly affects the suturing of the player into the game universe, because it directs the navigational interaction through meaningful sonic feedback.

Regarding the fascinating subject of voice-based communication in online multiplayer games, the term "anchor function" was introduced to designate an important aspect of the appearance of the players' voices in the game environment. This anchoring provides a kind of bridge that crosses the potential feeling of spatial disjunction and enables situation of the subject in the simulated environment, on the one hand, but also threatens to disrupt the consistent illusion based on fictional characters, especially in RPG games. The concept of the anchor function in relation to voice chat systems might provide a valuable starting point for the discussion of the wider implications of the changing role of the voice in digital online communities.

As has been shown, the impact of the voice in video and computer games manifests itself in very diverse yet at times overlapping domains. The digital entertainment and gaming landscape transforms itself with an enormous pace and experimental technologies, such as novel forms of voice communication, synthesis, and live DSP modulation, are finding their way into an increasing number of devices and games. A very interesting sign in this context is the planned integration of avatar lip-synching into the game *Little Big Planet* by the company media molecules. It is reasonable to assume that there will be a drive toward consolidation of the different voice chat systems, thereby integrating VoIP conversations in game environments or online universes like *Second Life*. This might lead to a much stronger blurring of the borderlines between play and work as well as between online and offline communities. For example, players might wish to follow events in game universes based on audio information and voice communication alone, just to keep track of developments in the game. Others might deliberately decide to opt out of voice communication due to the problems with maintaining the game's illusion, as discussed previously. Furthermore, voice acting is most definitely still gaining importance for Hollywood actors as the fields of film and interactive entertainment start to interpenetrate. As the technology continues to evolve, it is clear that the voice, one of our oldest means of expression, will continue to play a pivotal role in gaming.

Notes

1. Johnny Friberg, Dan Gärdenfors, "Audio Games: New Perspectives on Game Audio," (ACE Conference, Singapore, June 2004), http://www.cms.livjm.ac.uk/library/AAA-GAMES-Conferences/ACM-ACE/ACE2004/FP-18Friberg.johnny.audiogames.pdf, (accessed January 10, 2009); Mark Grimshaw, The Acoustic Ecology of the First-Person Shooter (doctoral thesis, The University of Waikato, 2007); Sander Huiberts, Richard van Tol, "IEZA: A Framework for Game Audio," Gamasutra.com http://www.gamasutra.com/view/feature/3509/ieza_a_framework_for_game_audio.php?page=1, (accessed January 10, 2009).

2. Matthew Belinkie, "Video game music: not just kid stuff," Video Game Music Archive 1999, http://www.vgmusic.com/vgpaper.shtml, (accessed January 10, 2009); Norman Chan, *A Critical Analysis of Modern Video Game Audio* (BA thesis, University of Nottingham, UK), http://www.gamessound.com/texts/chan.pdf, (accessed January 10, 2009).

3. Theo Van Leeuwen, *Speech, Music, Sound* (London: Macmillan Press, 1999), 128.

4. Troels Brun Folmann, *Dimensions of Game Audio*, http://www.troelsfolmann.com/blog/?p=16 (accessed February 8, 2008).

5. Axel Stockburger, "The Game Environment from an Auditive Perspective," (Level Up, Digital Games Research Conference, Utrecht, The Netherlands, Faculty of Arts, Utrecht University, November 4–6, 2003), 2.

6. Mark Grimshaw, *The Acoustic Ecology of the First-Person Shooter*, (Doctoral Thesis, the University of Waikato, 2007), 338.

7. Rob Bridgett, "Hollywood Sound: Part Three," Gamasutra.com, http://www.gamasutra.com/features/20051012/bridgett_01.shtml (accessed December 8, 2007).

8. Ibid.

9. Douglas Kahn, *Noise, Water, Meat* (Cambridge, MA.: MIT Press, 2001), 149.

10. Steve Meretzky, *Building Character: An Analysis of Character Creation*, Gamasutra.com, http://www.gamasutra.com/view/feature/3480/building_character_an_analysis_of_.php?print=1 (accessed December 8, 2007), 13.

11. Michel Chion, *The Voice in Cinema* (New York: Columbia University Press, 1999), 51.

12. Ibid.

13. Ibid.

14. Mark Grimshaw, *The Acoustic Ecology of the First-Person Shooter* (Doctoral Thesis, the University of Waikito, 2007), 81.

15. Douglas Kahn, *Noise, Water, Meat* (Cambridge, MA: MIT Press, 2001), 345.

16. Michel Chion, "Wasted Words," in Rick Altman (ed.), *Sound Theory Sound Practice* (New York: Routledge, 1992), 105.

17. Ibid.

18. Norman Chan, "A Critical Analysis of Modern Day Game Audio," (Doctoral Thesis, University of Nottingham, Department of Music, 2007), 13.

19. James Newman, *Videogames* (London: Routledge, 2004), 152.

20. Ibid.

21. Tony Manninen, "Interactive Forms and Communicative Actions in Multiplayer Games," Game Studies 3, 1 (2003), 7.

22. Roger Caillois, *Man, Play, and Games* (New York: The Free Press, 1961), 19.

23. Brandon LaBelle, *Background Noise: Perspectives on Sound Art* (New York: Continuum Books, 2006), 143–144; Steven Connor, *Dumbstruck: A Cultural History of Ventriloquism* (Oxford: Oxford University Press, 2000).

24. Mary Ann Doanne, "The Voice in the Cinema: The Articulation of Body and Space," in John Belton and Elisabeth Weis (eds.), *Film Sound: Theory and Practice* (New York: Columbia University Press, 1985), 170.

IV At the Human Limits of VOICE

The final section addresses a number of themes that have long haunted discourses of the voice.

Anthropologist Michael Taussig contributes an enchanting meditation on humming—a use of the voice, usually sung, which, he says, moves in and out of understandable language, and tends to work in tandem with body movement, whether in Iroquois ritual, or in the utterance of that great hummer Winnie-the-Pooh, who "walks through the forest humming proudly to himself" or "makes up a little hum as he is doing his Stoutness Exercises in front of the glass: *Tra-la-la-la*, as he stretches up as high as he can go." In this way, Taussig accentuates the creative force of the voice, its power to bring things about, ending with Allan Ginsberg's group chanting events about which Ginsberg declared, "A thousand bodies vibrating o-m can immobilize an entire downtown Chicago street full of scared humans, uniformed or naked."

Nermin Saybasili unshrouds the "uncanny," ghostlike quality of the disembodied voice, referring to Derrida's "hauntology." She analyzes disembodiment in art works dealing with immigration, such as Zarina Bhimji's film *Out of the Blue*, in which Bhimji returns to Uganda, filming the places she remembers from her youth, where, after Idi Amin expelled all Asians from the country, nothing now remains of the Asian culture in which she was raised. She then adds to these images the voices of those absent people and the sounds of that absent life. In Esra Ersen's video work *If you could speak Swedish*, this is reversed. We can now see the "ghosts," but not hear them, although "not hearing" is taken here in the metaphorical sense of "exclusion," as the immigrants are heard trying to express themselves in a Swedish language class. In Danica Dakíc's installation *El Dorado*, finally, the image and voices of immigrants are radically separated by being displaced in different locations.

Giselle Beiguelman starts with the Frankensteinian threat of the mechanical voice, as dramatized in films in which computers acquire emotions and a will of their own. But the art works she then considers move away from this tradition, no longer humanizing the computer voice, which can now emanate from anything—a room, for instance, or a book—and yet exercise significant power over our lives. In this way Beiguelman offers a vivid perspective on the "hybridization of man and machine" that differs from the traditional scenario, but is equally powerful.

Philip Brophy, finally, captures this theme in relation to music, with a wide range of examples in all of which the traces of what has usually been considered to make human voices "human" are removed. There are, for instance, the robotic voices of Kraftwerk's *Musique Non-Stop*; there is the machinic precision of Meshuggah's *I*, which is "inhuman because it is performed by humans," or there is Cornelius's *Point*, in which sampled and looped pitches are held for impossibly long times without any dynamic variation, in patterns which do not produce melodic phrases but only shifts of pitch. In all these cases, Brophy defiantly declares, "the haunting wispiness of a beautiful female aria, the stilling innocence of a child's nursery rhyme, the rugged honesty of a folksy male ballad (...) fall on deaf ears." Thus the book ends with the opposite of what it started out with, having moved from a mechanical voice articulating a humanist discourse of the "human" to a "posthuman" human voice stripped of the qualities traditionally associated with that discourse.

16   Humming

Michael Taussig

Bees hum. So does the traffic out my window five stories down, except for early morning when the garbage truck shrieks and groans, lifting and grinding, compressing and thumping. Interstitial sounds are they, bees and cars and even the shrieker, sounds that fill the void, sounds that don't really count, background, we might say, stuff for the likes of John Cage, who had trouble with the line demarcating sound from music. A dog whimpers and twitches in its sleep. The wind hums through the trees and the river has a humming, cruising sound that never stops as it runs over the rapids when I go upstate to the land without traffic or the shrieker. And then there's the pretty much continuous ringing in my ears, the ur-hum, the movement of the warm blood through the inner ear, that blends with the outside world so as to form the one great hum of the great bumblebee.

I look at this train of ideas and images and am surprised at how they themselves hum along like automatic writing. They form a sequence back and forth from animal to human as well as back and forth from machines to human. Most significant, I feel, is that the sequence comes to rest where you hear your body perched on the membrane of the ear where exterior meets interior.

There are few bees around now, less pollination and less food, fewer flowers, and less green. The hum of the great bumblebee is not what it used to be, as planet Earth falters and the ringing in the ear gets louder. Something is screaming even when I sleep. Is it outside or inside or both? Could this be the unconscious that was central to Nietzsche's definition of philosophy as the understanding, or rather misunderstanding, of the body?

Bees offer plenty to the allegorist. They appeal to me because their hum radiates through the vibrating heat of summer along with the meandering flight of butterflies, those other great pollinators, but although bees are considered industrious workers par excellence—the word "drone" comes to mind—butterflies are not. They are not industrious. They are flighty and they are unpredictable—a boss's nightmare. In their interaction with flowers, they are also held to be eminently sexual—as by that great utopian schemer, Charles Fourier. So, then, what of pollination? Does it not combine the industrious drone with the flighty flâneur and does it not disturb our notions of work, implicating it with sex and vice versa, to the benefit of what we sometimes call the "birds and the bees" and hence the regeneration of life?

Let us assume, for the sake of a larger argument, that pollination opens our eyes to the erotic quality of work as an interaction of materials no less than of the maker with the thing being worked on. And let us recall alongside this the vibrating heat of summer. You put your head close to the ground on a summer's day hearing a multitude of hummings and you are seeing wavy lines of colored heat rising and dancing along with the hums through which bees patrol and butterflies circle, while close to the surface of the river dragonflies hum as they copulate. Without shame. These vibrations of sight and sound, music and color, are certainly motive forces in the world, turning forms that are unpredictable, ephemeral, and frighteningly vulnerable. Think of van Gogh's last paintings, in which form surrenders to the vibrations of color, as when he writes his brother Theo how the "effect of daylight, of the sky, makes it possible to extract an infinity of subjects from the olive tree."[1] It was as if there was no such thing as the olive tree. It was more like a momentary artifact, a blaze of colors on their way to becoming blue flies and emerald rose beetles on their way to becoming leaves with that tinge of violet to be found on ripe figs.

All this humming, and this was the painter who cut off his ear.

There must have been some humming action with Sergei Eisenstein too, as when he tells us that "Disney is astonishingly blind, with respect to landscape—to *the musicality of landscape* and simultaneously the *musicality of color and tone.*"[2]

But then what is it to hum?

My Webster's dictionary is helpful here. It scans like a poem. A deep ecology poem. As etymological reckoning, it gives us "Middle Dutch," an exotic formulation, to be sure, the reference being the word *hommel* followed by the word *bumblebee*. Next comes an array of meanings relevant to today's usage, at least in American English. To hum can be to utter a sound that sounds like speech or to make the natural noise of an insect in motion or a similar sound. It can also mean singing with the lips closed without articulation, although my main interest is with that something that lies between words and sounds, no less than between singing and speaking. Humming is like alphabet soup, wetlands, where all manner of life forms thrive. Of course, there are hums of mine that are words such as

You always will be welcome
That cup of Bushells tea

which was an advertising jingle on the radio when I was a kid in Sydney in the 1940s. But when today I sing this, which is not often, the emphasis is more on the cadence of sound than on the words—which, to tell the truth, are meant to be picturesque and a little absurd. All of which brings out the undoubted fact, hideous as it may seem on account of its daylight robbery of childhood, how advertising exploits the hum and whatever else the hum assumes in terms of songs of innocence, birds, and bees to boot. But perhaps the days of the advertising jingle are over as it is too silly and too innocent for the serious business of consumer capitalism. And, to continue further with this historicizing, I doubt whether today young people hum and whether, given the ubiquity of the iPod, their membrane mediating inner and outer sound-worlds, has the function it used to have.

I must hasten to add that humming was a major component of the healing I got to know over twenty-five years visiting the Putumayo area of Colombia, South America, and this humming lasted all night and maybe the next and the one after as well. Of course some may object to my saying that this sacred music is humming, and therein lies a problem—maybe *the* problem. There were few words, or maybe none whatsoever, and the sounds came from the back of the throat with a strong and raspy feel to them, like the grinding of tree branches whipped back and forth against one another by a storm, at other times a whispering soft murmur of fairy dust falling from the stars. This was humming that got to you alright, deep in your bones. It is said that smell tends to obliterate the subject-object division. Well, that humming certainly did that, assisted as it was by hallucinogens such that your body as whole, eyes and thoughts included, would vibrate along with the great hum of the great bumblebee.

I have come to believe that singing is close to divinity and that by merely altering the sounds one makes with one's mouth and throat so as to diverge from speech achieves something forever strange. No doubt there are rhythms in language that the poet knows better than most and that song takes further.

Modes of singing that are like talking are fascinating, because they estrange this estrangement. They throw the field wide open, as does humming in its quiet way.

In indigenous North America, it seems like nothing much could happen out of the ordinary without being brought into the world by song or validated by song.

Commenting on the sense of a "mystic potence" known as *orenda* in the world of the Iroquois, being neither a god nor a spirit but a diffuse power informing all things, the Native American Anthropologist, J. N. B. Hewitt, son of a European trader and Huron mother, wrote in 1902 that shamans have *orenda* in abundance, as do successful hunters and gamblers. To exert his or her *orenda*, the shaman "must sing, must chant, in imitation of the bodies of his environment."[3] Indeed the very word *orenda* means to sing or to chant in the earlier speech of the Iroquoian people. Small wonder then that Hewitt repeatedly returns to sound, to music, singing, and the sounds of nature, as the privileged domain of *orenda* and magic.

Nietzsche would have been delighted. Didn't he say that music in Dionysian states had the capacity to intensify bodily states so that you discharge all your powers of representation, imitation, transfiguration, transmutation, every kind of mimicry and play acting, conjointly? In such a state, you possess to the highest degree the instinct for understanding and divining, the art of communication to the highest degree, entering into every skin, into every emotion, continuously transforming yourself.[4] But listen now instead to Hewitt and note how he uses the word "bodies" here, not the word "spirits":

The speech and utterance of birds and beasts, the soughing of the wind, the voices of the night, the moaning of the tempest, the rumble and crash of the thunder, the startling roar of the tornado, the wild creaking and cracking of wind-rocked and frost-riven trees, lakes, and rivers, and the multiple other sounds and noises in nature, were conceived to be the chanting—the dirges and songs—of the various bodies thus giving forth voice and words of beastlike or birdlike speech in the use and exercise of their mystic potence.[5]

So might I be permitted to think that humming, too, is not without its quotient of *orenda*?

In the case of my Putumayo friend, Santiago Mutumbajoy, it seems that the hum comes from the spirits of the hallucinogen, allowing the person humming—*the person thus hummed*, we might say—to work with power that lies beyond the visible.

This suggests to me that humming is connecting, not just the connection between insides and outsides, animal and human, machines and human, but the mediating medium that connection of any kind requires.

Humming often implies rhythm, meaning first of all the rhythm of the body in motion. When we walk and when we work at some repetitive task, we may hum. Nietzsche was a great walker, but we do not know if he hummed. Leslie Chamberlain says after the death of God, what was left for him was music and color. I wonder if humming should be in there too, along with Eisenstein's musicality of landscape that unfolds before and behind as you walk.

Speaking of repetitive tasks conducive to humming, and vice versa, Walter Benjamin thought the art of the storyteller was made easier by having listeners working at some repetitive task, which made it easier for them to recall and repeat the story when their turn came around, storytelling being but one side of the operation, story-listening being the other.

Speaking of stories, and more particularly of listening to stories, perhaps while you were falling asleep as a child, some of you may remember that Winnie-the-Pooh is a great hummer and it is instructive to study his humming, which surely has a lot to do with his love of honey, the stuff bees make. In fact, his first adventure, or misadventure, is to raid a beehive in search of honey. He is a child's Ulysses, this Pooh of ours, always ready to outwit the forces of nature in the approved Enlightenment manner, as he prepares an umbrella to act as a parachute so he can descend on the unsuspecting bees.

A great hummer, he has a day job as well—as an inert teddy bear who makes a noise as he is dragged downstairs then upstairs by his loving companion, an androgynous child named Christopher Robin. Bump, bump go the sounds as he is pulled first down and then, at the end of the tale, upstairs. Bump bump.

Yet in between these bumps, going downstairs then back upstairs, he comes alive as Winnie-the-Pooh. He is animated, we might say, and he speaks and he hums and he sings a lot. In the second chapter, which is when we get to really meet this transformed little bear, we read the first sentences:

Edward Bear, known to his friends as Winnie-the-Pooh, or Pooh for short, was walking through the forest one day, humming proudly to himself. He had made up a little hum that very morning, as he was doing his Stoutness Exercises in front of the glass : *Tra-la-la-la*, as he stretched up as high as he could go, and then *Tra-la-la-la, tra-la—oh, help!—la*, as he tried to reach his toes.[6]

Here is what I would like to point out. First, he is humming as he walks. He is humming proudly, conscious of what he is doing—humming, that is—and proud of the hum he has invented performing exercises in front of the mirror. Now he is walking and humming his hum and involved in repetitive bodily activity like when he was in front of the mirror watching himself. It is as if he is seeing himself from the outside, so to speak, yet the self he is observing is something like an unconscious self, not necessarily in the Freudian sense of the unconscious, but more like what I would call the bodily unconscious, and the humming facilitates this.

We might also note that this hum hovers between being nonsense syllables or sounds, on the one hand, and more conscious language, on the other, as when he exclaims "Oh help!" in the midst of his "tra-la" and "la." The exclamation rises up. It is like an eruption in a stream of humming.

Actually the hum is longer than I have indicated:

Tra-la-la, tra-la-la
  Tra-la-la, tra-la-la
Rum-tum-tiddle-um-tum
  Tiddle-iddle, tiddle-iddle,
  Tiddle-iddle, tiddle-iddle,
Rum-tum-tum-tiddle-um

What is more, as printed out, it occupies the bottom of a full page devoted to a drawing of Pooh looking very small and overwhelmed with his hands behind his back walking through the forest lost in thought looking up at the trees and the sky, somewhat like Heidegger, we might say, lost on one of those paths made by woodsmen and animals that go round and round.

As he hums, Pooh wonders what it feels like to be somebody else. It is as if humming frees him up to think big thoughts and even become somebody else. Humming facilitates speculation. Humming endows the mimetic faculty, the ability or the fantasy to be Other.

At the beginning of this scene, the narrator informs us that Winnie-the-Pooh is known as Pooh for short. This is an indication that language and naming are as much the subject of the story as is Edward Bear. Changing his name from Edward Bear to Winnie-the-Pooh is one sign of this. The name change represents the change from the adult world where he is known as a teddy bear, hence Edward, to that other world of the child-fairytale alliance where he now becomes Winnie-the-Pooh, and with this name become animated and breathe the life of make-believe. Games with language—or should I say games with names and language—are crucial to this book. And the fact that Pooh is the name of a person—or should I say of a teddy bear—yet is also the name of excretory matter, is another signal that names and games are plastic, entities that classify and give meaning to the world, yet are prone to change, if we so desire, and hence to misunderstanding.

Such plasticity is not achieved lightly, however. Names and words are meant to designate one thing and one thing only. Look at what happens to people who turn left instead of right or are caught cheating at Scrabble. Yet to sabotage language can be fun, and what is more, the definiteness of language depends on its being transgressed—the role allotted children and teddy bears and—dare I say it—humming. We sense this transgression with Pooh's name, which is scatology rendered sweet by the innocence of childhood. Thus occupying an in-between land of considerable ambiguity, it seems doubtful that *pooh* would make it past the censors of today concerned with child abuse.

Winnie-the-Pooh is a book that adventures with language as much as with bumblebees, honey, Heffalumps, and the lost tail of Eeyore the donkey. That is why there is so much attention paid both to spelling and to pronunciation. There is a love of misspellings and of mistaken meanings of words, such as ambush taken to mean a kind of bush. "Expedition, silly old Bear," explains Christopher Robin. "It's got an 'x' in it."[7] In other words, young Christopher Robin treats his beloved bear as he himself is probably treated by adults, because he has his adventures with language too, as with his spelling and love of making signs to be stuck up in the forest, such as his sign "PLS RING IF AN RNSWER IS REQIRD"—and is he not adult to his animal friends?[8]

The singular importance of writing is beautifully rendered when Piglet writes a message in a bottle that he casts onto the rising floodwaters, a message that is found days later by Pooh. "'Bother,' said Pooh as he opened it. 'All that wet for nothing. What's that bit of paper doing?' He took it out and looked at it. 'It's a Missage,' he said to himself, 'that's what it is. And that letter is a "P," and so is that, and "P" means "Pooh," so it's a very important Missage to me, and I can't read it. I must find Christopher Robin."[9]

That is what the story of Pooh is, a *missage* in a bottle thrown in the rising floodwaters of becomings—becomings between child and adult, child and animals, child and toys—most especially, that toy we call language, both spoken and written, both heard and read. That is the *missage* of Milne's book for children, much beloved by adults. It thus behooves us to think of humming as central to language, as a base state of the voice, humming being neither conscious nor unconscious, neither singing nor saying, but rather the sound where the moving mind meets the moving body—as when Winnie-the-Pooh walks lost through the forest dreaming of honey and the hum of the great bumblebee.

Hums and Cries

When Pooh exclaims "Oh help!" in the midst of his "tra-la" and "la," we are made aware that hums and cries form a combination of opposites. At one pole we have the hum, while at the other is the exclamation or cry, like an eruption spiking out from a smooth surface and then collapsing back into the steady hum as with the sugar-cane cutters I heard of in Colombia in the 1970s who—in contract with the devil, as well as with the large landowning corporations—were said to utter strange cries as they cut a swathe through the forest of cane, other cutters on either side, all advancing in a straggly line, the devil men plunging ahead with their unfair advantage—the devil being a type of obscenity, rendering the earth they worked on barren. I feel the sun; the monotony; the itch of the cane leaves; the sweat pouring; men in long-sleeved shirts, long pants, and hats. I hear the crunching of footsteps, the cutting of leaves, then the stalks, the thud as they are thrown into a pile with one's number cut into a marker, for here every man is paid separately, not much humming but the sound of cutting all day long and those weird screams from the men allegedly, secretly, in league with the devil who surely is running the whole damn show.

Or the tribal people beating the indigo in large vats in the 1850s in British Bengal, beating for hours at a time, the blue-green liquid up to their chests, in the stench of fomenting indigo and the heat of that land. They work in unison not just with each other but with the swirling back and forth of the liquid. Girded by a necklace of blue foam a foot high, the vat is in violent commotion.

As they advance and retreat along with this incandescent wave, their bodies blue, the tribesmen sing what my British eyewitness deems obscene songs and give voice to vehement cries.[10] Here the record halts. We can go no further. Why obscene, why songs, and why the vehement cries?

This is what I take from the anthropology of Africa, for instance, whether it be women at work or men at work, as described by Laura Bohannan from her time in Tiv land in Nigeria in the 1950s. Men were frightened to get too close to the women weeding together, singing their lusty songs.[11] "Many of them are too obscene for inclusion," noted Louise Cramer with respect to the West Indian work songs she collected in the Panama Canal Zone in the 1940s.[12]

Why this link between work and song and work and obscenity exists is a matter for prolonged debate, but what I would like to propose is that we understand obscenity as not only transgression of sexual boundaries or rules of pollution, defined in terms of the more obvious erotic zones, but as transgression of bodily propriety more generally understood—by which I mean the sexualized body of the world, including, of course, the human body within that body.

It seems like working on nature is to partake sexually, so to speak, in the inner life of materials. All labor has something of this quality, this eerie intimacy with things and with motions inseparable from the thing we call mind, only we take it for granted and rarely notice it until hit with a broadside from the colonies and from other sites of manual labor, where the mix of horror and the fabulous makes us sit up and take note. Magic is sometimes said to be just this dazzling fusion of the human with the thing-world, too, although the work is likely to be more involved with theater and incantation. But here in the Bengal vat, it is work, hideous and extreme—yet something beautiful and worth writing home about, no doubt. The collective nature of the work is an integral part of this, too. The bodies move like one as in a chorus line in time to the music, which brings the social and the natural worlds together.

It is the density and intimacy of the interaction with the inner life of the object-world that astounds me, the harmonies and self-transforming movements of animating materials confined by the vat, exploding into obscene song and color.

Strange, but not so strange, as if humming is the "sound of the world," the background hum of energy and movement to all that exists. I see

Nietzsche, who loved walking every day as part of his thinking, I see him pointing to the age-old magical power of rhythm, not only in prayer as a magical snare to make the gods pliable, but in mundane activities as well, such as rowing or bailing water from a boat. Still today, he thought, even "after millennia of work at fighting such superstition," this magical power of rhythm exerts itself.[13]

So I ask myself, is humming, then, a "magical snare" too, a rhythm of sounds without words making a prayer without any obvious Church or priest?

MR. WEINGLASS: Will you please state your full name?

THE WITNESS: Allen Ginsberg.

MR. WEINGLASS: What is your Occupation?

THE WITNESS: Poet.

...   .

MR. WEINGLASS: Will you explain to the Court and to the jury what chant you were chanting at the press conference?

THE WITNESS: I was chanting a mantra called the "Mala Mantra," the great mantra of preservation of that aspect of the Indian religion called Vishnu the Preserver. Every time human evil rises so high that the planet itself is threatened, and all of its inhabitants and their children are threatened, Vishnu will preserve a return.

MR. WEINGLASS: And what occurred in Lincoln Park at approximately 10:30, if you can recall?

THE WITNESS: There were several thousand young people gathered, waiting, late at night. It was dark. There were some bonfires burning in trashcans. Everybody was standing around not knowing what to do. Suddenly there was a great deal of consternation and movement and shouting among the crowd in the park, and I turned, surprised, because it was early. The police were or had given 11:00 as the date or as the time—

MR. FORAN: Objection, your Honor.

MR. WEINGLASS: What did you do at the time you saw the police do this?

THE WITNESS: I started the chant, O-o-m-m-m-m-m-, O-o-m-m-m-m-m-m.

MR. FORAN: All right, we have had a demonstration.

THE COURT: All right.

MR. WEINGLASS: Did you finish your answer?

THE WITNESS: We walked out of the park. We continued chanting for at least twenty minutes, slowly gathering other people, chanting, Ed Sanders and I in the center, until there were a group of maybe fifteen or twenty making a very solid heavy vibrational change of aim that penetrated the immediate area around us, and attracted other people, and so we walked out slowly toward the street, toward Lincoln Park.

MR. WEINGLASS: I now show you what is marked D-153 for identification. Could you read that to the jury?

THE WITNESS: Magic Password Bulletin. Physic Jujitsu. In case of hysteria, the magic password is o-m, same as o-h-m, which cuts through all emergency illusions. Pronounce o-m from the middle of the body, diaphragm or solar plexus. Ten people humming o-m can calm down one himself. One hundred people humming o-m can regulate the metabolism of a thousand. A thousand bodies vibrating o-m can immobilize an entire downtown Chicago street full of scared humans, uniformed or naked. Signed, Allen Ginsberg, Ed Sanders. O-m will be practiced on the beach at sunrise ceremonies with Allen and Ed.

MR. WEINGLASS: Could you explain to the Court and jury what you meant in that last statement of your message?

THE WITNESS: By "immobilize" I meant shut down the mental machinery which repeats over and over again the images of fear which are scaring people in uniform, that is to say, the police officers or the demonstrators, who I refer to as naked meaning naked emotionally, and perhaps hopefully naked physically.

MR. WEINGLASS: And what did you intend to create by having that mechanism shut down?

THE WITNESS: A completely peaceful realization of the fact that we were all stuck in the same street, place, terrified of each other, and reacting in panic and hysteria rather than reacting with awareness of each other as human beings, as people with bodies that actually feel, can chant and pray and have a certain sense of vibration to each other or tenderness to each other which is basically what everybody wants, rather than fear.

MR. WEINGLASS: Now directing your attention to the next day which is Sunday, August 25, what, if anything, did you do in the park?

THE WITNESS: First I walked around to the center of the park, where suddenly a group of policemen appeared in the middle of the younger people. There was an appearance of a great mass of policemen going through the center of the park. I was afraid then, thinking they were going to make trouble—

MR. FORAN: Objection to his state of mind.

THE COURT: I sustain the objection.

MR. WEINGLASS: What did you do when you saw the policemen in the center of the crowd?

THE WITNESS: Adrenalin ran through my body. I sat down on a green hillside with a group of younger people that were walking with me about 3:30 in the afternoon, 4o'clock Sat., crossed my legs, and began chanting O-o-m—O-o—m-m-m-m, O-o-m-m-m-m, O-o-m-m-m-m.

MR. FORAN: I gave him four that time.

THE WITNESS: I continued chanting for several hours.

THE COURT: Did you say you continued chanting seven hours?

THE WITNESS: Seven hours, yes. About six hours I chanted "Om" and for the seventh hour concluded with the chant Hare krishna/hare krishna/ krishna krishna/hare hare/ hare rima/hare rama/rama rama/hare hare.

MR. WEINGLASS: Now, directing your attention to Monday night, that is August 26, in the evening, where were you?

THE WITNESS: I was by a barricade that was set up, a pile of trash cans and police barricades, wooden horses, I believe. There were a lot of young kids, some black, some white, shouting and beating on the tin barrels, making a fearsome noise.

MR. WEINGLASS: What did you do after you got there?

THE WITNESS: Started chanting "Om." For a while I was joined in the chant by a lot of young people who were there until the chant encompassed most of the people by the barricade, and we raised a huge loud sustained series of "Oms" into the air loud enough to include everybody. Just as it reached, like, a great unison crescendo, all of a sudden a police car came rolling down into the group, right into the center of the group where I was standing, and with a lot of crashing and tinkling sound of glass, and broke up the chanting, broke up the unison and the physical—everybody was holding onto each other physically—broke up that physical community that had been built and broke up the sound chant that had been built. I moved back. There was a crash of glass.[14]

Back to Pooh

A dog whimpers and twitches in its sleep. The wind hums through the trees and the river has a humming, cruising sound that never stops as it runs over the rapids when I go upstate to the land without traffic or the shrieker. And then there's the pretty much continuous ringing in my ears, the ur-hum where insides meets outside in the one great hum of the great bumblebee. Forty years ago, a Poet of the people with his Reality Sandwich deflected the standard revolutionary wisdom of the West with his call not to arms but to o-m-ms.

At once profound and open, a Winnie-the-Pooh character if ever there was one, Allen Ginsberg updated that philosophy of history in which Walter Benjamin speaks of "chips of Messianic time," referring to what can happen when something from the traumatic past is suddenly brought into the present such that another world seems possible. To these chips I would like to add some humming, chips of *orenda*. Recalling a severe winter in the Dakotas in the 1870s, the Oglala Sioux Black Elk described a medicine man by the name of Creeping who cured people of snow blindness. "He would put snow upon their eyes," Black Elk is recorded as saying, "and after he had sung a certain sacred song that he had heard in a dream, he would blow on the backs of their heads and they would see again, so I have heard. It was about the dragonfly that he sang, for that was where he got his power, they say."[15]

Bees of the world, unite. You have nothing to lose but your chains.

Notes

1. W. H. Auden (ed.), *Van Gogh, A Self-Portrait: Letters Revealing His Life as a Painter, Selected by W.H. Auden* (Greenwich, Conn.: New York Graphic Society 1961), 396.

2. The quotes are from Sergei Eisenstein, *Non-Indifferent Nature: Film and the Structure of Things* (Cambridge: Cambridge University Press, 1998), cited by the editor Herbert Marshall in the "Notes and Commentary" section concerning Eisenstein on Disney, p. 98.

3. J. N. B. Hewitt, "Orenda and a Definition of Religion," *American Anthropologist*, New Series 4, no. 1 (January–March 1902): 40.

4. Friedrich Nietzsche, *Twilight of the Idols* and *The Anti-Christ*, trans. by R. J. Holingdale (London: Penguin, [1889] 1968), 84.

5. Hewitt, "Orenda and a Definition of Religion," 35–36.

6. A. A. Milne, *The World of Pooh: Containing Winnie-the-Pooh* and *The House at Pooh Corner*, illustrated by E. H. Shepard (London: Methuen Children's Books, 1982 [1926 and 1928]), 33.

7. Ibid., 111.

8. Ibid., 56.

9. Ibid., 133.

10. Colesworthy Grant, *Rural Life in Bengal* (London: Thacker, 1860), 129. The passage reads: "The operation of the beating continues for about two hours—the men amusing themselves and encouraging each other the while by sundry vehement cries and songs—generally not particularly distinguished for elegance or purity."

11. See Laura Bohannan (pseudonym Elenore Smith Bowen), *Return to Laughter* (New York: Random House, 1964 [1954]), 75–76.

12. Louise Cramer, "Songs of West Indian Negroes in the Canal Zone," *California Folklore Quarterly* 5, no. 3 (July 1946): 245.

13. Friedrich Nietzsche, *The Gay Science with a prelude in German rhymes and an appendix of songs*; edited by Bernard Williams; translated by Josefine Nauckhoff; poems translated by Adrian Del Caro (Cambridge, UK: Cambridge University Press, 2001 [1882]), 83–86.

14. Transcripts from the trial of the "Chicago 7," http://www.law.umkc.edu/faculty/projects/ftrials/Chicago7/Chi7_trial.html, accessed August 22, 2009.

15. John G. Neihardt, *Black Elk Speaks: Being the Life of a Holy Man of the Oglala Sioux* (Lincoln: University of Nebraska Press, 1979 [1932]), 14.

17 "Digital Ghosts": Voice and Migratory Hauntings

Nermin Saybasili

Introduction: "Ghosts" and Geographic Haunting in Digital Culture

In contemporary cities located at the crossroads of migratory routes, refugees or "illegal" immigrants are desperate to make contact with the world. In such inhospitable cities, Internet cafés are emerging as new "ghettos"; and in the era of cyberscape, a digital diasporic space is taking a new shape. A video documentary shot in such a place, Van, a Turkish city that borders Iran, provocatively defines the condition of a refugee as "having a life in the digital world." The documentary, *Search* (2005) by Yilmaz Ozdil, shows us that digital media are giving new meaning to Marshall McLuhan's optimistic idea of "the global village." In the documentary one of the "illegal" immigrants waiting to "move forward" says: "I couldn't remember my father's face; I saw it on a web-cam on the Internet. . . . I like the computer, because for the first time I saw my father on the computer. I like the computer. I can talk to my father."

The desperate immigrants in *Search* have proved that the virtual, in fact, is essential to the real, that it is no longer possible to fix the boundaries between the virtual and the real, between the digital and the material. In the film, the young boy who chats with his father on the Internet sees "something" like his father, but he does not really see him. Similarly, he hears "something" like his father, but they do not hear each other. The movement of virtual events, Jacques Derrida argues, "prohibit us more than ever . . . from opposing presence to its representation, 'real time' to 'deferred time,' effectivity to its simulacrum, the living to the non-living, in short, the living to the living-dead of its ghosts."[1] In the new world of the digital present, the virtual has become a supplement to the real; a simulacrum that holds ghostliness, gains its materiality and becomes more "real" than the real.

Although the world has become networked, this does not mean, as it might seem, that it is a timeless and placeless space. My point of departure in this chapter is that there is a new sort of movement and nomadism that actively facilitates new ways that the nation-state and its citizens are figured and configured in digital culture. I will argue that migration and disloca-tion remain distinctly human phenomena in this digitally mediated world, as "ghosts" remind us. I will investigate how the human voice haunts and is haunted in particular ways now in digital culture; I am particularly inter-ested in how that haunting is felt in migrant voices.

I will interrogate the "hauntology" of the digital domain in relation to audiovisual art practices, focusing on migrant subjectivity. I am interested in audiovisual works whose preoccupation is to register particular absence and/or presence in the field of vision through inventive and creative use of sound and voice. My aim is to make philosophical propositions about hauntology "sensible" (audible, visible) within digital culture. The migrant voices we will hear in the audiovisual art works that I will discuss will never simply occupy the digital domain; rather, they haunt both the visual and material space. Alternative or even countergeographical relations occur through the orchestration of diverse images and sets of aural data that rep-resent unseen perspectives and register dislocated, excluded, repressed, and unheard voices of the migrant populations throughout the world.

The appearance of "digital ghosts" in this chapter will mark the moments in which we make a journey from the geography of ontologies to the geog-raphy of hauntologies—where we come to hear the voices of migrants, thereby troubling our understanding of community as stable, fixed, and homogenous. Concerned with the contrast between the audio and the image, and the way in which the digitalization of the audio is used by the artists to produce migratory effects in audiences' minds leading to critical perceptions, I will examine the digital domain as the location for the poli-tics of audibility/inaudibility and visibility/invisibility.

By focusing on haunting and voice, I will argue, we also gain insight into haunting and the image. In particular, addressing the "materiality" of sound and voice in relation to vision enables us to consider a different way of seeing, a "performative" act of seeing, which offers an understanding of looking and listening as central to the process of inventive and creative interpretation of the world and the making of knowledge of the world.

In my focus on geographical haunting, searching for the possibility that something substantial can be made from things invisible and inaudible or hardly visible and audible, I particularly work with the approach of Jacques Derrida. In his book *Spectres of Marx: The State of the Debt, The Work of Mourning and The New International* (1994), Derrida developed the notion of the "ghost" and has proposed "hauntology" ("a science of ghosts" or a "science of what returns") as opposed to ontology. For Derrida, "A traditional scholar does not believe in ghosts—in all that could be called the virtual space of spectrality. There has never been a scholar who, as such, does not believe in the sharp distinction between the real and the unreal, the actual and the inactual, the living and the non-living, being and non-being ('to be or not to be,' in the conventional reading), in the opposition between what is present and what is not, for example in the form of objectivity. Beyond this opposition, there is, for the scholar, only the hypothesis of a school of thought, theatrical fiction, literature and speculation."[2]

In *Spectres of Marx*, Derrida splices ontology with its near homonym *hauntology*.[3] According to his conceptualization, the act of haunting is about the "traces" that oscillate between past and present, between here and there, without being reduced simply to one. Because the "ghost" introduces knowledge of a "supernatural and paradoxical phenomenality, the furtive and ungraspable visibility of the invisible,"[4] it introduces a fleeting modality to material being. Being half there and half not or half this and half that, it leaves a "trace" that marks the present with its absence in advance.

In my analysis, the notion of the "ghost" will emerge as a metaphor that operates by recalling a repressed absence that can be given life through the "presence" of digital voices demanding that the audience develop a strategy of listening. "Ghosts" represent the "unthought" of any given knowledge, the "invisible" of any given representation, and the inaudible of any given spectrum. They open up a new space within the familiar space, by resisting any closure or restful halt. By leaving room to imagination or dream, they shadow the "Truth" itself.

Following cultural theorist Mieke Bal's analysis of visual events[5] we can understand meaning as dialogic, performed between audience and audiovisual object. This means that to write about "ghosts" in the field of listening and vision is to develop a "performative" inquiry, because everything is triggered by what happens at the very moment of a troubling encounter.

Since "ghosts" are in between—in between the visible and the invisible, the material and the immaterial, here and there, the voice and the phenomenon—audiovisual analysis should be engaged with the "intelligibility" that slips in and out of auditory and visual sensory perception and empirical and representational concerns.

To be haunted by "digital ghosts" is what happens at the very moment of a troubling encounter; it is to question the limits of representation and to "enter a kind of disturbance zone where things are not always what they seem, where they are animated by invisible forces whose modes of operation work according to their own logics."[6] The artworks that I will engage with in this chapter do not attempt to represent conditions or reflect realities in terms of migration or dislocation. Rather, they propose what I understand as a digital aesthetic that synthesizes unseen images, repressed or unheard voices, unestablished or neglected relations, or unpredictable and uncontrollable forces. In this context, the act of haunting offers an aesthetic experience that transforms and stimulates shifts in our understanding of contemporary digital culture.

Haunting always implies a space, because by definition only space can be haunted. Moreover, space is understood as that which "houses." This is a point made by Mark Wigley, who argues that the word "haunting" is etymologically bound to that of "house." He points out that "haunting is always the haunting of a house. And it is not just that some houses are haunted: A house is only a house inasmuch as it is haunted."[7]

Haunted spaces and geographies are also uncanny spaces and geographies, just as haunting experiences are uncanny experiences. In his essay "The Uncanny" (1919), Freud claims that the uncanny (*unheimlich*) refers to the uneasy sense of the unfamiliar within the familiar, the unhomely within the home. We learn from Freud that when we have an uncanny experience, we feel like there are "ghosts" in our house.[8] I argue that the "ghost" is an "uncanny stranger," who has a presence that persists and cannot be effaced. This subject is therefore quite clearly related to borders and frontiers, to migrants and diasporic communities, to the colonized, to political refugees and to the consequent refiguring of notions of "home" and "nation."

In the following sections of this chapter, I develop these arguments about ghosts and geographical haunting by using voice as a way into three specific audiovisual works; this enables me to reexamine at the visual as well as to speculate on what is at the margins of our perceptions of the specters of migration. I examine Zarina Bhimji's video work "Out of Blue" (2002), Esra Ersen's video work "If You Could Speak Swedish" (2001), and Danica Dakíc's media installation "El Dorado" (2006–2007), in all of which sound and voice create their own place, a place which cannot be conceived of or experienced in visual terms: a haunting presence inseparably attached to vision and yet not visible or explainable through the visual. Concerned with the return of the voice of the migrant, we will make a journey from the geography of ontology to the geography of "hauntology," from actual presences to repressed absences, from comfortable familiarities to troubling strangeness. In a sense, this chapter is an attempt to read images and visual objects "symptomatically" through voice, in order to understand the most fundamental questions of social and political life in relation to dislocation and migration. Working with audiovisual materials in a cultural and a theoretical framework means finding new ways to intersect the voice with the visual and thus better understand each.

Sound in Silence in the Sonic Landscape of Haunting

Returning to her home country, Uganda, more than twenty years after her departure, in her video work "Out of Blue" Zarina Bhimji attempts to both visualize and auralize the presence of the postcolonial Uganda and the Ugandan diaspora. In the video, we are haunted by "mid-day ghosts." The camera wanders around the unpeopled topography of Uganda years after all the Asians were expelled from the country during the dictatorship of General Idi Amin. Every image in the video refers to an absence, but this absence becomes apparitional, as each filmic image is constantly haunted by the puzzling sounds and voices: sounds of a baby crying, of a woman screaming, of men laughing, of murmuring, of whispering, of burning fires, or of gunshots. Thus, these very absences articulate a presence through sound and voice.

The destabilization of sign and a certain crisis in meaning is the main operative logic of haunting. Bhimji's work recalls the limitations of direct signification as a means to capture presence. She is rather searching for the possibility that something substantial can be made from things invisible or hardly visible. Through her use of sound and voice, the artist tries to recall the instances in which a sign has become unstable. It stops doing what it is supposed to do; it stops signifying in a direct way. There are two implications of this: a sign is not there and/or a sign is not that. As the result of this certain type of crisis, both in the field of vision and the field of audio, as an audience, I am urged to find a way to activate an audiovisual field where there is an absence, but not the absence of meaning. I suggest that the crisis of meaning is always linked to the essential possibility of writing.

What the audience is listening to in Bhimji's film is not the occurrence of a signified, stable, and recognizable content that fully and successfully performs its task of deciphering, revealing, uncovering. He or she finds himself or herself in the place where the dispersed signifiers produce multiple meanings. In his conception of the "time-image," Gilles Deleuze has provided an analysis of the element of sound and voice in cinema as a complex "object." By drawing attention to the necessary and creative relation between visual image and what he calls "sound image," he writes: "The sound must itself become image instead of being a component of the visual image; the creation of a sound framing is thus necessary, so that the cut passes between the two framings, sound and visual."[9] In "Out of Blue," we endlessly move from the visual to the audio, and vice versa. Whereas the images, which do not follow one another in a linear fashion, depict the deserted streets and the abandoned buildings in the present topography of Uganda, and leave us with an unanswered question of "what happened?", the audio, which was composed by the logic of digital assemblage and seems to be autonomous from what we see on the screen, announces presences. Bhimji's digital assemblages offer us the creative representation of complexity that is at the heart of the realities of dislocation and migration, mixing together fragments of visual images and aural data that produce the bricolage of the connected forces, the repressed events, and the complex relations in a state of flux. Working with the premise that each piece of aural or visual data represents a fragment of information, the digital assemblage is conceived, built, and examined as a possible solution for reflecting how to represent the complexity of realities of the dislocation and migration. Thus in the video the visual and the audio that denounce the spatial and temporal restraints embody new signs that await our interpretation. There is a relation, a contact, between the visual and the audio. Deleuze has explained this complex process:

There will be the contact independent of distance, between an outside where the speech-act rises, and an inside where the event is buried in the ground: a complementarity of the sound image, the speech act as a creative story-telling, and the visual image, stratigraphic or archaeological burying. And the irrational cut between the two, which forms the non-totalizable relation, the broken ring of their junction, the asymmetrical faces of their contact. This is a perpetual relinkage. Speech reaches its own limit which separates it from the visual; but the visual reaches its own limit which separates it from sound. So each one reaching its own limit which separates it from the other thus discovers the common limit which connects them to each other in the incommensurable relation of an irrational cut, the right side and its obverse, the outside and the inside.[10]

In "Out of Blue," the visual and the audio refer to each other, they engage with an external space which does not belong to either of them, in order to signify the things that are beyond the visible and the audible.

As has already been noted, whereas the visual images in the large screen video projection depict the deserted topography of Uganda, the aural data, which consists of sounds and human voices, reveals the ghostly presence of the repressed, of the dislocated people. Thus Bhimji's "digital ghosts" signify an interval in time and space. Is not the "ghost" the one who disappeared in the past but appears, sometimes without any notice, to those with whom it used to be familiar? In *Spectres of Marx*, Derrida quotes from William Shakespeare's *Hamlet* to illustrate the temporality of ghosting. In Hamlet, the prince of a rotten state who encounters the apparition of the spectre of the king says: "The time is out of joint."[11] When the "ghost" appears, it tries to speak or to indicate something, even if it does not always manage to. It is, though, capable of doing at least one thing successfully: making us feel that something is going wrong in the present. In so doing, it makes us question the present. "If haunting describes how that which appears to be not there is often a seething presence, acting on and often meddling with taken-for-granted realities, the ghost is just the sign, or the empirical evidence if you like, that tells you a haunting is taking place."[12] This act of haunting is very important, for it has the force to put into crisis familiar social and political structures through the processes or the mediations it actively creates.

Bhimji's camera brings us to places and spaces as varied as the houses of the colonial power, ruined ancient graves, prison cells, deserted streets, military barracks, interior spaces whose walls are full of traces and shadows, and an abandoned airport. Bhimji's palimpsestic "audiovisual document" is about engaging with the "silence" caused by elimination, extermination, and erasure.[13] I will return below to the question of how the artist uses the sound in order to announce the production of a particular silence as the result of state terror and forced migration. But first I want refer to the public speech of General Idi Amin that was originally broadcast in a radio program one year after he came to power. In the video, we hear him say, "I have, therefore, today signed a decree revoking with effect from today, August 9, 1972, permits and certificates of residence granted to the above categories of persons. They are, however, permitted to stay in Uganda for a maximum period of 90 days from today."[14]

"Out of Blue" has a digital imaginary. Visually, it has a painterly quality. In contrast to the images, the audio makes things problematic. In this respect, Bhimji seems to play with the perfect imaginary that the digital technology can make possible, the assumption that something is more real the denser the distribution is, and more potential the more scattered is. Vilém Flusser points out: "What we call 'real,' and also perceive and experience as such, are those areas, those curvatures and convexities, in which the particles are distributed more densely and in which potentialities realize themselves. This is the digital world picture as it is being suggested to us by the sciences and presented to our eyes by computers."[15] But Bhimji interrogates what other possibilities the digital has. She seems to find the solution through the digital sound production. Sound and voice in "Out of Blue" provides a new ontology. Paradoxically enough, this happens through the haunting of the voice and sound. The "digital ghosts" haunt the full presence of "the real,"[16] in the form of a debt to the past and a promise of justice in the future. They haunt the filmic images that convey us the present-day topography of Uganda. Through the use of digital sounds and voices, the artist adds new meanings to what is known as digital culture, because she seeks to produce a creative knowledge for the digital world in which migratory hauntings give new forms to both digital and material space that starts to represent the heterogeneous and rupturing nature of the continuously shifting relationship between here and there, between material and immaterial, between voice and phenomenon. It is this new space that I believe offer new possibilities for conceptualizing and representing new ideas, generating alternative perspectives, and bringing unheard or repressed voices.

The "mid-day ghosts" are what have remained to be seen with the truth, what is needed to speculate with the truth that flickers on the screen. In *The Time Image*, Deleuze has written that political cinema should be centered on one basis: "the people no longer exist, or not yet . . . the people are missing."[17] In "Out of Blue," except for a silhouette or the reflected shadows of a group of people on the wall against which guns were leant, visually, we never catch a glimpse of any people throughout the film. Nonetheless, ghostly voices and sounds from the past register the presence of the displaced and now transnationally located Asian population in the present. Iain Chambers claims that by acknowledging the necessity of the dispersal of a single history, one can start to hear composite voices: "In the movement from concentrated sight to dispersed sound, from the 'neutral' gaze to the interference of hearing, from the discriminating eye to the incidental ear, I abandon a fixed (ad)vantage for a mobile and exposed politics of listening—for a 'truth' that is always becoming."[18] The fragmentary and heterogeneous forms of aural data in "Out of Blue" can become comprehensible and "unified" only through the audience's listening and viewing.

In this respect, "Out of Blue" requires a "double interpretation," which involves the concurrent readings of the two separate entities of the film: the visual and the audio. It requires an "audiovisual analysis" that Michel Chion proposed in his book *Audio-Vision: Sound on Screen*. Chion points out that "[a]udiovisual analysis aims to understand the ways in which a sequence or whole film works in its use of sound combined with its use of images."[19] In this analysis, "what do I see?" and "what do I hear?" become very serious questions, and in asking them we renew our relation to the world.[20] In discussing "audiovisual analysis," Chion writes:

We can discover both *negative sounds* in the image (the image calls for them, but the film does not produce them for us to hear) and *negative images* in the sound— "present" solely in the suggestion the soundtrack makes. The sounds that are there, the images that are there often have no other function than artfully outlining the form of these "absent presences," these sounds and images, which, in their very negativity, are often the more important.[21]

What Chion calls "negative images" and "negative sounds" are very useful formulations for our analysis of "Out of Blue." The images in the film depict a particular emptiness in the landscape of Uganda against which the audio of the film reverberates "loudly." The sonic sweeps through the frozen stillness of the muted, grave-like landscape, revealing a spectral density of the dislocated people and diasporic minorities that are paradoxically there and not there at the same time. Whereas the dialectics of visibility and invisibility in the act of haunting involve a constant negotiation between what we can see and what we cannot, the dialectics of sound and silence in the act of haunting require us to establish a link between what we can hear and what we cannot. Haunting always brings us to the recognition of our limits. Through her use of sound and voice, Bhimji seems to deal, in particular, with the limits of representation and description. "Out of Blue" urges us to realize that there is always something beyond the limits: there are always things that are about to emerge; things that can be made visible and that can be articulated. The creation of the audio—which recalls the events from the past that are in fact the "traces" in the Derridean sense—implies that there is more, more to see and more to hear.

Bhimji seems to claim that we should find ways of registering silence as the marker of another presence, a presence that adopts a voice that does not speak or utter words and that does not participate in the official record. Throughout the film, the only moment we encounter language is when dictator Idi Amin announces on the radio that all the Asians will be dispersed from Uganda. His voice speaks in the language of power which made the law. And years later, we see the effect of his "performative speech" in the topography of Uganda. What "Out of Blue" shows to us is that listening can direct us to a particular silence, to the absence of a voice. "Out of Blue" is therefore a journey into the past and the present—a journey into silence and a triumph. It maps out a long journey of the return and the repossession of the living voice. The "ghosts" within sound and memory point to where the voice of "the Other" finally becomes audible. Chambers has written: "In acknowledging silence, the interval of the unsaid (and the unsayable), the shadows of the subaltern are thrown across the transparency of words accustomed to ignoring the ontology of silence."[22] The more the artist allows us to hear "silence" (the absence of a voice), the more she indicates that we can think "the Other" only through its inaudible voices, as Derrida argues.[23]

In the installation, the excess of sounds that makes the aural space its own acquires a life of its own, somehow progresses toward the presence of a voice, and starts to exceed signification to some degree, both before the entry into language and after. The bearer of silence speaks the unsaid or unsayable, but this voice, to put it in Giorgio Agamben's words, speaks a "non-language." Agamben formulates "non-language" in discussing the way in which testimony contains a lacuna; "digital ghosts" in Bhimji's installation activate this lacuna by leading its audience to decipher the sounds accompanying the filmic images that can only depict the unpeopled topography of Uganda. According to Agamben, "it is impossible to bear witness to testimony from the inside—since no one can bear witness from the inside of death, and there is no voice for the disappearance of voice- and from the outside—since the 'outsider' is by definition excluded from the event."[24] He writes: "What is borne witness to cannot already be language or writing. It can only be something to which no one has borne witness. And this is the sound that arises from the lacuna, the non-language that one speaks when one is alone, the non-language to which language answers, in which language is born. It is necessary to reflect on the nature of that to which no one has borne witness, on this non-language."[25]

Agamben's arguments bring us to the recognition that we should broaden what we regard as language and voice. In "Out of Blue," except for Idi Amin's speech on the radio broadcast, we hear only sounds that are all anonymous and not speech. Haunted by "ghosts," we are urged to comprehend that it is necessary the senseless sound be, in turn, the voice of someone, because otherwise it is impossible to understand what happened in a particular moment in the history of a country, as the filmic images can show only the "traces" after the events.

By setting both sound and vision in motion and in dialog with one another, Bhimji refers to the condition of being neither simply inside or outside, but paradoxically, both inside and outside. The audiovisual story of displacement documented by Bhimji summons up a diasporic space that has resided in the "European psyche" for some time. This is because diaspora is not only a destabilized border[26] that powerfully rewrites the history of nation, but also is a site of traversals, through which the European history of conquest and colonization and the subsequent European cartographies of migration can be tracked.[27]

Bhimji's video work "Out of Blue" scrutinizes geographical haunting. It allows us to address—indeed, it demands that we address—the particular "phenomena" that occur with an act of haunting; the geopolitical boundaries and territorial identities are deeply disturbed, and what is called "home" becomes deeply unfamiliar. The conditions of haunting emerge when the illusion of coherence, stability, homogeneity, and permanence is faced with the shadowy reality of displacement, dislocation, and unbelonging, with all the layers of diasporic formations and migratory flows, with the crossover and overlap of cultures, and with the hybrid identities and new ethnicities that are constantly being formed. As Bhimji reveals in "Out of Blue," to engage with ghostliness and haunting is a matter of producing a hospitable memory—of encouraging memory to become present in order to give a historical counter-response. The returned voices of the dislocated, of the dispossessed, of the diasporic put the visible world to work in a different logic by challenging a certain "ontology," a value of full presence. By her use of sound and silent voice, the artist interrogates the way in which the migrant "belongs" to the vast geography of disappearance where "ghosts" reside, because the ones who stand on border zones, who cross borders, or who live in inhospitable cities have some kind of half-presence, an "illegal" presence or a not fully materialized presence. The migrant is therefore an elusive "specter" whose habitation without proper inhabiting is haunting.

Identities in Translation

Currently, it is becoming clear that we are living in a period in which the illusion of unity imposed by the nation-state is increasingly undone by civil war, ethnic cleansing, or wars of domination fought under the guise of liberation struggles. The more this occurs, the more those who as a result have been dislocated and forced into movement come to be seen as a "mass of people" circulating on or through borders and, consequently, as a "problem" to be contained. By discussing Esra Ersen's video work "If You Could Speak Swedish," I will suggest that what is *perceived* as a "problem" is in fact *produced* as a problem. The people who circulate on/through borders are seen as a "problem," because their existence disrupts the lines of exclusion, because there is no more a place to draw a line in order to exclude them as their movements actively produce a counter-cartography as they haunt the nation state. By focusing especially on the way in which through the use of language acts as a powerful tool for the application of power and subordination, Ersen makes the voices of migrants inaudible—like their disappeared bodies. Her work thus opens a way to understand what I call the "ghost citizen."

I am going to discuss Ersen's video work in detail, but first I want to refer to a particular scene (figure 17.1). In one of the opening scenes, Ersen's camera records a computer screen that covers almost the entire frame of the filmic screen. In the software program Adobe Photoshop, a selected tool in the bar decorates the clumsily written word "Irak" with a red heart. In the following scene of the video, an Iraqi man who attends a Swedish language

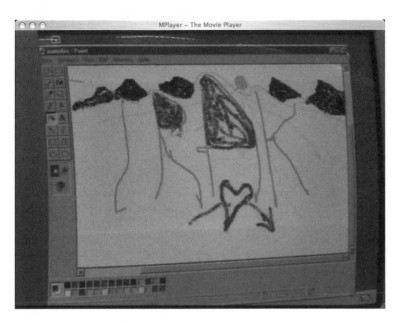

Figure 17.1
Esra Ersen, "If You Could Speak Swedish," video still, 2001.

course in a suburb of Stockholm tries to say in Swedish: "Ah, beloved Bagh-
dad, a city that was my refuge from evil. When I left it, I felt like Adam did
when he was forced to leave the Kingdom of Heaven." Digital space has
been figured and foregrounded here. But in Ersen's work, the unseen, invisible user does not seem to benefit from the freedom of the current digital
computerized environment. In this case, his or her digital design is directly
related to his condition in the real world. It is not clear whether the Iraqi
man who is reading the sentences written on a piece of paper in front of
the camera is the anonymous user of the Photoshop program who digitally
paints his or her wish and desire for belonging and longing for his or her
homeland. For me, the opening scenes of "If You Could Speak Swedish"
relate to the concept "ghost citizen," referring to the immigrant, the refugee, and the asylum-seeker whose particular "absence" from their originating community creates some kind of new community. This is a community
that we might refer to, as Michael Hardt and Antonio Negri do, as "multitude."[28] The multitude cannot be localized within a unified world. It is what
is left over from the process through which the nation-state constitutes its
citizens. As a multitude, these ghost citizens make the nation-state leak.

The "ghost citizen," the refugee or an immigrant, has a life, but is without a personal life or individual property. "Not without identity (the ghost is a 'who,' it is not of the simulacrum in general, it has a kind of body, but without property, without 'real' or 'personal' right of property),"[29] writes Derrida. His or her body, like that of a "ghost," is not fixed into one identity, but searches for a meeting point in various networks of identities. He or she inhabits an extensive "relational geography."[30]And what are the voices of these ghost citizens; what language do they speak?

In her video work "If You Could Speak Swedish," Esra Ersen deals with the failure of the immigration policies applied by the European counties by focusing on language that, as cultural form, can become a powerful instrument for the fortification of the border between "us" and "them." In her artistic practices, Ersen often examines the tension between stable and delineated locations and the uncontrollable flux of migration. In "If You Could Speak Swedish," she examines this tension by focusing especially on the complex processes of integration and assimilation immigrants have to cope with in relation to the subtle way of the use of power of language over foreigners. For the work, Ersen collaborated with immigrants and asylum-seekers attending a Swedish language course in a suburb of Stockholm.

At the beginning of the film, we see two signs at the entrance to the language course in InfoKomp, Huddinge. The courses, which are organized according to what is called an integration (not immigration) policy,[31] are designated for "two types of participants." One sign indicates the way to a language course reserved for those whose visa applications have been accepted and the other leads to other courses in the same building that are designated either for those whose applications have not yet been accepted or for immigrants who are permitted only a limited stay in the country. Ersen, herself attending the course for one term, asked the immigrants who were participating in these language courses to write down, in their mother tongues, what they would like to say if they could speak Swedish. These texts include personal, emotional comments and political statements, and were translated into Swedish from a variety of languages, such as Arabic, Russian, Spanish, and Chinese.

The apparent vocal as well as visual uneasiness of the students as they try to read their own sentences in Swedish in front of the camera and the perceptible incongruity in the environment hint at the impossibility of inhabiting a foreign language or being able to fit into an already existing community and its cultural values and norms. This is especially noticeable in the lack of harmony between the posters hung on the classroom walls, such as one showing a beautiful Stockholm with bright skies and a blue sea, and the real condition of the immigrants standing in front of the posters, struggling to "express" themselves. If the nation-state is haunted by these migrants, they in turn are haunted by the nation-state. The haunting existence of the language teacher, who is offscreen, is heard in her voice correcting the students' pronunciation, again and again asking for words to be repeated until they are correct, conveys a kind of aggression. Jacques Lacan remarks in "Function and Field of Speech and Language in Psychoanalysis" that "I identify myself in language, but only by losing myself in it like an object."[32] Lacan emphasizes here that speech produces absence, not presence. He also draws attention to the fact that at the moment the subject enters language, she or he undergoes a phenomenal "fading." He claims that language preexists and coerces speech and voice.[33] What Esra Ersen's work shows us is that whoever is outside the language cannot appear or cannot be heard in the hegemonic representation of language. Thus the teacher's interruptions of their speeches double the immigrants' foreignness and bring us face to face with the haunting and dominating "European presence" for the ghostly multitude. Ersen's camera makes it possible to double the quality of the recording sounds in the environment of the classroom, and thus adds an odd dialectic of presence and absence, where the presence of recording can register a particular absence; a haunting presence of the performance in the frame of the filmic scene; a distance which is both here and there, both near and far. Listening and hearing thus become a critical moment in which we come to reconsider the materiality of embodied speech in the age of digital recording technologies.

One wonders whether an immigrant speaking in Swedish can convey its intended meaning, not only to us, but also to the author of the sentences. Seated before a colorful poster filled with a rich selection of fruits and vegetables (some have a clear resonance of "exoticism"), an Iraqi man reads: "When he sought to make me one of his tools of oppression I declined. He sought to make out of me a murderer of innocent and unarmed people. . . . I left my friends and family and came to Sweden." It is not difficult to notice the fact that while he is speaking his translated text, his own sentences became suddenly strange to himself. It becomes quite clear that his voice cannot really be heard in a completely different sign system and under the pressing power of cultural codes that come from outside. By positioning the subject in the regime of representation, the language, in this case, has the power to make the immigrants see and experience themselves as "the Other."

There is a particular resistance that takes its power from the particularity of the voice of the "foreigner" that cannot be "erased" and that signals the presence of "ghosts" that inhabits the difference between the same, thereby making the claim of the unified, stable, and fixed identity impossible and only illusionary. As Ersen's video work powerfully reveals, for an immigrant, acquiring a new language represents a process of "integration" into the coordinates of a completely new cultural system, an attempt to translate them to a new, fixed identity, just as they are meant to translate their voices into a new language, as if it is just the same (although better).

We should take into consideration Ersen's camera, which takes the digitally produced and reproduced images hung on the classroom walls into its framing. For instance, standing in front of a digitally produced aerial poster of Stockholm, with yellow-bronze houses, light-blue sky, blue water, and white sailing boats, a young man from Iran has chosen to describe his arrival at Sweden in these words: "I saw beautiful forests, rivers and lakes that resembled a beautiful work of art created by a skilful artist, using different colors on a large canvas." As he is speaking, one cannot miss the visual harmony between the colors in the poster and the colors in his clothing and his face" (figure 17.2) Has the dream of a "Photoshop asylum-seeker" been managed? Has this man who—like a canvas—is willing to be painted over with the respective values and norms of the European culture become an European? The answer is "no," because the auditory space of the film tells another story. When the camera shows a real—yet imposed and fabricated—condition in which the migrants who are "speaking" in Swedish have found themselves, the video, through the effect of the disjunction between the visual and the aural, hints to the fact that haunting is the product of an asymmetrical relation and an irreversible condition. The video's imaginary resonates with a certain phenomenon as the product of digital culture: the rich and the refined possibilities of production, reproduction, and manipulation of images lead to a certain "dematerialization" in the real world. If the constructed aesthetics and narrations generated and constructed by digital technologies paint a colorful, peaceful, and transparent vision of the world, as we experience in "If You Could Speak Swedish,"

Figure 17.2
Esra Ersen, "If You Could Speak Swedish," video still, 2001.

then the aural is stubbornly insistent on illustrating the fact that in the real world there is always "noise."

The Transvocal Soundscapes of Migrancy

I have been arguing that Derrida's notion of the "ghost" offers a theoretical figuration with which to better understand contemporary migrant subjectivity, as it involves the idea that being is never present or pregiven. It helps us not only to tackle the idea of a singular, self-contained, and unified identity, but also to imagine a future yet to come. Derrida's spectral, coming future is definitely antinationalist.[34]

So, haunted by near or distant pasts, we have finally arrived at the threshold of potentialities. To conclude, I will discuss Danica Dakíc's media installation *El Dorado* (2006–2007), which "imprisions" its audiences in the enduring present and captures them in the continual return of the "ghosts."

Dakíc's installation, which was shown in *Documenta XII* in Kassel, consists of a photographic work, a video work, and a fourteen-channel sound installation. The photographic work and the video installation were shown in Schloss Wilhelmshöhe; the fourteen-channel sound installation was displayed in the German Museum of Wallpaper (Deutsches Tapetenmuseum). In Schloss Wilhelmshöhe, the photograph, presented as a transparency in a light-box, invited the audiences to enter into the dark room where the video was shown. The video had been shot in the German Museum of Wallpaper. The offscreen voice of a migrant in the video engaged the audiences with the acoustic world of migrancy. The sound installation displayed in the German Museum of Wallpaper permeated all the museum spaces, and led its audiences to move through transvocal soundscapes. The fourteen-channel sound installation in the Museum, which houses a collection of wallpapers from different periods and from various styles such as arabesques, Biedermeier, chinoiserie, Bauhaus, designer wallpaper, Pompadour style, velour wallpaper, drapery wallpaper, and so on, makes the audiences take a performative tour in the twelve rooms of the museum, as the sensors trigger sequences of different audio tracks that haunt the space as well as the audiences.

In this complex work, the artist deals with an "in-between" domain of difference. The title of the installation is taken from the panoramic wallpaper from 1849 that is now on display in the German Museum of Wallpaper in Kassel. For the project, Dakíc collaborated with young people from the Hephata home for unaccompanied minor refugees, the Schlachthof youth center, the Carl-Schomburg-Schule's dance class in Kassel, and adolescents from Kulturbunker Bruckhausen in Duisburg as well as from the region of Münster and Düsseldorf. In the work, the panoramic wallpaper depicts four continents from left to right, beginning with Africa, where the pyramids stand in the middle of exotic planting; continuing with America, where the city of Veracruz lies at the foot of snow-covered mountains; then Europe, where a peacock sits on a balustrade; ending with Asia where a masque stands, serving as the metaphorical opening into culture in which the stereotyped social narrations, expectations, and fantasies are constructed. Dakic seems to question the way in which culture is our backdrop locating us in a place, shaping us, telling us who we are, and providing us a window through which to look at the world. If the wallpaper defines a cozy, domestic enclosure, then the artist pressures us to disclose its surface in order to discover alternative formations within the familiar, within the constructed and the imagined. She locates her viewers/audiences in a space where a series of transformational encounters happen. These encounters that produce a dynamic in-between space mark the moment at which the boundaries that seemingly tell us who "we" really are appear incoherent, fragmented, fluid, and on the move.

The photographic work depicts a group portrait of teenagers, who stand in front of a wallpaper that depicts the wilderness landscape of a forest (figure 17.3) At the back lies a highway. The composition in which the young migrants are located in a deserted area reflects upon not only their vulnerability and fragility but also their stubborn resistance to be there, not to be excluded, repressed or ignored. In the video work, the panoramic wallpaper in the German Museum of Wallpaper, which depicts the world as a pristine and heavenly garden, provides the backdrop for the same migrant teenagers who all seem to insist on appearing and taking their parts against the deserted and peaceful utopian landscape: one runs, a couple dances,

Figure 17.3
Danica Dakíc, transparency in light box, from the media installation *El Dorado*, 2006–2007.

one fights, one sings a traditional song, one tries to find his way out, and one just sits and waits (figure 17.4 and figure 17.5). All these performances in the Museum that appear on the screen are aurally attached to an off-screen voice of a young man who recounts his "illegal" journey, which started from Africa and ended up in a place in Germany where the refugees and asylum-seekers are temporarily housed. His bodiless voice invites us to search for his absence, as none of the scenes in the film shot in the museum space show us his face or his body, until—toward the end of the film—the owner of the voice comes into view, saying, "Now I am alone and I have to work hard to make life. I have to make new life. Life doesn't end."

Compared to the two audiovisual works that I discussed earlier in the chapter, this sound piece has a more evident digital construction, as the whole environment of the museum space is turned into a mixing desk through the movements of the audiences from one place to another by the sensors. The audiences have become "nomads" hearing the "diasporan mixology"[35] of sounds that the artist has recorded and captured for our ears. The installation therefore constitutes a distinct form of digital aesthetics:

Figure 17.4
Danica Dakíc, video still from the media installation *El Dorado*, 2006–2007.

Figure 17.5
Danica Dakíc, video still from the media installation *El Dorado*, 2006–2007.

it is interactive and participatory. We, the audiences, are there in order to activate an aural field where "sounds and voices migrate from microculture to microculture, assembling new lines of communication as they go and creating sonic spaces that alter as we traverse or are traversed by them."[36] Through the existence of diasporas, the "root" metaphors that are fixed in place are replaced by mobile metaphors. Dakíc uses digital media in order to make the whole environment material for diasporic formations. Just as the dissolution of origins occur in the digital production techniques, diasporan sounds and voices mark the moment of the loss of an absolute origin and of the authenticity establishing a dynamic dialog with here and there, past and present, near and far.

The sound installation is therefore dialogical, as it engages us with the vast "geography of disappearance" where the "ghosts" reside by inserting us in an auditory culture. Walking into a dynamic space, penetrated by nomadic sounds and voices, we turn the aural environment into a material one. Sounds and voices in the sound installation put our knowledge and our way of looking into question as they locate us in an in-between space.

For instance, while voices are predominantly and loudly repeating the word "El Dorado," we suddenly hear a woman's voice saying, "It is a paradise where everybody wants to be," then another woman's voice asks, "Do you think there is such place?" The voice thus always reminds us of the fact that the subject matter remains "out of sight," that we should make our own pictures and create our own contents. The work puts the observer in a new and indeterminable position between seeing and hearing. The museum space, in which the wallpapers seem to promise a cozy and familiar space, is filled with multiple languages such as English, German, French, Turkish, Spanish, Chinese, Persian, Italian, Ethiopian, Sudanese, Greek, Arabic, and so on. These voices thus powerfully turn the familiar into unfamiliar. The multiple languages haunt like "ghosts" without inhabiting any particular space. When a "ghost" appears, what it addresses is always a spectator. The ghost voices in Dakíc's sound installation suggest that the perspective has to be reversed: the "ghost," which is sensuous/nonsensuous, visible/invisible, sees us.[37]

"Ghost-voices" in Dakíc's sound installation trace out an alterity that refuses to fix the meaning in the frames of the wallpapers displayed in the museum. The "transvocality" of the piece leads us to a transnational space that heralds the dynamic, emergent, geographically and temporarily fluctuating pattern of presences of the migrant population in the very domesticity of Europe. The transnational space, which recalls diasporic formations, migratory flows and mobility, provides what Maharaj calls a "scene of translation." Maharaj writes of a desire to

move toward reindexing the international space which I should like to describe as the "scene of translations." Beyond the demand for assimilation, beyond absolutist notions of difference and identity, beyond the reversible stances of "self and other" in which the Eurocentric gaze fashions itself as the other . . . we have come to see the international space as the meeting ground for a multiplicity of tongues, visual grammars and styles.[38]

Conclusion

The "digital ghosts" in this chapter are what resist being domesticated or excluded. By interrogating the way in which a distributed presence emerges in the films and a sound installation, I have focused on the complex interplay between virtual and physical existence and between image and voice that affects our understanding of the world and our making knowledge of it. A "ghost" is always the "uncanny" guest, and I have argued that the uncanniness of the voice of the foreigner is that he or she is never simply alien to and separable from the social body, which he or she already haunts. The voices of the migrants that we hear in the works that I have discussed in this chapter never simply occupy the digital domain, but elusively haunt both the visual space and the material space. To hear the repressed voices, the silenced voices, the voices of "the Other" is an attempt to inspire a deeper rethinking of the relationship between the stranger or the foreigner and the citizen. "Digital ghosts" thus promise a future that would open up a scene of migrancy and that would map out transnational linkages and formations.

Notes

1. Jacques Derrida, *Spectres of Marx: The State of the Debt, The Work of Mourning and The New International* (London: Routledge, 1994), 169.

2. Ibid., 11.

3. Ibid., 51.

4. Ibid., 7.

5. Mieke Bal, "Visual Essentialism and the object of visual culture," *Journal of Visual Culture* 2, no.1 (2003): 9.

6. Avery Gordon, *Ghostly Matters: Haunting and the Sociological Imagination* (Minneapolis: University of Minnesota Press, 1997), 46.

7. Mark Wigley, *The Architecture of Deconstruction, Derrida's Haunt* (Cambridge, MA: MIT Press, 1997), 163.

8. Sigmund Freud, "The Uncanny," in *The Standard Edition of the Complete Works of Sigmund Freud*, vol.17 (London: Hogarth Press and the Institute of Psycho-Analysis, 1919), 225.

9. Gilles Deleuze, *Cinema 2: The Time-Image* (London: The Athlone Press, 1989), 278.

10. Ibid., 279.

11. Derrida, *Spectres of Marx*, p.18.

12. Gordon, *Ghostly Matters*, 8.

13. Efza Evrengil (ed.), *Poetic Justice*, Exhibition Catalog of the 8th International Istanbul Biennial (Istanbul: Istanbul Foundation for Culture and Arts, 2003), 77.

14. Ibid., 552.

15. Vilém Flusser, "Digital Apparition," in Timothy Druckrey (ed.), *Electronic Culture: Technology and Visual Representation* (New York: Aperture Foundation, 1996), 244.

16. As one of Jacques Lacan's categories, "the real" is that which is beyond the "symbolic" and the "imaginary." The real is the unknown that exists at the limit of the sociosymbolic. In contrast to reality that is associated with the symbolic order or "social reality," "the real" is beyond the realm of appearances and images, and is in constant tension with social reality.

17. Deleuze, *Cinema 2: The Time-Image*, 216.

18. Iain Chambers, "Signs of Silence, Lines of Listening," in Iain Chambers and Lidia Curti (eds.), *The Post-Colonial Question: Common Skies, Divided Horizons* (London: Routledge, 1996), 52.

19. Michel Chion, *Audio-Vision, Sound on Screen* (New York: Columbia University Press, 1994), 185.

20. Ibid., 186.

21. Ibid., 192.

22. Iain Chambers, "Signs of Silence," 51.

23. Ned Lukacher, "Introduction," in Jacques Derrida, *Cinders* (Lincoln: University of Nebraska Press, 1991), 14.

24. Giorgio Agamben, *Remnants of Auschwits, The Witness and The Archive* (New York: Zone Books, 1999), 35.

25. Ibid., 38.

26. Jana Evans Braziel and Anita Mannur, "Nation, Migration, Globalization: Points of Contention in Diaspora Studies," in Jana Braziel Evans and Anita Mannur (eds.), *Theorizing Diaspora: A Reader* (London: Blackwell, 2003), 8.

27. Etienne Balibar, "The Borders of Europe," in Pheng Cheah and Bruce Robbins (eds.), *Cosmopolitics: Thinking and Feeling beyond the Nation* (Minneapolis: University of Minnesota Press, 1998), 225.

28. Michael Hardt and Antonio Negri, *Empire* (Cambridge, MA: Harvard University Press, 2000), 103.

29. Derrida, *Spectres of Marx*, 41–42.

30. Irit Rogoff, "Engendering Terror," in Ursula Biemann (ed.), *Geography and the Politics of Mobility* (Vienna: Generali Foundation, 2003), 57.

31. Soren Grammel, "Butterflies," in *Esra Ersen*, Exhibition Catalog (Stockholm: Moderna Museet, 2001), 19.

32. Jacques Lacan, "The Function and Field of Speech and Language in Psychoanalysis," [1977] in *Écrits: a selection* (London: Routledge, 2004 [1989]), 94.

33. Kaja Silverman, "Body Talk," in *The Acoustic Mirror, The Female Voice in Psychoanalysis* (Bloomington: Indiana University Press), 43–44.

34. Derrida, *Spectres of Marx*, 65.

35. Sean Cubitt, *Digital Aesthetics* (London: Sage Publications, 1998), 120.

36. Ibid., 120.

37. Derrida, *Spectres of Marx*, 101.

38. Sarat Maharaj, "Perfidious Fidelity: The Untranslatability of the Other," in Sarah Campbell and Gilane Tawadros (eds.), *IVAnnotations* 6 (London: inIVA, 2001), 26.

18 Media Voices: Beyond Talking Heads

Giselle Beiguelman

It is not that words are imperfect, or that, when confronted by the visible, they prove insuperably inadequate. Neither can be reduced to the other's terms: it is in vain that we say; what we see never resides in what we say. And it is in vain that we attempt to show, by the use of images, metaphors, or similes, what we are saying; the space where they achieve their splendor is not that deployed by our eyes but that defined by the sequential elements of syntax.[1]

The man-machine relationship, mediated by a voice command, is a recurrent theme in twentieth-century science fiction. The onboard computers of the USS *Enterprise* spaceship in the *Star Trek* television series, which premiered in 1966; the friendship between the robot B-9 and Will Robinson in the series *Lost in Space* (1965–1968); Stanley Kubrick's mythic HAL 9000 (*2001: A Space Odyssey*, 1968); and the robot boy of *AI: Artificial Intelligence* (Spielberg, 2001, who not only speaks but also suffers are some examples of the recurrence of that theme.[2]

In spite of their different plots and narratives, the presence of the voice in the artificial beings those fictions portray manifests the utopia of hybridization of men and machines, which could culminate in an approximation of universes (inorganic and organic) starting from a particularly human trait: the voice.

The interest in investigation of ways to synthesize artificial sound is not new. Synthesized sound has long been explored in the field of music, and has been produced industrially since the late nineteenth century, gaining sophistication during the twentieth century. Landmarks of that process include the invention of the telephone by Alexander Graham Bell (1876); the phonograph patent by Thomas Edison (1877); the creation of the carbon microphone by the Anglo-American musician David Edward Hughes (1878); the magnetic recording, whose principle was first demonstrated by the Danish engineer Valdemar Poulsen in 1900; and the stereo reproduction, in the late 1950s.[3]

In the decade after 1960, the first program to synthesize music was produced at Bell Labs, and in 1984 a set of parameters was established to convey musical information in digital format between a synthesizer and a computer. However, it was only in 2000, with the specification of the VoiceXML standard by the World Wide Web Consortium (W3C) that the desire for human-computer communication through voice emerged from both research labs and science fiction screens and became part of our daily life, making viable the communication not only between humans and computers, but also within a computer network.[4] In this chapter, I will discuss voice and media art within computer networks. I will concentrate particularly on voice and the emergent condition of the networked body in net art, wireless art, and cybrid spaces, spaces between on- and offline networks.

Voice and Media Art

In the media art field, research directed to the exploration of the voice gained importance in the late 1980s and the 1990s, with emphasis on voice synthesis technologies. Good examples of this tendency include the following: *Huge Harry* by Arthur Elsenaar and Remko Scha (1990 to the present), a speech synthesis machine that presents lectures about algorithmic art; *Inquiry Speech Theatre* (1986) by Stephen Wilson, a drama in which four programmed computer personalities conversed with viewers via synthesized speech and voice recognition; and *I Have Never Read the Bible* (1995) by Jim Campbell, in which the complete text from the King James version of the Bible is whispered, one letter at a time.

The use of the voice in digital art works intensified from the year 2000,[5] with real-time works exploring a combination of different technologies (such as natural language processing and algorithmic translation of sound in other language formats), images, and the possibility of interaction through the Web. Evidence of that process can be found in several projects by Ken Feingold, realized since 2001, such as *If/Then* (2001), among many others; *Messa di Vocce* (2004) by Golan Levin, Zachary Lieberman, Jaap Blonk, and Joan La Barbara; and *Tampopo* ("dandelion" in Japanese), by Kentaro Yamado (2005).[6]

Regarding net-art—that is, projects conceived for the Internet environment—some significant works include *net song* (2000), by Amy Alexander; *Voice Mosaic* (2004), by Brazilian artist Martha Gabriel; and *IP Poetry* (2004), by Argentinean Gustavo Romano. All those projects, which will be discussed in this chapter, explore the Web as an informational space and use the voice to interrogate the emergent condition of the networked body.

In wireless art, I highlight here *Net Aura* (2007), by myself and Mauricio Kusamo, with programming by Rodrigo Cruz, and *Cellphonia* (2006), by Scot Gresham-Lancaster and Steve Bull. Those projects also investigate the networked body through the use of the voice, but, because of their mobile attributes, link the networked body to different social contexts.

Concerning cybrid spaces, it is fundamental to mention and to discuss *Tactical Sound Garden* (2005–present), by Mark Shepard, which combines locative media and sound spatialization processes (3D sound); *The Living Room* (2001), by Christa Sommerer and Laurent Mignonneau, which explores camera tracking, sound, and voice recognition systems; and *Reler* (*Reread* 2008) by Raquel Kogan, which combines quadraphonic sound and superposition of prerecorded audio books. In all these art pieces, the voice plays the role of a connecting tool between varied systems and distributed networks.

This discussion will concentrate on these latest areas (net-art, wireless art, and cybrid spaces), seeking to analyze the epistemological implications of the human-machine relationship, mediated by voice command. I will argue that those projects point to new cognitive patterns and sociocultural features because they suggest and make us to deal with an extra-human repertoire (imaginary and aesthetic) that may emerge from that relationship. By doing so, they reverse the market trend and a cultural anthropocentric tradition cultivated since the Renaissance that concentrates only on the reproduction of human features in machines. The point of departure for this latter approach is the assumption that man is and always will be superior to machines forever.

It is a fact that word recognition and text synthesis are today functions that can be performed by any home computer and that the ability to register or produce sounds or words does not give them meaning. However, we cannot forget that "if there are lacks in artificial senses, there are also compensations, because the natural senses have limitations" to which artificial devices offer extra-human abilities, such as infrared vision that penetrates darkness, and the sonar used by submarines to scan the environment.[7]

That evidence indicates two major research trends being applied to the exploration of artificial sound: the search to reproduce human features in interfacing with machines, and the effort to approach the extra-human repertoire (cognitive, imaginary, and aesthetic) that may emerge from the human-machine relationship. On one hand, industrial creativity (from the microphone to VoIP, or Voice-over-Internet Protocol, technology) seems to be mobilized toward freeing us from the baffling "grooming [toilette] of the dead" to which the transcription of words into written text seems to condemn us, and which the muteness of machines tries to consecrate. On the other hand, artistic projects and top-level scientific research—without which industrial creativity does not exist—point to an almost opposite direction, namely the investigation of the extra-human unfolding of the human-machine relationship.

Roland Barthes, who defined the process of transcription under that funereal figure of "grooming [toilette] of the dead,"[8] pointed out that

What is lost in transcription is very simply the body—at least this external body (contingent), that, in a dialog situation, casts towards another body, as frail (or confused) as itself, intellectually empty messages, whose only function is, in a way, to retain the other (even in the prostitutor sense of the term), and to keep it in its state of partner.[9]

But it is exactly this status of the body—ever more contingent, as Santaella has pointed out—that recent scientific discoveries and technological inventions (artificial life, robotics, neural networks, and genetic manipulation, among others in the so-called digital revolution) are redefining as the biocybernetic body, which is breaking down the barriers between artificial and natural life.[10] This biocybernetic body demands a questioning not only of the limits between organic and inorganic, but it also calls upon us to expand our thinking on the human-machine vocalic interface beyond trying to reintroduce the biologic body into the scene where the machine makes of us an accessory agent and vice versa.

Otherwise, one would do little more than new attempts to unhaunt, through the voice, the alphanumeric code, hence restoring phonetics and confirming the point of view that subordinates writing (which, to Derrida, is a technology to process ideas in several formats, such as text, painting, photography, films, etc.) to the level of an effect of the original "thought-sound." A point of view that would have, also according to Derrida, instituted an inside and an outside of language, and condemned writing (textual, pictorial, cinematographic, etc.) to the condition of mere figuration of speech.[11]

Otherwise, also, one would not advance beyond the twentieth-century ambitions to emulate the sounds of human speech. Unlike eighteenth-century automata and nineteenth-century industrial products, today's projects that include voice try to differ from the processes that generate sounds in the human body and thus counter the idea of being a mere simulacrum of nature, that is, a mechanism of production of undifferentiation between the real and the unreal, the natural and artificial, through the staging of a hyperreality.[12]

As the artist and researcher Remko Scha, coauthor of the virtual and interactive speaker *Huge Harry*, has declared:

In the 20th century, we see an entirely different approach: digital technology which calculates the shapes of sound signals and then uses loudspeakers to make them audible. The voice is no longer imitated, but its output is faked. The algorithm computes signals that evoke the image of a physical process that never occurred. The 18th century automaton is a mechanical body, a piece of clockwork claiming the qualities of life. In 20th century computer simulation, the mechanics is abstract, the machine dissolves into mathematics. The body has disappeared.[13]

Digital Voices and Networked Bodies

It is exactly that dissolution of the body that is announced in projects such as *net song*, *IP Poetry*, and *Voice Mosaic,* and that is rethought as an ambivalence between presence and absence in *Living Room, Re-Read, Tactical Sound Garden, Cellphonia,* and *Net Aura.* These projects also engage with the emerging dynamics between public and private that are revealed with mobile communication.

The project *net song,* as Amy Alexander states on her website, is:

the song of the web, as performed by a web search engine robot. When provided a search term, the net song bot will search for this term in a search engine, then choose a page from the search results and begin following links from that page. It will continue to follow links from the resulting pages indefinitely, backing up and rerouting if it hits a dead end.[14]

The result is "a unique lyricalness and poignant narrative of the web." In sum, "not content to merely surf the information superhighway, the netsong bot makes it music."[15] *net song*'s music points to new formats of

agency between human and nonhuman entities that are at the core prem-
ises of the actor-network theory (ANT) of Bruno Latour, Michel Callon, and
John Law.[16] These new formats also imply new paradigms of interaction
and relationship in a "disquieting liminal zone between the living and the
dead, the animate and the inanimate," as Kathy Cleland has pointed out.[17]

In *Voice Mosaic*, Martha Gabriel maximizes that approach, taking as a
point of departure a series of dualities (oral/visual, individual/collective,
active/passive, and human/machine, among others) that for centuries in
western culture have been understood as oppositions, and treating them
instead as forces that interpenetrate. The work appropriates speech synthesis and voice recognition technologies—used in electronic call centers by
banks, airline companies, institutions, and client attendance services. The
website offers some phone numbers that participants must call to receive
instructions. Basically, one must choose one color and to record a message.
The chosen color will become a tile in the collective mosaic of voices.

By clicking on the colored tiles, it is possible to hear the messages
recorded by the people who form the mosaic. People's tiles can be found in
the mosaic via the phone number from which they called to participate. It
is possible to find a person's tile or your own tile by searching for the phone
number. It is also possible to search for all people within the same area by
searching the area code and leaving the phone number blank.

Although it is possible for the message emitter to recover his or her own
participation, the eclectic mosaic of recorded messages, on being heard or
viewed by the visitor, erases the traces of its origins, appearing as a diminu-
tive monochrome audiovisual among others. So Gabriel creates an interesting friction between the real, biological persona (the one who conveys
the voice), and the virtual, cybernetic persona (the one that mingles with
the data offered in the mosaic), enunciating their relationship of complementarity, without creating identities or continuities between the online
(public) or offline (private) spaces.

The disturbing character of the liminal zone between the animate and
the inanimate to which Cleland refers shows up particularly clearly in *IP
Poetry*, by Gustavo Romano, in which a similar process to that of *net song* is
realized, with the final result of orally recited poems, created from a real-
time text search on the Internet. However, the game between the human
and nonhuman elements in the work is distinct. Those texts, defined on
the project's site by interactors, who also choose the parameters of com-

position, are converted into sound that animates prerecorded images of a human mouth reciting phonemes (figure 18.1).

The combination of the interactors' selection of and instructions for text composition along with the processing done by the robotic agent, the "IP Bot," and the video image of a mouth reciting phonemes, to which are attached the recited poems, result in a disturbing portrait of a post-anthropomorphic device that haunts and charms those who see/read/watch the generated IP poems.

It is precisely the presence of telematic entities—partially human, but not at all anthropomorphic—that is at the center of Christa Sommerer and Laurent Mignonneau's *The Living Room*. As the artists describe on the project website:

The Living Room is an intelligent, interactive image, sound and voice environment. It becomes "alive" and starts to "sense" when users enter and interact with this room. Like in a perfect surveillance system, all sounds, voices, gestures and motions of the users are detected through state-of-the-art camera tracking, as well as sound and voice recognition systems. When the various users start to interact and communi-

Figure 18.1
IP Poetry installation view at Bienal del Fin del Mundo, Ushuaia, Argentine, 2007.

cate with each other within this room, they will also start to communicate with *The Living Room.*[18]

The Living Room interprets the speech data collected on the Web and displays it in form of images in the exhibition space and uses those data to generate and broadcast new sound and voices. By doing so, the project creates a dynamics of multiplied doubles within which the limits between natural and artificial, on- and offline are undone, to consolidate the reality of networks that, according to Bruno Latour's definition, don't have an inside and an outside, but rather points of connection.

And it is exactly this deep approach to the networked experience that guides the *Reread* project by the Brazilian artist Raquel Kogan. The installation is composed of one wood bookstand filled with fifty untitled books, otherwise similar to any traditional library. All the books are apparently the same, same color, all of the same width and height, identified solely by the golden number engraved on the spine. But they are not usual books. They are books to be heard and not read. Moreover, they are not mere audio books. Each volume is filled with short excerpts of the favorite books of fifty people invited to participate in the execution of the installation, with each book having an owner and a voice.

In the exhibition space, visitors choose a book and upon opening it have their faces illuminated by a small LED installed in the traditional page place. Simultaneously, a built-in audio recording system with integrated circuit plays back the prerecorded voice of the one who selected that excerpt reading from his favorite book for a maximum of four minutes.

At the same time, all of the texts being "read" from the opened books are added one to another by one interface connected with a computer, forming the quadraphonic sound of the ambient in real time and creating a palimpsest of voices, timbres, and languages that continually changes as new books are removed and returned (figure 18.2).

By doing so, the project transforms the presence of the "reader" in the room into a player of a discrete orchestra of fluid personal memories that will compose the ephemeral voice of the installation, situating it in a unique cybrid experience. There, while listening to other people's voices, the individual dissolves itself and becomes a temporary node in a network of different spaces (like the private space of each of the fifty people invited to participate in the books' recording and the public space of the reading room), temporalities (like the narrative temporality of each audio record

Figure 18.2
Reread installation at the 4th Art and Technology Biennial, Sao Paulo, Brazil, 2008.

and the machine reading time of each audio book), and textual individual memories translated into collective "databodies" voices of a delicate dataspace.

Digital Voice and Data Bodies

Today, with the multiplication of connected and connectivity spaces through the growing presence of Wi-Fi systems and the popularization of mobile devices, such as cell phones and PDAs, dataspace is confused with the very urban space and the human body. As a matter fact, we can say that the proliferation of iPods, cell phones, and mobile technology in general has transformed the human body into part of a circuit of connections integrated to global telecommunications networks.

The project *Tactical Sound Garden* (2004–2008) by Mike Shepard explores this emerging dataspace creating a relationship between the city's inhabitants with the sound that surrounds and permeates them. As the artist explained in an interview with Marcus Bastos, *TSG* "is not a specific sound composition or a sound art work, but a technology that allows the public participation in the creation of a collaborative sound sculpture."[19] In a certain sense, one can say that *Tactical Sound Garden* is an exercise of giving voice to the city through the "audio selections" operated by the project's participants.

Shepard explains:

The TSG Toolkit enables anyone living within dense 802.11 wireless (Wi-Fi) hot zones to install a sound garden for public use. Using a Wi-Fi-enabled mobile device (PDA, laptop, mobile phone), participants plant sounds within a positional audio environment. These plantings are mapped onto the coordinates of a physical location by a 3D audio engine common to gaming environments—overlaying a publicly constructed soundscape onto a specific urban space. Wearing headphones connected to a Wi-Fi-enabled device, participants drift though virtual sound gardens planted by others as they move throughout the city.[20]

At the project's website, one can access the conceptual and technical documentation and also download the software needed for the urban interventions (figure 18.3). In addition, the site has interactive maps that document the experiments done and that work as virtual gardens, adding new public dimensions to the personalized urban experiences.

The relation between intimacy/individuality and the voice is approached with irony in the amusing work *Cellphonia* by Scot Gresham-Lancaster and Steve Bull. This work promotes the collective composition and performance of "operas" on daily themes, such as the threat of exhaustion of the planet's water and the avalanche of news, that result in intriguing "mobile karaokes." In *Cellphonia in the News*, launched in San Jose during the First Zero One Festival (2006), for example, the public would access the project's voice interface by phone and would hear a robot singing the main headlines of the day. The song lyrics were taken from an RSS newsfeed provided by the *San Jose Mercury News*. To the prerecorded voices, interactors would add their words. The soundtracks available on the site record the choir formed by the junction of machine and human voices, by the integration of an automatic libretto—based on RSS news feeds—music precomposed and algorithmically generated by the news feeds with the real-time recording of the voices. This multimedia and multilanguage system—real people's voices and programming languages—results in an intriguing biocybernetic opera that transforms the mobile phone caller in a post-human performer.

The stimulus to the creative use of mobile phones, which are more and more popular, is the justification of *Cellphonia* and was also that of *Net Aura*, a project based in voice synthesis and recognition that allows the participant to record an audio message by phone or any VoIP system and to receive an animation that translates the message sent into an image.

When calling the project's phone, the participants' voices are recorded in Waveform Audio Format (WAV) converted to Musical Instrument Digital

rhinoceros.mp3 | very loud | once a day | lat: 40.70851135 | lon: -73.99899292

runningBrook.mp3 | soft | once a minute | lat: 40.70851342 | lon: -73.99899010

sayYes.mp3 | soft | once only | lat: 40.70851342 | lon: -73.99899010

Figure 18.3
TSG concept diagram.

Interface (MIDI) format, and archived in a database that communicates with another server. In this second server, the audio is read by an algorithm, from instructions that associate the tones to a palette of thousands of colors and to vertical, horizontal, and sinusoid lines. Those parameters are included in a video file that is generated in Windows Media Video (WMV), converted into Flash Video (FLV) and 3GP (a cell phone video format), published on the project's site, where one can view the recorded aura (and all the others), send the aura to someone by e-mail, and download it to a computer or to a mobile phone. A third database identifies the mobile number used in the recording (when it is done through mobile) and sends a text message (SMS) to the emitter, notifying the availability of his or her "Net Aura."

In Brazil, according to data collected in 2006, there are around ninety million mobile phone users—with 87 percent being from class A (the richest class), 85 percent from B, 69 percent from C, and 43 percent from D and E (the poorest classes)—whose activities are still mainly speech (74.5 percent) and text messaging (47 percent).[21]

Starting from this information, the project has tried to design an accessible system (using the mobile phone's main functions from the Brazilian public's point of view—speech and text message) that would stimulate the formation of a cycle in which the emitted message in an ordinary phone call could return, artistically, to the emitter, to be published and circulate among other devices. Beyond that investment in the possibility of creation of message migration cycles, the project tried to explore the relationship between the voice individuality and its algorithmic translation into an image artificially created by the different conversions of media and format.

In this way, *Net Aura* dialogs with the other projects analyzed in this chapter. Like them, it is concerned with voice interface as a reflection on the human/machine relation, focusing on the possibility of hybridization of the human body with the machine, merging organic and inorganic universes without denying their differences, but considering them as fluid territories in temporary connections. As Felix Guattari states: "We need to free ourselves from a solitary reference to technological machines and expand the concept of machine so as to situate the machine's adjacence to incorporeal Universes of reference."[22] From that perspective, the projects presented in this chapter stress the necessity of understanding the digital voice not merely as an upgraded version of the human voice or its translation into a technological device, but as a more complex approach to technology and the presence of the networked body in our daily life.

Notes

1. Michel Foucault, *The Order of Things: An Archaeology of the Human Sciences*, (London: Routledge, 2002), 10.

2. For an interesting history of artificial beings in literature and in films and examples of their human attributes, including voice, see Sidney Perkowitz, *Digital People— From Bionic Humans to Androids* (Washington D.C.: Joseph Henry Press, 2004), 17–50.

3. Ibid., 79–80, and *Encyclopaedia Britannica Online*, s.v. "Hughes, David," http://www.britannica.com/eb/article-9041424 (accessed July 29, 2008).

4. Martha Gabriel, "Interfaces de Voz em Ambientes Hipermidiáticos" [Voice Interfaces in Hypermediatic Environments] (MA diss., University of São Paulo, 2006), 15. For the VoiceXML specification at the time it was released (2000), see *"Voice eXtensible Markup Language (VoiceXML) version 1.0,"* (W3C, 2000), http://www.w3.org/TR/2000/NOTE-voicexml-20000505/ (accessed July 29, 2008).

5. Those explorations are contemporary of important projects related to sound art that involve experiments in the area of electroacoustic music, installations, and performances that evade the scope of this work. Among others, nonetheless relevant, one could indicate *OP_ERA: Sonic Dimension* (2005–2007), from Brazilian artists and researchers Daniela Kutschat end Rejane Cantoni, an immersive and interactive installation designed as a music box. The box is a black, open cube filled with hundreds of visually identical violin-like strings. Tuned with the specific tension, each virtual string vibrates with a visual-sound frequency (light and sound waves) that varies according to its relative position and mode of interaction. See http://www.op-era.com (accessed July 29, 2008).

6. For a detailed and encompassing scrutiny of artistic projects related to the theme, I recommend the links compiled by Stephen Wilson at "Intersections of Art, Technology, Science & Culture—Links," http://userwww.sfsu.edu/~infoarts/links/wilson.artlinks2.html#speech (accessed July 29, 2008).

7. Sidney Perkowitz, *Digital People—From Bionic Humans to Androids* (Washington D.C.: Joseph Henry Press, 2004), 81.

8. I refer here to *The Grain of the Voice*, a volume that gathers most interviews given by Barthes between 1962 and 1980, and that includes, in the opening, the introduction written by him in 1974 to the transcription of the *Dialogues,* produced by Roger Pillaudin for France-Culture, and published by Presses Universitaires de Grenoble.

9. Roland Barthes, *O Grão da Voz* [*The Grain of the Voice*], trans. by Teresa Meneses and Alexandre Melo (Porto: Edições 70, 1982), 11.

10. Lucia Santaella, *Culturas e Artes do Pós-humano. Da Cultura das Mídias à Cibercultura* [Post-human Arts and Culture—From Media Culture to Cyberculture] (São Paulo: Paulus, 2003),180–199.

11. Jacques Derrida, *Gramatologia* [Of Grammatology], trans. by Renato Janine Ribeiro and Miriam Chnaiderman (São Paulo: Perspectiva, 1973), 38.

12. Jean Baudrillard, "Simulacra and Simulations," in Mark Poster (ed.), *Jean Baudrillard, Selected Writings* (Stanford: Stanford University Press, 1998), 166–184, http://www.stanford.edu/dept/HPS/Baudrillard/Baudrillard_Simulacra.html (accessed July 29, 2008).

13. Remko Scha, "Virtual Voices," *Mediamatic* 7, no. 1 (1992), http://www.mediamatic.net/article-8340-en.html (accessed July 29, 2008).

14. Amy Alexander, *net song*, 2000, http://www.netsong.org (accessed July 29, 2008).

15. Ibid.

16. Bruno Latour, "On Actor Network Theory: A few clarifications," *Nettime mailing list archives*, 1997, http://www.nettime.org/Lists-Archives/nettime-l-9801/msg00019, and John Law, "Notes on the Theory of the Actor Network: Ordering, Strategy and Heterogeneity," Centre for Science Studies, Lancaster University, 2003, http://www.lancs.ac.uk/fass/sociology/papers/law-notes-on-ant.pdf accessed July 29, 2008).

17. Kathy Cleland, "Talk to me: getting personal with interactive art," *Proceedings of the Interaction Systems, Practice and Theory Symposium*, University of Technology Sydney/ Powerhouse Museum, Sydney, November 16–19, 2004, http://research.it.uts.edu.au/creative/interaction/papers/interaction04_43.pdf. (accessed July 29, 2008).

18. Christa Sommerer and Laurent Mignonneau, *The Living Room,* 2001, http://www.interface.ufg.ac.at/christa-laurent/WORKS/CONCEPTS/TheLivingRoomConcept.html (accessed July 29, 2008).

19. Marcus Bastos, "Jardins sonoros da bit-lônia (entrevista com Mark Shepard)" [Sound Gardens of Bit-lon—interview with Mark Shepard], *arte mov—revista*, no. 7 (August. 2007), http://www.artemov.net (accessed July 29, 2008).

20. Mark Shepard, "Tactical Sound Garden [TSG] Toolkit," *306090–09: Regarding Public Space* 9 (2005): 64–71.

21. Regarding the use of mobile phones to access music and video, excepting ringtones, Internet, and multimedia messages, the numbers drop sharply—respectively, to 10 percent, 5 percent, and 8.75 percent. For all the information related to the use of cell phones in Brazil cited here, see: *Survey on the Use of Information and Communication Technologies in Brazil ICT HOUSEHOLDS and ICT ENTERPRISES 2006* (São

Paulo: Brazilian Network Information Center, 2007), http://www.cetic.br/usuarios/tic/2006/rel-semfio-01.htm (accessed July 29, 2008).

22. Felix Guattari, *Chaosmosis: an ethico-aesthetic paradigm*, trans. by Paul Bains and Julian Pefanis (Bloomington and Indianapolis: Indiana University Press, 1995), 31.

Art Works

Alexander, Amy. 2000. *net song*. http://www.netsong.org

Beiguelman, Giselle and Mauricio Kusamo. 2007. *Net Aura*. http://www.netaura.org

Bull, Steve and Scot Gresham-Lancaster. 2006. *Cellphonia*. http://cellphone.el.net

Campbell, J. 1996. *I Have Never Read the Bible*. http://www.jimcampbell.tv/MW/MWBible/index.html

Cantoni, Rejane and Daniela Kutschat. 2005–2007. *OP_ERA: Sonic Dimension*. http://www.op-era.com/index_eng.htm

Elsenaar, Arthur and Remko Scha. 1990–present. *Huge Harry*. http://www.iaaa.nl/hh/cv.html

Feingold, Ken. 2001. *If/Then*. http://www.kenfeingold.com

Gabriel, Martha. 2004. Voice Mosaic. http://www.voicemosaic.com.br/

Kogan, Raquel. 2008. *Reread*. http://www.raquelkogan.com

Levin, Golan, and Zach Lieberman, with Jaap Blonk and Joan La Barbara. 2004. *Messa di Voce*. http://tmema.org/messa/messa.html

Romano, Gustavo. 2006. *IP Poetry*. http://ip-poetry.findelmundo.com.ar

Shepard, Mark. 2006. *Tactical Sound Garden*. http://www.tacticalsoundgarden.net

Sommerer, Christa e Mignonneau, Laurent. 2001. *The Living Room*. http://www.interface.ufg.ac.at/christa-laurent/WORKS/CONCEPTS/TheLivingRoomConcept.html

Wilson, Stephen. 1991. *Synthetic Speech Theatre, Inquiry Theatre*. http://userwww.sfsu.edu/%7Eswilson/

Yamada, Kentaro. 2005. *Tampopo*. http://www.kentaroyamada.com/works_tampopo.php

(All art works accessed on July 29, 2008).

19 Vocalizing the Posthuman

Philip Brophy

Prologue: Breath

The voice is corrupted by being human. The evolutionist assumption that "voice" inevitably implicates a human producer limits the potential breadth of its definition. The human-centric notion that a voice is both the organ of intelligible transmission and the inalienable vessel of human emotion submits to a most vain image of the voice. A wealth of transhistorical discourses and intercultural myths forms a formidable front to ensure the voice remains a gilded talisman that—like the mimetic oval of the human face—will assure all that it is an essentialist sign of the human. This essay chooses to disregard that the voice is such a mirage. We will investigate the voice (1) as auditory signification of the limits of its presence in the human zone, and (2) as material evidence of how recognizable and identifiable traces of the human can dissolve before our very ears.

The voice can subsume nonhuman appellations and contort into multiple characterizations beyond itself. It can mimic the giggle of a baby and the approach of a steam engine, it can control an unruly crowd through truthful exposure, and it can whisper erotic lies into the ears of a lover. It innately tends toward illusion and fallacy, for truth and lies are primarily vocal in their occurrence due to acts of "saying." The human voice readily becomes its Other through vocalization. Conversely, the face retains its visible base onto which are mapped the mannered means for shaping itself into facial variations. The pulled face, the disfigured face, will always be marked by its human physiology. The voice—through the multiplicity of its invisibility—will always locate itself in adverse directions beyond the origin of its generation and production. Like the thrown voice coming from somewhere else, the voice sings, speaks, screams, and states its residence in Otherness.

Ultimately, the voice can reach far beyond itself, and hence beyond the limiting definitions of being human. Three observations lead to this position. First, the voice is the body's most powerful tool for engineering the posthuman: a figure of the human reconstituted not according to humanist dogma, but through a play with abject materiality and a handling of fluid morphology integral to the voice's performative energy. Second, the voice manifests itself this way more by relinquishing control than it does by mastering itself. Arcing from being unrefined to being manicured, malnutritioned to bloated, the voice stretches beyond normative degrees of qualification. Though it is often stabilized in a middle ground of technical execution and aesthetic perfection, the voice just as often diverges from that zone through inability to control itself or refusal to be controlled. And third, the voice opens itself up to these applications by refuting its solitary positioning and unique stamping—the self-gratifying idea that it can trumpet individuality in the human—and in place explores how it can be many things at once. In its voiding of soloistic function, the voice expands its field of apparition, welcomes its Others, and maintains its posthuman composition.

There is only one way in which the voice is human, and that is through its breath. If one desires humanist contact and human-centered discourse, then breath is the sign of life one seeks. It is the audible rhythm of living in the world, of inhaling and exhaling the spatial cosmos of social exchange. If life is precious, than so is breath. When the body is at the threshold of being extinguished, breath is its sonic lifeline—so silent it is best registered as a visual atmospheric upon the mirror held under the nose. Neither voice, words, nor language are required or expected at this penultimate stage of life. The articulate singing voice that projects an image of the conscious human—capable of language and social expression—is the voice masquerading as a living force. Its recourse to language remits it to symbolically celebrate its distance from death, from the primal scream of the baby birthed into bright light to the unheard death rattle of the aged in the dark of night. But that same remit blocks the articulate singing voice from confronting voice at its elemental, its guttural, its expulsive. Posthuman vocalization thus refers precisely to how the voice returns to breath—not merely as an attempt to escape language, but as an open embrace of how breath is the vital fuel that prompts the body to sing.

The haunting wispiness of a beautiful female aria; the stilling innocence of a child's nursery rhyme; the rugged honesty of a folksy male ballad—such apparitions of the human voice fall on deaf ears in this essay. We will instead audit the choruses of posthumans who have sung the body in alien and alienating ways. The intention of this essay is to construct a basic matrix for perceiving how the voice in song and performance flashes and fleets between fixed nodes of self-identity to define a host of Others in its slippery recourse to not be the container of a singular human.

Five procedures will be detailed.

• *Multiplication: schizophrenic multitracking*   How the voice becomes all that it cannot be in order to engineer choruses of mirrored selves (Cornelius, Destiny's Child, Michael Jackson)

• *Addition: linguistic cross-talk*   How the voice captures and stages a performative space and modulates semantic linearity with poetic verticality (John Cooper Clarke, Scott Walker)

• *Subtraction: granular override*   How the voice corrupts its material identity to generate an aural apparition of its voided self (Yoko Ono, Meshuggah, Luciano Berio)

• *Division: textual refraction*   How the voice governs the interlocking of song narrative through quotation and referencing the prespoken (Daniel Steven Crafts, Grandmaster Flash, Grandmaster & Melle Mel)

• *Expansion: exponential assemblage*   How the voice declares its encoding to vocode a cosmetic simulation of itself (Kraftwerk, Daft Punk, Perfume)

The performers' works selected will exemplify key tendencies within each procedural subset. Neither artistic persona nor musical style are determining factors in the selection, and in all cases only recordings of single compositions will be discussed by means of close materialist analysis. All titles included are extant recordings from the last forty years, and collectively result from self-conscious phonological experimentation and practice. As exemplars of studio-based applications of the voice, they intellectually and/ or intuitively investigate ways in which the recorded voice becomes something else—something other to its acoustic state. Accordingly, our basic matrix for perceiving posthuman vocalization will be constructed from analyzing the phonological aura contained in these recordings.

Multiplication: Schizophrenic Multitracking

Cornelius's "Point" (2002, Japan) is the title track from a "meta-pop" album that can be aligned with a postmodern lineage that starts with the Beatles'

Sergeant Pepper's Lonely Hearts Club Band (1968), continues through Brian Eno's *Taking Tiger Mountain by Strategy* (1974) and pans out to ABC's *The Lexicon of Love* (1982). But though such a lineage is largely built on layers of wit, irony, play and perversity in the interplay of lyric and song, "Point" shifts such strategies into a domain of wordless vocals and paralinguistic experimentation. Sounding like the Beach Boys' wordless harmonies deconstructed through Japanese melodic logic, the song "Point" features a shimmering surface redolent of pop's classic "ooh-aah" verbiage, sheathed in alien skin.

A key device throughout "Point" is the digital sampling and looping of a held vocal pitch, which is used to simulate the effect of the voice singing perfectly for impossibly long durations without dynamic variance. This operation is then multitracked with various voices undergoing the same procedure. The end result is a static sustained choir singing fixed chord clusters heavy with second, fourth, fifth, and sixth harmonic intervals. No melody lines are articulated; pitch is figured purely as a vertical phenomenon, with no gestural motifs or sequences. The effect has remarkable psychoacoustic ramifications, as the inhumanly held note leaves one waiting for cessation in the eternal choir. The release ironically comes in the form of key changes, when the voices instantaneously and in unison sound a new dense choral cluster. Ultimately, the approach in "Point" to pitch is a matter of large-scale stratification, conveyed through the tonal landscape wholly stepping up or down according to the key changes. Its nexus of postmodern lineage and posthuman genus rests upon the way the human voice—specifically, the wordless cooing of pop—is textured into an apparition of itself. Less a ghostly illusion and more a genetic allusion, the humanist visage in "Point" is but the razing of its voice to pitched breath.

Destiny's Child's "Apple Pie à la Mode" (2001, U.S.) commences with a term long used to dismiss acts of speech by women: "girl talk." In the throats of Destiny's Child, though, a pop-feminism (and all implicated by that term) is ironically deployed as the three singers talk about a guy they are eyeing. This introduction—a preamble of gossip—is emblematic of Destiny's Child's stratagem in utilizing the feminine vox to their own ends. First, they place you completely in the corporeal point of view: they describe and discuss in speech and song an unseen male, one we are invited to imagine, but one whose presence is extinguished by the erotic gushing of the three singers. The effect is like an adult-movie actress grabbing the camera and focusing things on her alone during the male climax: the egocentric pulsations of "Apple Pie à la Mode" place Destiny's Child central to the spectacle of their singing. Second, their sung descriptions are often quite plain sentences detailing the physical presence of the male object of their attention. But their harmonized flows are braided and cascaded with such lurid complexity and charged physicality that, again, our listening perspective is sited within their being, not the corpus of their object.

This is not the standard ethnographic pleasure afforded by classical black R&B female vocal gymnasts such as Aretha Franklin and others. "Ethnographic" here refers to the lineage of black voices "faithfully captured" in the recording so as to display them at a safe remove, like beautiful but dangerous beasts singing their body phonographic. Counter to this, Destiny's Child are the posthuman extension and reinvention of classical models like the Supremes, and as such they fracture, multiply, diffuse, meld, and atomize their selves and their voices through choral arrangements and technological rendering. R&B purists tend to draw a line in the sound when hearing processed ornamentation augured by contemporary R&B acts like Destiny's Child. This chapter celebrates their refusal to keep themselves "faithfully captured," and notes "Apple Pie à la Mode" is imbued not simply with a progressive freedom borne of singing out loud, but with a liberation from being solely human.

Pop music—especially songs by vocal harmony groups—is often ostentatious in its pulping of grand narrative and symphonic forms. Yet pop is strengthened by its resistance to subtlety and restraint. "Apple Pie à La Mode" starts off simply with idle chatter, but this is a contrived prelude to how the song will evolve into an ornamental scaffolding assembled by layered lines of the singers' vocal multitracking. With phrasing continually running counter to the hiccupped drum programming, Destiny Child's voices are continually detached from their "backing." Their singing effectively disrupts the rhythm track, causing it to skip and halt its entrainment in a perverse play of *jouissance*. And not only do the vocals puncture rhythm; they also replace most musical instrumentation by sung motifs and ostinatos that bubble underneath the foregrounded harmonies. This is no kitsch pomp: the interweave of linear melodies vertically thickened and thinned by choral harmonies is no mere dress-up for these pop mannequins, but a dimensional theater within which their posthuman harmonization dances and roams.

Michael Jackson's "Don't Stop 'Til You Get Enough" (1978, U.S.) starts with a spoken intro. Jackson mumbles awkwardly, unsure of himself as he expresses a mystical connection to the object of his affection. The "force" he talks of is beyond comprehension, yet equally undeniable in its power to bind Jackson with his unnamed lover. And then the "force" erupts: music starts and Jackson is transformed into a supreme Other. Michael Jackson is possibly the most important artist to be discussed in relation to notions of vocalizing the posthuman, and this early song is writ large with vocal cryptograms that embody corporeal posthumanism as it has phenomenally developed over the last thirty years.

On the one hand, Jackson's "coming alive" to music is standard cabaret fare: a stage performer always orgiastically erupts into action once the backing energizes a performative presence. But for Jackson, this "coming alive" is Frankensteinian, not Creationist. He is electrified, yelping and shrieking with a smattering of erotic gulps and coughs (a hallmark of his vocal identity that would become more pronounced over successive years). For Jackson—once dormant sans music, now all-singing and all-dancing—proves to be a volatile being whose life force is set alight by music. When he sings in hybrid falsetto curlicues, he self-immolates, obliterating himself to become one with the music. In this sense, his posthuman state—that is, his escape from staking his humanity over and above the power of music that transforms him—is Animist. This orients broader readings of his performance with a doctrine that notably bypasses Baptist associations largely embraced by black R&B. Granted, "Don't Stop 'Til You Get Enough" does rhetorically defer to Baptist modes of affirmation: testimonial and congress through Jackson's call-and-response, phrase repetition, and cheering collective chatter. But the bulk of these voices are Jackson's alone. In this sense, his solitary self-created status is energized by his ability to also become a community for himself through multitracking.

Jackson's posthuman vocalization is qualified by the difference in his mouth's operation—a mode antithetical to orthodox assessments of vocal music. In conventional appraisals of the voice, mysticism in exceptional singing is expressed by the "magic" that happens all at once when the singer's mouth is opened. Like a streamed vocal cornucopia of unbridled humanism, the mouth simply has to open to allow for this phenomenal transition to occur. It does so usually as a seamless effortless affair, like a perfectly conjured magician's trick. Jackson is not this kind of performer.

He is continually gripped by an excess of energy—emotional, physical, psychological, musical—and he just as continually fights to ride the energy. He never controls it; he always acknowledges its control of him. Herein lies the crux of both his Frankensteinian diagnosis and his Animist prognosis.

Far from being a central emission point, Jackson's mouth is but a limited aperture for the total emotionalism of that which energizes the voice. When the "beautiful singer" employs the mouth to focus all experience on vocal melodiousness, the sung is qualified as what could be termed an "aural visible": a means by which the listener is conscious of the voice alone as generator of the audible effect. Conversely, Jackson allows the "aural invisible" to be enunciated between, across, and underneath the sung melodic line. His glottal explosions corrupt language, disrupt breath, fractalize rhythm. We audit the workings of his corporeal machinery as he sings, granting us the experience not simply of him singing, but of him actualizing song. This movement between visibility/inaudibility and invisibility/audibility is highlighted by the multi-microphonics of the recording and production of "Don't Stop 'Til You Get Enough." His falsetto lines are slightly displaced from the mic and blurred through overdubbing; the interjected lower-pitched responses are single-tracked and close-miked. Jackson's corpus is definitively posthuman through this sense of being in multiple places at once, effecting multiple means of vocal emission which compose a microphonic field for sounding his multiplicity.

Addition: Linguistic Cross-Talk

John Cooper Clarke's "The Cycle Sluts" (1978, UK) is a ferocious version of how the posthuman is formed by contra- and supra-linguistic actualizing of words. Recorded live in a London club, "The Cycle Sluts" is a "piss de resistance" of British punk poetry. Nominally, it is rooted in a tradition of bawdy English folk rhyming. Cooper's tale-spinning riffs on the postwar tradition of comedic banter developed in Northern English industrial town working men's bars. Against such a rugged manly terrain, Cooper's anemic body intensifies his live performances. His amphetamine-driven bloody verbiage is paradoxically laced with inventive rhyme, colorful meter, devastating drollness, and dense semantic threads. That he carries this off at a breakneck speed earns Cooper a posthuman status. However, his incisive collision of literature and orality—of the authored and the uttered—illuminates

how the voice's sounding of text replays territorial conflicts in the definition of the English language.

The English language is a particularly oppressive form of communication. On the one hand, held as a magisterial marker of the heights that
literature can attain through its masterful control; on the other hand,
wielded as a viciously class-determined tool for orally labeling the illiter-
ate as inferior beings. Speaking "the King's English" has been historically
instated in Great Britain through the usurpation of grammar, accent, and
speech as a license for exclusivity and exclusion. Yet many strains of resistance—mostly vocal and oral—contest that supremacy. Notably, English
slang embraces the profane, the vulgar, the ungrammatical, and the fluid,
promoting language as social force rather than scriptural force. "The Cycle
Sluts" is a modern testament to the former over the latter.

To this day, the championing of literacy is a ghostly reminder of how
"speaking like the written" signifies the attainment of a prescribed social
stature more than a demonstration of advanced vocabulary and comprehension. The English-speaking intelligentsia may take umbrage to the
assertion that English—well-delivered, clipped-toned, plum-mouthed—is
potentially oppressive. For those not offended by the notion, John Cooper
Clarke's "Cycle Sluts" performs like an emancipated being, verbally playing
language back on itself in order to show its class roots while forwarding a
literacy that promulgates "improper English." This essay is hypersensitive
to the processes by which a posthuman entity is formed through vocalization, and a counterlinguistic antilyric subtext lines most observations
delivered here. Clarke—a living, breathing Mancunian punk incarnation of
Chaucer—exemplifies how a posthuman can be molded by a resistance to
the best the English language has to offer.

Scott Walker's "The Cockfighter" (1995, UK) shuns the world and creates
a phonological space for the voice to withdraw and refuse contact with
humanity. The song is an obtuse therapeutic manual for this hermetic operation, rendered audible by Walker's angular faceted vocal projections. The
opening is a haunting incantation from the world where Walker's voice
originates. We hear him muttering almost inaudibly: the sound of someone addressing himself, not us. In the distance, intermittent vocal-like sus-
tains, resembling barge horns in their funereal pulse. Elsewhere, a pregnant

empty ambience. This is all so vague and indistinct that one might even miss it.

Suddenly, the song erupts, erasing any sense that there was a phantom prelude: hissing percussive shakers, metallic snare rimshots, distorted guitar noise, low-end rumbles. And Walker's voice: a distinctive quavering of double-tracked harmony that alludes to his previous incarnation as one of the Walker Brothers—a genetic fabrication from the past, now an aural fabrication in Scott Walker's solo recordings. Like a number of songs discussed here, "The Cockfighter" explodes after a down-toned introduction. But unlike other examples, it is born in flames, screaming in white light after the womblike darkness of its introduction. For Walker's bombastic spectacle has nothing to do with us. Its tersely posthuman condition results from nullifying the prospect that we as listeners exist. Impenetrable lyrics, clouded vocal projection, misty arrangements, cavernous spatialization— "The Cockfighter" is the world of Scott Walker alone. We are interred there for the duration of his vocalization, hearing ghostly suggestions of melodies whose utterance speaks their uncertain existence. More a confined ward with frighteningly imaginary corridors than any architectonic construction, the blaring clarion horns and devolved guitar solo evoke a walled self being decimated. In the rubble, Walker is more thing than being, wracked by the sound of his song.

"The Cockfighter" obfuscates at every turn. The listener is continually aware of the disconnection between vocal flow and musical tracing. Never does one coincide with the other's momentum; always, one halts the other to determine access or regress. All is negotiated, parsed, rationed, exchanged: voice and instruments are schizophrenically separated from each other. This is a supremely inhuman feat, for music is a powerful force in binding humans—metaphorically, socially, symbolically, aurally. Yet "The Cockfighter" never sounds like Walker is "singing along" to anything except himself. His archly melodramatic vocal technique creates superlative arcs which are continually flattened by existential slumps of organ clusters and antiharmonic devices. The music voids its contents as a mess of unformed half-processed effluvia in a Gloria to nothingness. Walker's strangely heroic intonation suggests he can sing by himself despite all that peels away from him, thereby formulating a formidable testament to empowerment in posthuman vocalization.

Subtraction: Granular Override

Yoko Ono's recording of "Why" (1971, Japan/U.S.) with the Plastic Ono Band theatricalizes the conspiracy theory that she single-handedly broke up the Beatles. A twelve-minute jamming rock-out with Ono repeatedly wailing "Why?", its hedonistic looseness combined with her acidic shrill is jettisoned from the Beatles' experiments in expanding pop form. Pertinent to our ruminations on voice, Ono's vocals function as a violent insertion into the Beatles' harmonic apparatus, one that ruptures its constituency from multiple axes. Within its ill-fitting environs, her screams sound like an uncontrolled allergic reaction to her surroundings. The rhythm section of "Why" chugs indifferently, like a musical cage for her incarceration as she questions her existence. Her high-pitched screams are less Janis Joplin–style bourbon-doused gravelly blues wails, and more an abrasive modernization of Japanese kabuki sung narration. Considered from every possible angle, Ono's vocalization in "Why" signifies her Otherness to pop.

Apart from being symptomatic of an anti-body within pop, "Why" casts Ono as a meta-being wholly dispelled from chauvinist Rock discourse. Her voice alternates between straight-jacketed nymphomaniac, assailed witch, possessed mother, and embattled sorceress—each modulated via her defeminized vocal technique. In an impressive array of screeching archetypes, Ono stages a psycho-drama that presents her voice as Woman dehumanized within rock heroism. John Lennon's over-amped slide guitar mimics her animalistic screed, their call-and-response soon devolving into a pitched domestic battle of the sexes as each spits noisy jabs at the other. The band's energy is eventually dissipated, exhausted like the aftermath of a marital fight, leaving Ono to babble like a demoness squawking in tongues. Though Yoko Ono is not immediately apparent as a posthuman figure, her placement within the intersecting fields of pop and rock signpost how posthuman vocalization is primarily determined by context.

Meshuggah's "I" (2004, Sweden) is metal "none more blacker." Like the bulk of metal music dispersed through thirty years of manifold subgenres, Meshuggah accept the artifice of Occult practice and its theater of affected alchemy. But Meshuggah cast their "blackness" not as a stage mechanism, but rather as an apparition behind which they hover so as to rupture image with sound. This is a stance they share with much post-1990s "New Metal" mostly emanating from the European continent: numerous bands have grown up fans of the British Metal cannon and its carnivalesque flirtation with the black arts, but now have musically and sonically pushed their performance and sound into an explosive postmusical terrain. Meshuggah's lead singer Jens Kidman exhibits the prerequisite guttural howls typical of those biblical "men who walk with beasts," but it is the means by which his voice is integrated into the pummeling music that evidences the band's move beyond human corporeality.

"I" is a single twenty-one-minute song released as a standalone EP. It contains numerous sections, and resembles a microsymphonic suite in its complexity and interlocking parts. The opening of "I" is a tautly stretched sequence of polymath pugilism generated from bass, guitars, and the kick and deep toms of the drum kit rhythmically charging onwards. The precision alone is inhuman, but as with much New Metal, the machinic precision is inhuman because it is performed by humans. This inversion of human enterprise is epicentral to Metal's doctrine of identifying with all that humanism excludes from its dogmatic definitions. Mythologically, this identification with ostracism qualifies why metal finds parallel discourse in Satanism and other demonic worship, as metal aligns itself with the long history of all that the church fears and expels. Succinctly, the fast machinic percolation of "I"—sounding not unlike an idling engine wracked with accented shudders while holding a constant pitch—serves to declare that Meshuggah, as producers of this sound, have crossed over to an inhuman performative domain.

After a minute and a half of this grinding bass-laden drone, a snare crack halts all sound. A split-second later, Kidman inhales a single gulp of atmosphere, then lets rip with an impossibly extended scream. The timbre and tone of the scream is notably absent of any effects processing: this is the voice as heard from within the throat, audibly traumatized by oxidation. Like holy water on the possessed, the scream leaps to an anguished plateau of pain. Fused with this voice is the hissing of cymbals, the supersonic paradiddling of the double-kick pedal, and dual guitars sculpting a wall of densely clustered noise. Opposite to the angel sighing reverberantly in the ether, this is the human voice embalmed in granite, screaming under carbonized pressure. Then, after twenty long seconds of this mammoth wail, all cuts to stillness as if the band has been collectively extinguished into nothing. The rest of "I" moves through a series of apocalyptic soundscapes—a description not aligned by mere biblical metaphor. Across the music's atonal wasteland, the sections in "I" figure the voice as a dislocated node impaired of control yet governed by the postmusical assemblage of its backing, portraying Kidman as a postapocalyptic survivor. Upon such other worldly terrain, all normative musical structure and meter conforms to alien algorithms. Kidman thrives in this sulphuric sonorum through being spastically rhythmatized by the music's posthuman construction.

Luciano Berio's "Visage" (1961, Italy) encapsulates our prefatory discussion of the physiognomic relational effects perceivable in both face and voice. *Visage* pointedly cites the face as its subject, and through the part-scored/part-improvised multitracked vocal performance of mezzo-soprano Cathy Berberian, sculpts an oral persona. While Berio's score, conduction, and accompanying electronic manipulation execute the Promethean task of realizing his magnetic tape maiden, it is Berberian's voice that provides the energy vital for signaling the success of his alchemical craft. Indeed, Berberian's presence in "Visage" resides at the crossroads of classical and modern approaches to the feminine vox.

Counter to both classical and romantic tendencies in opera which tightly regiment female vocal technique in order to mold an often morbid contortion of grotesque femininity in grand claim of "beauty," modern and postmodern approaches to the female voice in the higher arts tend toward exposing the power plays implicit in exploiting the female voice as a vessel of beauty. Berberian's performance in "Visage" is founded on her powerful projection of hysteria and its schizophrenic fringing through multilingual tongues. Mixing both *sprechgesang* and *sprechstimme* in Italian, German, and French, her voice is always feverish, always frenetic; it continually sounds like it is casting itself beyond the energy of its projection, leaving it to sound on the verge of breathlessness. This relentless exhaustion—itself a fascinating performative paradox—is a subliminal sign of how excessively manipulated the female voice is within histories of high-art music. In "Visage," we are hearing the psychological sonorum of the woman who otherwise would be defeated by decorum to emit a pure uplifting aria that hides her inner scars.

Berio's "Visage" invigorates a posthuman from Berberian's performance in two ways. First, his *musique concrète* "mannequinization" of the female character in "Visage" effects a superhuman performance. The sharp contrasts in Berberian's tone and delivery are mostly intensified through tape edits; microphone placement allows for audible ranges of proximity to be similarly contrasted through tape edits; and multitracking contributes recognizable and abstracted sensations of choral multiplicity. Her posthuman status is then formally a matter of Frankensteinian assemblage, simpatico with the modern ethos of this composition. Second, Berberian's theater of schizophrenia is violently extrapolated from the micro mood swings managed by clinically sane people. Her persona in "Visage" is a superhuman conflation of multiple personality disorder. But just as the tape edits construct an impossible performance, so do they in concert with her extreme vocalizations construct an impossible psyche. The deafening madness connoted by her barrage of peaking moods constructs a superhuman through its power to sustain a psychological framework for their interconnectivity.

Division: Textual Refraction

Daniel Steven Crafts's "Soap Opera Suite I: The Essence of Melodrama" (1982, U.S.) could be misinterpreted as hitting an easy target in its tape cutup of fragments from morning soap operas on American television, but the effects generated from this simple concept grant us quantum considerations of the voice. The etymology of "melodrama" lies in its merger of music and drama, extending from the formal incorporation of interspersed songs in a dramatic play, to the ways in which dramatic action itself can adhere less to a structural paradigm and more to a linear flow typified by the ontology of music. "Lyrics" shares a similar etymology, derived from spoken words phrased and enunciated in a way that either melds with or simulates the strum of the lyre. Indeed, the act of articulating words (in reality or on a stage) can be viewed as a rationalist halting and processing of the voice's inclination to sing, cry, scream, laugh, sigh. The praise accorded the beautiful singing voice can likewise be viewed as a guilt-driven acknowledgment of how the voice has been prioritized as an instrument for social communication over and above self-centered expression. Listening to "The Essence of Melodrama" unexpectedly gives rise to these notions, as the collage of banal script, emphatic delivery, and clichéd musical interludes resembles an injunction against delivered language. The modern intelligentsia's eternal distaste for the "melodramatic" testifies to an unwillingness to allow language to slide into the mire of over-emotional gesture: could there be a more septic pool than daytime soap operas?

"The Essence of Melodrama" is an exhausting listen. A barrage of snatches, each lasting around five seconds, the effect is like having the whole pathetic world vent its middling insignificant woes. Each declared sentence is an embarrassing reveal of a threadbare human, squirming help-lessly like an emotional slug. This composition's unending parade of his-trionic humans clinically reveals humanism as a hysterically egocentric program. The characters void themselves upon the televisual stage, self-immolating in the glare of the spot light they draw to themselves. No sing-ing to an audience here, nor any ruminations on interiority. In place, a spiraling snake of disconnected dialog, each montaged actor speaking to someone whose response is disallowed. The voice is sublimely posthuman in "The Essence of Melodrama," because when this cast of hundreds voice their concerns through spoken dialog, they nullify themselves as defen-dants and implicate us as judicators exercising the power to not care about someone else.

Grandmaster Flash and the Furious Five's "The Adventures of Grandmaster Flash on the Wheels of Steel" (1981, U.S.) is an overload of voices scratched, mixed, and overlaid upon each other. On the one hand, this can be tech-nologically qualified as the meeting of modernism (the technology of turn-tables) and postmodernism (the quotation and appropriation of source material). But what a withered hand that is. The other hand—truly, a hand of the Other—would be to site this work (more a record than a song) as an exemplar of how we listen to the overloading of voice. In turn, we can audit how modernist and postmodernist claims to respectively destroy or deflate music are never substantiated, due to our capacity to listen to all that music can be. "The Adventures of Grandmaster Flash on the Wheels of Steel" is a particularly prescient indicator of how we can unproblematically embrace the vocalization of the posthuman.

Let us detail the manifold devices by which "The Adventures of Grand-master Flash on the Wheels of Steel" aligns itself with posthuman expres-sion. Formulated as a biographical metatext, the song is an inverted Tower of Babel, composed of tightly interlocked fragments of extant recordings. Two primary levels of reference can be discerned. The first is dedicated to telling the story of mixer Grandmaster Flash and his involvement with the rap quintet the Furious Five. Simply, any call-out to Flash on a recording by the Furious Five is scratched into "The Adventures of Grandmaster Flash on the Wheels of Steel." Additionally, when Flash is roll-called by other artists like Blondie, the relevant passage is also segued into the composition. The second is dedicated to stamping Flash's name upon this layer of self-referencing. Flash's use of the half-second cry of "Good" from Chic's seminal disco anthem "Good Times" (1977, U.S.) is alternately dropped, cut, scratched, or run into the mix. Like an aural graffiti tag, "Good" is "Flash" is Grandmaster Flash, and all three are fused through his machinic instatement of himself in the material dimensions of the music. From these two sedimentary layerings, "The Adventures of Grandmaster Flash on the Wheels of Steel" builds a complex scaffolding to showcase Flash's technical mastery and creates a phonological family tree.

Here is where the posthuman is disrobed of its Nietzschian cloak and shuns binary opposition to humanism's maudlin baggage. "The Adventures of Grandmaster Flash on the Wheels of Steel" is a celebratory testament to communality, genealogy, and shared legacies. Despite being urban, electrical, industrial, technological, noisy, and flashy, it is essentially folk music. Most importantly, its folk idiom is materialist in nature: the "turntabilist" means by which it is produced determines its awareness of context, cognizance of influence, and intelligence of audience. This is a folk text not authorially separate from its aural aura (as in, to cite a white maxim, the Woody Guthrie legacy), but folk as a holistic dissolution of the individual into the group (a key operation in the indigenous, ethnic and transcultural formations of Afrocentric musics). Flash's multiplication of himself is neither schizophrenic nor supremacist, but a sign of this genealogical dissolution via the turntable's employ as a portal to history. At one point, we hear an actor from a radio drama about to tell young children the story of his life, saying "It went pretty much like this—". Immediately, he is cut off as Flash scratches in a sharply dissonant brass burst that rips the record apart before launching into another section of Flash's quotational life on record. This is the sound of history breaking the levee of the present, overloading it with the past; this is the sound of Flash becoming the sound of all that precedes him.

Grandmaster & Melle Mel's "White Lines (Don't Do It)" (1983, U.S.) is a song from the eve of the Regan-era "Just Say No" war aimed most dramatically at the upsurge of crack cocaine usage. Celebrated as a "message song" in line with hip-hop's social critique of urban injustice engulfing

African-American communities, the song is noticeably devoid of didacticism. Instead, it resounds with hieroglyphic encoding within the striate lines of voice and music which score its form. "White Lines" is a peak in subsuming social politique into social sonority, which it undertakes through musicological and semiological operations.

Musicologically, "White Lines" adheres to hip-hop's extension of jazz's willful eclecticism and melting-pot heterogeneity. The song stirs the bass and congas of contemporary urban busking with the nostalgic sounds of corner doo-wop. The former summons an Afrocentric lineage through its message drums and low-end bias, while the latter beckons a Baptist lineage via the soulful choir. Both musical genres express a desire for transcendence from the urban/mortal plane of existence, and both connote a *musica povera* through their modest means of production. The doo-wop component is most pertinent. Even though it relates to a prefabricated nostalgia embraced by white American culture, its signification in this song shuttles the listener back to the escapist yearning experienced by black slave culture. As Melle Mel facetiously urges us to "get higher" through drugs, the doo-wop harmonies build into a tiered chord, reaching to the heavens. The fallacy of this "higher plane" is tersely held as a fatal delusion in contemporary urban life. Similarly, the white lines mentioned are sometimes linked to highways and the lure of the open road. Again, this is racially posited in the song. The highway in black mythology is the terrain not of a white privileged beat journey to self-discovery, but a reminder of the emancipated negroes and itinerant hobos who wandered for work before settling in whichever urban center they could.

Semiologically, two streams of symbolic discourse are evident: one playing with coded argot, the other playing with musical mnemonics. The slang infection of innocent words transforms Melle Mel's rap into a semantic mirror maze of the early 1980s. This is antiliterature by implication, exercising the recourse to ambivalently speak multiple lines with the single phrase, as opposed to employing well-crafted language to clarify distinct statements. "Freeze!" is the B-Boy moment when dancers hold a gravity-defying position, as well as what police officers bark at suspect blacks; "Rock!" is early hip-hop's punchy embrace of dance music, as well as a raw form of cocaine; "Bass!" is the lifeblood of Afrocentric music, as well as baselining cocaine for heightened impact; and "White" is white cultural oppression, the speeding highway's lines, powdered cocaine on the table, and the deathly white light at the end of the tunnel. These single words are often shouted as tags, performing like aural hieroglyphs compacting linguistic density into a hardened symbol. Interlocuting the vocabulary in "White Lines" is the mnemonic function of its instrumentation. Hi-hats hiss like sniffling noses; echoed bass bubbles like bongs; digital keyboards tinkle like angel dust of a nefarious kind. Collectively, this instrumentation paints a visual backdrop for the scenarios being detailed by the rap.

Perhaps the most haunting moment in "White Lines" occurs in its conclusion. Melle Mel cries out, "Don't do it, baby!" but the phrase is virtually eaten up by the digital delay, which simulates a machinic stuttering. Seminal rap technique explored how the human voice could be its own beat box, mimic arcade game robotic effects, and generally appear more humanoid than human. The stuttering specifically simulates ways in which vocal fragments are scratched back onto themselves in the mix. Melle Mel's warning is overcome by technology undoing his words, symbolizing the descent into overpowering drug abuse. "White Lines" is thus underscored by a solemn awareness of how the human is voided under such all-consuming circumstances.

Expansion: Exponential Assemblage

Kraftwerk's "Musique Non-Stop" (1988, Germany) is an obvious portrait of the posthuman, with its mannered pleasure in banning all human endeavor from its glistening metallic composition. But the precision with which this song holds its robotic stance affords a full means to consider the broader implications not of pretending to be robots, but pretending to not be human. "Musique Non-Stop" employs a panoply of humanoid voices. Sounding like an exposition of the evolution of digital speech synthesis, the song has no singular voice, and therefore no assertive type of speech to authorially govern its gathering.

Among the song's multi-vocalese, we can audit two major developments in synthesizing speech: the first focusing on bluntly joining labials to vowels, the second drawing pitch intonation across those phonemes. Whereas the first phase concentrates on producing discrete syllabic components to replicate the building blocks of vocabulary, the second phase aims to "humanize" that vocabulary's delivery. Put another way, the stilted blocking of syllabic reproduction is akin to the abstracted written word, whereas the modulating pitch curve overlaid on concatenated syllables is akin to the concrete spoken word. The core perversity of digital speech synthesis is that it progresses from the former to the later—and in the same process proves that it did not progress at all. The cavalcade of syncretic and synthetic speech in "Musique Non-Stop" exponentially diminishes the voices' implied degrees of human veracity, thereby celebrating that no voice was human after all.

The more human voices in "Musique Non-Stop" are gendered female, and the more robotic tones are gendered male. The female voices maternally speak with reassurance, helpfulness, concern—but they smack of falsity and insincerity. In fact, the more "human" they sound, the deeper the quandary they instigate for the listener, as we become acutely aware of the humanoid grain of these non-human speakers, calmly intoning that our pleasurable consumption of music will be "non-stop." The grain of the voice has long been held as a forensic trait of the formed human, bearing its genealogy through accent, delivery, phrasing, and tone. Far from providing a eugenic "voice print," synthesized speech blares its algorithmic formulation. Indeed, synthesized speech always sounds like a voice in extreme close-up—so close that its internal essence distorts its external appearance. And then in Mobius-strip fashion, the vocal algorithm calculates its own character and becomes familiar through repetition.

The music of "Musique Non-Stop" is a heavily accented terrain of bleeps and clicks. Bass, keyboards, and percussion exist as absences marked by electronic tags. The musical matrix outlaid is completely nodal, in that it performs like a schematic blueprint for where music would occur. But for Kraftwerk, the fastidious planning of music overrides the need for actualized music. Just as the vocal entities never existed, so too does the programmed music never pre-exist. This is precisely the posthuman pleasure of "Musique Non-Stop": it celebrates how music, song, and voice can eternally sound in the electronic forest without any need for humans to hear its occurrence.

Daft Punk's "One More Time" (2001, France) salaciously flaunts its aural artifice as android disco crowned by an electronic voicebox. Yet this is a camp affectation of mannequined music, as both the backing and voice are actual, not virtual. Building upon the idea of "pretending to not be human," "One More Time" actively dehumanizes extant recordings of human production in order to inure an empathetic reading of the resulting posthumanism. The song bears decidedly "human" attributes: warm, soulful, melodic, pleasing—mostly resulting from the vocals provided by Romanthony. Yet these same vocals are deliberately corrupted through the recording undergoing digital pitch correction. Via extreme compression, sibilance exaggeration, and all-round "aural excitation," Romanthony's vocal grain is microscopically rendered to evidence its self-corrupting digital artifacts. His breath is perfectly artificialized, while the pitch-stepping perfectly decimates his natural glissandos and human projection.

Soulful singing by African-Americans remains a fixture of humanist deposition, partly from white guilt of colonialist slavery and partly from black cultural approaches to singing technique. It may not be outright racist to slap some black vocals on a song, but the effect generated certainly exploits its humanist baggage. In "One More Time," Romanthony's Baptist-inflected gushing is almost parodic of this recourse; however, it is also implicated in a "racial robotization" contextualized by a long history of French anthropological plunder. The ultimate irony is that pitch correction is needed in expressive African-American vocal techniques only if you wish to remove the "blackness" from the sound. Daft Punk's production amounts to a laryngeal taming of overtly soulful singing, perversely creating a posthuman who does not sing as much as it technologically aspirates.

Perfume's "Chokoreito Disuko" (2007, Japan)—a sparkling, piercing, ingratiating example of hypersynthetic idol pop—requires some contextualizing comment on pop history to ward off any dismissal the reader may direct to the song. A most amazing feature of pop—among its vast garden of artificial delights—is its genetic conflation of rejuvenation and regurgitation. Its old is its new and vice versa—simultaneously. This alone leans it toward fluxile ahistoricist qualifications, but even tagging pop "postmodern" is a disservice to how unending pop's rotations have been for the last century. In terms of vocalization, the posthuman in pop has always shimmered phantasmally behind the iconicization granted the human voice as it warbles on the phonographic surface. Yet the greater half of pop music (from the Tin Pan Alley revolution of the 1920s to the transistorized auralization of the 1960s) exhibits a humanist strain in capturing the erotic delicacy of vocal grain in order to release it through mechanical reproduction. This teleology of pop's encoding of the voice echoes nineteenth-century poetics dedicated to the pursuit of truth (the recording as documentation), beauty (the singing voice as harmony), and nature (the human presence spiritually existing within the recording technology).

But by the 1960s, the triangulation of pop's industrialization, marketing, and consumption becomes intensified so as to produce a strain of pop that narcissistically mirrors its own formal procedures over and above any humanist appraisal. This is the genesis of pop many love to hate. Internationally, 1960s pop embraces mock-Wagnerian all-girl groups, cry-baby boy balladeering, toy-like bubblegum concept-ensembles, and whispering sexpot ingénues. Wacky sound effects, ungainly instrumentation, excessive studio production, and all manner of sonic novelty are concentrated and consolidated across the 1960s, serving to adorn, dress, and idolize the voice in aural costumery. It is an epoch that sheds the recorded voice's humanist skin to allow the emergence of a prepubescent posthuman in pop. Thus contextualized, Perfume's "Chokoreito Disuko" can now be discussed as a sign of the advanced stages of the posthuman in pop.

"Chokoreito Disuko" ("Chocolate Disco") is a nightmare for those claiming to be allergic to pop music. This song is so genetically modified, chemically concocted, and artificially flavored that it is like acid on the eardrum awaiting pure unadorned vocals. Yet "Chokoreito Disuko" needs to be ingested whole if we are to come to terms with where the posthuman currently resides in pop. As per the purpose of pop production, it is intended for initial impact, so allergic responses are understandable: the song's hyper-saccharine assault is instantaneous and constant. Perfume's trio of female voices are encased in a fireworks display of richly harmonized cadences and modulated flows. Here note must be made of the song's Japanese context, to qualify its excessively patterned harmonization as emblematic of Japanese pop music. Seemingly Baroque in its detailing, Japanese patterning is less about mystical calculus and mathematical sublimity to intimidate the Self, and more about how background and foreground merge into complexly interlaced environments which engulf the Self. Though this has been readily noted in discourses on visuality in Japanese traditional arts, the same principles guide Japan's digestion of Western harmony. "Chokoreito Disuko" is truly kaleidoscopic in this respect.

But ultimately, Japanese idol music is about enshrining the human within a quasi-mystical portmanteau, posing the singer like a faux-deity or "god-child" (in the non-Judeo-Christian sense). Perfume are typically amateur and untrained in their delivery of the song. This "human" aspect of their composure is integral to their transformation into "idols": the contrast between their naïve, frail vocals and the awesome non-humanness of the musical staging is mandated by their deification. Their vocals sound "pitch-corrected," but a closer listen reveals that such inhuman perfection might be illusory. Their "pseudo-vocoding" is achieved through (a) hyperflattened acoustics which stridently despatialize the voice (in contrast to long Judeo-Christian histories that grant the voice cathedral reverberation), combined with (b) the removal of all breathing between phrases. This is in further keeping with the posthumanism of idol music, in that the resulting idols are transient figurines: not simulacra, but evacuated icons declaring the absence of any corporeal human. Psychoacoustically, the compound effect of technical procedures and cultural processes in "Chokoreito Disuko" is impressive in its allowance of the human voice to be intensely human while framing it in a highly fabricated model. This audible displacement disconnects the voice from social discourse, manufacturing music that is not simply inhuman, but supremely solipsistic in its capacity to be so comfortable in its artificial enshrinement. The "Chokoreito Disuko" vocals thus mark an apotheosis in posthumanism, joyfully offered up for human consumption.

Epilogue: Death

In one sense, posthumanism is very simple: it is all that has ever been described, proscribed, and inscribed as being indelibly human—erased. When one asks of another, "Are you listening to me? Can you not hear what I'm saying?" the plea is to comprehend not mere words, but the reason for uttering words. When voice is theatrically, dramatically, and/or musically imbricated in such communiqués, it is forced to perform in ways that essentializes the need for an articulate point of view—irrespective of what the voice could do otherwise. In other words, the instrumentality of voice as the means of imparting speech posits voice as a prime device in celebrating the humanist enterprise of language. For discourses intent on that celebration—through the actions of performing and singing especially—voice is thus shackled with a performative function that channels its aurality and vocality through abstract thought and systematized literacy.

But voice can also be the prime means of bypassing these directives. Voice can be most powerful not simply when it chooses to affect an imaginary "prelinguistic" universalism through emotive babble, but when it explores ways in which its sonic essence can direct its phenomenological reception. In a sense, this already happens when we audit the predictable beauty in tropes like soaring female arias, innocent children's rhymes, and earthy male ballads: they all "move" through their palpable materialization of mere words.

Yet our aural perception can advance beyond being pleased by mirror images of our idealized selves. In place, we can make contact with the "host of Others" detailed in this essay: pitched breathers, rhythm disruptors, Animist emitters, language resistors, schizophrenic heroes, defeminized screamers, apocalyptic survivors, super-human mannequins, emotional slugs, genealogical declarers, undone rappers, algorithmic speakers, racial robots, and Japanese idols. When the posthuman is vocalized through these figures (and many more besides), the egocentric human in us responsible for reading itself solely in its own image can die a warranted death. Only then can the posthuman be heard.

Contributors

Mark Amerika is an interdisciplinary artist and Professor in the Department of Art and Art History, University of Colorado in Boulder (http://www.markamerika.com).

Isabelle Arvers is a new media curator, critic, and author based in France (http://iarvers.free.fr).

Giselle Beiguelman is a media artist teaching in the Graduate Program in Communication and Semiotics, Catholic University of São Paulo (http://www.desvirtual.com).

Philip Brophy is a musician, composer, sound designer, filmmaker, writer, graphic designer, educator, and academic based in Melbourne (http://www.philipbrophy.com).

Ross Gibson is Professor of Contemporary Art, Sydney College of the Arts, University of Sydney. He makes books, films, and art installations.

Brandon LaBelle is an artist and writer teaching at Bergen National Academy of the Arts, Norway (http://www.errantbodies.org/labelle.html).

Thomas Y. Levin is Associate Professor of German, Princeton University.

Helen Macallan is a filmmaker and research associate in the Creative Practices Group, University of Technology, Sydney.

Virginia Madsen is Lecturer in Media, Music, and Cultural Studies at Macquarie University, Sydney. She is also a radio producer and writer.

Meredith Morse is completing a PhD in art history in the Department of Art History and Film Studies, University of Sydney.

Norie Neumark is Professor of Media Studies, La Trobe University, Melbourne. She is also a sound and media artist (http://www.out-of-sync.com).

Andrew Plain is a film sound designer at Huzzah Sound and filmmaker (http://www.huzzahsound.com/flash_site/flash_site.html).

John Potts is Associate Professor in Media, Music, and Cultural Studies, Macquarie University, Sydney. He is also a radio producer and sound artist.

Theresa M. Senft is Senior Lecturer in Media Studies, University of East London (http://www.terrisenft.net).

Amanda Stewart is a poet, writer, and vocal artist based in Sydney, Australia.

Nermin Saybasili is Assistant Professor, Department of Art History, Mimar Sinan Fine Arts University, Istanbul.

Axel Stockburger is an artist and theorist who lives and works in London and Vienna, where he is a scientific staff member at the Department for Visual Arts and Digital Media/Academy of Fine Arts (http://www.stockburger.co.uk).

Michael Taussig is Professor of Anthropology, Columbia University.

Martin Thomas is Research Fellow, History Department, University of Sydney.

Theo van Leeuwen is Professor of Media and Communication, University of Technology, Sydney.

Mark Ward is Head of the Sound Department at the Australian Film Television and Radio School, Sydney.

Index